The Japanese Prime Minister and Public Policy

Kenji Hayao

UNIVERSITY OF PITTSBURGH PRESS

Pittsburgh and London

Published by the University of Pittsburgh Press, Pittsburgh, Pa. 15260
Copyright © 1993, University of Pittsburgh Press
All rights reserved
Manufactured in the United States of America
Printed on acid-free paper

Library of Congress Cataloging-in-Publication Data

Hayao, Kenji.
    The Japanese prime minister and public policy/Kenji Hayao.
      p. cm.
    Includes bibliographical references and index.
    ISBN 0-8229-3736-0. — ISBN 0-8229-5493-1 (pbk.)
    1. Prime ministers—Japan.   2. Japan—Politics and
government—1945–   3. Nakasone, Yasuhiro, 1918–   . I. Title.
JQ1641.H42   1993
354.5203'13—dc20   92-25278
                                        CIP

A CIP catalogue record for this book is available from the British Library.
Eurospan, London

Contents

Preface

I*n most countries*, much attention is focused on the top political leader—
the president, the prime minister, or the chancellor—and virtually
everyone recognizes the central role that leader plays. But the scholarship on government at the top has trailed behind other concerns in
political science, such as legislative behavior, political parties, and
voting behavior. Remarkably little has been written on heads of government, and few of those studies are in any way comparative. The study of
the U.S. presidency, which has produced hundreds if not thousands of
books and articles, is of course the notable exception. But even here,
scholars have bemoaned its lack of development. Hugh Heclo has written
that, considering its size, "the field is as shallow as it is luxuriant."[1]
Anthony King made a similar comment: "To read most studies of the U.S.
presidency . . . is to feel that one is reading not a number of different
books but essentially the same book over and over again."[2]

Luckily, this state of affairs is improving. Recent studies, individual
and comparative, of the presidencies and prime ministerships of various
countries have started to fill the void. In the United States, the empirical
studies of Paul Light, Mark Peterson, and others have revealed much
about the role and influence of the president in the policy process.[3] Bert
Rockman and Richard Rose have been putting the U.S. presidency in
comparative context.[4] Studies of heads of government of other countries
include: Richard Rose and Ezra Suleiman's edited volume on the presidents and prime ministers of eight Western countries; Patrick Weller's
comparative analysis of the prime ministership of Westminster systems
(Great Britain, Canada, Australia, and New Zealand); and, most recently,
George Jones's edited volume on West European prime ministers.[5]

The literature on the Japanese prime ministership has unfortunately
remained largely undeveloped; it is almost completely ignored in studies
of decision making. Haruhiro Fukui's standard review of the literature on
Japanese policy making, for example, barely mentions the prime minister

vii

as a significant actor.[6] Though many have written descriptive accounts of the administrations of individual prime ministers and some have written journalistic analyses, virtually no one has made a systematic study of the postwar premiership let alone put it in comparative perspective.[7]

This lack of literature is unfortunate for at least two reasons. First, Japan is an important country, and a better understanding of the prime minister's role and influence in the policy process will give us a better idea of the possible directions and impact Japan will have on other countries, including the United States. Some of the most serious problems in U.S.-Japanese relations have been the result of misunderstandings about the prime minister's ability to effect change in policy.[8] Second, although a number of the so-called newly industrializing countries, such as South Korea and Taiwan, are becoming more democratic and more industrialized, Japan is still the only non-Western country among the advanced industrialized democracies. With its non-Western cultural heritage it provides a unique look at a different pattern of politics and in particular at the role of political leadership in a modern society.

The purpose of this book, then, is to analyze in a systematic way the Japanese prime minister's role and influence in the policy process. The problem is deciding how to approach this large and mostly uncharted territory. The prime minister's role and influence in the policy process, and in the political system more broadly, is very complex. Each premier is unique, and the circumstances of each period of tenure also unique. Hence making generalizations on the subject in any concise and understandable way is more than a little difficult.

Scholars studying the U.S. presidency have taken many different approaches. There are numerous textbooks that survey all the different roles or "hats" of the president. Other studies are much more specific; they concentrate either on the president's relationships with other actors or on his role in specific policy areas. Given the infancy of the research, the approach to the study of the Japanese prime ministership has to be somewhere in between. No one work can hope to cover all areas well. Too many gaps exist in the available information for more than a superficial survey of all the premier's different roles. But it is also too limiting to concentrate on too specific a topic, some fragment of his policy-making functions, when so little has been written. Like the blind men's study of only one part of an elephant, the study of only a small part of the prime ministership could lead to a wildly inaccurate impression of the whole animal.

The emphasis of this study is on analyzing the Japanese prime minister's role and influence in the policy process and to try to identify major patterns of that influence. It concentrates on two fairly broad questions: What are the issues in which prime ministers are most involved? And how do they influence the course of these proposals in the policy process? I believe this approach, while not comprehensive, does provide an understanding of the premier's potential for making an impact on the course of issues in the policy process. This research tries to throw some light on these questions as a first step toward a more comprehensive explanation.

Chapter 1 argues that, although the major models of Japanese policy making do not consider the prime minister to be an autonomous actor in the policy process, he nevertheless can play a major if not critical role in bringing about change in policy. But his leadership is different from what is considered usual for other leaders. Rather than being strong and assertive, he tends to be reactive.

The rest of the book addresses three sets of questions regarding this reactive leadership. First, why is the role reactive? What has shaped the position in this way? Second, given that the prime minister is not a major initiator of policy change, how is he able to bring it about? How is he able to make his impact felt, and under what conditions? And third, what are the consequences of this rather weak leadership? How does the Japanese political system function without the strong, assertive leadership that we commonly assume to be important in the West?

One would suppose that the relative passivity of the prime minister is the result of strong political checks. Yet, as chapter 2 shows, when we compare his political resources to those of heads of government of other countries, we discover an interesting puzzle: he seems to be in a stronger position than most. Factors that seem important in other countries do not help much in explaining the Japanese prime minister's relatively passive leadership.

Before delving into the puzzle directly, we need to look at some actual cases of the prime minister in action in order to have a better feel for the type of limitations on him. Chapters 3 and 4 provide in some detail specific examples involving Prime Minister Nakasone and two of the biggest issues he dealt with. These chapters look at how he became involved in the policy issues and how he affected the process. In the first case, Nakasone wanted a comprehensive reform of education to liberalize government administration. In the other, reform of the tax system, he picked up an issue that was being pushed by the Finance Ministry and already had considerable support among party leaders. Chapter 4 also gives some attention to Prime Minister Takeshita Noboru's success in enacting an indirect tax similar to the one that was dropped under Nakasone.

These cases were not picked to be representative of prime ministerial involvement in issues. In fact, they are quite atypical. First, they were big and well publicized, and they were chosen in large part because it was relatively easy to collect information. The proposals were constantly in the news, and many books and articles on the two cases were written by journalists, experts, and many of the participants. Certainly, relatively few questions are so well covered. The issues were also atypical because they involved Nakasone, who was a rather atypical prime minister. He was more of an activist than most of his predecessors and, more than any of them, he tried to participate in all aspects of the policy process.

The two cases, then, are atypical: they were among the top issues of an especially activist prime minister. But their atypicality helps make them worthy of study. Because they are characterized by unusually high levels of prime ministerial involvement, they highlight both his resources and his constraints. Nakasone was pushing the resources at his disposal to the limit; thus we can get a better idea of how far a prime minister—if he is willing—can go in influencing the policy process.

The book then examines a number of broad forces that seem important in explaining the prime minister's role in the policy process.[9] The first major factor, the subject of chapter 5, is the process of determining who becomes the leader, which can have a powerful effect on behavior through selection and socialization. The next two chapters explore the second factor: his relationships with other important actors in the political system. Chapter 6 looks at the prime minister in the context of party politics, that is, his relationship with the Liberal-Democratic party (LDP) and the opposition parties, and analyzes the limitations placed on him by party politics and the resources that he can use as leverage.

Chapter 7 focuses on the prime minister's relationship with subgovernments. These are particularly strong in Japan and can be a major restriction on his ability to influence the policy process. Chapter 8 concentrates on the third major force shaping the prime ministership, the incumbent's human resources. His staff includes the "inner staff," the Cabinet Secretariat, the Management and Coordination Agency, and an informal network of advisers, and it helps him in four main ways: providing secretarial services (e.g., arranging his schedule), carrying messages, gathering information, and offering advice and expertise.

No president or prime minister alone brings about major changes in policy. Analyzing the role and influence of a head of government is especially difficult given that the process leading to policy change is generally long and complicated. Very often, landmark legislation is the result of years of political agitation. Prime ministers often are not even in office long enough to see the process from beginning to end, let alone to be involved in all the phases. Japanese prime ministers may not be as powerful as their counterparts in other countries; nevertheless, they *can* make a difference. Chapter 9 addresses the questions of where and how in this process they are most likely to participate.

The role and influence of the Japanese prime minister go against most normative theories of leadership. Most studies stress that forceful leaders are necessary to prevent organizational stagnation. The conventional wisdom is that assertive leadership at the top is crucial to national success. Yet the Japanese government has been able to function well without a powerful head of government. How is this possible? Chapter 10—the conclusion—looks into the reasons for this anomaly.

Inevitably, the study does not pursue a number of questions, important though they may be. It does not look at the prime minister's impact on areas outside the policy process, such as party affairs, elections, or Japan's image abroad. Nor does it concentrate much on the unique circumstances of any particular prime minister. For example, a study analyzing the differences in personality between prime ministers, and the effect of these differences on their prime ministerships, would be fascinating. In particular, given the striking contrasts between the three premiers of the 1980s, Suzuki Zenkō (1980–82), Nakasone Yasuhiro (1982–87), and Takeshita Noboru (1987–89), one would certainly want to know more about how each approached and shaped the office in his own individual way. These are worthy and interesting questions, but they will have to wait for another time and perhaps another person.

One further qualification must be added: this study concentrates exclusively on the prime ministership in the context of conservative-controlled LDP governments and, in particular, on prime ministers since 1974 (since Miki Takeo). The LDP has maintained its majority in the National Assembly's House of Representatives since the party was formed in 1955 and hence has supplied all prime ministers since then.[10] If the LDP were to lose its majority there, one can at best only speculate about the ways in which the prime ministership would inevitably be changed. The position would certainly be transformed, for example, if a member of one of the other political parties, such as the Japan Socialist party (JSP) were to succeed to it. This study does not consider what would happen in such cases; and, for better or for worse, this situation is not likely to arise anytime soon. Despite numerous scandals, the LDP's long-term majority in the House of Representatives seems secure for the foreseeable future.

Inevitably, this study has its gaps and flaws. But despite its limitations, I hope that it will help stimulate more research not only of the role of Japanese prime ministers but also of leadership more broadly. And if it does that, then I will feel I have done my job well.

A few notes regarding conventions used here: Japanese words and names are romanized according to the modified Hepburn system. Macrons are used for long vowels, except for *Tokyo* (which should be *Tōkyō*) in order to follow normal English spelling. Japanese names normally appear in the Japanese order—family name first and given name second. The exception is when I cite authors whose English-language publications give the author's name in Western order (e.g., Michio Muramatsu). In addition, when referring to Japan's legislature, I use *National Assembly* instead of *National Diet* or *Diet* wherever possible. Although the official English name of the legislature is the National Diet, the term, as Hans Baerwald rightly complained, is outdated.[11] "National Assembly" is a more literal translation of the Japanese name, *Kokkai*. I also continue to refer to the *Nihon Shakaitō* as the Japan Socialist party. Even though the party changed its official English name in 1991 to the Social Democratic party of Japan its Japanese name was left unchanged, and the former English name is a more accurate translation.

Finally, figures in yen have not generally been converted to U.S. dollars. The yen-dollar exchange rate has fluctuated wildly over the past twenty years. The dollar's value was 360 yen before the Bretton Woods system broke down in the early 1970s, and it has since fluctuated between 120 and 250 yen. From 1989 to 1992, the exchange rate has been relatively stable. For the most part, the U.S. dollar has ranged between 120 and 140 yen. If one works at the rate of US$1 = ¥125, then ¥1,000 = $8.00 (see the following conversion table).

Yen	Dollars
1 thousand	8
1 million	8 thousand
1 billion	8 million
1 trillion	8 billion

Acknowledgments

W*ithout the support* of a number of individuals and organizations, this book could not have been completed. First, I wish to thank John Campbell, Martha Feldman, Roger Hackett, John Kingdon, Ellis Krauss, Marc Landy, Steve Reed, and Jack Walker for their helpful comments on various drafts of the manuscript. In particular, I am deeply appreciative for the strong support and guidance from my friend and teacher, John Campbell, who first suggested this topic to me many years ago. Without his help throughout this project, this book would never have been finished.

I am grateful to the Fulbright Commission, the University of Michigan's Horace H. Rackham School of Graduate Studies, and the Lilly Foundation for their generous financial support through the various stages of the project. In Japan, I wish to thank Professor Okazawa Norio of Waseda University, who helped me while I was in Tokyo doing my field research. For their intellectual and moral support, thanks also go to my friends and colleagues of the Michigan-*batsu*, particularly Ryōsei Kokubun, Yoshi Nakai, Seiichirō Sakata, Miranda Schreurs, and Yoshi Soeya, and to my friends and colleagues from the Ph.D. Kenkyūkai, particularly Steve Anderson, David Arase, Tom Berger, Jim Foster, David Morris, Greg Noble, Skip Orr, Ed Pratt, Mark Tilton, and Bob Uriu. I am grateful to those from the University of Pittsburgh Press, in particular Bert Rockman, Catherine Marshall, Frank Moone, and Irma Garlick, who made the publication of this book possible.

I would especially like to thank my wife, Victoria, who helped make the writing of this book far more enjoyable than it would have been otherwise. Finally, I dedicate this to my parents: To my mother, who encouraged me throughout the many years of this project. To the memory of my father, who was not able to see me finish but was nevertheless a source of much inspiration.

Abbreviations and Japanese Terms

CEC	Central Education Council
DSP	Democratic Socialist Party (Minshatō)
hakuchū	Situation of near parity of seats in the National Assembly between the LDP and the opposition parties
JCP	Japanese Communist Party (Nihon Kyōsantō)
JNR	Japan National Railway (Kokutetsu). Became Japan Railways after it was privatized in 1986.
JSP	Japan Socialist Party (Nihon Shakaìtō)
Kantei	The prime minister's official residence. It houses his office and his inner staff. It is the Japanese equivalent of the U.S. president's White House or the British prime minister's 10 Downing Street, and is distinct from the PMO.
Keidanren	Federation of Economic Organizations. One of the major big business federations.
Kokkai	Japan's National Assembly (also known as the National Diet)
Kōmeitō	Clean Government Party. A political offshoot of Sōka Gakkai, a Buddhist organization.
LDP	Liberal-Democratic Party (Jimintō), the ruling party
Maruyū accounts	Tax-exempt small-lot savings accounts. These accounts lost their tax exemption as part of the tax reform of 1987.
MITI	Ministry of International Trade and Industry (Tsūsanshō)
MPT	Ministry of Posts and Telecommunications (Yūseishō)
naikaku sanjikan	Cabinet adviser
naikaku shingikan	Cabinet councillor

Nisshō	Japan Chamber of Commerce and Industry
NPA	National Police Agency
PARC	Policy Affairs Research Council (Seichōkai)
PMO	Prime Minister's Office (Sōrifu)
Rinchō	The Second Ad Hoc Council on Administrative Reform
Rinkyōshin	National Council on Educational Reform
san'yaku	The three top LDP executives (i.e., secretary general, chairman of executive council, chairman of policy affairs council)
VAT	Value-added tax
zoku	Literally "policy tribes." Group of politicians who are influential in a particular policy area, such as education, tax, commerce, posts and telecommunications, construction, and agriculture.
zoku-giin	A *zoku* politician. *Zoku* politicians are usually, but not exclusively, LDP legislators.

Agencies and Organizations

Agriculture Ministry. (Nōrinshō). Full official name is the Agriculture, Forestry and Fisheries Ministry. Established in 1925.

Administrative Reform Promotion Council. (Gyōkakushin). Successor to the Second Ad Hoc Council on Administrative Reform.

Cabinet Advisers' Office. (Naikaku Sanjikan Shitsu). Part of the Cabinet Secretariat. Handles the staff work for cabinet meetings.

Cabinet Councillors' Office on Internal Affairs. (Naikaku Naisei Shingi Shitsu). Part of the Cabinet Secretariat. It replaced the Cabinet Councillors' Office in 1986. Its main function is to coordinate government policy on internal affairs.

Cabinet Councillors' Office on External Affairs. (Naikaku Gaisei Shingi Shitsu). Part of the Cabinet Secretariat. Established in 1986 to coordinate government policy on international affairs.

Cabinet Security Affairs Office. (Naikaku Anzen Hoshō Shitsu). Part of the Cabinet Secretariat responsible for assisting the Security Council of Japan in crisis management. Established in 1986.

Cabinet Information Research Office. (Naikaku Jōhō Chōsa Shitsu). Part of the Cabinet Secretariat in charge of coordinating the gathering of intelligence from the information organizations in the government. Before the 1986 reorganization, it was known as the Cabinet Research Office.

Cabinet Office of the Director General of Public Relations. (Naikaku Kōhōkan Shitsu). Part of the Cabinet Secretariat in charge of supplying information about the government to the nation and abroad, and in particular to provide public relations for government policies. Before the 1986 reorganization, it was known as the Cabinet Public Relations Office.

Cabinet Secretariat. (Naikaku Kanbō). Primary support organization for both the prime minister and the cabinet. Reorganized in 1986 to improve the government's coordinative capability. The chief cabinet secretary is a state minister, and the position has become an important stepping stone to the prime ministership.

Central Education Council (CEC). The primary advisory body to the Education Ministry.

Clean Government Party. (Kōmeitō). Centrist, and the second largest opposition party. A political offshoot of Sōka Gakkai, a Buddhist organization. After the 1989 election it holds the balance of power in the House of Councillors.

Construction Ministry. (Kensetsushō). Established in 1948.

Defense Agency. (Bōeichō). A cabinet-level state agency, which oversees the SDF.

Democratic Socialist Party (DSP). (Minshatō). Centrist party, established in 1960 when a group in the JSP defected. It is often allied with the Kōmeitō.

Economic Planning Agency. (Keizai Kikakuchō). A cabinet-level state agency, which is responsible for the coordination and planning of economic programs and policies.

Education Ministry. (Monbushō). Established in 1871. Responsible for overseeing Japan's education system. Its officials generally succeeded in using Nakasone's reform effort to pursue their own proposals on education.

Environment Agency. (Kankyōchō). A cabinet-level state agency, established in 1971. Responsible for the coordination and planning of policies relating to environmental protection. Much of the agency was originally part of the Health and Welfare Ministry.

Federation of Economic Organizations. (Keidanren). One of the major big business federations.

Finance Ministry. (Ōkurashō). Established in 1869. Oversees the budget and the financial and tax systems. The minister's post is considered one of the main stepping stones to the prime ministership. Finance officials were among the leading supporters of the VAT.

Foreign Ministry. (Gaimushō). Established in 1869. Official English name is the Foreign Affairs Ministry. The minister's position is considered one of the main stepping stones to the prime ministership.

General Council of Trade Unions of Japan. (Sōhyō). Formerly a major association of labor unions. It was disbanded in the late 1980s when it merged with the Japan Confederation of Labor to form the Japan

Trade Union Confederation.

Health and Welfare Ministry. (Kōseishō). Established in 1938. Formerly part of the Home Ministry.

Hokkaidō Development Agency. (Hokkaidō Kaihatsuchō). A cabinet-level state agency, established in 1950. Responsible for the promotion of development in Hokkaidō.

Home Affairs Ministry. (Jijishō). Formerly the Local Autonomy Agency from 1952 to 1960, when it was upgraded to ministry status.

Home Ministry. (Naimushō). Powerful prewar ministry that was dismantled in December 1947 by the U.S. occupation. Agencies with roots in the ministry include the ministries of Construction, Labor, Health and Welfare, and Home Affairs, and the agencies of Environment and National Police.

House Management Committee. (Giin Unei Iinkai). Determines to which house committee legislative bills are assigned.

International Trade and Industry Ministry (MITI). (Tsūsanshō). Established in 1925, but known as the Commerce and Industry Ministry in the prewar period. Primary organization overseeing Japan's famed industrial policy. The minister's position is considered one of the major stepping stones to the prime ministership.

Japan Chamber of Commerce and Industry. (Nisshō). One of the major associations of business groups, but one that tends to represent the interests of smaller businesses.

Japan Communist Party (JCP). (Nihon Kyōsantō). Leftist. It is often allied with the left-wing of the JSP.

Japan Confederation of Labor. (Dōmei). Formerly one of the major associations of labor unions that was closely aligned with the DSP. It was disbanded in the late 1980s when it merged with the General Council of Trade Unions of Japan to form the Japan Trade Union Confederation.

Japan Council for Economic Development. (Keizai Dōyūkai). One of the major business organizations.

Japan Federation of Employers' Association. (Nikkeiren). One of the major big business groups.

Japan National Railways (JNR). (Kokutetsu). Became Japan Railways after it was privatized in 1986.

Japan Socialist Party (JSP). (Nihon Shakaitō). Leftist, established in 1955 by the merger of two socialist parties. Since then, it has remained the largest opposition party. In 1991, the party changed its official English name to the Social Democratic Party of Japan, although the Japanese name remains unchanged.

Japan Teachers' Union. (Nikkyōso). Closely aligned with the Japan Socialist and Japan Communist parties.

Japan Trade Union Confederation. (Rengō). Formed in the late 1980s from a merger of several labor union federations, including Dōmei and Sōhyō.

Justice Ministry. (Hōmushō). Established originally in 1871. Became a cabinet-level state agency during the U.S. occupation and regained its ministry status in 1952.

Kansai Economic Federation. (Kansai Keizai Rengōkai). One of the major big business associations.

Labor Ministry. (Rōdōshō). Established in 1947, formerly part of the Health and Welfare Ministry and before that the Home Ministry.

Legislative Affairs Committee. (Kokkai Taisaku Iinkai). A political party's committee responsible for formulating legislative strategies.

Liberal-Democratic Party (LDP). (Jimintō). Conservative, established in 1955 by the merger of the Liberal and Democratic parties. It has controlled the government continuously ever since.

Management and Coordination Agency. (Sōmuchō). An external organ of the PMO to provide central management and coordination of government operations. It was established in 1984 from the merger of the Administrative Management Agency and parts of the PMO. Its head, the director general, is a state minister.

National Assembly. (Kokkai). Japan's national legislature. The official English name is the National Diet.

National Council on Educational Reform. (Rinkyōshin). Government commission formed in 1984 to propose reforms in the education system.

National Land Agency. A cabinet-level state agency, established in 1974. Responsible for the coordination and planning of policies concerning national land use.

National Police Agency (NPA). (Keisatsuchō). Agency responsible for overall supervision of police activities. Attached to the National Public Safety Commission, which is a cabinet-level state agency. Part of the Home Ministry before the war.

New Liberal Club. (Shin Jiyū Kurabu). Political party formed in 1976 by a group of younger parliamentarians who defected from the LDP. It disbanded soon after the 1986 general election.

Okinawa Development Agency. (Okinawa Kaihatsuchō). A cabinet-level state agency, established in 1972. Responsible for the promotion of development in Okinawa.

Policy Affairs Research Council (PARC). (Seichōkai). One of the main decision-making bodies in the LDP. Its chairman is one of the top LDP leaders, along with the secretary general and the chairman of the party executive council.

Posts and Telecommunications Ministry (MPT). (Yūseishō). Called the Communications Ministry in the prewar period, it became MPT in 1949. Oversees the postal service and the telecommunications networks. It also oversees the postal savings system.

Prime Minister's Office (PMO). (Sōrifu). Umbrella government organization that includes administrative agencies not affiliated with any of the ministries. It includes the secretariat supporting the prime minister. This is distinct from the Kantei, which houses the prime minister's office and his inner staff.

Science and Technology Agency. (Kagaku Gijitsuchō). A cabinet-level state agency, established in 1956. Responsible for the coordination and planning of policy on science and technology.

Second Ad Hoc Council on Administrative Reform. (Rinchō). Government commission formed in 1981 to recommend reforms in administrative organization and practices. The First Ad Hoc Council is referred to as the First Rinchō.

Security Council of Japan. (Anzen Hoshō Kaigi). Cabinet council which replaced the National Defense Council in 1986 to serve as Japan's main coordinative body for crisis management.

Self-Defense Forces (SDF). (Jieitai). Japan's defense forces. It consists of three branches: the Ground, Maritime, and Air Self-Defense Forces.

Social Democratic League. (Shaminren). A minor political party that split off from the JSP in 1977.

Transportation Ministry. (Unyushō). The Railroad Ministry in prewar period. Became Transportation Ministry in 1945.

The Japanese
Prime Minister
and Public
Policy

The Japanese Prime Minister:
Reactive Leadership

The role and influence of the top political leader have always been important concerns in political science, from Plato's *Republic*, to the *Federalist*, to studies of the modern U.S. presidency: "The need to give direction to government is universal and persisting. Every country, from the Egypt of the Pharoahs to contemporary democracies and dictatorships, faces the challenge of organizing political institutions so that leaders can make authoritative decisions about collective problems of society."[1] This seems even more true today than ever before, as many countries address again the problems of governability.

From the United States to the major European countries of Great Britain, Germany, and France, to other countries around the world, the focus of the political system has increasingly been on the top political leader—the president, the prime minister, or the chancellor. In the United States, the story of the twentieth century is the rise of presidential government in meeting new demands for waging hot and cold war, creating welfare programs, managing economic recovery and growth, and protecting civil rights. Margaret Thatcher, during her eleven years as prime minister, had a profound impact on British politics and public policy, with her aggressive style in pushing market capitalism as the solution for her country's economic ills. In Germany, Helmut Kohl, as chancellor, led the way in forcefully promoting the reunification of East and West Germany. For the French, the problems of the Fourth Republic seemed to prove the need for a strong leader. With Charles de Gaulle providing the impetus, the succeeding Fifth Republic was founded in 1958 on a strong presidency.

Even in Asia, where the cultural heritage emphasizes the collectivity over the individual, the politics of many countries have been dominated by strong and often charismatic leaders: Mao Zedong and Deng Xiaoping in China, Chiang Kai-shek in Taiwan, Lee Kwan Yew in Singapore, Sukarno and Suharto in Indonesia, and Jawaharlal Nehru and Indira Gandhi in India.[2] The conventional wisdom, around the world seemingly, is that strong leadership is critical to national success. And a change of leadership in any of these countries, East or West, generally brings about major political changes.

It is surprising, then, how little attention is paid to the head of Japan's government, the prime minister, especially given the growing interest in the country's economic success and increasing impact on international affairs. The prime minister, particularly his role and influence in the policy process, is almost completely ignored in writings about policy making. Part of the reason for this is that Japanese prime ministers, with the recent exception of Nakasone Yasuhiro, are almost always seen as uncharismatic, colorless figures. Edwin Reischauer noted, "There is a strong prejudice against the sort of charismatic leadership commonly sought in a president of the United States."[3] The typical Japanese prime minister appears to be a remarkably weak and passive figure. He is the one who tends to be lost or forgotten when the pictures are taken at the annual summit conferences of the advanced industrialized democracies. As one reporter commented, "when photographed together, the other leaders might be paired up, apparently sharing some private joke, while successive Japanese Prime Ministers typically stood apart, scrutinizing the nearby foliage."[4]

Japan is, unlike most other countries, "a nation without a pantheon of political heroes."[5] It has no equivalent of such leaders as Franklin Roosevelt, Charles de Gaulle, or Mao Zedong. Changes at the top seem more to confirm Japan's political stability than to signify any major political changes. Even though the conservatives have ruled for almost the entire post-1945 period, it is surprising to find that Japan has had more instability at the top than virtually any other country.[6] Under the postwar constitution, promulgated in 1947, there have been nineteen prime ministers—if one counts Yoshida Shigeru twice, since he held the office on two separate occasions (see table 1.1). By comparison, during the same period, Australia, Canada, and Sweden have each had nine; Great Britain, eleven; and New Zealand, which has had an unusually rapid turnover during the last few years, twelve. The United States has had ten presidents. West Germany, since 1949, has had only six chancellors. France has had only four presidents since 1958, when the Fifth Republic was founded. Only Italy and Switzerland have a higher turnover rate than Japan's. Italy, with its unstable cabinets, has had twenty-nine prime ministers, while the chairmanship of Switzerland's national executive, the Federal Council, rotates annually among its seven members.

Moreover, the few activist exceptions seem to prove the rule of weak and passive Japanese prime ministers. Postwar, Yoshida Shigeru certainly had the most impact. He was by no means simply a tool of the Americans, but the source of his strong rule was the absolute authority of

TABLE 1.1
Postwar Prime Ministers: Terms of Office

Higashikuni Naruhiko	8/17/45–10/9/45
Shidehara Kijurō	10/9/45–5/22/46
Yoshida Shigeru	5/22/46–5/24/47
Katayama Tetsu	5/24/47–3/10/48
Ashida Hitoshi	3/10/48–10/19/48
Yoshida Shigeru	10/19/48–12/10/54
Hatoyama Ichirō	12/10/54–12/23/56
Ishibashi Tanzan	12/23/56–2/25/57
Kishi Nobusuke	2/25/57–7/19/60
Ikeda Hayato	7/19/60–11/9/64
Satō Eisaku	11/9/64–7/7/72
Tanaka Kakuei	7/7/72–12/9/74
Miki Takeo	12/9/74–12/24/76
Fukuda Takeo	12/24/76–12/7/78
Ōhira Masayoshi	12/7/78–6/12/80[a]
Suzuki Zenkō	7/17/80[a]–11/27/82
Nakasone Yasuhiro	11/27/82–11/6/87
Takeshita Noboru	11/6/87–6/2/89
Uno Sōsuke	6/2/89–8/8/89
Kaifu Toshiki	8/8/89–11/5/91
Miyazawa Kiichi	11/5/91–

a. Following Ohira's death and until Suzuki's appointment, Itō Masayoshi served as acting prime minister.

the U.S. occupation.[7] More recently, Nakasone raised many expectations with his attempts to "presidentialize" the prime ministership so that the incumbent would become more activist and influential. Clearly, his style was different; he was active in a more public way than other recent prime ministers. Yet he, too, was heavily constrained in many areas, such as defense, education, and trade frictions with the United States.

The leadership of the Japanese premiership, then, seems quite different from what is considered typical of the top leadership in the United States and the West, or even in the rest of Asia. The purpose of this chapter is to determine what sort of leader the prime minister is. It first reviews the literature on the Japanese policy process and how it relates to the prime minister. It then looks at the different possible ways the prime minister can affect the policy process, and, in particular, it outlines three potential types of leadership in that arena. And finally, on the basis of an analysis of prime ministerial issues such Miki Takeo (since 1974), the chapter concludes that the Japanese prime minister's leadership can best be described as reactive.

Literature on Policy Making in Japan

The conventional wisdom—to the extent there is one, given the state of the literature—is that the Japanese prime minister is exceptionally weak and passive compared to other heads of government. Japanese prime ministers are regularly lambasted in foreign countries and at economic summits for their inability to ease trade frictions. Prime Minister Kaifu Toshiki was heavily criticized both in Japan and abroad for his government's weak response to the Iraqi invasion of Kuwait. Frequent changes in prime ministers, as was mentioned above, seem more to confirm Japan's political stability than to signify any major political changes. This view is further reinforced if one looks at the way people view decision-making and policy processes in Japan.

The Japanese, as is well known, value consensus and harmony. Decision makers within their group or organization try to avoid conflict if possible.[8] Rather than forceful, top-down leadership, which tends to be viewed as illegitimate, Japanese tend to favor bottom-up styles of decision making.[9] Chie Nakane, in her classic analysis of Japanese society, writes, "Superiors do not force their ideas on juniors; instead, juniors spontaneously lay their opinions before their superiors and have them adopted."[10] Rather than the strong and independent leaders who are favored in the West, the Japanese have traditionally favored articulators of consensus. Nakane argues that "the leader is expected to be thoroughly involved in the group, to the point where he has almost no personal identity."[11] Leadership, therefore, tends from the outside to be "invisible":

> The effective actor in Japanese society is the selfless arbitrator between conflicting interests and opinions, the messenger and negotiator who, in a flurry of activity, smooths away all disputes, differences, and injured feelings, all the while maintaining a pure detachment and neutrality. . . . His role is not to find new solutions, but to seek accommodation among old ones, and this privately, behind the scenes so that the dispute can be contained as much as possible. Hence the leader in Japan remains invisible.[12]

The view of Takeshita Noboru, a former prime minister, is typical: "It is the role of the leader today not to pull people along, it is to get the consensus of the people."[13]

This view of weak and passive prime ministers is further reflected in the two quite different models of the Japanese policy process that dominate the literature, one of which sees power as highly centralized in the hands of a coherent elite, and the other of which sees it as highly fragmented with no central power capable of making decisions. Both models reflect important aspects of Japanese politics, but they leave little room for the prime minister to play an autonomous role.[14]

Japan, Inc.

The prevailing view of Japanese politics, at least until quite recently, has been that power is centralized in the hands of "Japan, Inc."—a ruling triad made up of leaders of the bureaucracy; the ruling conservative party, the LDP; and big business (commonly referred to in Japan as the *zaikai*, literally the "financial world"). In this view, the ruling triad is united in promoting high economic growth above all else while at the same time subordinating Japan's defense and foreign policy more generally to that of the United States. Indeed, probably more than most of the industrialized democracies, Japan has had, and to a large extent still has, an unusually cohesive and stable political elite.

This centralization of power is attributed to two broad factors. First, Japan has, as will be shown in detail in the next chapter, the major ingredients of a majoritarian government: a unitary government and a parliamentary system with a disciplined, long-term ruling party. Second, in comparison to other countries, Japanese society, and particularly the ruling elite, is very homogeneous. The cohesion is fostered by school ties, particularly Tokyo University and to a lesser extent Kyoto University, that form a pervasive "old boy" network throughout society. Graduates of these two schools dominate the bureaucratic and big business elite and form a substantial part of LDP leadership. An overwhelming majority of the elite bureaucrats, especially in the more important ministries such as the Finance Ministry, continue to be graduates of one of the two schools.[15] Of the postwar presidents of Keidanren (the Federation of Economic Organizations, widely considered to be the leading big business group), a majority have also been Tokyo University graduates.[16] Of the nineteen postwar prime ministers, ten were graduates of these schools (nine from Tokyo University), serving thirty-three of the forty-six postwar years.

The cohesiveness of the elite is further strengthened, it is argued, because each element of the triad is a dependent on the other two groups. The LDP depends on the bureaucracy for policy expertise, while the bureaucracy relies on the party to pass its proposals in the National Assembly. The LDP counts on big business for electoral funds; in return, big business depends on the LDP for support of capitalism, a favorable business climate, and political stability. Finally, the bureaucracy relies on business for jobs after retirement (a practice the Japanese refer to as *amakudari*, literally "descending from heaven"), while business depends on the bureaucracy for favors in the drawing up and implementation of legislation.[17]

For most of those who favor this view of Japanese politics, the bureaucracy is the key actor, particularly in the policy process. The basis for this argument is as follows: First, the bureaucracy has had a long tradition of rule in Japan. It was set up in the mid-1800s well before the National Assembly was established in 1890, and it continued to have the upper hand through the rest of the prewar period. Many argue that the civil service, particuarly the economic ministries, maintained and even strengthened its near monopoly on policy expertise even after the war. As

Chalmers Johnson points out, the economic ministries survived the U.S. occupation nearly intact, while most of the other prewar elites, particularly the military and the *zaibatsu* (the prewar big business conglomerates), were eliminated.[18] The politicians are dependent on the bureaucracy because they—and the prime minister, as will be shown in chapter 8—have little support staff of their own to draw up policy proposals and thus are forced to rely on bureaucrats for most of their information and expertise. Under one of the early postwar governments, the cabinet ministers were reportedly "so lacking in expertise and so unfamiliar with legislation that everyone had his vice-minister sitting next to him in the cabinet room in order to advise him on what to do."[19]

Second, the power of the civil service is supposedly reinforced by the practice of high-ranking bureaucrats moving into politics or business after retirement. This provides another link between a ministry and its main clients and "contributes to a common orientation" between government and business.[20] The fact that most of the prime ministers from Yoshida through Satō Eisaku, Fukuda Takeo, and Ōhira Masayoshi were former elite career bureaucrats is often given as further evidence of the dominance of government officials over the system. Indeed, from 1955, when the LDP was formed, to 1980, former elite bureaucrats dominated the prime ministership, serving a total of nineteen out of the twenty-five years.

"Japan, Inc." models generally view politicians not as leading the government but as merely the tools of the bureaucrats. The politicians' primary role is to serve as "supreme ratifiers" of the bureaucracy's policies. Beyond this, their role is to insulate the bureaucracy from pressure by political and interest groups so that it can autonomously implement policies fostering high economic growth.[21] This generally meant acting as safety valves by satisfying the main group of voters supporting the LDP, farmers and other rural constituents, with agricultural supports and public works projects.[22]

The prime minister, in this model of Japanese decision making, is not an important autonomous actor. He is either irrelevant because he is part of the consensus or powerless to make an impact in changing the consensus: the constraints of the bureaucracy, the LDP, and big business, according to Taketsugu Tsurutani, reduce prime ministers "to near impotence" in influence.[23] For example, Donald Hellmann argues that

Nakasone's attempt to fashion a more assertive role for Japan in international politics failed because elite consensus on national policy inhibits change.[24]

Fragmentation in Policy Making

The "Japan, Inc." model of decision making continues to be the predominant view in most popular accounts, and it still is important in much of the scholarship on Japanese politics. However, scholars increasingly question whether this model continues to describe politics accurately. They have come to see the current process as much more pluralist than was previously believed. Research using case studies across a number of policy areas indicates that more social interests than just big business, farmers, and other conservative groups have access to and influence in the system.[25] In particular, there is a growing consensus that the process is more fragmented or sectionalized than it is cohesive or unified.

Most of those who see the current system as fragmented believe that, though the cohesive, united view may have been accurate in the 1960s, "Japan, Inc." since then has become "unbundled."[26] In particular, the overwhelming consensus of the early 1960s on promoting economic growth began to unravel by the late 1960s. Economic successes led to a "new middle mass," which stressed issues related to the quality of life. Pollution became a major political issue in the late 1960s and early 1970s, to be followed by demands for expanded welfare programs in the early to mid-1970s. In addition, the international environment favoring high-growth policies also changed. The United States began to apply more pressure in matters of trade and defense. Richard Nixon pushed Japan to limit exports of textiles to the United States, abruptly abandoned the postwar Bretton Woods system, which supported a yen-dollar exchange rate that greatly undervalued the yen, and urged Japan to beef up its military forces.[27] Then in 1974 came the first of the two major oil shocks, which brought an end to the high-growth era in Japan.

As a result of the changes in the domestic and international environments the dominance and cohesiveness of the conservative camp in Japan began to come apart. First, the opposition parties gained in influence. During the mid-1970s, the LDP's majority in both houses of the

National Assembly dropped to razor-thin margins. After the 1976 election, for instance, it maintained its majority only after a number of conservative independents joined the party. The LDP was forced to make more concessions to the opposition parties in order to pass important pieces of legislation.

Second, the conservative camp lost much of its coherence. As T. J. Pempel notes, "there are important divisions among powerful conservatives within Japan over almost all elements of foreign, economic, and defense policy."[28] A major reason for this is that the LDP, in order to stay in power, broadened its electoral base beyond just farmers and industrialists. Over the years, it became a catchall party, expanding its base of support to include virtually all parts of society.[29] According to Gerald Curtis, by the 1980s the LDP had become so dependent on the support of a diverse coalition of social interests that the need to avoid alienating any significant element itself acts as a powerful check on the party's policies.[30] These interests are mostly represented in the party's Policy Affairs Research Council (PARC) by groups of LDP legislators generally known as *zoku* ("policy tribes"), who specialize and have particular influence in specific areas of policy, such as taxes, education, construction, and agriculture.[31] Many now see these politicians as rivaling and often exceeding the influence of bureaucrats.

While the research shows that more social interests are being represented in the system, it also suggests that government institutions have structured the access of social interests in a way that limits the extent of pluralism, especially because the cleavages caused by the bureaucracy's long-recognized sectionalism are being reinforced by the development of LDP *zoku*. According to this model of Japanese politics, policy making is dominated by subgovernments. Decision making is sectionalized into separated arenas each of which involves a ministry or a bureau, its related policy group or *zoku* in the LDP (which is somewhat akin to a congressional committee in the United States), and interest groups. Although strong subgovernments and subgovernmental conflict are hardly unique to Japan, they do seem to be particularly prominent.[32] Satō Seizaburō and Matsuzaki Tetsuhisa argue that subgovernments are even stronger in Japan than in the United States.[33] Instead of seeing Japanese decision making as highly centralized and unified, then, the tendency now is to emphasize the system's fragmentation. Michio Muramatsu and Ellis Krauss call it "patterned pluralism": "Policymaking conflict under patterned pluralism are *pluralist* in that many diverse actors whose alliances may shift participate, but *patterned* in that the shifting coalitions occur within the framework of one-party dominance and of a bureaucracy that procedurally structures the types of possible alliances and policymaking patterns."[34]

The effect of this fragmentation is that Japan has a strong bias toward maintaining the status quo. The main role of the *zoku* politicians is to act as brokers between bureaucrats and interest groups. But the energy of these politicians is usually concentrated less on initiating change in policy than on preventing their clienteles from being hurt. At best, the prime minister is seen as a mediator of last resort. In Murakawa Ichirō's description of the policy process, the prime minister, as LDP president, becomes involved only when lower bodies are deadlocked and cannot make a decision.[35] At worst, the premier is hardly able to do even that. Karel van Wolferen, in his controversial article "The Japan Problem," goes so far as to argue that the Japanese prime minister has less influence than the head of government of any Western country.[36] He asserts that the Japanese political system is so fragmented that it is incapable of making decisions in its best interest; it is, he says, a "government without a top."[37]

The Prime Minister and Models of Japanese Policy Process

As we have seen, neither of the two paradigms has much to say about the prime minister's role and influence. Both models virtually ignore the premier as an influential autonomous political actor. In "Japan, Inc." models, the prime minister is reduced to "near impotence" by the ruling triad made up of the party, the bureaucracy, and big business. In models of fragmentation, particularly as envisioned by van Wolferen, the prime minister lacks the influence to counter the centrifugal forces of the fragmented system. Van Wolferen argues that change in Japan's trade practices will occur only when the United States and other countries apply intense pressure for change.[38] But both models, by concentrating on the constraints, overlook the cases in which the prime minister has been important, often critical, in bringing about policy change.

Even during the 1960s, when the "Japan, Inc." model applied best, politicians played more important roles than simply being ratifiers and safety valves. They often dominated important areas of policy other than those directly related to economic growth. In fact, much evidence supports the view that bureaucratic dominance of industrial policy was an exception rather than the norm. Kent Calder's study of various areas of policy through the postwar period shows that, long before the 1970s, entrepreneurial conservative politicians played far more activist roles in many areas, including agricultural, regional, and public works policy, than they are given credit for.[39] In foreign policy, prime ministers in the postwar period have often established and then accomplished major personal goals during their tenure: Hatoyama Ichirō reestablished diplomatic ties with the Soviet Union; Kishi Nobusuke renegotiated the United States–Japan Security Treaty; and Satō reestablished relations with South Korea and negotiated the return of Okinawa to Japanese sovereignty.[40] Haruhiro Fukui concludes in his study of the reestablishment of relations with China in 1972 that the "central role of the prime minister was abundantly clear."[41]

Even in economic policy, politicians were not simply the tools of bureaucrats in pursuing economic growth. Michio Muramatsu and Ellis Krauss emphasize that political leadership was critical in establishing and institutionalizing the conservative line emphasizing high economic growth.[42] As they point out, the conservatives were not unified on the conservative line; many wanted to push policies favoring traditional values and military power.[43] Although the conservative line was initiated by Yoshida while he was prime minister during the late 1940s and early 1950s, the conflict between the two conservative camps was not resolved until Ikeda Hayato became prime minister in 1960. He consolidated the conservative policy line with his "low-posture" politics, thus reducing the confrontation between the conservative and progressive camps.

Politicians were crucial in overriding the caution of what is regarded to be Japan's most powerful ministry, the Finance Ministry, in developing budgetary policies critical to the country's expansionist economic policies. In the beginning, it took an activist prime minister to persuade Finance Ministry officials to support the highly expansionist economic policies.[44] John Campbell's study of the budgetary process reveals that in formulating subsequent budgets the LDP leadership often overrode objections from the Finance Ministry. For instance, the ministry worked hard—and failed—to control increases in the 1968 budget because it could not resist the pressure from the LDP.[45] Thus it is clear that politicians, particularly prime ministers, were much more than simply safety valves for the bureaucracy even in economic policy during the 1960s, when "Japan, Inc." was supposedly at its peak.

Models emphasizing Japan's fragmentation also are flawed. In particular, they tend to exaggerate the deadlock of the system. A number of important changes in policy occurred without significant subgovernmental conflict, such as the new and expanded welfare programs under Tanaka. These models also neglect a number of cases in which conflict between subgovernments has been resolved or at least contained. Administrative and fiscal reforms of the 1980s brought down a huge chronic government deficit that was, in the late 1970s, even larger in terms of gross national product than that of the United States. Takeshita played an important part in opening two important agricultural markets, those in oranges and beef. As will be shown in chapter 4, both Nakasone and Takeshita played leading roles in reforming the tax system despite intense public opposition. As Daniel Okimoto argues, despite the fragmented nature of the system, "the state still seems capable of rising above petty politics to take action in the public's and nation's best interests."[46]

Japanese prime ministers, then, have figured prominently in a number of cases of policy change. By virtually ignoring this prominence, both models underestimate the possibility of policy change and the role that the prime minister can potentially play in bringing it about.

Leadership and the Policy Process

We are presented with a puzzle: the Japanese prime minister is certainly not a strong and assertive leader; nevertheless, there is much evidence to suggest that he can and often does play an important role in policy change. The solution to the puzzle lies in widening our view of the role of leadership in the policy process. The process leading to policy change, after all, can be long and complicated; most major legislation is the result of years of effort. A leader's role and influence in the process, therefore, can also be quite complex. The question, then, is, Where and how in this process are prime ministers most likely to be involved?

The usual approach is to "measure" influence in terms of "power," that is, whether a person gets his or her way. This is particularly true in much of the literature on the U.S. presidency; for example, much of the discussion on presidential power focuses on "boxscores" that tally the president's wins and losses vis-à-vis Congress. The president either wins or loses the battles.[47] But this approach is too narrow a framework to analyze the many possible ways in which the head of government can affect the policy process.

To understand an actor's role and influence, we need a broader framework than is generally used. The policy process includes at least the following three parts: agenda setting, determining the content of change, and the enactment of change.[48] In addition, change can follow different types of process, which may be divided into three major categories: rational, political, and garbage can models.[49] Building on these approaches, one can postulate that leadership can be categorized into three major types: technocratic, political, and reactive.

Technocratic Leadership

Technocratic leadership involves problem solving. The leader's task is to search for solutions that best solve the problems at hand, monitoring the environment, and, when a problem arises, searching for alternative solutions, systematically comparing them, their costs and benefits, and choosing the best. The classic model of rational choice requires perfect information about all the alternatives and the ability to calculate the consequences of each. But, as many have noted, this is impossible because of the substantial time and resources needed to acquire information.[50] Decision makers are at best "boundedly" rational; they inevitably must cut the costs of following a rational process and settle for the first satisfactory alternative that comes along. For the purposes here, leadership is technocratic as long as it approximates a unitary actor being able to make a decision based on well-defined goals.

What this model implies is that, first, the leaders have the power to make the decisions without interference from other actors and, second, goals are clear and unified. Technocrats, Joel Aberbach, Robert Putnam, and Bert Rockman have noted in their study of bureaucrats and politicians in Western democracies, tend to emphasize continuity, stability, and predictability.[51] Leaders in this case are not involved in setting the agenda—the goals are assumed. Rather, the leader's main role is to find the appropriate solutions to the problem at hand to bring conditions back to some sort of equilibrium. A relatively pure example of technocratic leadership is the role of the chairman of the Federal Reserve, who monitors the economy and adjusts interest rates depending on changing economic conditions.

But Aberbach, Putnam, and Rockman found that the emphasis on technical problem solving is more representative of bureaucrats than of politicians.[52] Bureaucrats, particularly in nonpoliticized issues, often have a great deal of autonomy to pursue specific goals. Thus one would expect to see technocratic leadership in highly centralized, bureaucratically dominated societies with a strong consensus on goals. One major example of this was Meiji Japan, where the leaders had the power and the desire to advance policies to modernize and industrialize the country in an attempt to catch up to the Western powers.[53] A more recent case of technocratic leadership is France in the late 1970s, when Raymond Barre, prime minister under the presidency of Valéry Giscard d'Estaing, implemented policies to restrain government deficits.[54]

For most top political leaders, however, so pure a technocratic role is unusual. In most cases, even if they have strong coherent goals, they must compete with other significant actors in the process. Leadership in this case would be political.

Political Leadership

In political models choice is a result of individuals and groups with different interests, perceptions, and resources. That is, goals within camps are unified, and change is the result of conflict among the participants who have a stake in the outcome. The leader plays a forceful part in pushing for change; he has clear goals and pursues those goals using the resources at his disposal to overcome opposition. Political leadership, in other words, is top-down leadership. Enactment may be an important part in political leadership; ultimate success is determined by whether the leader is able to have policies adopted. But the emphasis is on initiating policy change, that is, agenda setting. The assumption is that the leader has a program of change to carry out. Aberbach, Putnam, and Rockman conclude in their study of bureaucrats and politicians that politicians contribute "direction, energy, and a modicum of idealism" to the policy-making process; their role is to "articulate society's dreams."[55]

As is suggested above, this type of leadership is the one that is emphasized in the United States, particularly in studies of the presidency. David McKay, for example, argues that modern presidents have exercised a high degree of control over the initial design of domestic programs.[56] Presidents can pursue their own preferences, formulate coherent policies, and seize opportunities for innovation not available to other institutions in a fragmented political order. A number of other studies of policy making seem to confirm that the president's primary role is the initiation of policy rather than the determination of the content or even the enactment of change.[57]

It is also the type of leadership ascribed to party governments in Europe. Richard Rose argues that, in Great Britain, taking initiatives is "often the most important thing a party does to influence government policy."[58] European parties are "likely to have a long-term commitment to a statement of principles, the support of a relatively stable group of voters, and a manifesto of pledges for action by government."[59] Party leaders push these policy platforms to win elections, so that on entering office, the prime minister has a strong commitment to the programs outlined in the party manifesto. Rose's study of British parties found that the great majority of the nearly one-hundred pledges made at each election were put into effect by the winning party.[60]

Reactive Leadership

One of the main assumptions of the political model is that the behavior of actors is the result of their pursuit of well-defined goals. But these assumptions do not hold in many situations.[61] Not only are preferences often unclear, but they are "discovered through action as much as being the basis of action."[62] Members of an organization may have only a fragmentary and rudimentary understanding of why they are doing what they are doing, and with what effect. For many reasons participants vary in the amount of time and energy they put into the process. Michael Cohen, James March, and Johan Olsen refer to these situations as "organized anarchies," which result in a "garbage can" style of organizational choice.[63]

Choice in an organized anarchy depends on more than just the political power of the actors. It is highly contextual, depending substantially on the pattern of flows in four streams that run through organizations: problems, solutions, participants, and possible choices. Each of the streams is largely independent of the others. Participants may generate solutions because they want to expand the activities of their jobs or that of the unit, rather than as responses to problems. They drift in and out of decision making; their attention to an issue is not-necessarily fixed, because other demands upon them may impinge on their time. Choice, therefore, is viewed as a somewhat fortuitous confluence of the streams.

In this sort of situation, the leader has relatively little influence. His role "is a bit like the driver of a skidding automobile. The marginal judgments he makes, his skill, and his luck may possibly make some difference to the survival prospects for his riders. As a result, his responsibilities are heavy. But whether he is convicted of manslaughter or receives a medal for heroism is largely outside his control."[64] When a leader has no clear policy goals and thus no agenda to advocate, he will instead apply his energy to issues that happen to be salient at the moment. He does not take the initiative for change. Neither is he involved directly in the content of change. When he takes up issues that are at hand and applies his energy to them, his role is simply to try to resolve them in some way. This leadership can be described as reactive. Although without a say in determining which issues are attended to or the content of proposed changes, the leader can be important in deciding whether any choice occurs, and therefore which issues are resolved.

Although this is not the typical view of leadership in the West, it is not by any means unknown. In Germany, Renate Mayntz comments: "While there are variations in the internal balance in the executive, the dominant pattern is one of checks and countervailing powers. The need for consensus building and conflict resolution is correspondingly high. . . . The pattern of executive leadership in the Federal Republic of Germany seems . . . to make more for a stable than for a very powerful government."[65] Meanwhile, in Italy, Sabino Cassese claims: "The leadership exercised is more the result of mediation among factions, pressure groups, and parties, than the result of elaboration, promotion, and planning by responsible and expert ministry officials. . . . The Italian system is more suited to reaching agreement about problems as they gradually emerge than to ensuring positive guidance and direction."[66]

Indeed, scholars increasingly describe American presidential leadership in similar ways. Because of changes in the American political system in the last twenty years, leadership has become more difficult and complex, which makes it much harder to predict "what the consequences of one's actions will be."[67] As Hedrick Smith writes in the *The Power Game*, we tend to see the president as John Wayne, but in reality we have a fluid system of power in which power floats to and then away from the president.[68] Presidential government, Hugh Heclo argues, is an illusion. "Far from being in charge or running the government, the president must struggle even to comprehend what is going on."[69] This perception is even stronger under the presidency of George Bush with his "just-in-time" foreign policy: he is often accused of reacting to events rather than trying to take advantage of opportunities in order to shape them.[70]

Prime Ministerial Issues

What sort of leader, then, is the Japanese prime minister? As a first step, a logical approach is to look at the proposals in which recent incumbents have been most involved. By developing lists of these, one can discover a number of things about the prime minister's role in the policy process. The number of issues on a list gives an idea of the breadth of his involvement—whether he participates in many or relatively few. The list also provides an indication of whether his involvement is in important issues or in minor ones. And finally, it offers some idea of the way he participates in the process—whether he helps put these proposals on the agenda or becomes involved after they are there. The lists were developed on the basis of analysis of headlines in the *Nihon Keizai Shimbun* (Japan's equivalent of the *Wall Street Journal*, usually referred to as *Nikkei*), and a content analysis of two other major newspapers: *Asahi*

Shimbun and *Yomiuri Shimbun* (see appendix A for details of the methodology). Major issues are indicated by an *x*.

<table>
<tr><td colspan="2" align="center">Miki Takeo</td><td colspan="2" align="center">Fukuda Takeo</td></tr>
<tr><td>x</td><td>Lockheed scandal</td><td>x</td><td>Economy</td></tr>
<tr><td>x</td><td>Clean politics</td><td>x</td><td>China peace treaty</td></tr>
<tr><td>x</td><td>Economy</td><td>x</td><td>Trade frictions</td></tr>
<tr><td>x</td><td>Antimonopoly bill</td><td></td><td>ASEAN/Fukuda Doctrine</td></tr>
<tr><td>x</td><td>China peace treaty</td><td></td><td>Energy</td></tr>
<tr><td></td><td>Right to strike</td><td></td><td>Administrative reform</td></tr>
<tr><td></td><td>Revenue bills</td><td></td><td>USSR fishing treaty</td></tr>
<tr><td></td><td>Welfare/life cycle</td><td></td><td>Party reform</td></tr>
<tr><td></td><td></td><td></td><td>Education</td></tr>
</table>

<table>
<tr><td colspan="2" align="center">Ōhira Masayoshi</td><td colspan="2" align="center">Suzuki Zenkō</td></tr>
<tr><td>x</td><td>Fiscal reform</td><td>x</td><td>Fiscal reform</td></tr>
<tr><td>x</td><td>Energy</td><td>x</td><td>Administrative reform</td></tr>
<tr><td>x</td><td>U.S. relations:</td><td>x</td><td>Defense expenses</td></tr>
<tr><td></td><td>[Trade, defense,</td><td>x</td><td>Trade frictions</td></tr>
<tr><td></td><td>Iran, Afghanistan]</td><td></td><td>Foreign aid</td></tr>
<tr><td></td><td>Economy</td><td></td><td>Economy</td></tr>
<tr><td></td><td>Political ethics</td><td></td><td>Ethics/party reform</td></tr>
<tr><td></td><td></td><td></td><td>Textbooks</td></tr>
</table>

<table>
<tr><td colspan="2" align="center">Nakasone Yasuhiro</td><td colspan="2" align="center">Takeshita Noboru</td></tr>
<tr><td>x</td><td>Trade frictions</td><td>x</td><td>Tax reform</td></tr>
<tr><td>x</td><td>Defense</td><td>x</td><td>Recruit/political reform</td></tr>
<tr><td>x</td><td>Tax reform</td><td>x</td><td>Trade frictions</td></tr>
<tr><td>x</td><td>Economy</td><td>x</td><td>Land reform</td></tr>
<tr><td>x</td><td>Administrative reform</td><td></td><td>Foreign aid</td></tr>
<tr><td>x</td><td>Education reform</td><td></td><td>Hometown revival</td></tr>
<tr><td>x</td><td>Fiscal reform</td><td></td><td></td></tr>
<tr><td>x</td><td>Kokkai representation</td><td></td><td></td></tr>
<tr><td></td><td>Yasukuni Shrine</td><td></td><td></td></tr>
</table>

Analyzing the Lists

What do these lists suggest about the prime minister's role in the policy process? One is that he is not particularly activist: he is involved in relatively few issues. The premiers surveyed generally concerned themselves with three to four primary issues during a two-year term. Nakasone, generally considered to be the most activist of recent prime ministers, participated in more, but he also served five years—more than double the time of any of the others.

The lists also suggest that the prime minister is involved in major issues, the ones that dominated the political agenda: foreign crises such as trade frictions with the United States, political scandals such as Lockheed and Recruit, and major domestic issues such as administrative and fiscal reform. These all showed up on the front pages of the newspapers. In this sense, the prime minister is involved in important issues. The major omission is industrial policy, which is widely regarded as an important area of public policy; however, the prime ministers surveyed were not particularly involved, although some did concern themselves with it as part of their involvement in economic issues (e.g., Fukuda).

Finally, the lists provide some idea of the prime minister's degree of involvement. The issues divide into three categories.[71] First are those that the prime minister cannot ignore. Second are those that were already major political questions when he became involved. These are issues that the prime minister would have a hard time turning away from. Third are those over which he has discretion: in other words, he chooses to participate. This analysis gives some insight into the prime minister's role in policy, in particular the extent to which he has discretion over matters of policy in which he is involved.

Obligatory Issues   The prime minister must often deal with policy crises that entail systemwide conflicts within the political system. As head of government and party president, he is the only person who can coordinate broad policy programs and resolve major conflicts. Thus he must deal with any large-scale flare-ups that occur during his term. There are three main types of obligatory issue that make it to the prime minister's agenda: political scandals, international crises, and economic problems. (Note that brackets indicate secondary issues.)

Miki Takeo	Clean politics, economy, Lockheed, [right to strike]
Fukuda Takeo	Economy, trade frictions
Ōhira Masayoshi	Energy crisis, U.S. relations, [political ethics]
Suzuki Zenkō	Defense, trade frictions, [textbooks]
Nakasone Yasuhiro	Trade frictions, defense, economy
Takeshita Noboru	Recruit scandal/political reform, trade frictions

Some of the biggest issues that prime ministers have had to deal with were scandals. Miki Takeo not only had to attend to the Lockheed scandal, which dominated his second year in office, but he also pursued his goal of clean politics as the result of the public's furor over Tanaka's "money power politics." Takeshita had to cope with the Recruit scandal, which dominated the latter part of his tenure.[72]

International crises, in particular those involving Japan's relations with the United States, also pushed themselves onto the prime ministers' agendas. Almost all have had to deal with some sort of crisis in that area. Only Miki seems to have been largely exempt. In particular, the trade friction between the two countries was one of the top items for every prime minister from Fukuda to Takeshita. In addition, Ōhira and Suzuki Zenkō have had to face demands for more defense spending. Almost all of Ōhira's agenda was taken up by problems in the Japanese U.S. relationship: there were not only the usual trade frictions and defense demands, but also the U.S. push for sanctions on Iran for taking U.S. hostages and on the Soviet Union for invading Afghanistan.

The U.S. relationship is quite special for the prime minister: his speeches in the National Assembly inevitably include a section reaffirming that the United States is the cornerstone of Japan's diplomacy. He meets the U.S. president about twice a year, once alone in Washington (or occasionally in Tokyo) and once at the summit of industrialized democracies. Arranging a trip to the United States is nearly the first task for a new prime minister.

These meetings often provide the stimulus for the prime minister to deal with the problems of relations with the United States. So that the meeting will go as smoothly and harmoniously as possible, he does his best to ease any frictions that may exist at the time. This is reflected in the Nikkei index, which shows that prime ministerial involvement in trade or defense issues increases sharply with the approach of a planned trip to the United States or the economic summit and decreases sharply afterward. Nakasone, for example, had scheduled a meeting with President Reagan in 1987 as a farewell visit to help cap his final year in office, but trade frictions increased as the date approached. (Congress often uses the prime minister's visit to press for Japanese trade concessions.) Nakasone needed to show the president and Congress that Japan was taking concrete action to ease the trade imbalance. The number of Nikkei headlines mentioning Nakasone in conjunction with trade issues went from zero in January 1987 to a peak of nineteen in May, when he made his visit. It then dropped to four in June.[73]

Such situations arise not only with the United States. Suzuki became involved in a problem because of a planned trip to China. In the summer of 1982 proposed revisions of Japanese high school history textbooks exploded into a major diplomatic issue as much of East and Southeast Asia, particularly China and South Korea, made clear its opposition to them. Suzuki had scheduled a trip to China that fall, and he worked to have the Education and Foreign ministries settle matters before he left for his visit.[74]

The third type of obligatory issue is economic. The prime minister must deal with economic matters both because they are important and because they usually go beyond the jurisdiction of any one ministry or agency. Economic questions, although not always obligatory, were on the agenda for almost every prime minister in the period surveyed. Tanaka Kakuei had to cope with the economic crisis brought on by high inflation following the oil shock. Economic problems continued from the middle to the late 1970s, as the economy suffered from stagflation, and were major issues for Miki, Fukuda, and Ōhira.[75] Ōhira also faced the inflation caused by the second oil shock. In addition, Nakasone had to deal with the economic slowdown to the dramatic rise in the yen's value against the dollar in 1986–87.

Incidentally, in two cases the prime minister passed on the responsibility to someone else, in both instances Fukuda Takeo. In 1973, Tanaka brought in Fukuda to take over the Finance Ministry to tackle inflation; and in 1974, Miki appointed him deputy prime minister and director of the Economic Planning Agency, as well as head of a cabinet council in charge of economic problems. Despite his giving Fukuda much of the responsibility for developing and coordinating economic measures, the economy still ranked as one of the top issues for Miki himself.

Overall, obligatory issues tend to take up a large portion of the prime minister's agenda. Three of the top five issues for Miki can be considered obligatory, and the proportion for other prime ministers is similar. For Fukuda, the proportion is two out of three; for Ōhira, two out of three; for Suzuki, two out of four; for Nakasone, two (or three, if defense is included) out of eight; and for Takeshita, two out of four. In addition, there were a number of shorter-term problems beyond their control that demanded their attention, such as the textbook controversy under Suzuki, and various scandals and other political controversies that virtually all prime ministers have had to deal with at some point during their tenure.

Continuing Issues   Prime ministers also concern themselves with major continuing political questions, that is, issues over which prime ministers have some discretion—they could decide not to get involved—but it would be difficult for them to ignore. In effect, they would have to make an effort to stay out of them. Issues that are already on the national agenda generally take up one or two places on the prime minister's personal agenda.

Miki Takeo	—
Fukuda Takeo	China peace treaty, [party reform]
Ōhira Masayoshi	—
Suzuki Zenkō	Fiscal reform
Nakasone Yasuhiro	Administrative reform, fiscal reform
Takeshita Noboru	Tax reform, land reform

Many of these are tasks left unfinished by the previous administration. Fukuda took over a number of problems from Miki, including negotiating a peace treaty with China, revising the antimonopoly law, and reforming the party. Suzuki continued Ōhira's efforts at fiscal and administrative reform, which then became Nakasone's centerpiece issue of administrative reform. Takeshita's efforts at tax reform were a continuation of those of Nakasone. Another example, outside the period under scrutiny, is Uno Sōsuke's promise in 1989 to double Japan's foreign aid; this was a continuation of Takeshita's Global Contributions plan.

Much of this continuity can be explained by two factors: succeeding prime ministers were from the same party, and to some extent the party's priorities are also the prime minister's; and new prime ministers often were important figures in the administrations of their immediate predecessors, even in promoting these particular issues. Fukuda was deputy prime minister in the Miki cabinet and head of the cabinet council dealing with economic issues. He had also helped Miki push for party reform at the end of Tanaka's tenure as prime minister. Ōhira's concern for the national deficit was in part due to his having been finance minister under Miki and secretary general under Fukuda.[76] Nakasone was the director general of the Administrative Management Agency in Suzuki's cabinet and was central in starting the Second Ad Hoc Council on Administrative Reform (Rinchō), as well as supporting Suzuki on fiscal reform. Takeshita served as finance minister and secretary general in Nakasone's administration and played a strong supporting role in advocating tax reform. And Uno, as foreign minister under Takeshita, helped in Takeshita's Global Contributions plan to increase Japan's foreign aid.

Discretionary Issues   If one assumes that in most of the items in the first two categories, prime ministers had relatively little discretion, then the remaining issues on the lists can be considered discretionary—ones in which they chose to become involved.

Miki Takeo	China peace treaty, Antimonopoly, |welfare/life cycle|
Fukuda Takeo	|ASEAN/Fukuda Doctrine|, |administrative reform|, |education|
Ōhira Masayoshi	Fiscal reform
Suzuki Zenkō	Administrative reform, |foreign aid|
Nakasone Yasuhiro	Tax reform, education reform, |Yasukuni Shrine|
Takeshita Noboru	|Foreign aid|, |hometown revival|

Often the prime minister has had a long-standing interest in these, frequently since well before becoming head of government. Miki, who pushed for the signing of a peace treaty with China, was one of the main supporters of Tanaka's recognition of China in 1972. Ōhira's efforts at fiscal reform, as I mentioned above, was in large part the result of his concern for the increasing budget deficits incurred while he was finance minister under Miki and secretary general of the party under Fukuda. And Nakasone's attempt to reform the education system was something he had called for well before becoming prime minister.

These issues, however, are a relatively small portion of the primary agenda of prime ministers and range from zero to two issues per incumbent. Miki and Nakasone each had two; and Ōhira and Suzuki each had one. Fukuda and Takeshita had none, although all had one or more issues of lesser priority that can be considered discretionary (the issues in brackets). In addition, for the most part, the prime ministers did not get very far with these problems. Miki failed to accomplish either of his two initiatives while in office (although both were accomplished under Fukuda); Ōhira was forced to back down on fiscal reform; and Nakasone accomplished little with education reform and managed to pass only a relatively minor part of his tax reform plan (although most of the remaining plan was passed under Takeshita).

On the basis of the analysis of the lists, one can make three conclusions about the prime minister's participation in the policy process. First, given that the number of primary issues on the lists is small, he is not particularly activist. Second, with the possible exception of industrial policy, he is involved in the questions that dominate the political agenda. And third, the lists suggest that the prime minister's agenda is dominated by issues over which he has little discretion. Almost inevitably, at least two of the top problems are ones he is forced to deal with, and there is usually one more that he would have difficulty ignoring because it already is of major political importance. Moreover, these two types of issue tend to be at the very top of his agenda. Only a few arrived there by his choice.

Conclusion

The typical Japanese prime minister is, by the standards of most other countries, a remarkably weak and passive figure. Prime ministers have come and gone with more rapidity than in virtually any other country, and they are almost completely ignored in writings about the policy process in Japan. Neither of the two major models of this process that dominate the literature—one of which sees power as highly centralized and the other of which sees it as highly fragmented—view the premier as an influential autonomous political actor in the process. Indeed, Japan has had few examples of strong, assertive leadership. Yet, despite this, prime ministers have often played a central part in bringing about change in policy. The leadership of the Japanese prime ministership, then, seems quite different from what is considered typical in the West or in the rest of Asia.

What sort of leader, then, is the Japanese prime minister? There are three possible types: technocratic, political, and reactive. Japan is often thought of as a technocratic state because of its strong bureaucracy. Many ascribed this sort of leadership to the former bureaucrats who entered politics, in particular, Ikeda and Satō. Technocratic leadership may be strong at the lower levels, particularly in policy areas in which the bureaucracy is the leading actor, such as the Ministry of International Trade and Industry (MITI) in industrial policy. But, at least since Miki, prime ministers have generally not been involved in issues that one would generally associate with technocratic leadership. Most of the problems they were forced to deal with, for instance, were political scandals and international crises, rather than technical matters.

Prime ministers sometimes provide political leadership. In the past a number of prime ministers have taken initiatives. During the 1950s, Hatoyama and Kishi pushed ideological issues, such as rolling back some of the more liberal Occupation reforms. In the early 1960s, Ikeda pressed for economic growth as a priority. Heads of government have also been central in foreign policy, for example, Hatoyama's initiative to reestablish diplomatic ties with the Soviet Union, Kishi's renegotiation of the United States–Japan Security Treaty, and Tanaka's recognition of China. But, at least since Miki, these sorts of initiative have been relatively few. Japanese prime ministers have not been important agenda setters; their leadership in this sense has not been particularly political.

Prime ministers, therefore, have not tended to be either technocratic or political leaders. Most of the issues they deal with are those that are already on the agenda. They have tended to become involved in them as the result of outside factors, such as foreign pressure on trade and security policies, domestic and international economic problems, diplomatic crises, and political scandals. The prime minister, then, has tended to be reactive.

2

The Japanese Prime Minister in Comparative Perspective

T *he prime minister* is not a particularly dominant figure in Japanese politics. His role, as was shown in chapter 1, seems to be reactive and constrained, especially when compared to that of heads of government of other major countries. This would suggest that he has fewer political resources to influence policy than most other leaders. The purpose of this chapter is to put the Japanese prime ministership in comparative perspective to see whether this is true.

Comparative analysis is important because it provides a broader perspective to the nature of the political leadership at the top of government. As Richard Rose argues, "differences between national political institutions create more variation in the office of prime minister than do differences of personalities and circumstances within a country."[1] Two factors seem to be important in determining the role and influence of central political leaders. One is the degree to which power and authority are centralized in the hands of the leaders. The other is the effect of contemporary trends on the leadership of heads of government. On both counts, contrary to what one would think given his reactive role in the process, the prime minister should have the resources to be an influential if not dominant figure in Japanese politics.

Japan as a Majoritarian System

A major difference among democracies is the extent to which they have significant constraints on majority rule.[2] At one end of the spectrum are majoritarian systems, such as those in Great Britain and New Zealand, which have few constraints. There the head of government generally has a greater capacity to bring about change in policy. Leadership strategy is essentially "mechanistic."[3] That is, it is a matter of pressing the buttons to direct the system. Margaret Thatcher, for instance, was able to take advantage of the majoritarian British system and push through many of her programs despite resistance not only from the opposition parties but also from within her own party.[4]

At the other end of the spectrum are consensual democracies, such as Switzerland and Belgium, which have strong limitations on majority rule. Power is dispersed so that any major change in policy generally requires the support of much more than just a simple majority of the representatives in the legislature. The head of government is often not much more than a figurehead. The chairmanship of the Swiss executive, the Federal Council, for instance, is rotated yearly among the members of the government coalition: "In his or her year at the top, the Swiss Premier is not expected to . . . lead or to manage competing coalition partners but to express amicable agreement when it is arrived at by coalition partners themselves, or to interpret a consensus that may not otherwise be expressed."[5]

Richard Rose argues that two variables are critical in differentiating majoritarian from consensual democracies: whether the constitution centralizes power or disperses it broadly throughout different institutions of government, and whether there is single-party government or a multiparty coalition government.[6] On the basis of these two criteria, Japan, while not as extreme as Great Britain or New Zealand, should be considered much more a majoritarian system than a consensual one, which should make the Japanese prime minister a strong leader of government.

Japan's Formal Structure of Government

One of the main factors that shapes the capability of political leaders is the degree to which formal government authority is centralized.

Democratic systems vary significantly in the extent to which they institutionalize responsibilities in different parts of government. Whereas formal authority in majoritarian systems tends to be concentrated, it tends to be dispersed in consensual democracies. The more the authority is centralized in the control of the top political leader, presumably the more impact he or she is likely to have. Conversely, the more the leader is distanced from many of the government's activities, the less impact he or she is likely to have. But authority is centralized or decentralized in varying ways. Three levels of centralization are particularly important: (1) the division of authority between the central government and local governments; (2) the effective authority of the executive within the central government; (3) the degree of centralization within the executive.

Local Governments   The first major way of dispersing authority is to give lower levels of governments autonomy from the central government. In federal systems, such as in those of the United States, Canada, Australia, and Germany, the constitution guarantees the division of power between central and local governments.[7] Central governments are limited in their ability to control local governments. The head of a federal government finds certain areas of policy off limits because they are the jurisdiction of the local governments. Thus the president or prime minister, pursuing "national" policies, often has to deal with local governments and their leaders. In the United States, Ronald Reagan's efforts in the early 1980s to cut back the size and scope of government activities in the domestic sector were negated in part by the response of many states that offset the federal cuts.[8] Given the large degree of autonomy of provinces in Canada, the federal prime minister is even more limited: attempts to deal with many issues, such as pollution, education, labor, agriculture, and economic regulation often become, as one scholar put it, a "weary confused jurisdictional wrangle with the provinces."[9]

Almost all other industrialized democracies, including Great Britain, France, Italy, and Japan, are unitary states. Local governments in these countries have less authority than under the federal system. In extreme cases, such as in Great Britain, local governments can do only what the parliament specifically allows them to do. The British parliament can take back any or all of the powers from local governments if it so chooses. France is another highly centralized state: the grant of power to the provinces is narrow and is not written into the constitution; it is simply set down in statutes.

In comparison to the most highly centralized unitary states, Japan's postwar constitution gives local governments a grant of authority that is relatively generous (see Articles 92–94). The U.S. occupation authorities attempted to make local governments more autonomous, and in the Constitution they gave residents the right to set up local assemblies and elect by direct popular vote the chief executive officers of the local governments. Prefectural governors, for instance, are now directly elected, instead of being appointed by the central government, as was the case before the war. But the conventional wisdom is that, despite these attempts, the central government is not very constrained in its dealings with local governments.[10] Steven Reed in his study of prefectural governments concludes that the distribution of authority in Japan is similar to that in other unitary states, even if Japanese local governments have somewhat more authority than those in a typical unitary state.[11] The central government in Japan, therefore, is not restricted in dealing with many issues, such as education, law enforcement, and economic regulation, which would largely fall under the jurisdiction of local governments in many federal systems.

Central Government   The second level of centralization is that within the central government. There are two main types of central government, commonly known as presidential and parliamentary governments. The United States, of course, has a presidential system, in which authority is not concentrated in any one institution; it is a system in which institutions check and balance the power of one another. The president and members of Congress are elected separately, and both the president and Congress have a hand in the legislative process, as well as in administrative and judicial processes. As a further limitation, Congress is bicameral; the two houses have somewhat different constituencies but similar powers. In addition, the Supreme Court, with its right of judicial review— the right to rule on the constitutionality of laws—serves as a further check. A law must have the support of a majority of both the House and Senate, the assent of the president, and the acquiescence of the Supreme Court. Any one of the other institutions can block the passage of a bill sponsored by the president. As Richard Neustadt wrote in his classic *Presidential Power*, the United States has a government of "separated institutions *sharing* powers."[12] Countries with a well-developed system of checks and balances, then, tend to be more consensual than majoritarian, which puts restrictions on the influence of the head of government.

Most of the other industrialized democracies, including Japan, Australia, New Zealand, and virtually all of the West European countries, have a parliamentary system. France and Ireland, with their hybrid types combining a strong presidency with a parliamentary government, are the major exceptions (although many of the democratizing countries in Eastern Europe have adopted similar hybrids). Parliamentary government works on a different principle. Instead of having a system of checks and balances, it tends to concentrate formal authority in the legislature, usually called the parliament, which then delegates effective power to the executive, embodied in the cabinet. In return, the prime minister and the cabinet are dependent on the confidence of the parliament. It is a form of constitutional democracy in which "executive authority emerges from, and is responsible to, legislative authority."[13] The British parliament, for example, is the supreme constitutional body, and thus few limitations are placed on it by other institutions (although Britain's membership in the European Community means that Parliament's supremacy is somewhat qualified).

In theory, the legislature in parliamentary systems puts an absolute constraint on the prime minister and cabinet—it can oust them at any time. In practice, because the prime minister is elected by and has the support of a majority in the legislature, the constraints on the executive are generally much less than in the U.S. form of government. Such legislatures have rarely brought down a government: only one no confidence vote has been passed in Britain since 1945 (in 1979), only one in France since 1958 (in 1962), and, surprisingly, since 1945, only one in Italy, where governments resign regularly even though they are under no constitutional obligation to do so.[14]

Many argue, therefore, that a more appropriate term for parliamentary government is *cabinet government*, because it is the cabinet, not the parliament, that is the dominant actor. The overwhelming majority of the bills that are proposed and passed in parliaments are sponsored by the cabinet rather than by individual members. Richard Rose argues that, unlike the U.S. system, parliamentary systems have in the cabinet a unifying force that provides a center in which ultimate authority resides.[15]

Japan's form of parliamentary government in this sense is very much like other parliamentary systems. The postwar system was largely modeled after the British type. The Constitution (Article 41) makes the Kokkai (the National Assembly, also known as the National Diet), "the highest organ of state power," and "the sole law-making organ of the State." It gives the power to select the prime minister (who must be a member of the National Assembly) to the legislature, particularly the House of Representatives (Article 67), and it makes the cabinet collectively responsible to the National Assembly (Article 66). In order to remain in office, the prime minister and the cabinet must maintain the support of the House of Representatives. If that body passes a no confidence resolution or rejects a confidence resolution, the cabinet must resign en masse within ten days, or it must dissolve the lower house, call an election, and then resign following the opening of the National Assembly (Article 69). Although the opposition parties often bring up no confidence votes, passage is extremely rare. In the postwar period it has happened three times, and only once since 1955.[16]

As in most other parliamentary systems, then, the Japanese cabinet is dominant in the relationship between the executive and the legislature. The prime minister, as the representative of the cabinet, "submits bills, reports on general national affairs and foreign relations to the National Assembly" (Article 72). The overwhelming majority of the bills passed in the legislature—between 80 and 90 percent—are sponsored by the cabinet.[17] The cabinet also has the power to determine the convocation of extraordinary sessions of the Kokkai and to enact cabinet orders to execute the provisions of the Constitution and laws.

The cabinet's dominance of the legislature is further enhanced by its right to dissolve the House of Representatives and call elections at any time (Article 7), a power that by no means all cabinets in parliamentary systems possess. Neither the Netherlands nor Norway gives the prime minister or the cabinet such power.[18] In Germany the chancellor and the cabinet cannot dissolve the legislature unless they first lose a vote of confidence. In Australia the decision is ultimately in the hands of the governor general, who has, on several occasions, either dissolved Parliament on his own initiative or refused a request by the prime minister to do so.[19] The prime minister and the cabinet also have considerable influence over the judiciary: they have the power to select the chief justice and the other judges of the Supreme Court and to appoint the judges of the inferior courts from a list nominated by the Supreme Court (Articles 79–80).

Although parliamentary systems tend to concentrate authority in the main legislative chamber, they are usually not without some sort of checks, even if they do not always exactly balance the authority of the parliament. There are typically four types of constitutional constraint on the main chamber (and therefore the cabinet): constitutions, second chambers, judiciaries, and heads of state.

The first major type of formal check on majoritarian rule is the Constitution.[20] Some countries, such as Great Britain and New Zealand, have very flexible constitutions, which may be changed by normal parliamentary majorities.[21] Most others make amendments to the Constitution at least a little more difficult. Some require approval by a national referendum, in addition to a majority vote by the legislature.[22] Others require a special majority before the Constitution can be amended, thus giving veto power to a minority of a minimum given size. Amendments to the U.S. constitution, for example, generally require a two-thirds majority in both house of Congress and approval by three-quarters of the states (the president has no formal role in the amendment process). Thus it cannot be amended unless there is an overwhelming consensus.

Japan's postwar constitution, in this regard, is closer to the American than it is to the British. Constitutional amendments require approval by a two-thirds majority in both houses of the National Assembly and a majority of the vote in a national referendum. In fact, the postwar constitution has never been amended, in over 45 years, and it seems unlikely that any amendment will be made in the foreseeable future. The LDP has endorsed constitutional reform in the past, particularly in the 1950s and 1960s, but it has never had the necessary support to pass amendments.[23] The so-called peace constitution has strong public support, so that even if the LDP had enough votes in the National Assembly to change it, the party would still be reluctant to push reform for fear of a public backlash. In particular, public support for Article 9, the peace clause, has inhibited the growth of the military and has likely prevented Japan from obtaining certain types of weapons that would have offensive capability (e.g., aircraft carriers, bombers, ballistic missiles).

Besides making amendments to the Constitution more difficult, most democracies also have a second chamber (often referred to as the upper house) to serve as a check on the main legislative chamber (also known as the lower house).[24] The most powerful of these is the U.S. Senate, which the Founding Fathers set up in large part to serve as a check against what they thought would be a populist and radical House of Representatives.[25] The Senate's unusual influence is the result of two factors. First, it has equal powers with the House of Representatives in determining legislation—all bills must be passed by both houses of Congress—and it has additional powers in other areas, such as the ratification of treaties and the confirmation of many of the president's appointees to the executive and judicial branches. The Senate is also influential in large part because it represents slightly different interests than does the House. Its members serve six years (in staggered terms) compared to the House members' two, and each state is represented equally, regardless of its population. Thus the Senate was set up to thwart the passions of the moment as well as prevent the most highly populated states from dominating the smaller ones.

In virtually all other bicameral systems, the upper house is not as influential as the lower house because it either has weaker constitutional powers or represents a similar constituency, or both. Italy's upper house, the Senate, for example, has powers equal to that of the lower house, the Chamber of Deputies, but it represents nearly the same interests. In other cases the interests represented are very different from those of the lower house, but the upper house's power is so weak that its influence is virtually insignificant. The members of Great Britain's House of Lords and Canada's Senate, for example, are appointed and not at all representative of the people, but their power is weak: they can delay legislation, but they cannot stop it. And even this power is rarely used.

Among the parliamentary systems with relatively strong bicameral systems are Germany and Australia. Germany's upper house, the Bundesrat, is made up of members of the Länder governments (it is as if governors and other high state officials in the United States were automatically given seats in the Senate). For many periods, including the present, the ruling coalition in the Bundestag, the lower house, has not had a majority in the Bundesrat, which has given the opposition added influence against the government. The Bundesrat, however, does not have the full legislative powers given to the Bundestag. It has an absolute veto power over legislation affecting the Länder, but in other issues its veto can be overridden with as little as a simple majority vote in the Bundestag. Australia's Senate is even stronger: apart from initiating money bills, it can do in practice everything the lower house can do.[26] Moreover, the majority party in the House of Representatives does not, and for the foreseeable future will not, control the Senate.[27]

Until recently, Japan's second chamber, the House of Councillors, has been a relatively weak, although by no means powerless, body. The Constitution makes the House of Representatives, the lower house, more powerful (it selects the prime minister, controls the budget, and ratifies treaties), and, for most of the time since the party was formed in 1955, the LDP has enjoyed an absolute majority in the upper house, as it has in the lower house. The House of Councillors, however, is not impotent. Most legislation must be passed by both houses. The lower, with a two-thirds majority, can override a bill that is rejected by the upper house. Thus passage of a bill can be assured only with either a majority in both houses or a two-thirds majority in the lower house. Since 1989, when the LDP lost its majority in the upper house, the House of Councillors has become much more important.

The judicial branch provides another potential constitutional check. The United States, with its system of separation of powers, has one of the most judicially active courts. The Supreme Court's right of judicial review allows it to strike down any law or regulation that violates the Constitution, a right that it has used and asserted a number of times. In parliamentary systems, however, the judicial branch is generally constitutionally inferior to the legislative branch. In a number of European countries, such as Great Britain, Switzerland, Belgium, and the Netherlands, the courts do not have the power of judicial review.[28] In Great Britain, Parliament ultimately decides whether a law is constitutional. But some parliamentary systems, such as in Germany, France, Italy, and Ireland, give their courts powers that rival those of the U.S. Supreme Court to rule on constitutional issues, and the courts have, at least on occasion, asserted those powers.[29] Japan's Supreme Court is in theory quite powerful. The Constitution (Article 81) gives it the right of judicial review (a right that even the U.S. constitution does not explicitly provide). However, the conventional wisdom, supported by Hiroshi Itoh's study, is that the Supreme Court is self-restrained and conservative: "Where a given law or ordinance is amenable to more than one interpretation, a court tends to adopt an interpretation that would uphold its constitutionality."[30] This is particularly true in cases involving the cabinet or the National Assembly. In a large majority of decisions, Itoh writes, "there were no changes in the policies of either the Supreme Court or political branches; the Court dismissed appeals challenging acts and actions of the political decision makers."[31] He adds, however, that the Supreme Court is not completely self-restrained. "The statistics that nearly half of the divided grand bench decisions characterized the Court as activist vis-à-vis the political branches is significant enough to qualify the widely held view that the Supreme Court has blindly followed the policies and actions of the LDP-dominated government."[32] In one particularly significant case the Supreme Court in 1985 ruled that the imbalances in representation in the House of Representatives were unconstitutional.[33] This ruling forced the government to pass in the Kokkai a redistricting bill that satisfied the Supreme Court criteria before it could call another election.

Finally, the prime minister in many parliamentary systems sometimes must deal with the head of state, either a monarch or a popularly elected president. In presidential systems, the head of state—the president—is also the head of government (with the exception of France and Ireland, which both have a strong president *and* a prime minister). As head of state, the U.S. president has prestige that prime ministers do not have. But in most parliamentary systems among the industrialized democracies, the head of state is separate from the head of government. The head of state typically has at best symbolic powers and rarely intervenes in any autonomous way in the political process.[34] The only real power given to heads of state is the naming of the prime minister, but even this is rarely exercised. The head of state usually has some discretion only when the parties in the legislature are unable to form a government on their own. In Japan's case the emperor is only a symbol of state; he is technically not even the head of state. The constitution does not allow the emperor to have any direct political influence. All his functions are purely ceremonial: he is not permitted to make any initiatives and has no discretion in fulfilling his roles. For instance, he does not even have the relatively nominal role of nominating a prime minister. He is limited to appointing the prime minister designated by the National Assembly (Article 6). His political role, therefore, is much weaker than that of even the British monarch and other heads of state.

The Executive   The final level of centralization that has to be considered is the executive. In the United States, at least in relation to the rest of the executive branch, the president's position is preeminent. He has the power to hire and fire not only cabinet secretaries but also officials in the top several levels of each department. Moreover, the president's control over the executive branch has been centralized further with the growth of the modern White House staff and other coordinating, budgetary, and monitoring organs of the Executive Office.[35] The president has, as Richard Nathan argues, the ability to shape the bureaucracy to reflect his policies.[36]

Unlike presidential systems, parliamentary ones do not make the prime minister the preeminent head of the executive. Instead, executive authority is generally concentrated collectively in the cabinet. In this regard, Japan's is very much like other parliamentary systems. The postwar constitution makes the cabinet the highest executive authority (Article 65).[37] It authorizes the cabinet to exercise control and supervision over various administrative branches of the government, prepare the budget, conduct the affairs of state, manage foreign affairs, administer the civil service, and, with the National Assembly's approval, conclude treaties (Articles 72–73).

And as in most other parliamentary systems, Japan's constitution makes the cabinet collectively responsible to the National Assembly; that is, all members of the cabinet are jointly responsible for any policy or decision officially made by it. For the prime minister, collective responsibility is a double-edged sword. On the one hand, it binds the members of the cabinet to decisions made by that body—any member seriously dissenting is expected to resign or face dismissal by the prime minister. But on the other, it also constrains the prime minister from straying very far from the consensus of the cabinet. This is particularly important in Japan, where consensus is greatly valued. Because the cabinet is a collective body, the prime minister's position is often described as only "first among equals."

Influence over the executive, therefore, largely depends on the prime minister's relationship with the rest of the cabinet. In particular, according to John Macintosh and Richard Crossman's analyses of the British system, two levers are important in giving the prime minister advantages over colleagues in the cabinet.[38] The first and more important is the power of patronage, that is, the prime minister's right to appoint the members of the cabinet. In most parliamentary democracies the majority, if not all of those the prime minister appoints, are members of the legislature, although some countries prevent ministers from simultaneously holding a seat in the legislature. Most prime ministers also have, besides the power to appoint ministers, the constitutional power to dismiss them. The exceptions here are in Italy and the Netherlands.[39]

In both regards the Japanese premier's powers are typical: the postwar constitution (Article 68) requires that a majority of the ministers be members of the National Assembly, and it gives him the power not only to appoint but also to dismiss them. Under the current Cabinet Law, the prime minister may appoint up to twenty people to cabinet posts and, in addition, an equal number of parliamentary vice ministers.

The second major lever is the prime minister's ability to control the cabinet's structure and proceedings. In Great Britain, Crossman and Macintosh argue, the prime minister's influence over the cabinet derives in part from the ability to control access to it through the agenda, to chair the meetings, to summarize the decisions, to decide the composition and subject matter of cabinet committees, and to limit decisions to meetings of inner or partial cabinets. "These powers can seldom be used to flout what is clearly the collective will of the majority; but they can always be used, including by a British prime minister, to nudge—sometimes even to steer—collective decisions in a desired direction."[40]

Under the Cabinet Law, the Japanese prime minister has similar powers: the authority to control and supervise the administrative branches, to decide the jurisdiction of issues, and to suspend temporarily ministry orders pending cabinet action, although not to give directives to ministry officials without the backing of the full cabinet.

The Japanese prime minister, however, does not have the British prime minister's relatively unusual power to determine which administrative departments of state will exist and which functions of state will be assigned to them.[41] Margaret Thatcher, for instance, abolished the Civil Service Department in 1981, remerged the Department of Trade and the Department of Industry, abolished the Central Policy Review Staff in

1983, and "culled" a number of secondary institutions.[42] The Japanese premier, and most other heads of government, does not have this power. The reorganization of ministries and agencies requires legislation. In other words, it requires the support not only of the cabinet but also of the National Assembly. The effect of this constraint was apparent when the original plan to establish a new central coordinating agency was significantly watered down in 1985.

The Japanese prime minister's control over the executive, then, does not come close to that of the U.S. president. And it is inferior to that of the British prime minister—he does not have the power to reorganize the executive. But he does have the important constitutional power of hiring and firing cabinet ministers and additional powers that he can use as leverage. His position in the executive, therefore, does not seem significantly different from that of his counterparts in most other parliamentary systems.

Party Government in Japan

The formal structure of government makes up only part of the environment in which the head of government operates. Great Britain and Belgium are both parliamentary systems, but they operate in quite different ways: Great Britain is a majoritarian system while Belgium is a consensual democracy. Even in a single country, changes occur between and even within administrations. The strong presidencies of Franklin Roosevelt, Lyndon Johnson, and Ronald Reagan are in contrast to the less influential ones of Gerald Ford and Jimmy Carter. The main factor that explains these differences is the party system. Party systems in majoritarian types of government generally have a single party that controls a majority of the seats in the legislature. Consensual democracies, however, tend to have many parties, none of which commands a majority. The head of government tends to be strong when his party commands a majority, and weak when it does not.

This seems to be true in both presidential and parliamentary systems. Most recent studies show that the most important predictor of the U.S. president's overall rate of legislative success is the strength of his party in Congress—Paul Light calls it the "gold standard" of congressional support.[43] Other factors such as the president's personality, legislative skills, and public popularity in comparison are all marginal. In Light's analysis, the major difference between John Kennedy's early legislative failures and Lyndon Johnson's successes in 1965 was the massive increase of House Democrats following the 1964 election: "Neither institutional prerogatives nor bargaining skills explain Johnson's dramatic success."[44]

In parliamentary systems, the number of seats controlled by the prime minister's party is, if anything, more important. George Jones, in his analysis of West European prime ministers, argues that the number and nature of parties are the most important variables in determining a prime minister's power.[45] Particularly important is whether a majority party rules or not. Great Britain and other Westminster systems generally have single-party majority governments, with the prime minister serving as the head of both the government and the majority party. The prime minister in these countries tends to be more influential because single-party governments tend to concentrate power. "[A] party with just over half the seats in Parliament can enjoy 100 percent of the power of government. As the leader of that party, a Prime Minister can expect to exercise a disproportionate amount of influence upon the overall direction of government."[46] This does not mean that the prime minister is necessarily dominant. Influence over the party depends on the prime minister's ability to maintain the confidence of party members. Anthony King points out that in the case of the Great Britain, the prime minister is ineffective if the party feels that it is being led to electoral defeat.[47]

Because most of the literature on prime ministers, particularly in English, concentrates on Westminster systems, particularly Great Britain's, many assume that they are representative of most other parliamentary systems. The truth is that most prime ministers do not enjoy single-party majority support.[48] Some countries, such as Germany, Italy, Sweden, Norway, and Belgium, have majority governments only rarely. Some, such as the Netherlands, Denmark, and Finland, have never had one. In all of these, governments are generally made up of either a coalition of political parties or a minority party. Recent studies of Italy, Spain, and the Netherlands suggest that prime ministers who do not have majority party support are considerably weaker than those who do.[49] A prime minister who does not represent a majority of votes in the legislature, then, is "enfeebled."[50]

In this regard the Japanese premier should have the strongest base of any head of government. He presides over a ruling party that is unsurpassed in its longevity—the LDP has now been in power continuously for over thirty-five years.[51] Although it lost its majority in the upper house, it has maintained its majority in the more powerful House of Representatives since the party was formed in 1955. It even won a rather comfortable victory in the 1990 general elections despite the taint of numerous scandals. With the current disarray in the leading opposition party, the JSP, the LDP does not seem to be in any danger of losing control of the government in the foreseeable future.

The prime minister's ability to maintain the confidence of the party, then, would seem to be relatively great. Contrary to the situation in a two-party system, his party would seem to have less fear of being electorally vulnerable. Moreover, party discipline in the National Assembly is quite strong. The rank and file has never crossed over in any significant numbers during a roll call vote, as has happened on occasion in Great Britain, particularly during the 1970s. The prime minister, as head of the party, also has powers of patronage in addition to those already provided by the Constitution. He appoints the speaker of the House of Representatives, as well as the top executive officers of the LDP.

The party does exercise certain constraints on the prime minister's patronage powers. The LDP is highly factionalized, and the prime minister must balance the cabinet according to the relative strengths of the factions (more on this in chapter 6). In this sense the party is a greater limitation in Japan than it is in Great Britain, where such considerations, while not ignored, are certainly less important. But the Japanese prime minister's position is not unique and not always inferior when compared to others. The German chancellor, even in a one-party government, is also forced to include members of important factions within the party.[52] Unlike the prime ministers of Canada, Australia, and Italy, the Japanese prime minister does not have to consider region when choosing the cabinet.[53] And the LDP is certainly not as restricting as the Labour parties in Australia and New Zealand. Prime ministers who head Labour governments there have had their formal patronage powers taken away altogether: in both countries the party elects the cabinet.[54]

Long-term Trends

The Japanese prime minister's position should also be strong because, in modern times, the top political leaders in virtually all countries have become much more central figures.[55] This argument has been most developed in the literature on the U.S. presidency, but it is also increasingly prevalent in the literature on other political systems.[56] In Great Britain, John Mackintosh and Richard Crossman have argued, cabinet government has been replaced by prime ministerial government.[57] Denis Smith and, more recently, James Simeon have argued that Canada's prime ministership had become "presidentialized."[58] Patrick Weller writes that in Australia "belief in overpowerful prime ministers has become orthodox."[59] Even in Italy, where the executive is weak and unstable, many scholars believe that the premiership has become more important.[60]

Two reinforcing factors seem to be driving this trend. First, modern governments face increased demands for government action, for example, in the areas of welfare, inflation, unemployment, national security, and the negative effects of international economic interdependence. "Prime ministers and presidents, not legislators, were asked to supply the innovation and integration that those situations demanded."[61] Second, modern technology, particularly in transportation, communications, and the media, has enhanced the visibility of the top political leader.[62] In the United States, it has long been argued that increased public demands for an activist national government, along with the emergence of the mass media, have increased public expectations of the president. Modern trends "have made presidents more central figures in our political and governing constellation, central enough to publicize agendas, to articulate visions and ideals, to command presence, and to be magnets for criticism."[63]

With increased public expectations, heads of government have enlarged their personal staffs and increased their control of the bureaucracies. In the United States presidents have centralized control of the government in the White House, and consequently the White House staff has grown and the bureaucracy has become politicized.[64] This has also been true in Great Britain, where Margaret Thatcher set up a personal policy staff known as the Downing Street Policy Unit and showed that the prime minister could dominate Whitehall (the civil service).[65] Similar trends seem to exist also in Canada, Australia, Italy, and Germany.[66]

One can also see many of these trends at work in Japan. Demands on the government have increased in similar ways. Although Japan was long considered a welfare "laggard," public demand has now put the welfare system at least on par with that of the United States.[67] The adverse effects of high economic growth led to pressure on the government to alleviate problems caused by pollution, inflation, and urban crowding. And with the continued growth, liberalization, and internationalization of the economy, demands on government have become even greater and more complicated.[68] International pressures have likewise increased. As was mentioned in chapter 1, the United States and other trading partners increasingly demand that the prime minister reduce Japan's trade surplus with them. Reinforcing these demands is the development of modern technology, which Japan has experienced to a greater degree than most other countries. Japan's mass media, with both national newspapers and television networks, is perhaps more national in its coverage and more widespread in circulation than those of virtually any other country.

Those trends seemed particularly evident during the prime ministership of the activist Nakasone Yasuhiro, who tried to fashion a "presidential-style prime ministership."[69] He was able to use his public popularity to maintain his base in the LDP and in addition worked on developing a personal staff by making use of private advisory committees and government commissions in pushing his policy goals. Also, he reorganized the Cabinet Secretariat and other administrative organizations to provide for more effective coordination and control of the domestic and international policy processes.[70]

Conclusion

Comparative analysis suggests that the Japanese prime minister's position should not be significantly weaker than that of most other heads of government. In many ways his position should be similar. For instance, he should be a more central figure because Japan is experiencing the same modern trends that have led to the emergence of presidents and prime ministers as the central force in government in virtually all countries around the world.

The analysis, in fact, suggests that although his constitutional powers may not be as strong as the British prime minister's, his position is considerably stronger than the position of some. In particular, Japan has the primary ingredients of a majoritarian system, which should give the prime minister the tools to provide forceful direction to government. It is a unitary state; the prime minister does not face the constraints that he would in a federal system. Nor does he face those that he would encounter under a system with strong checks and balances. The cabinet is relatively unconstrained by the House of Representatives; the Supreme Court is generally passive in dealing with issues involving the cabinet or the Kokkai; and the emperor no longer plays any active political role. Only the amendment process to the Constitution and the current control by the opposition parties of the House of Councillors put any formal limitation on the cabinet. And the prime minister has formal powers over the cabinet, in particular, that of patronage, that should make him a relatively powerful head of government.

Perhaps most importantly, the party system provides for majority party rule. In comparison to presidents who face legislatures controlled by opposition parties or to prime ministers who head coalition or minority governments—and most democracies regularly experience one or another of these situations—the Japanese prime minister has a much more solid base in the legislature from which to give direction to government. Hence one would expect that, much like his counterpart in Great Britain, he would be in an advantageous position to be an effective leader.

Yet as we have seen in chapter 1, the Japanese premier is not a particularly strong leader. His leadership is generally reactive. Before trying to explain this puzzle, it will help to examine some studies of the prime minister in action. The next two chapters provide two such studies.

3

Nakasone and Educational Reform

T*he Japanese prime ministership* presents a puzzle. On the basis of factors that are considered important in determining the influence of heads of government elsewhere, the prime minister should be in a relatively strong political position and thus be able to make a strong impact on the policy process. Yet, as we have seen, his role tends to be reactive. He tends to get involved in the process only after an issue is already on the agenda. Before we analyze the main factors that explain this, it may help to consider in some detail a couple of concrete cases. This chapter and the next concentrate on two such issues, both involving Nakasone Yasuhiro: this chapter traces the development of educational reform; chapter 4 focuses on tax reform.

In many ways these two cases are unusual and are therefore not at all representative of prime ministerial involvement in the policy process. First, both were big, well-publicized issues. Few issues, including other prime ministerial ones, have received so much attention. Second, both involve Nakasone, who was more of an activist than virtually any of his predecessors. He became prime minister in November 1982, fulfilling his longtime, if not life-long, ambition. With the support of two other major factions—those of Tanaka and Suzuki—in addition to his own, he easily won the election for the LDP presidency. And with the backing of the ruling LDP, he easily won the National Assembly election for the prime ministership. He remained in office for the next five years, serving longer than any prime minister since Satō Eisaku. What made him stand out among recent predecessors was his style. In contrast to the passive style of leadership usually associated with Japanese prime ministers, Nakasone consciously tried to exercise forceful top-down leadership as a "presidential" prime minister. He tried to participate in all aspects of the policy process, and the two cases of educational reform and tax reform highlight both the resources and constraints of the office. Thus they offer a better view of how far a prime minister—if willing—can go in influencing the policy process. In particular, these two chapters look at how Nakasone became involved in and how he affected the process of these questions. Each of the two chapters pays special attention to his role and influence in the process, from setting the agenda to the deliberation of the issues and the enactment of changes in policy.

Educational reform is a particularly interesting case because Nakasone was so personally concerned with it: it is one of the clearest cases of a Japanese prime minister trying to exercise strong leadership on a specific policy. This reform effort started during Nakasone's first year in office and for the most part had died by the time he left office five years later. More importantly, Nakasone's role in educational reform was hardly reactive: he played an active part in virtually every aspect of the process. He helped get the issue on the agenda, and he led the way in establishing the National Council on Educational Reform (generally known in Japanese as the Rinkyōshin), which was to develop the proposals for the reform of education. Moreover, Nakasone had very specific ideas about what should be reformed and how. In particular, he wanted to liberalize government administration of education. That is, he wanted to weaken the government's, especially Ministry of Education's, control over the system. Despite his efforts, however, he accomplished little of what he wanted to get done. Not only was he unable to get his main ideas enacted, but his efforts were also in some ways counterproductive. Many of the proposals that were adopted were actually the opposite of what he had in mind. The case of educational reform, then, suggests a number of the limits the Japanese prime minister faces in exercising top-down leadership.

Educational Reform Reaches the Agenda:
Nakasone Looks for an Issue

Educational reform was not one of Nakasone's first priorities when he became prime minister. But it did not take long during his first year in office before it became a major topic of discussion not only by the prime minister, but also by the Education Ministry, the LDP politicians specializing in education (the LDP education *zoku*), all of the major opposition political parties, and a number of interest groups. How did educational reform make it to the political agenda? The explanation is in three parts. First, juvenile delinquency became headline news as a result of successive violent incidents involving school-age children. Second, Nakasone seized upon it for use in election campaigns and broadened it to bring in other concerns. And third, a number of political actors jumped in to push their views on how the whole matter should be handled.

The Problem: Juvenile Delinquency

In February 1983 there were two well-publicized especially violent cases of juvenile delinquency. In the first, reported in the news on February 12, a group of about ten 14–16 year olds in Yokohama attacked sleeping vagrants in parks and underground shopping malls. The police suspected that the gang was involved in a number of assaults that resulted in a total of three deaths and thirteen injuries. And then, on February 15, a few days after the Yokohama incidents came to light, a teacher in a junior high school just outside Tokyo stabbed a student in self-defense.

These two incidents helped to focus attention on the state of education, already a matter of some public concern, even if it was not yet a political issue. The number of incidents of juvenile delinquency, particularly acts of school violence involving junior high school students, was rising.[1] According to National Police Agency (NPA) statistics, the number of incidents of assaults on teachers in 1982 was well over four times the number for 1978, and that for 1982 was double that for 1981.[2] Through the early 1980s the press reported numerous incidents of student gangs defacing school property and assaulting teachers. In addition, more and more students played truant from school. Competition over admission to senior high schools and universities was increasing, forcing more and more students to go to private cram schools in addition to regular school.

In January 1983 a *Mainichi Shimbun* public opinion poll on education revealed that one-half of those surveyed expressed some level of dissatisfaction with schools.[3] Moreover, perhaps the only aspect of school that the respondents felt had improved since their school days was the facilities. In just about all other areas—the quality of teachers and instruction, the quality of the curriculum, the emphasis on entrance examinations, the contact between teachers and students—most felt that schools had gotten worse.

Nakasone Looks for an Issue

While the incidents of juvenile delinquency were making the headlines, Nakasone was in need of a new issue to use in upcoming election campaigns for local governments and the upper house.

At the beginning of his administration, Nakasone pushed a number of controversial issues, such as increasing defense spending, strengthening the U.S.-Japanese security alliance, and revising the Constitution. His statements on these three topics, however, proved to be too controversial: newspaper polls showed not only strong public opposition to his hawkish statements themselves but also a marked decline in public support for his cabinet and the LDP as a whole.[4] Largely as a result of the public opposition, most of the heads of other factions also publicly disapproved of Nakasone's hawkish statements.[5] They feared that, with local elections in April and the upper house elections that summer, a public backlash would lead to a major LDP setback.

The drop in approval in the polls and the resulting criticism reportedly shocked Nakasone and his aides. He started to look for domestic issues to soften his hawkish image.[6] Although he considered a number of ideas, such as cancer research and doubling greenery in urban areas, he focused most of his attention on juvenile delinquency largely because of the two violent incidents described above.[7]

At this time, however, Nakasone did not emphasize educational reform. In fact, his chief cabinet secretary, Gotōda Masaharu, suggested that the government's countermeasures to juvenile delinquency would *not* involve the education system.[8] Rather, Nakasone viewed the problem mostly as a family one. But he did not have any concrete policy ideas on how to approach it from this angle. When he directed the Prime Minister's Office (PMO) to work out comprehensive measures to deal with the problem, officials there were reportedly at a loss as to what to do.[9]

Other Actors Define the Problem

As a result of the attention that the media and Nakasone were giving to juvenile delinquency, a number of other actors—the education sub-government (primarily the Education Ministry and the LDP education *zoku*) and several interest groups—took up the question, all pushing their own ideas. They helped make what initially was a problem of juvenile delinquency into an issue involving virtually all aspects of education.

Using the problem of juvenile delinquency, the Education Ministry and the LDP education *zoku* pressed for a number of changes that they had been advocating since the U.S. occupation.[10] In particular, they wanted more emphasis on moral education, stricter controls over the licensing and training of teachers, and tighter screening of textbook contents. These were sensitive political issues. For example, they wanted closer scrutiny of textbooks in order to revise accounts of Japanese actions during World War II in high school history textbooks and thus put Japan in a more favorable light.[11] LDP politicians also wanted to have more emphasis on patriotism in schools and change the one-track, 6-3-3 school system to include multiple tracks.[12] The Central Education Council (CEC), the primary advisory body to the Education Ministry, was already investigating two of these ideas, textbooks and reform of the 6-3-3 system to include an elite track. These were also supported by the Japan Federation of Employers' Associations (Nikkeiren), a big business group, in a report it published on school violence.[13]

In addition, the four major opposition parties—the JSP, the Democratic Socialist Party (DSP), the Japan Communist Party (JCP), and Kōmeitō (Clean Government party)—and the Japan Teachers' Union (Nikkyōso) proposed measures, centered on schools, to counter school violence and juvenile delinquency. The JSP, the JCP, and the teachers' union wanted fewer students per class, less emphasis on tests for entrance into high schools and universities, and fewer regulations for students. The union also wanted fewer administrative controls on teachers.

The interesting point is that most of the activity had little to do with Nakasone's emphasis on family issues. The groups that joined the action either were involved in some way with education or, in the case of the political parties, made statements that centered on education. The lack of response on the family side is largely because there are no groups pushing for public policy changes in this area. In essence, the activity of the groups defined the problem of juvenile delinquency as an education issue, rather than as a family problem. Nakasone then changed his emphasis and started concentrating on educational reform. First, on March 29, 1983, a little over one month after his first public statement on juvenile delinquency, he announced his intention to review the education system. He later proposed setting up an ad hoc council to study educational reform, similar to the one for administrative reform, rather than leaving the issue in the hands of the Education Ministry. Then, during the election campaign for the House of Councillors, Nakasone appointed a private panel of advisers to study educational reform in terms of preparing Japan for the twenty-first century. And during the election campaign for the lower house in December, he unveiled his seven-point plan to reform education, in which he included the high school entrance examinations.[14]

The question of educational reform proved to be extremely popular, with practically all the political parties climbing on the bandwagon in the campaign first for the upper house election on June 26 and then for the lower house election on December 18. A *Mainichi Shimbun* survey of candidates for the upper house revealed that in terms of the issues they wanted to raise during the campaign, education had priority over all others except social welfare.[15] Indeed, during the campaign, all the major political actors stepped up their efforts at educational reform.

Thus by December the debate over educational reform had attracted a wide range of issues as well as participants. Not only were Nakasone and education-related groups (such as the LDP education *zoku*, the Education Ministry, and the Japan Teachers' Union) involved, but also virtually all of the political parties and a number of big business groups.

Establishing the National Council
on Educational Reform

Nakasone was thinking of making educational reform a centerpiece of his second cabinet. If the LDP had done well in the election, he would likely have gone ahead immediately to press for an ad hoc council on education. The party, however, did unexpectedly poorly, winning only 250 of the 512 seats and maintaining its majority only with the addition of conservative independents and an alliance with the New Liberal Club. The poor election showing weakened Nakasone within the party and made it difficult to override the education *zoku*'s opposition to the ad hoc body. Thus, at first, Nakasone gave up the idea: in a press conference during the New Year holidays, he announced that the Education Ministry's Central Education Council (CEC) would handle the issue.

But by the middle of the month, he had changed his mind. First, he was able to persuade three members of his faction who were influential members of the education *zoku* not only to accept an ad hoc body but also to persuade the other *zoku* members to go along.[16] And then on January 17, in meetings with the heads of the opposition parties, Nakasone picked up support for an ad hoc council from two parties, the Kōmeitō and the DSP.

Nakasone then persuaded Mori Yoshirō, whom he had appointed as education minister following the lower house election, to agree. Mori and other members of the LDP education *zoku* were at first opposed. He announced on January 17 that the Education Ministry would commission its advisory group, the CEC, to deal with the issue. In part, the opposition of Mori and other *zoku* members was due to factional infighting; many of its important members were from the rival Fukuda and Kōmoto factions, which did not want Nakasone to be able to take credit for educational reform in his drive to be reelected in the fall as president of the party. Mori, as a member of the Fukuda faction, could not immediately agree with the prime minister, but he was in a delicate position because he had promised Nakasone on entering the cabinet that he would cooperate in carrying out educational reform. On January 22, Mori decided that he would go along and also help in persuading the other *zoku* members. In addition to being a *zoku* member, he was a rising politician in the LDP. Mori felt that he could make a name for himself by identifying himself with educational reform, in a somewhat similar fashion to the way Nakasone had used administrative reform to establish himself as the leading candidate to succeed Suzuki Zenkō as prime minister.

Thus Chief Cabinet Secretary Fujinami Takao and Education Minister Mori met with two other *zoku* leaders, Mitsuzuka Hiroshi (Fukuda faction) and Kaifu Toshiki (Kōmoto faction) at a Tokyo restaurant to discuss the establishment of an ad hoc council. Both Kaifu and Mitsuzuka were opposed, but Fujinami let them know that the prime minister's position was firm and emphasized the opportunity this presented to carry out a comprehensive reform of education. Mori promised in addition that, if the ad hoc council were established, it would be run under the Education Ministry, rather than under the prime minister. With this, Kaifu and Mitsuzuka were persuaded to agree.

The next day, Kaifu visited the prime minister and relayed to him the news that the party would formally accept the establishment of the ad hoc body on condition that he respect the responsibility of the Education Ministry and past reports of the CEC. Thus on February 1 the prime minister and the education minister formally agreed to establish the National Council on Educational Reform, the Rinkyōshin.

Even with the agreement of the *zoku*, Nakasone still faced opposition in the party. On February 6 in his policy speech to the Kokkai, he included educational reform as one of three domestic reforms he planned to push in the coming year, but in the formal question period following the speech, Fujio Masayuki, the chairman of the LDP Policy Affairs Research Council (PARC), harshly criticized Nakasone's attempt to establish an ad hoc council: "The party already has splendid organs in its education division and research council and the National Assembly already has a standing committee on education to handle educational reform." But by appointing Nikaidō Susumu, a senior member of the Tanaka faction, as vice president of the party, Nakasone was able to consolidate his position in the party and thus silence criticism of him and his plan.

In order to draft the bill to establish the Rinkyōshin, Nakasone had to negotiate with the Education Ministry. The ministry, on the one hand, wanted to maintain as much of its autonomy over the reform effort as possible and therefore wanted to limit the tenure and number of its members. Nakasone, on the other, wanted to strengthen the council as much as possible. The resulting draft of the bill was a compromise. The council was to consist of twenty-five members appointed for three years, rather than twenty appointed for two years, as advocated by the ministry. In order to increase support for the bill not only among ministry officials but also among opposition parties, Nakasone agreed that the council would try to reform education "in the spirit of the Fundamental Law of Education."[17]

The bill was presented to the legislature at the end of March, and Nakasone had expected to have it passed by mid-June and to inaugurate the council by early July. But the bill faced unexpected difficulties in both houses. The JSP and JCP were wary about the intentions of Nakasone and the LDP and constantly questioned what the council would investigate, thus delaying passage.[18]

In addition, the original strategy was to allow the House of Councillors to amend the bill to include a condition that the appointments to the Rinkyōshin be approved by the National Assembly—an amendment previously agreed upon by the LDP, the DSP, and the Kōmeitō. But because the deliberations in the House of Representatives were taking longer than expected, the amendment was added there. Members of the upper house felt that their position was being usurped by the lower house and therefore delayed their deliberations. Moreover, just as the upper house was taking up the bill, two bribery scandals involving section chiefs of the Education Ministry surfaced, which forced the bill to be shelved for a while.

The bill nevertheless passed on August 7, 1984, the last day of the legislative session.

The National Council on Educational Reform

The National Council on Educational Reform (Rinji Kyōiku Shingikai, abbreviated to Rinkyōshin) issued four reports over the span of three years, before disbanding on August 20, 1987.[19] The discussions involved virtually every conceivable facet of education, from preschool to primary and secondary to higher education to lifelong learning. And within each level, members discussed what should be taught, who should teach, the facilities of the institutions, and the role of the government in administering education. The council reached a consensus on a number of recommendations with relatively little trouble: for example, promotion of international student exchanges, better use of computers for educational purposes, more physical education,[20] and an expansion of part-time schools and correspondence courses to allow those adults without high school education to earn their diplomas. These were relatively uncontroversial within the council. In other cases, such as the recommendation for a university council to handle issues of higher education, the Rinkyōshin put off most of its discussions and simply recommended the establishment of another deliberative body.

But deliberations were also often heated. Nakasone had hoped that the Rinkyōshin would present proposals to overhaul the education system, while the Education Ministry and its allies in the LDP wanted to make some changes but maintain the basic system. This difference was reflected both in struggles over the appointments to the council and in its deliberations. It is these differences that are emphasized here.

Council Membership

After the law to establish the council was passed, the first step was to appoint the members. For the chairmanship, Nakasone wanted someone from outside education. He felt strongly that only outsiders would push for fundamental reform. He first looked for guidance from the private sector, in particular big business, which had helped bring him success in administrative reform.[21]

Nakasone, however, faced opposition from the LDP *zoku*, the Education Ministry, and the opposition parties. The DSP and Kōmeitō, which provided crucial support for the passage of the bill establishing the council, were against having a chairman from big business. Both the Education Ministry and the LDP education *zoku* urged the prime minister to appoint someone who was well versed in the administrative affairs of education.

As a compromise, Nakasone settled on Okamoto Michio, a former president of Kyoto University. Okamoto was chairman of Nakasone's private advisory council on youth issues, and Nakasone reportedly was pleased with his performance. In addition, Okamoto was well known in the education field, having been head of the committee investigating reforms of university entrance exams. The appointments of the two deputy chairs were balanced by Ishikawa Tadao, president of Keiō University, who represented private schools and had served on Nakasone's private advisory group on education and culture; and Nakayama Sōhei, a senior adviser to the Industrial Bank of Japan, who had served as a member of a number of Nakasone's private advisory groups over the years and likely would have been his first choice for chairman.

Nakasone also battled with the Education Ministry over the appointment of the twenty-two other regular members of the council plus the twenty specialist members (*senmon iin*). The result was a compromise. Eight of the regular members (out of twenty-five) and five specialist members were considered to be close to Nakasone, while the Education Ministry had six members and six specialists.[22] The appointments to the remaining seats were made to represent various other interests.[23]

The tug-of-war between Nakasone and the Education Ministry extended even to the physical location of the Rinkyōshin's secretariat, which did much of the staff work. The secretariat was made up of about fifty members from various ministries and agencies and was headed by the Education Ministry's administrative vice minister, Sano Bun'ichirō. Education Ministry officials wanted the secretariat to be housed in the ministry, so that they could watch the workings of the council more closely, but at Nakasone's insistence it was housed in the same building as the PMO.

The Rinkyōshin's Deliberations

The council members decided to divide themselves into four subcommittees, each responsible for developing proposals on a certain aspect of education, although the final decisions regarding the reports outlining the Rinkyōshin's proposals had to be approved by the full council. The first subcommittee was responsible for studying reforms of the educational system to meet the needs of Japan in the twenty-first century; the second concentrated on the role of education in society, particularly working to deemphasize the importance that Japanese society gives to school background; the third focused on elementary and secondary education; and the fourth concentrated on higher education.

Two of the four main issue areas were due in part to Nakasone. The reform of the education system to respond to the needs of Japan in the twenty-first century was originally brought up by Nakasone and was the major topic of discussion of his private advisory council on education, and many of the members belonging to the first subcommittee were members of Nakasone's brain trust. And the discussion of reforms in higher education was particularly concerned with the university entrance examination system. University examinations were not handled by the Central Education Council, which generally concentrated on the primary and secondary levels. Nakasone, however, made reform of university examinations one of his main promises during the campaign for the 1983 lower house election.

In writing the reports, the Rinkyōshin was often divided between Nakasone's appointees and those who were closer to the views of the Education Ministry. Thus the tug-of-war between Nakasone and the Education Ministry continued through their proxies in the deliberations of the council. This was particularly evident in the two issues Nakasone was advocating most strongly: liberalization and the elimination of the national and public universities' first-stage entrance examination.

Liberalization

The division within the Rinkyōshin soon became apparent as the first and third committees battled over liberalization. This was the main topic of the deliberations even though it was not included explicitly in the reports. The subject was proposed by the first subcommittee, where most of Nakasone's appointees were concentrated. In essence, certain members of that subcommittee, particularly Kōyama Ken'ichi, wanted education to be run under free market rules: school districts would be enlarged or abolished altogether so that parents and children would be allowed to choose the school they thought would best serve their needs, and the licensing of private schools would be significantly liberalized, thus allowing private cram schools to operate as accredited schools rather than just as institutions offering supplemental schooling. The effect of the proposal, if implemented, would have meant that the control of the Education Ministry over the education system would have been greatly weakened.

Liberalization was first espoused by the Kyoto Study Group on Global Issues, chaired by Matsushita Konōsuke, in a report released in March 1984.[24] Nakasone later appointed a number of members of this group to the Rinkyōshin as either regular members or specialists.[25] In addition, he appointed other people who supported liberalization: Kōyama Ken'ichi, Tawara Kōtarō, and Yayama Tarō.

The proposal was fiercely opposed by the Education Ministry and other members of the council, in particular Arita Kazuhisa, the chairman of the third subcommittee, which was studying reform of primary and secondary education. It was also opposed explicitly both by the Education Ministry and the LDP education *zoku*. Takaishi Kunio, chief of the Education Ministry's primary and secondary education bureau, submitted to the first subcommittee on January 23, 1985 a statement opposing liberalization. The LDP Special Research Commission on Education Reform, headed by Mori Yoshirō (the previous education minister), criticized liberalization as departing from the original theme of dealing with violence in schools. The LDP *zoku* and Education Ministry officials generally wanted tighter, not looser, controls over schools.

The proposal to liberalize education initially received strong support from Nakasone. He announced publicly in the National Assembly that he was a "liberalization person," thus encouraging supporters of liberalization to continue to push for their proposal despite opposition from the other members of the Rinkyōshin and the LDP. Nakasone, however, eventually abandoned the issue; he was unable to arouse public opinion to support his view. Moreover, Sunada Shigetami, a member of Nakasone's own faction—one of those in it who helped persuade the other members of the LDP education *zoku* to go along with the establishment of the ad hoc council—went to Nakasone to request that he drop his support for the liberalization proposal. Without the support of Nakasone, its supporters could not persuade the other members of the Rinkyōshin, and the proposal was dropped from the first report.

The issue of liberalization continued to come up during deliberations for later reports, particularly in terms of school districts and textbook screening. Kōyama was able to get the reports to endorse in limited form the principle of liberalization. One of the main themes in the final report was the principle of stressing individuality: "The educational policy and system should be made more flexible and decentralized."

There were, however, few concrete proposals for such liberalization. Kōyama and others on the first subcommittee proposed that the textbook screening system be completely liberalized—that textbooks be published and adopted for school use without intervention by the

Education Ministry. This suggestion was adamantly opposed by the third subcommittee. The Education Ministry and the LDP *zoku* were interested in tightening the screening process further. The final proposal seemed to suggest that there was a move toward liberalization, recommending that the textbook screening process be simplified from the three-step system then in use to a one-step review process, and left open the possibility that the system could be liberalized in the future.[26] The Rinkyōshin also recommended that schools consider the possibility of not subjecting some high school textbooks to any sort of screening.

But most experts believed that the simplified system would actually give the Education Ministry more control over the screening process, not less, because it would deprive authors and editors of the ability to negotiate with textbook examiners before a final decision was made.[27] In addition, the education minister would still have the final authority to approve or reject school textbooks, as well as the right to order revisions of those that initially failed the screening.

Another example is the proposal from the third report for an increase in the number of school districts where students have two or more options, so that they would have more choices in the selection of public schools for compulsory education. Kōyama advocated that parents and their children should be able to choose schools. Those on the third subcommittee argued that such a system would make the management of schools difficult. The resulting proposal was something of a compromise. The Rinkyōshin recommended that boards of education try to expand the choices, but it left the existing system intact.[28] This meant that the local boards of education would be able to prevent any large-scale transfers of students.

University Entrance Examinations

In addition to liberalization, Nakasone also wanted to have the first-stage entrance examinations for national and public universities abolished. The system was started in 1979 to ease pressures on students trying to enter universities. It provided a preliminary exam that would help inform them which universities' entrance exams they should take. But because private universities never joined the system, students wishing to apply to both public and private universities were forced to take *more* exams

than previously. Hence Nakasone wanted to abolish the first-stage examinations, claiming that they intensified "examination hell."

The Education Ministry, however, wanted to revise the system rather
than abolish it, and the Rinkyōshin's draft proposal took the ministry's
position, largely because Iijima Sei, chairman of the subcommittee
responsible, worked with the Education Ministry's higher education
bureau in drafting it.[29] Iijima was one of the ministry's appointees to the
Rinkyōshin and was formerly a member of the Council of National
Universities special committee on improving entrance examinations and
of the CEC.

When the Rinkyōshin presented its draft proposal, Nakasone wanted
it changed, but the council did not do so. Okamoto, the chairman of the
Rinkyōshin, was often referred to as the "father of the preliminary exam";
the council, therefore, found it difficult to call for its outright abolition. It
proposed a compromise whereby it would be replaced by a new "common" test (*kyōtsū tesuto*) that would be utilized voluntarily by any university, national, public, or private. The Rinkyōshin members tried to
appease the prime minister by suggesting that the meaning of the
proposal could be interpreted to include the abolition of the preliminary
test, but Nakasone not surprisingly remained unconvinced. He met with
then Education Minister Matsunaga Akira five days before the first report
was to be issued to complain, "The proposal for the new common test is
just a continuation of the preliminary test. Do you call this reform?"[30]

The Proposals of the Education Ministry and LDP Education Zoku

Meanwhile, the Education Ministry and the education *zoku* were able
to include proposals that they had been pushing for many years. The
ministry was interested in three things in particular: increasing control
over teachers, greater emphasis on moral education, and reform of the
curriculum—all of which were included in the Rinkyōshin reports. The
second report, for instance, called for a teacher apprenticeship system in
which all newly recruited teachers would be under the supervision of a
senior teacher for a probationary period of one year. The justification was
to make them better teachers, but it also would help weaken the Japan
Teachers' Union because teachers would be socialized by nonunion
teachers. The introduction of this system alone would have made the

whole effort at educational reform worthwhile for the ministry,[31] for, starting before the war, it had tried many times—without success—to introduce just such a system.

Most of the Rinkyōshin's proposals regarding primary and secondary education followed past CEC reports. The Education Ministry is responsible for setting national standards for the curriculum for each school level.

The LDP *zoku* was able to include two proposals: the six-year secondary school and a greater emphasis on the teaching of patriotism. LDP legislators have long sought a reform of the one-track 6-3-3 system. Members of the party's *zoku* were unhappy that the Education Ministry failed to pursue a 1971 CEC proposal to set up another track alongside the 6-3-3 one. The Rinkyōshin's first report included a proposal to allow local governments to set up six-year secondary schools at their discretion.

In addition, the fourth report recommended that school education emphasize the teaching of patriotism so that "people can understand and respect the meaning of the national flag and national anthem." This part was included apparently at the request by Education Minister Shiokawa Masajurō, but not before considerable discussion in Rinkyōshin meetings.[32] But this proposal was already being handled by the Curriculum Council, an advisory body to the Education Ministry.

Assessing the Proposals

The consensus among almost everyone involved is that the Education Ministry was able to use the council to promote some ideas that it had advanced in the past. As one reporter put it, "The proposals made me wonder why the Rinkyōshin was needed. I think that the Central Education Council would have come up with the same proposals."[33]

The Education Ministry was certainly satisfied with the reports. The three things it wanted most were included: teacher apprenticeship, curriculum reform, and moral education. The *zoku* members were also satisfied. In addition to moral education, the reports proposed greater emphasis on the teaching of patriotism and a reform of the uniform 6-3-3 system to include six-year secondary schools. Nakasone, on the other hand, had little reason to be happy. He often criticized the council for the "lack of content" of its proposals.[34] In particular, his wish for the liberalization of education administration made little impact. Amaya Naohiro, chairman of the first subcommittee that suggested more comprehensive reforms, admitted, "I thought we could accomplish big things, but the conservative forces were stronger than the ones pushing for reform."[35]

Enactment of Proposals

The Rinkyōshin only developed proposals for educational reform; it was not responsible for putting them into effect. Once it was disbanded in August 1987, having completed its three-year mission, the question was who was to oversee the enactment of the proposals: the prime minister, through another ad hoc commission, or the education subgovernment? Both worked hard to gain control over the process. And in the end it was the education subgovernment, particularly the Education Ministry, that won. It was able to press for the proposals it wanted and sit on those it did not.

Follow-up to the Rinkyōshin: Nakasone vs. the Education Subgovernment

Nakasone called for the establishment of an organ under the prime minister to follow up the Rinkyōshin proposals, as was done after the Second Ad Hoc Council on Administrative Reform (the second Rinchō). This was opposed by Education Minister Shiokawa and other LDP *zoku* members, all of whom wanted the reform effort to be handled by the ministry through its advisory body, the CEC. In the meantime, the ministry established headquarters for the implementation of education reform, headed by the education minister, as part of its attempt to takeover. But Nakasone managed to persuade key members of the *zoku* and was thus able to get cabinet approval to establish an "ad hoc body for facilitating the implementation of educational reform."[36]

The new ad hoc body, however, was never realized. Nakasone stepped down as prime minister soon after the cabinet decision, and his successor, Takeshita Noboru, did not pursue it. According to one member of the *zoku*, with Nakasone no longer prime minister, no one was willing to advocate passage of legislation needed to set up the new body.[37] Thus the enactment of the proposals was left in the hands of the education subgovernment, particularly the Education Ministry, which reinaugurated the CEC as it had originally intended to do.

The Education Ministry, therefore, was in large part able to determine which proposals were put into effect. It implemented some almost immediately and referred others to one of its advisory groups to flesh out. While tabling proposals it did not want, the ministry quickly moved to enact the three it wanted most: teacher apprenticeship, reform of the curriculum, and greater emphasis on moral education.

As I mentioned above, the ministry wanted more than anything else to be able to introduce the teacher apprenticeship system. Hence it was one of the first things that the ministry took up even though it was listed in the second, and not the first, report. Immediately after the second report was issued, the ministry entrusted the recommendations for apprenticeship to its advisory body, the Education Personnel Training Council, to develop into concrete proposals. It also started apprenticeship on an experimental basis in thirty prefectures and metropolitan areas, including Tokyo and Osaka, covering 6 percent or about 2,130 of the newly recruited teachers. The new system was formally passed into law in 1988 and introduced across the country in 1989.[38]

The Education Ministry also proceeded with reforms of school curricula and moral education. It inaugurated the Curriculum Council in September 1985, which submitted its report in December 1987 on new national standards for the curriculum of kindergarten, primary, and secondary school. The ministry issued revised courses of study in September 1988 for primary and junior high school and in February 1989 for senior high school. The new courses of study will be introduced into schools by 1992 for primary schools, 1993 for junior high schools, and 1994 for high schools. The new curriculum puts more emphasis on moral education[39] and on patriotism by forcing schools to fly the Hinomaru flag and sing the national anthem, "Kimigayo," at school events. The ministry is being opposed by a number of groups that claim that the flag and anthem are symbols of Japanese militarism, and the new curriculum is being challenged in the courts as unconstitutional infringement on the freedom of speech.[40]

The third report recommended that textbook authorization be simplified to one step. The Education Ministry immediately began to prepare for the introduction of the new screening system. Primary and middle school textbooks submitted to the ministry came under the new rules in 1988, and high school textbooks from 1989. The newly authorized textbooks were introduced into primary schools in 1990. It appears that the new system is strengthening the ministry's control over textbooks, as had been feared. In 1988 the ministry became even more involved in the details of the textbooks' content. It requested that content follow national policy; for example, it wanted textbooks to support the use of nuclear power. Thus not only is the ministry seeking deletions of offensive passages, as it has done in the past, but it is now apparently also directing the publishers to add certain items.[41]

One case in which the Education Ministry is dragging its feet is the proposal advocated by the LDP *zoku* to establish trial six-year secondary schools. In order to establish the new schools, the School Education Law and the Teacher Certification Law have to be amended and the curriculum for the new type of school has to be drawn up. The ministry set up a research council to study the idea and asked the Curriculum Council and the Education Personnel Training Council to look at the question from their respective angles. But the ministry is not really interested in the new schools because they go against its policy of maintaining one track for compulsory education.[42] Thus neither the Curriculum Council nor the Education Personnel Training Council have spent much time on the six-year schools, and it seems unlikely that the new schools will start anytime soon.

The Education Ministry established in July 1985 the University Entrance Examination Reform Council (Daigaku nyūshi kaikaku kyōgikai), headed by Uchida Kenzō, who was also a member of the Rinkyōshin. In July 1986 the council outlined a "new test" that all universities, national, public, and private, would be able to use voluntarily. In May 1988 the National School Establishment Law was amended to introduce changes in the functions of the National Center for the University Entrance Examination so that it will not only handle the new test but also serve as an information source for high school students and others wishing to take the exam.[43] At the urging of Nakasone the new test was originally scheduled to be introduced by 1989, but the council decided on a one-year delay because of the Council of National Universities (Kokuritsu daigaku kyōkai) and high schools wanted more time to prepare for it.[44] Although one of the main reasons for introducing the new test was to include private universities, only 4 percent of them participated in 1990.[45] They are afraid to compete directly with the more prestigious national universities.

In addition, the Council of National Universities in 1987 divided the schools of national universities into two groups that would have the second-round entrance exam on different days to allow students more choices and opportunities to test at universities, as was recommended in the Rinkyōshin's first report. Problems arose, however, when some of the more prestigious schools did not go along with the plan. Some law departments, including the prestigious department at Kyoto University, did not want to hold their exams on a day different from Tokyo University's for fear that the vast majority of those accepted at both would choose the latter. But because of pressure from the LDP education *zoku*, the Council of National Universities revised the system again for the 1989 test. In addition, some or all the departments of nine national universities concentrated in western Japan have set up another system, the "separate partitioned entrance examinations" (*bunri bunkatsu nyūshi*), in which students have two opportunities to take a university's entrance examination.[46]

In the enactment and implementation of proposed reforms, the Education Ministry was even more dominant than it was in drafting of Rinkyōshin's proposals. Certainly, Nakasone did not make much of an impact. In part this was because he stepped down as prime minister just after the proposals were submitted and because he supported few of them anyway, since his personal proposals were not reflected in the reports.

Conclusion

What was Nakasone's impact on the process of educational reform? Although it was one of his top priorities, his impact was limited. He felt that a comprehensive reform could be accomplished only by an ad hoc council similar to the one for administrative reform because the Education Ministry would not push for major reform.[47] But the proposals did not reflect the prime minister's expectations. And it would be difficult to identify what effect he had on education given the way the education subgovernment, particularly the Education Ministry, took control of the issue of reform.

This is not to say that Nakasone had no impact in the process. Clearly, he did. He was able to help direct attention to the issue in a general way, first by emphasizing the problem of juvenile delinquency and later by setting up the Rinkyōshin. He highlighted some problems, such as "examination hell," and presented some solutions, such as liberalization, which were discussed even if they were eventually discarded.

But, ultimately, little happened in the way of the comprehensive reforms that he had advocated. The development of proposals and their enactment were handled almost exclusively by the education subgovernment made up of the Education Ministry, the LDP education *zoku*, and some of the interest groups. Members of this subgovernment did not necessarily agree with one another, but they were all opposed to the prime minister's intervention. Even the Japan Teachers' Union, which is in constant battle with the Education Ministry, opposed the establishment of an ad hoc council and preferred that educational issues be handled by the CEC.

Still, Nakasone might have been able to make more of an impact on the deliberations had he been able to enlist more support for his views, as he had done with administrative reform. Then, he had received help from a "center structure" alliance consisting of the Finance Ministry, LDP leaders, and big business which had the shared objectives of eliminating the national deficit.[48] Had Nakasone been able to muster some support from the LDP, the public, and interest groups (e.g., big business), as he did with the Administrative Reform Council, he might have had more sway over the deliberations of the council and later in the drafting of legislation. But with education he was not able to do this. There was no other ministry interested in education, and there was no one among the LDP leadership who strongly advocated liberalization. And although some of the big business groups originally expressed interest, it seemed to wane, perhaps because education was peripheral to their interests. With virtually no outside help, those appointed by Nakasone had little effect. Amaya Naohiro, for instance, complained that they were outsiders.[49]

Thus, the education subgovernment, in particular the Education Ministry, was able to dominate the drafting of the Rinkyōshin proposals. With members appointed by Nakasone unable to advance their ideas, the process was taken over by those close to the ministry who also had a great deal of experience and expertise in education issues. Saitō Tadashi, a former administrative vice minister of education, for example, was responsible for drafting the proposals involving primary and secondary education. The Education Ministry, therefore, was able to use the council to promote some of its ideas. One of the main members confessed, "Even if the council had not been set up, proposals would have been almost the same had the Education Ministry done the work itself."[50]

Nakasone also had little impact in the enactment and implementation of the proposals since there were few that he wanted to push, and he left office before he could set up another deliberative council. Thus the Education Ministry and the LDP education *zoku* were able to dominate this part of the process also. This is not surprising since many of the more concrete proposals were ones that the ministry supported and in many cases helped draft and because it was able to flesh out many of those that were left rather vague through its advisory councils.

But the education subgovernment might hve been able to dominate the enactment and implementation of proposals regardless of what was in the Rinkyōshin reports. A member of the LDP education *zoku* commented: "I don't have any interest in the council. If the council comes out with reports that do not fit with our policies, we will not let them be realized."[51]

The case of Nakasone's involvement in educational reform, therefore, suggests that the prime minister faces major constraints when trying to go against a well-defined subgovernment such as the one in education. He has difficulty because the subgovernment defines the issues, has well-developed proposals for change, and controls the actual drafting and implementation of change. A prime minister can try, as Nakasone did, to bring in outsiders, but they have a hard time making an impact. They generally lack the resources, expertise, and persistence that the permanent actors possess.

4

Nakasone and Tax Reform

T _ax reform was arguably_ the most important domestic policy issue of the last half of the 1980s. One of the major reasons for tax reform was to stabilize the government's revenue base in preparation for the increased expenditures expected with the aging of Japan's society. But tax reform was controversial: the attempts to introduce a large indirect tax set off protests nationwide. The tax reforms that the National Assembly ulti-mately introduced in 1987 and 1988 affected virtually every person in Japan. And there were widespread political implications: the introduc-tion of the consumption tax, a value-added tax (VAT), along with the Recruit scandal, helped lead to the loss of the LDP's majority in the House of Councillors (the upper house) for the first time since the party was formed in 1955.

Even though the reform he was able to accomplish while in office was limited, Nakasone played a central role in pushing tax reform. In the previous case, the education subgovernment was able to stop his efforts to liberalize education administration even before any legislation was drafted. He was able to take the process for tax reform considerably further, in large part because he was taking up proposals supported, rather than opposed, by the main actors responsible for tax policy, the LDP tax _zoku_ and the tax officials in the Finance Ministry. But Nakasone and later Takeshita faced other obstacles in trying to get the tax reform bills passed in the Kokkai. The case shows some of the difficulties the prime minister can face not only in overcoming resistance from opposition parties but also in keeping his own party in line.

This chapter follows the development of the issue of tax reform from late 1984, when the LDP started to consider introducing a new indirect tax, to December 1988, when Takeshita was able to guide legislation introducing the VAT through the National Assembly. It looks at how the issue of tax reform reached the agenda; the deliberations of the two main bodies, the Government Tax Council and LDP Tax Council, responsible for developing the proposals for tax reform; and the attempts to pass the bills in the National Assembly. In particular, the chapter focuses on the role and impact that Nakasone had at each stage of the process.

Tax Reform Reaches the Agenda

Nakasone's first statement on tax reform came on December 3, 1984, when he revealed that he was considering tackling it as one of his medium- and long-term policy goals in his second administration. Those dealing with tax policy in the LDP and government had already started to consider seriously the introduction of some sort of large indirect tax—a uniform tax on almost all commodities and services—as a solution to various problems.

Members of the Finance Ministry had been studying indirect taxes since about 1970, soon after a number of the European Community countries started various forms of VAT, a form of indirect sales tax paid on commodities and services at each stage of production or distribution, based on the value added at that stage. Finance officials began promoting the introduction of some form of indirect tax in Japan to counter a growing budget deficit.[1] Then, in 1979, Prime Minister Ōhira Masayoshi announced plans to introduce a VAT before a general election.[2] This was a complete disaster for Ōhira: the proposal led to massive public opposition and splits within the party.[3] And even though he backed down during the campaign, the LDP still fared poorly in the election, and Ōhira and his tax proposal received most of the blame.

The result of the 1979 election was that a new indirect tax was not seriously considered for several years. In December 1979 the National Assembly adopted a resolution at the start of its session that fiscal reform would not rely on a new tax. Ōhira's successor, Suzuki Zenkō, made a public promise to reconstruct the nation's finances without new taxes.[4] Nakasone, Suzuki's successor, continued the policy by adopting very austere guidelines for budget requests.

By 1984, however, there was widespread sentiment in both the Finance Ministry and the LDP that Nakasone's austerity policy should be changed. The ministry was proposing to raise 300 billion yen in national taxes starting in fiscal year 1985 by abolishing the tax exemption on small-lot savings in the so-called *maruyū* system[5] and by collecting more taxes from corporations, partly through the imposition of a 5 percent excise tax on the sale of office automation equipment (e.g., office and personal computers, word processors, electric typewriters, electronic calculators, photocopiers, and facsimile machines). Both efforts, however, failed because of strong opposition from interest groups that would be affected.[6]

The Finance Ministry advocated the tax not only for the revenue but also as a strategy to highlight the distortions of the indirect tax structure and to persuade the *zaikai* (big business groups) to support a new indirect tax. When the postwar tax system was set up in 1950, the government's revenues came almost equally from direct taxes (income and corporate) and indirect taxes (on commodities such as automobiles, liquor, and tobacco).[7] Because of changes in the structure of the Japanese economy since 1950, the government's revenues became increasingly dependent on direct taxes; the percentage from indirect taxes fell from 45 percent of all revenues in fiscal year 1950 to 27 percent in fiscal year 1986.[8]

Because legislation was required to specify new taxable commodities, the Finance Ministry faced the problem of keeping up with the introduction of all the new products. The battle over the tax on office automation equipment was only one example that showed how hard it had to fight to tax any new items. The commodities tax structure, therefore, became distorted. Golf equipment was taxed, for instance, but tennis equipment was not; water skis were taxed, but snow skis were not; conventional televisions were taxed, but liquid crystal ones were not. Hence the Finance Ministry wanted a new indirect tax, preferably a VAT similar to the ones used by the European Community, which would assess a uniform tax on all commodities and services, with exceptions for items such as food, to counter the political pressures involved in trying to assess taxes on each specific item.[9]

The mood within the LDP toward Nakasone's austerity policy was changing as well, as many felt that new taxes were needed either to ease the budget deficit or to finance politically popular public works spending. A group of the party's tax experts, headed by Murayama Tatsuo, released a report calling for continued efforts to eliminate the dependence on government bonds by fiscal 1990 through reductions in government spending and increased taxes.[10] And then, toward the end of November, three of the party's heavyweights, Finance Minister Takeshita Noboru, Kanemaru Shin, the LDP's secretary general and mentor of Takeshita, and Fujio Masayuki, the chairman of the LDP's PARC, began to speak out on the need for the introduction of a large indirect tax.[11]

Thus there was consensus toward the end of 1984 among those in government and the LDP who dealt with tax policy that the tax system needed to be reformed and that tax increases of some sort were needed. On December 18 both the LDP Tax Council and the Government Tax Council proposed that a comprehensive review be made of the tax system. Both councils noted the necessity of securing additional revenues and of introducing an indirect tax in order to correct the over-reliance on direct taxes for revenue.[12] On December 19 the LDP adopted the LDP Tax Council report and decided that the party should make a comprehensive review of the tax system, which would include the introduction of a large indirect tax after fiscal year 1986.

Shaping the Agenda

In the midst of the debate on his austerity policy, Nakasone, on December 3, 1984, revealed that he was considering tackling tax reform as one of his medium- and long-term policy goals. He had been reelected as party president at the end of October, and he was looking for a new issue to mark his second term as LDP president.

Nakasone's proposals for tax reform, however, were rather different from those of other participants in the discussion at that point. First, he reemphasized that he was sticking with his policy of rebuilding the deficit-ridden national finances without tax increases. In other words, his tax reform plan would be revenue neutral. Second, he stressed cuts in direct taxes. He announced that he wanted to implement an income tax cut for middle-income households, those with annual incomes between

3 million and 8 million yen, but did not specify how the cut would be financed except to say that it would not be covered by government bonds. He also wanted to reduce the number of tax brackets from fifteen to about five, to lower the top bracket from 70 percent, and reduce corporate taxes.

A number of factors seemed to prompt Nakasone's ideas. First, his emphasis on simplicity and fairness coincided with the U.S. Department of the Treasury's proposal for tax reform, which was released just a month before he made his first public statement on the subject. In particular, the ideas of reducing the number of tax brackets and lowering the top bracket were very similar. Nakasone, therefore, was probably stimulated by President Reagan's effort at tax reform.[13]

In addition, Nakasone was picking up on public dissatisfaction, particularly among salaried workers, with the uneven burden of the tax system, the so-called *ku-ro-yon* (9-6-4) problem. The numbers 9-6-4 refer to the relative amount of taxes said to be paid by salaried workers, self-employed businessmen, and farmers. It was estimated that salaried workers paid income tax on *nine*-tenths of their income; self-employed businessmen on only *six*-tenths, and farmers on only *four*-tenths. Public dissatisfaction with the tax system was reflected in an Economic Planning Agency survey published in October 1984 in which respondents put "fair taxation" at the top of the list of those things that they thought had not been achieved. Three years earlier, fair taxation had been listed fourth in a similar survey. In addition, the survey revealed that 56 percent of the people interviewed replied that the current tax system was "not equal" as against only 9 percent who supported the existing system as "appropriate."

Nakasone helped push tax reform along in the LDP and the government by advocating massive cuts in income and corporate taxes. Finance officials and leaders of the LDP Tax Council were afraid that the prime minister would try to cut taxes without making up the revenue through increases elsewhere and hence make the deficit worse. They therefore decided to press for a package that included tax cuts as well as the introduction of an indirect tax. The ministry calculated that a broad-based indirect tax of 1 percent would raise 1 trillion yen, which would mean that the government could make a major cut in income taxes. In addition, the package would help correct the overreliance on direct taxes by lowering them and raising indirect taxes.

The drafting of proposals for tax reform was formally handled by the Government Tax Council and the LDP Tax Council. In particular, the latter's final report would serve as the party's proposals and be the basis for the drafting of legislation by the Finance Ministry. The final report, however, was not to be made until December 1986, about two years after attention had started to be focused on the issue. The reasoning for this was that the LDP did not want to make any hard choices regarding taxes, especially any that involved the introduction of a large indirect tax, until after the next set of elections for the Kokkai. The upper house elections were to be held in the summer of 1986, and the chances were considered good that Nakasone would try to hold the lower house elections at the same time.

Even though the final report was not to be made until December 1986, a number of actors within the LDP started in 1985 to influence the debate. First, a policy group of the Tanaka faction released its proposals;[14] and a private advisory council to Fujio, the chairman of the PARC followed suit.[15] In essence, the two reports presented proposals very much along the lines of Nakasone's in that they called for large cuts in income and corporate taxes and a simplification of the tax structure. But they also emphasized that the cuts had to be offset by the introduction of an indirect tax and the elimination of the *maruyū* system.

One very important supporter of reform was Kanemaru, then the LDP's secretary general and one of the most influential members of the Tanaka faction, who endorsed the proposal to eliminate the *maruyū* system. Of particular importance was that Kanemaru was considered the head of the LDP postal *zoku* and in 1980 had led the drive to overturn the so-called green card law, which was intended to restrict tax evasion on *maruyū* accounts.[16]

Nakasone tried to influence the debate of the Government Tax Council more directly than by just advocating his views in public: he placed many of his personal advisers on the council. He had been advocating cuts in both income and corporate taxes for fiscal 1986, but the Finance Ministry was resisting the idea, fearing that the cuts would not be covered by other revenues. Instead, the ministry wanted to postpone the cuts at least until fiscal 1987. Thus Nakasone's move was to shake up the Government Tax Council, which had been viewed as a mouthpiece for the Finance Ministry, to make it more responsive to LDP electoral needs.[17]

When the Government Tax Council restarted its deliberations on September 20, 1985, Nakasone asked it to put together a two-stage reform package in which tax cuts would precede tax increases. In addition, he emphasized that the reform be revenue neutral. He expressed his strong desire for tax reform as one of the big reforms of the postwar system and expressed his determination "to push for reform with strong leadership, and with resolve and boldness." He emphasized that the main focus should be to lower taxes on personal income, particularly for salaried workers, corporate income, and inheritances. Nakasone seemed to have two reasons for advocating tax cuts: to help stimulate the domestic economy and thereby ease trade frictions with the United States; and to help him win a third term as LDP president by helping the party's chances in the upcoming National Assembly elections.

In April 1986 both the LDP Tax Council and the Government Tax Council released their interim reports. Both proposed that the progressive income tax structure be flattened somewhat, particularly for salaried workers, who felt the burden the most.[18] The intent of the proposed reforms was to cut down the number of tax brackets that most salaried workers would pass through from the time they are hired out of college or high school until the time they retire. Under the existing system there were about eight. Katō Mutsuki, the chairman of the LDP Tax Council, proposed that at most there be two or three brackets for most salaried workers. In particular, the tax councils wanted to reduce the burden for salaried workers around the age of forty-five, who have housing loans and children's educational expenses to worry about.

The reports, therefore, listed proposals for tax cuts but did not mention how they would be financed, whether through deficit bonds or increased taxes. In particular, the proposals were aimed at attracting the votes of salaried workers for the upcoming upper house elections as well as to stimulate domestic demand as requested by the United States. The reports, then, followed the strategy put forth by Nakasone to propose tax cuts in the spring—before the election—and tax increases in the fall—after the election.

Nakasone's Campaign Promise

Part of Nakasone's strategy to win a third term as LDP president—and thereby another two years as prime minister—was to call a double election (a stimultaneous election for both the upper and lower houses of the National Assembly) in the summer of 1986 and have the LDP regain the comfortable majority it lost in 1983. After overcoming some obstacles, he managed to call elections for July 6.[19] Nakasone's effort to use tax reform as a campaign issue was complicated when Fujio, chairman of the PARC, acknowledged that the party was considering, as part of tax reform, the introduction of a large indirect tax and the elimination of the *maruyū* tax-free savings system.

Fujio's statement made taxes a major issue during the campaign as opposition parties did their best to capitalize on the public's resistance to increases. In order to quiet the controversy, Nakasone announced that he was not thinking of introducing a "large indirect tax that would be opposed by the people and by the LDP." In addition, he vowed to maintain the *maruyū* system for old people, families headed by single mothers, and other disadvantaged members of society. Many other LDP candidates picked up on the prime minister's promise not to introduce a large indirect tax and made similar pledges during their individual campaigns.

The LDP went on to win an overwhelming victory in the double election. The 304 seats won in the House of Representatives were far above even Nakasone's highest hopes, and it was clear that the party would amend its rule limiting its presidents to two consecutive terms and would grant Nakasone at least one more year as president. Nakasone almost completely changed the makeup of the cabinet and the *san'yaku* (the top three party executives). He appointed to the top two party positions two of the three major candidates for the party presidency. Takeshita, who was finance minister in the old cabinet and had helped push for the Finance Ministry's view of tax reform, was appointed to the top party post of secretary general; and Abe Shintarō, previously the foreign minister, became chairman of the party's executive council. Itō Masayoshi, a member of the Miyazawa faction and a politician with close ties to Nakasone, was appointed chairman of the PARC. The other major candidate for the party presidency, Miyazawa Kiichi, was named finance minister; and Nakasone reappointed Gotōda Masaharu as his chief cabinet secretary. In addition, he chose Hara Kenzaburō, a senior member of his faction, as speaker of the lower house.

Nakasone also made one other important appointment. He asked Itō to appoint Yamanaka Sadanori, a member of the Nakasone faction, as chairman of the LDP Tax Council. Itō's first choice would probably have been Murayama Tatsuo, who, like Itō, was a member of the Miyazawa faction and head of Fujio's private advisory research council. The choice of Yamanaka rather than Murayama for the post was crucial because Yamanaka was known for his desire to enact tax reform and was somewhat infamous for ignoring political pressures, whereas Murayama was generally believed to be less assertive.[20] It should be pointed out that although Yamanaka was a member of the Nakasone faction, he had a reputation of being very independent-minded; he was not a Nakasone proxy.[21]

After the election was over, Nakasone continued to press hard for tax reform, and he made it clear that he took seriously his election pledge not to introduce a large indirect tax that was opposed by the public and the LDP. In particular, he started promoting a manufacturer sales tax (also called a shipment tax) over the VAT, the one preferred by the Finance Ministry.[22] Nakasone felt that, because a manufacturer sales tax is not a multistage, all-encompassing tax (the tax is assessed only on manufactured goods at the time of delivery from the factory), it would not violate his election pledge.[23] When the Finance Ministry seemed to be promoting the VAT, Nakasone called in two top finance officials and scolded them, "I want the Finance Ministry bureaucrats to study more about what I said during the election."[24]

The main public reaction to the debate on indirect taxes came from business groups. On August 23, Suzuki Eiji, chairman of the Federation of Economic Organization's (Keidanren's) tax committee, announced that Keidanren supported a VAT and was against the manufacturer sales tax. Retailers, however, were adamantly opposed to a VAT; they felt they would bear most of the burden. Kiyomizu Shinji, chairman of the Japan Chain Stores Association, immediately after Suzuki's testimony, handed a formal letter of protest to Saitō Eishirō, the chairman of Keidanren. The Japan Chamber of Commerce and Industry (Nisshō) headed by a member of Nakasone's brain trust, Gotō Noboru, also opposed the VAT.

Nakasone seemed to be getting his way on the indirect tax issue and other aspects of tax reform during his meeting on October 18 with the leaders of the LDP Tax Council. First of all, he obtained their agreement that the government would not introduce a large indirect tax. He and party officials said that they would continue to study indirect taxes that could be introduced without violating the prime minister's campaign promise. In addition, they agreed that the tax reform would be revenue neutral, even though Yamanaka had been pressing for an overall increase to help ease the national deficit, and they agreed to a simplification of the graduated income tax structure similar to that passed in the United States. And finally, Yamanaka promised Nakasone that his commission would submit its final recommendations for tax reform in time for the compilation of the fiscal 1987 budget, which meant by December 1986.

On October 28 the Government Tax Council submitted its final report to Prime Minister Nakasone. The council called for cuts in income and residential taxes totaling approximately 2.7 trillion yen, a reduction in the number of brackets in income and residential taxes, cuts in corporate taxes totaling approximately 1.8 trillion yen, and the elimination of the *maruyū* system, which would raise 1 trillion yen in revenues.[25] The council also proposed that an indirect tax be introduced but was unable to obtain a consensus on the type. Instead of one proposal, it listed three (a manufacturer sales tax, a retail sales tax, and a VAT), although the report said it preferred a VAT that would cover a wide range of items at a low tax rate, which, if set at 5 percent, would raise about 4 trillion yen in revenues. Overall, then, the council proposed equal amounts in tax increases and cuts of close to 5 trillion yen.

The LDP Tax Council Deliberations

As soon as the Government Tax Council finished its report, the LDP Tax Council started its deliberations, which culminated in its proposals for tax reform released on December 5, 1986. On the same day as the LDP Tax Council decided on the fundamental outline of tax reform, the party's PARC and executive council formally approved the policy. The tax reform plan, which proposed to introduce a 5 percent VAT, eliminate the *maruyū* system, and cut income and corporate taxes, thus became official LDP policy.[26]

Cuts in Income and Corporate Taxes

The LDP Tax Council first decided on the tax cuts. There was little problem in reaching the decision; the council more or less adopted the proposals of the Government Tax Council. The package of cuts—2 trillion yen in income tax, 700 million yen in resident taxes, and 1.8 trillion yen in corporate taxes—was estimated to total about 4.5 trillion yen. It would reduce the maximum personal income tax rate from the present 70 percent to 50 percent and the effective rate of corporate taxes from 52.92 percent to 50 percent. The council also decided to reduce the number of income tax brackets from fifteen to six.

The Decision to Introduce the VAT

The Government Tax Council in its proposal had listed three types of indirect taxes and recommended the VAT as the one most preferred by its members. The LDP Tax Council, after a tug-of-war between Nakasone on the one side and the leaders of the council and the three so-called new leaders (Takeshita, Abe, and Miyazawa) plus Keidanren on the other, decided on December 5 to adopt the VAT with a 5 percent rate, with exemptions for businesses with total annual sales under 100 million yen.

Who were the actors in this struggle? The commerce and industry *zoku* is one of the most popular among the many policy *zokus* in the LDP, so one might expect that it—or at least its leaders—would play a major role in the negotiations. The *zoku*, however, played almost no part in the choice of indirect tax because the groups it represented were badly divided over the question. The *zoku* in actuality is a collection of groups clustered around each industry and around the distributors. There is a group supporting textiles, another supporting the petrochemical industry, another supporting retailers and shopowners, and so on.[27]

On one side were the manufacturers represented by Keidanren, which saw a need for tax reform and wanted a cut in corporate taxes. They were not opposed to an indirect tax as long as it was not a manufacturer sales tax. On the other side were the distributors, represented by Nisshō, who were strongly opposed to any indirect tax but felt they could live with a manufacturer sales tax. They were obviously opposed to the retail sales tax, which was not seriously considered, but they were also strongly opposed to the VAT. The ministry concerned, MITI, did not take a strong stand one way or another; it primarily wanted a cut in corporate taxes.

Nakasone, as I previously noted, was opposed to the VAT and supported the manufacturer sales tax instead. But those in favor of the VAT were stronger. They included the leaders of the LDP Tax Council and the Finance Ministry, who both felt that the VAT was the best way to gain revenue; the major manufacturers, represented by Keidanren, did not want to bear the brunt of a manufacturer sales tax; and Takeshita, Abe, and Miyazawa, the three main contenders to succeed Natasone. The three contenders supported the VAT both because of the revenue it would provide and to support Keidanren in hopes of garnering political contributions that would be needed to win the presidency of the LDP. Nakasone ended his resistance in mid-November when he met with Saitō Eiji and Hanamura Ninhachirō of Keidanren, and Hanamura reportedly told Nakasone pointedly, "Mr. Prime Minister, you understand, don't you? Keidanren supports the VAT."[28]

The LDP Tax Council decided to set the VAT at 5 percent and exempt businesses with less than 100 million yen in annual sales. That level was higher than expected and considerably above the 20 million yen level proposed in Ōhira's plan in 1979.[29] The high ceiling was out of consideration for Nakasone's election campaign pledge. The Finance Ministry estimated that if the tax exemption point was set at this level, 87.1 percent of all enterprises would be free from the tax, but the expected revenue would be only 8.7 percent smaller than if all businesses were subjected to it.[30]

After the LDP Tax Council decided on the VAT, the opposition parties continued to grill Nakasone on his pledge not to introduce a large indirect tax. Nakasone replied on December 9 before the lower house Cabinet Committee and on December 10 before the upper house plenary session that a large indirect tax is one that is "multistage, comprehensive, which covers everything like a net," and that in his view the proposed tax was not a large tax. In particular, he claimed that it did not violate his election campaign promise because of exemptions for businesses with sales of less than 100 million yen and for nine types of goods and services including necessities such as educational materials, medical care, and food.[31]

Nakasone, in his desire to make it acceptable to the public, opened up the tax to more exemptions, but the process snowballed, so that the original list of nine exemptions eventually grew to fifty-one.[32] Once one item was exempted, it became difficult to resist other requests. For example, postal services were granted an exemption, so private express mail companies also demanded and received one. Since farmers were granted exemptions on the sale of their farmland, fishermen argued that fishing boats were their "land" and should therefore also be given exemptions. Used car dealers pressured the LDP to give exemptions on used cars, arguing that if a 5 percent tax were to be applied, potential buyers would resort to private transactions and the dealers would become bankrupt.

The resulting tax proposal was flawed in two ways. First, the high number of exemptions meant that the rate would have to be higher to bring in the same amount of revenue. The second and more damaging flaw was that the tax did not have provisions to avoid tax duplications involving tax-exempt middlemen, who would not have tax vouchers to pass on the deductible amount to the next stage of transaction. In other words, the tax exemption would make them less competitive because their customers would have to pay tax on the full value of the item, rather than just the value added. This turned out to be one of the major reasons why this version of the VAT was never passed, for it hit the small businesses and distributors that made up a big part of the LDP's traditional constituency.

The Decision to Eliminate Maruyū

The most difficult decision for the LDP Tax Council was whether to eliminate the *maruyū* system of tax-free small-lot savings accounts. The Finance Ministry and the Ministry of Posts and Telecommunications (MPT) had engaged in bitter clashes over postal savings a number of times, most recently in 1984, but each time the MPT, with the support of the LDP postal *zoku*, managed to stave off efforts to tax interest from or to restrict the illegal multiple use of the tax-free accounts.[33] This time, however, the leaders of the LDP postal *zoku* changed sides and came out in favor of abolishing the tax exemption. Of particular importance was the switch by Kanemaru, who was considered the top leader of the *zoku* and had played an important role in fending off the two previous efforts to reform or eliminate the *maruyū* system.

Starting at the end of November, the administrative vice minister of finance, Yoshino Yoshihiko, and the administrative vice minister of posts and telecommunications, Sawada Shigeo, entered into negotiations over the future of the *maruyū* system. The compromise plan is said to have been drawn up by the management and coordination director, Tamaki

Kazuo, with the approval of MPT Minister Karasawa Shū'nirō, Finance Minister Miyazawa, and Chief Cabinet Secretary Gotōda.[34] The plan was seen as a fair trade between the two ministries.[35] In particular, the MPT, in return for the elimination of the tax exemption on *maruyū* accounts, received more control over the deposits in postal savings. The Finance Ministry, on the other side of the deal, was able to assess a uniform 20 percent tax on all interest income from *maruyū* accounts, which it estimated would bring in approximately 1.6 trillion yen.

The three top LDP executives—Takeshita, Abe, and Itō—approved the compromise on December 5 after making sure that all the major parties concerned were in agreement.

The First Attempt to Pass the Tax Reform Bills

With the three major party rivals to Nakasone as well as other party leaders behind the tax reform bills, the main tasks in the legislature were keeping the LDP in line and trying to neutralize the opposition parties. Neither proved easy. Although opponents to the VAT were not organized soon enough to prevent the LDP leadership's decision to introduce it, opposition forces grew during the months afterward and were eventually successful in forcing the LDP leadership, and Nakasone in particular, to abandon the effort to adopt the tax bills during that legislative session. Opposition to the VAT was broad-based: it included not only all of the opposition political parties, but also many LDP members of the Kokkai and traditional LDP supporters.

Opposition from the Opposition Parties

During the 1986 double election the opposition parties as a whole made their worst showing since the early 1960s. In particular, the leading opposition party, the JSP, saw its number of seats in the lower house drop to below one hundred for the first time, and it could put up virtually no resistance to the bill privatizing Japan National Railways (JNR). This was a crucial defeat because the JNR's labor union had been one of the JSP's most important supporters. The tax bill, however, provided an issue behind which all of the opposition parties could rally against the LDP. Particularly important was the role played by the *Kōmeitō's* secretary general, Yano Tōru, who served as the bridge between the JSP and the DSP in creating an alliance consisting of the three parties plus a minor group, the Social Democratic League (Shaminren). The Japan Communist Party (JCP), although just as opposed to the VAT, was outside this tripartite alliance.

On December 18 the JSP, the Kōmeitō, and the DSP decided to join together in opposing the introduction of the VAT and elimination of the *maruyū* system. On December 26, in separate meetings with the prime minister, the leaders of each opposition party pressed Nakasone to withdraw the VAT. And on January 16, 1987 the JSP, the Kōmeitō, the DSP, and the Shaminren inaugurated the Council to Crush the VAT on the day when the cabinet approved the outline of the tax reforms. The strategy of the opposition parties to force the withdrawal of the tax reform bill consisted of two parts. The first was to delay any deliberations of the bill in the legislature, and the second was to use the issue in their campaigns for the local elections to be held nationwide in April.

The opposition first boycotted the legislative sessions after Nakasone, in his policy speech to the National Assembly on January 26, neglected even to mention the VAT plan as part of the tax reform package. After a week of boycotts, the opposition parties returned after Nakasone agreed to announce before the legislature that the planned tax reform included the introduction of a VAT.[36] The opposition parties again boycotted the legislative budget committee sessions when the LDP decided to schedule unilaterally the public hearings that are required before the budget can be formally approved. The opposition parties feared that once the public hearings had taken place, the LDP would use its majority and force the 1987 budget through the National Assembly. In essence, the opposition parties were holding the budget hostage to pressure the LDP to withdraw the tax reform bills. Nakasone needed to have the budget passed because he was planning to visit the United States in May, and the budget contained measures to stimulate the domestic economy and help alleviate some of the trade frictions with the United States.

The second part of the strategy to block the introduction of the new tax was to gain public support for their opposition and use the issue to campaign against the LDP in the upcoming quadrennial unified local elections. On February 1 about eight thousand unionists, consumers, and shop owners held an outdoor protest rally in Tokyo, thus starting a series of joint actions by opposition parties and labor organizations against the tax.

Opposition from Traditional LDP Supporters

One factor keeping the LDP from using its majority to force passage of the tax reform bills was that the norms in the legislature and LDP support consensus in decision making.[37] For fear of a public backlash, the leadership of the LDP does not take lightly the decision to force passage of legislation. Nevertheless, Nakasone and the LDP leadership gave many indications that they were willing to try to do just that. For instance, they took unilateral action on the budget a number of times: first, they set a date for public hearings, and then they forced the bill through the lower house budget committee.

Had the resistance to the VAT been limited to the opposition parties and their supporting labor groups, the LDP might well have been willing to force the tax reform bills through the legislature, despite the inevitable public criticism. Opposition to the tax, however, was much more broad-based than that. Not only were the opposition parties united, but a large number of traditional supporters of the LDP joined in the opposition.

The Nisshō, headed by Gotō Noboru, a member of Nakasone's brain trust, actively opposed the tax and held a demonstration. On February 6, Gotō revealed that over one-third of the 455 chambers across the country had officially voted against the VAT, and he predicted that more would follow. In addition, another business group, the Kansai Economic Federation (*Kansai Keizai Rengōkai*), urged the LDP not to submit the tax bill to the legislature because of the business recession caused by the steep rise in the value of the yen. Retailers and wholesalers, in particular, were vehement in their opposition. Japanese department and chain stores announced in February that they were stopping political contributions to the LDP in protest.

Similar types of pressure were being applied at the local level. In late January wholesaler groups from Tokyo handed out questionnaires to all LDP members of the National Assembly. Takeshita, the party's secretary general, and Itō, chairman of the PARC, instructed the party members to be "cautious" in their answers, suggesting that they simply not reply. Most took the advice. But six members representing districts in Tokyo, including a parliamentary vice minister, not only replied but also expressed their opposition to the introduction of the VAT. These representatives were particularly vulnerable to the group's pressure, because many of the executive members of the wholesaler groups were important backers.[38]

Besides sending the questionnaire, wholesalers and retailers held numerous rallies. On February 6, seventeen hundred wholesalers from Tokyo's Nihonbashi and Asakusa districts held a demonstration and vowed not to vote for LDP politicians who favored the introduction of the tax. Tokyo's Ōta ward merchants also held a rally, which was attended not only by representatives of the opposition parties, including one from the JCP, but also by the two LDP members representing the district in the lower house.

And on February 24 representatives from 151 business and labor groups met in Tokyo at Nisshō headquarters to form the National Conference on the Tax System to orchestrate a campaign against the tax. On the same day, the national organization of cosmetic retailers decided that its twenty thousand members would secede from the LDP en masse if the government and the LDP did not scrap the proposal.

Other junior LDP members of the National Assembly also publicly expressed their opposition. Iwai Tomoaki and Inoguchi Takashi note that although the LDP's overwhelming victory in 1986 had strengthened the party, it also meant that many freshmen and other junior representatives would be especially vulnerable during the next election.[39] A Kyōdō news service survey of LDP members of the Kokkai Assembly revealed that twenty-one of them expressed opposition to the planned tax and another fifty-four wanted the plan revised or felt that the government "should make efforts to gain the public's understanding of the tax."[40] None of those who responded felt that there was strong support for the tax. Given that LDP representatives are required by party rules to abide by official policy in replying to any surveys, the number willing to express their opposition was a clear indication of a real party revolt.

The Upper House By-Election in Iwate Prefecture and Local Elections

On March 8 the party leadership's efforts to introduce the VAT received a devastating blow. In a by-election to fill an upper house seat in

Iwate prefecture, the JSP candidate, Ogawa Jin'ichi, won an overwhelming victory—a two to one margin—over the LDP candidate, Isurugi Rei. This was the first National Assembly election fought over the government tax plan and represented an overwhelming victory for the antitax forces. The JSP victory was particularly significant because Iwate was considered an LDP stronghold: this was the first time the JSP had won an upper house seat in Iwate since 1968.

Ogawa's victory came as a great shock to the LDP leaders. The LDP had expected to win not only because Iwate was a conservative stronghold, but also because its candidate was the widow of Isurugi Michiyuki, the LDP politician whose death vacated the seat. In addition, Isurugi Rei was herself from a prominent political family. Generally, sympathy for the widow would be enough to ensure election, but the tax issue over-whelmed any sympathy for Isurugi. It was clear that many of the groups that traditionally supported the LDP had this time supported Ogawa. Eight of the ten chambers of commerce and industry in the prefecture passed resolutions against the tax, and there was a joint conservative-progressive citizens rally opposing it. Over thirty organizations of res-taurant owners and retailers who had previously supported the LDP supported Ogawa, claiming that the "LDP had betrayed" them and that it would not "listen to what the small shop owners have to say."[41]

The defection greatly weakened what support there was for the tax. Most of the prefectural assemblies—thirty-seven out of the nation's forty-seven—passed resolutions either opposing it or asking for more prudence in pursuing tax reform.[42] The election also caused some LDP leaders to have second thoughts about the tax plan. Kanemaru, the deputy prime minister and one of the most influential figures in the party, expressed in a meeting with Gotōda, the chief cabinet secretary, his opinion that the government should take a more flexible stand on the issue. In addition to Kanemaru, other members of Takeshita's faction were sounding out leaders of other factions about modifying the tax bill.

Nevertheless, Nakasone continued to defend the tax reform pro-posals. He had the party leaders officially reiterate that the party would continue with the tax bill witout modification, although they decided to postpone public hearings on the budget and not to try to pass the budget until after the first set of local elections. But much of the party clearly had misgivings. The unpopularity of Nakasone's stand was clear when none of the LDP-backed candidates for local office asked him to campaign on his or her behalf.

The first set of local elections was held on April 12. At stake were thirteen gubernatorial seats and two mayoral seats, and control of forty-four prefectural and nine municipal assemblies. LDP leaders were hopeful that, at the very best, the party would gain back the gubernatorial seat it had lost in Fukuoka four years before. The party felt it had a good candidate and, with the backing of the Kōmeitō and the DSP, felt it should win. Public opposition to the tax, however, resulted not only in the LDP's failure to win back the Fukuoka governorship, but also large losses in prefectural assemblies.

The Lower House Speaker's Mediation Plan

After the April 12 elections, the leaders of the LDP and the government decided to force the budget through the lower house budget committee on April 15 and through the lower house, if necessary, by April 21. On April 15, as planned, the LDP forced it thorugh the committee.

The party, however, did not have the unity needed to force the bill through the legislature. On April 16, a number of backbenchers led by Shionoya Kazuo started a petition drive to demand the withdrawal of the bill. The group quickly gathered signatures from 90 of the LDP members of the House of Representatives, including a number of former cabinet ministers. By the next day, it had the support of a total of 150 LDP members of the National Assembly.

More importantly, some of the top party leaders started to seek some sort of facesaving compromise, in particular, to entrust the VAT bill to the care of the speaker of the lower house, Hara Kenzaburō. The idea originated with those close to Takeshita and Hara, but it also had strong support from elements in both the LDP and opposition parties. Takeshita, working with Hara's aides, outlined a three-point compromise plan in which (1) the tax bill would be entrusted to the speaker; (2) a deliberative body made up of members of both the LDP and the opposition parties would be set up to discuss tax reform; and then (3) the VAT would be dropped. On April 20, Takeshita's trusted lieutenant, Ozawa Ichirō, took this draft over to the opposition parties to sound them out and received a favorable response. The JSP even started to select its members for the new body. But during a meeting with the secretaries general of the opposition parties, Takeshita did not give them absolute assurances that the LDP would drop the tax bill, saying he did not have the authority to do so. That compromise, therefore, fell through.

Takeshita continued to work on a compromise. He met with Hara, Tagaya Shinnen, vice speaker of the lower house (and a member of the JSP), and Ochi Ihei, the chairman of the lower house rules and administration committee, to work on a draft. Tagaya passed along an idea from Yamaguchi Tsuruo, the JSP's secretary general: the addition of an oral agreement that the VAT would be dropped. Nakasone, however, still refused to go along with the compromise plan. Gotōda, following the wishes of Nakasone, relayed to Itō, the chairman of the PARC, that Nakasone would not accept the compromise draft because it clearly stated that the tax bill would be dropped. Gotōda emphasized that deliberations on the bill had to go forward. Itō then wrote Takeshita a letter saying that he agreed with Gotōda. This attempt at accommodation, therefore, also fell through.

The decision on whether to go ahead with the compromise along the lines advocated by Takeshita and Kanemaru or take Nakasone's hard-line stand was left to the speaker, who has broad formal powers in handling legislation (though he rarely exercises them). Hara sided with Nakasone, and the National Assembly started its first all-night session in ten years. On April 21, as the LDP tried to force through the budget, the opposition parties dragged out the voting process through the use of "cow-walking" tactics, a filibustering technique in which opposition members, spaced at long intervals, walked at an excruciatingly slow pace to the podium, where they cast their votes.

Kanemaru, however, continued to try to work out some sort of accommodation. On April 22 he met with Tanabe Makoto, a former JSP secretary general. The two agreed on a compromise whereby the speaker would clearly state in an oral acknowledgment that the VAT would be dropped but would also say that the LDP and the opposition parties would continue to deliberate on tax reform, thus allowing Nakasone to save face. Kanemaru then telephoned Nakasone that evening and again the next morning to urge him to accept the compromise, but both times Nakasone refused, hinting that he was willing to wait to pass the budget until after his trip to the United States.

On April 23, Takeshita and Fujinami went to the speaker's official residence, where they confirmed that Hara would not exercise his right to force the budget through the lower house because this would lead to chaos in the legislature, and that there was no other way to achieve a breakthrough except the compromise to let the speaker mediate and drop the VAT. The two then went to meet with Nakasone and Gotōda. This time, Takeshita was able to persuade Nakasone to accept the compromise.[43] He promised that in return he would set up a deliberative body in the legislature to discuss tax reform and that he would work to extend the legislative session. He also promised that, even if there was no clear conclusion to the deliberations, he would open up a path to reform while Nakasone was still in office.[44]

With this agreement, the opposition parties ended their stalling tactics and allowed the LDP to pass the budget in the House of Representatives that night, which meant that it would be enacted by May 23 regardless of what happened to it in the House of Councillors. Nakasone, therefore, was able to proceed with his trip to Washington, D.C. during the Japanese Golden Week holidays (from April 29, the Shōwa emperor's birthday, to May 5, Children's Day) and show the United States that Japan was taking concrete action to stimulate its domestic economy. With the close of the session on May 27, the tax bill was officially dropped.

The Second Attempt to Pass the Tax Reform Bills

Even after it became clear that he would be forced to drop the tax bill, Nakasone worked hard to keep the tax reform effort on track. In return for dropping the bill, he at least gained two concessions. First, he managed to get a commitment from the opposition parties to establish a joint panel in the lower house to negotiate ways to reform the tax system, including a reexamination of the ratio between direct and indirect taxes. This was no assurance that anything would be done about tax reform, but at least it kept open a multipartisan forum for tax reform. Second, he was able to get support from both the LDP and the opposition parties for an extraordinary session of the legislature that was to last a relatively lengthy 65 days, from July 6 to September 8, on the pretext of compiling a supplementary budget to stimulate domestic demand.[45] This gave him the time to have some sort of tax package passed.

Then Nakasone used the joint panel to help press for legislation to reform the tax system. The important thing for him was to have it complete its deliberations quickly so that there would still be time to submit bills to the National Assembly and get them passed. Two people helped in this. The first was House Speaker Hara, whose mediation allowed for the establishment of the joint panel and who had the participants complete their deliberations within two months. The second was Itō, chairman of the LDP's PARC, who was appointed chairman of the new group.[46] The appointment was important to Nakasone because Itō was very sympathetic toward tax reform and the need for a new indirect tax: he had been a close friend of the late Ōhira Masayoshi and had helped in the failed attempt to introduce a VAT in 1979. Itō also had personal ties to Nakasone, and Nakasone had confidence in him. According to an aide, "the Prime Minister intends to entrust the management of the Nakasone tax reform to Chairman Itō."[47]

The tax panel's deliberations on reform originally involved three main topics, which were carried over from the previous legislative session: the size and type of tax cuts; the introduction of an indirect tax; and the abolition of the tax-exempt small-savings system. Consideration of an indirect tax was soon dropped when, at the Venice summit, Nakasone committed Japan to 1 trillion yen in tax cuts and the elimination of the *maruyū* system as part of the attempt to restructure its economy to stimulate domestic demand and reduce its trade surplus with the rest of the world.[48] As a result of this commitment, the LDP proposed to the opposition parties on the tax panel that the cuts be linked to the elimination of *maruyū* and dropped any talk of enacting an indirect tax.

The opposition parties, however, still opposed eliminating the *maruyū* system. They criticized the LDP proposal, saying that there were many other parts of the tax system that needed to be corrected. They proposed that, instead of abolishing *maruyū*, the tax cuts be financed through the surplus in tax revenues from fiscal 1986, the sale of government-owned stocks of Nippon Telephone and Telegraph, and corrections in the unfair tax system. Thus, when it was time for the panel to submit its report to the speaker of the House of Representatives on July 24, the two sides agreed only that there should be a sizable cut in income tax. They did not agree on the size of the cut or how it was to be financed. The LDP proposed that the reduction be about 1 trillion yen, while the opposition parties wanted about 2 trillion yen, and they continued to disagree on whether to maintain the *maruyū* system.

But the important thing for Nakasone was that the tax reform panel had finished its deliberations with the submission of its report. With that, the LDP went ahead with plans to submit legislation on tax reform despite protests from the opposition parties, which claimed that the report was not really valid since it did not offer any agreement. And in the next week, Yamanaka, Itō, and Miyazawa met several times to work out a new tax package.

The important points were the size of the tax cut and whether to revise the original plan for eliminating *maruyū*. They quickly agreed to cut income taxes by about 1.3 trillion yen and delay the elimination of the *maruyū* system from October 1, 1987 to January 1, 1988. More troublesome was whether to revise the proposal to eliminate *maruyū*. Yamanaka was against any revision, while Itō felt that some was necessary in order to obtain the opposition parties' acquiescence. But after a telephone call from Nakasone, Yamanaka agreed to Itō's proposal for *maruyū*, in which the nontaxable ceiling was raised from 6 million to 9 million yen for certain people, such as those aged sixty-five and over and fatherless families. The leaders of the government and LDP then met to give their formal approval to the agreement.

With the approval of the party leaders, the cabinet approved a package of four bills that included a cut in the income tax of 1.3 trillion yen, reductions in the residential tax by 500 billion yen in 1988 and 660 billion yen in 1989, and the elimination of the *maruyū* system. When these were submitted to the legislature, the opposition parties protested by boycotting the deliberations. They demanded that income taxes be cut by 2 trillion yen in the current fiscal year and that the *maruyū* system be retained, but their position was not entirely unified. The JSP wanted to maintain a hard line and continue to oppose the elimination of *maruyū*, but the DSP and the Kōmeitō soon let it be known that their position on *maruyū* was flexible if the LDP offered more in tax cuts.[49] And when the DSP and the Kōmeitō defected, the JSP felt it could not stand alone and it, too, went along.

There were a number of reasons for the flexibility of the DSP and the Kōmeitō. First, important supporters of the parties, the labor unions, in particular Dōmei (the Japanese Confederation of Labor), wanted large tax reductions more than they wanted to maintain the *maruyū* system. Second, there was little public outcry over the proposed elimination, which was in dramatic contrast to the large demonstrations earlier in the year over the proposed VAT. And third, the two parties wanted to set up a good working relationship with the administration succeeding Nakasone's and build some capital with Takeshita. It also helped that the main negotiators for the two parties, Ōkubo Naohiko of the Kōmeitō and Ōuchi Keigo of the DSP, were friendly with Takeshita.

Takeshita and Itō met on August 6 to discuss what to offer the opposition parties in terms of a compromise. They decided to increase the tax cut by 200 billion yen to 1.5 trillion and to delay the elimination of the *maruyū* system from January 1, 1988 to April 1, 1988. In a meeting on August 7 with the secretaries general of the JSP, the DSP, and the Kōmeitō, Takeshita was able to persuade them to accept the proposal and to end their boycott with the promise that he would make further efforts to increase the tax cut.

The agreement that brought the opposition parties back to the legislative deliberations came as a big relief to Takeshita. He had worked hard in the negotiations to help make up for the defeat of the VAT bill, and he was under time pressures. Given the schedule of the legislature, he had to get the opposition parties to agree to resume deliberations before the ten-day recess for the *Obon* festival if the tax reform bills were to have a chance of getting through the legislature without an extension.[50] If he had failed, his chances for the prime ministership would have been severely damaged. Kanemaru tried to help by calling Nakasone, asking that Takeshita be given more room to maneuver.[51]

Still, the negotiations were not over because the opposition parties demanded an even bigger tax reduction when the deliberations resumed. They wanted to increase the cut in income taxes by another 100 billion yen to 1.6 trillion yen. Takeshita, however, was given very little leeway, with both Nakasone and Miyazawa ruling out larger cuts. The reason for the hard line had to do largely with the politics of succession. Takeshita had the biggest faction and was generally viewed as having the best chance to become the successor to Nakasone. Thus the opposition of Miyazawa to further tax cuts was seen as an effort to hold him in check, while Nakasone did not want to lose his leverage in the determining his successor by making Takeshita too obviously the front-runner. Because the party left him very little room for further compromise, Takeshita had no choice but to persuade the opposition parties to back down in their demands for bigger cuts. Kanemaru called the leaders of the opposition parties on August 19 to tell them that the LDP was unable to make further concessions.[52]

Finally, on August 26, the LDP and the three major opposition parties (the JSP, the DSP, and the Kōmeitō) agreed to increase the proposed income tax cut for 1987 by 40 billion to 1.54 trillion yen and to raise the minimum taxable income from 1.2 million to 1.5 million yen. In return, the opposition parties agreed not to boycott the deliberative sessions, which meant that they would acquiesce in the passage of the tax reform bills, including one to abolish the *maruyū* system. The passage of the tax reform bills was now more or less assured. With the LDP majority, they passed fairly quickly through the lower house and were sent to the upper house. The National Assembly's session had to be extended to give the upper house time to deliberate and vote on them, but this time there was no resistance. The House of Councillors passed the bills on September 19, and they became law.[53]

Epilogue: Tax Reform Under Takeshita and Kaifu

In October 1987, Takeshita succeeded Nakasone as prime minister, and he made tax reform his top priority. He stated that he would take the political responsibility if he failed to get the bills through the extraordinary legislative session in the fall of 1988. The tax package included the introduction of a revised version of the VAT, termed a consumption tax, which was offset by cuts in direct taxes and the ending of commodity taxes.[54] The centerpiece of the package was the VAT. Takeshita had confidence that he could succeed with it where Nakasone had failed. He had a solid base in the party, and there was a consensus among all the party leaders for the tax. There were no divisions in party unity.

Moreover, he believed that he could avoid the mistakes that many thought had led to the previous defeat. One reason often given for that defeat was that Nakasone did not explain the need for it sufficiently to gain the understanding of the people. Thus Takeshita started going around the country explaining the need for the tax, in effect, campaigning for it. Another reason often given was the opposition of small businesses, which were traditionally LDP supporters. Hence the new version of the VAT was designed to make it easier for them to accept. Unlike the previous version, the new one included provisions to avoid tax duplication for transactions involving tax-exempt middlemen. Real tax exemptions were given to businesses with annual sales below 30 million yen, and there were reduced rates of between 0 and 3 percent for those with sales above 30 million yen but below 60 million yen. In addition, there were no vouchers. The system was based on the bookkeeping method, and there was a simplified method of tax payment for firms with total annual sales of less than 500 million yen that significantly reduced the amount of paperwork involved. The VAT was revised in other ways. The tax rate was set at 3 percent instead of the previous 5 percent. And in order to counter political pressure to exempt certain items, the new tax allowed virtually no exemptions.[55] Among the items taxed were even necessities such as food and housing.

Much of the political discussion, however, was diverted from tax reform by the Recruit scandal (and to a lesser extent by the Shōwa emperor's illness), which started to develop during the summer of 1988. Thus, during the extraordinary session of the Kokkai in the fall, there was little deliberation on the tax bills, with the opposition parties focusing their attention instead on the scandal. Takeshita was able, despite the scandal, to pass the tax package by keeping the Kōmeitō and the DSP (although not the JSP and the JCP) in the legislative process. The bills to reform the tax system passed the lower house on November 16 and became law when they passed the upper house on December 24. The new tax went into effect on April 1, 1989.[56]

Takeshita and other party leaders certainly hoped and expected that, once the new tax went into effect, the public would no longer actively oppose it. Although few demonstrated against this tax, in contrast to the previous one, public dissatisfaction started to grow and helped lead to the backlash against the LDP during the election for the upper house, in which the LDP lost its majority for the first time since the party was formed in 1955. What made the issue particularly sensitive to the public was the Recruit scandal. The effect on the public of the two issues was probably much more than simply additive. The combination proved explosive because the public felt that it was being forced to make the sacrifice of paying a new tax at the same time as the LDP leaders seemed to be on the take.

The new tax remained a major issue on the political agenda under the new prime minister, Kaifu Toshiki. Before calling a general election in February 1990, the LDP proposed to revise the tax by including more exemptions, for example, for food, education, and other basic necessities. When the LDP did much better than expected in the election, it was able to resist opposition demands to drop the tax.[57]

Conclusion

Nakasone's main impact on the issue of tax reform came in the enactment process, that is, in trying to pass bills in the legislature. He attempted and failed with his version of the VAT, but he did manage to get a lesser but still important tax package, which included the elimination of the *maruyū* tax-free savings system, passed in the following legislative session.

It is important to note that tax reform was something that the Finance Ministry had been pushing for years. In particular, finance officials wanted to introduce a comprehensive indirect tax and eliminate *maruyū* in order to get higher and more stable revenues. By 1984 they were already starting to get a sympathetic ear from a number of LDP party leaders at the time Nakasone became involved, and the broad outline of tax reform was already largely in place. He was picking up on an issue that already had quite a bit of backing in both the Finance Ministry and the LDP leadership. This is in contrast to Nakasone's limited impact on educational reform, in which he had tried to promote an idea, liberalization, that had virtually no real support in the party, the bureaucracy, or powerful interest groups.

Nakasone was primarily concerned about getting something passed and much less about the content of the tax bills. His impact on the contents of tax reform derived from his political strategy for getting an indirect tax passed: making tax reform revenue neutral, advocating big cuts in income and corporate taxes and having the proposals presented before the election, pledging during the double election not to introduce a large indirect tax, pressing for the manufacturer sales tax over the VAT, raising the tax exemption ceiling for small businesses, and opening up exemptions to a greater number of items.

Although he was not able to get the VAT bill passed, he nevertheless came pretty close. The bills were submitted with cabinet approval. That he failed does not mean that the prime minister's impact was small. Quite the contrary, given the massive public demonstrations not only by groups that traditionally supported the opposition parties but also by those that were considered LDP supporters, it was not surprising that Nakasone failed. But this was an extreme case. There are few issues that have aroused such opposition. That Nakasone came so close to succeeding suggests that the prime minister's influence on the process is far from insignificant.

After failing to get the tax passed in the regular legislative session, Nakasone persisted and was able to keep the tax reform issue on track and eventually to get a lesser tax package passed before stepping down in October. He succeeded in this even though his term was about to end and after his credibility had been badly damaged by the tax debacle. He used the succession issue to his advantage in advancing the issue by keeping his party rivals in line. In particular, he was able to get Takeshita to get the tax reform package through the National Assembly.

In conclusion, the tax bills would have had no chance without the active support of the prime minister, given the strong tendency toward the status quo. Nakasone's main impact on the process of tax reform, in other words, was getting the tax bills enacted. He was able to produce policy change by taking an issue behind which there was already considerable support and then adding his own.

The two cases of prime ministerial involvement in the policy process described in chapter 3 and here suggest that a number of different forces are at work in shaping the prime ministership. The next four chapters analyze these broad forces in detail, beginning with the process of selecting a prime minister.

5

The Process of
Selecting a Prime Minister

O*n November* 5, 1991, Miyazawa Kiichi fulfilled a long-held ambition. After more than a decade of trying, he was finally elected prime minister by the Kokkai, replacing Kaifu Toshiki, who formally stepped down earlier in the day. How did he become prime minister and what does the selection process say about the office? The answer is important for a number of reasons. The selection process can affect the style and personality of the incumbent, the types of issue he becomes involved in, and the effect he has on these issues.

As in other parliamentary systems, the head of government in Japan is selected indirectly by the people through their representatives in the legislature, in particular the House of Representatives, rather than popularly elected, as is the case in the United States and other presidential systems.[1] Given that the LDP has a majority in the lower house, the person who becomes party president—the top leader in the party hierarchy—is virtually assured of also becoming prime minister.[2] Hence Miyazawa's election by the House of Representatives generated no suspense, because he had been elected as the party's president a few days before. The answer, then, to the question, Who becomes prime minister? lies in how the LDP determines who becomes party president.

This chapter describes the process in two steps. First, it analyzes who can become serious candidates for the top post, what sorts of LDP politicians they are, and how this part of the process affects how prime ministers perform in office. Second, it looks at the actual LDP presidential selection process and at the races for the presidency, particularly at how one candidate prevails over the others, and how the races affect what prime ministers do in office. In particular, this chapter argues that while LDP presidents tend to be very experienced in virtually all areas of national politics—from party and factional politics to government affairs—the selection process makes it difficult for them as prime ministers to be major agents of policy change.

Becoming a Candidate for the Party Presidency

The LDP's majority in the lower house means that, out of the 764 members of both houses of the National Assembly who are constitutionally eligible to be prime minister, the effective pool of candidates is limited to 400 or so.[3] But only a very few in this pool have much of a chance of becoming party president. What sets the few apart from the rest is that they have become the heads of major LDP factions.

As Nathaniel Thayer explains, the intraparty factions were formed as support groups to help their leaders become party president.[4] Virtually all past LDP presidents and serious candidates for the presidency were either the formal head or the acting head of their faction.[5] There have been two exceptions to this rule: Uno Sōsuke and Kaifu Toshiki, the two successors to Takeshita Noboru.[6] They became party president when the Recruit scandal had tainted the heads of the four largest factions.[7] But even they were both among the very top leaders of their respective factions. Uno was part of the leadership group in the Nakasone camp, and Kaifu had long been regarded as the likely heir to the Kōmoto faction. Current party rules also reinforce this norm by restricting the field of formal candidates to those who file petitions with a minimum number of signatures—currently set at 30—of fellow LDP members of the legislature.[8] This requirement normally restricts the field of candidates to heads of factions because only they have enough supporters to gather the required number of signatures without outside help.

However, explaining how and why one person, among the dozens in a faction, takes over or inherits leadership of it is not easy. So far, there are no studies on this. But one can still narrow considerably the field of likely candidates. Haruhiro Fukui analyzed the career patterns of past party presidents (see the list of LDP presidents below)[9] to project likely future prime ministers. Tahara Sōichirō and other political journalists have analyzed the promotion of current party leaders, including those who were, in the late 1980s, considered within the party to be likely candidates for its presidency through the 1990s (see table 5.1).[10] This section uses a similar method and also looks at how the LDP views the process; in addition, it supplements the data on past party presidents with data on current politicians.

LDP Presidents (1955–1992)

Hatoyama Ichirō
Ishibashi Tanzan
Kishi Nobusuke
Ikeda Hayato
Satō Eisaku
Tanaka Kakuei
Miki Takeo
Fukuda Takeo
Ōhira Masayoshi
Suzuki Zenkō
Nakasone Yasuhiro
Takeshita Noboru
Uno Sōsuke
Kaifu Toshiki
Miyazawa Kiichi

The Profile of Likely Candidates

The LDP currently has quite a rigid promotion system that applies to all incoming party members of the National Assembly. Three aspects of it shrink the pool of LDP politicians who can be considered possible candidates for the party presidency. First, a serious candidate must be a member of the more powerful lower house, as all past party presidents have been and as all those now considered to be possible candidates are.[11] Although there are no constitutional laws or formal party rules that prohibit members of the upper house from becoming prime minis-

TABLE 5.1
Future Prime Ministerial Candidates

Mitsuzuka Faction	Miyazawa Faction	Takeshita Faction	Watanabe Faction
Mitsuzuka Hiroshi	Katō Kōichi	Hashimoto Ryūtarō	Watanabe Michio
Abe Shintarō[a]	Kawara Tsutomu	Hata Tsutomu	Fujinami Takao[b]
Katō Mutsuki[c]	Kōno Yōhei	Kajiyama Seiroku	Yamaguchi Toshio
Mori Yoshirō		Obuchi Keizō	
		Ozawa Ichirō	
		Watanabe Kōzō	

Source: Itō Masaya and Fukuoka Masayuki, *Korekara 10-Nen Sengoku Jimintō* (Tokyo: Daiichi Kikaku Shuppan, 1988), 92.
   a. Abe was the head of the faction until his death in May 1991.
   b. Fujinami was implicated in the Recruit scandal in 1989 and has since resigned from the faction and party.
   c. Katō Mutsuki was expelled from the faction in 1991 as part of the power struggle he had with Mitsuzuka over control of the faction following Abe's death.

ter, the practice has been that only members of the House of Representatives can advance very far in the party hierarchy. For example, none of the top party executive positions (including the secretary generalship, the chairmanship of the executive council, the chairmanship of the PARC, and, if the position is filled, the party vice presidency) and only two or three of the cabinet posts (and for the most part minor ones at that) are given to upper house members. In addition, no member of the House of Councillors has served more than one term in the cabinet since the early 1970s. If they are excluded, the pool of candidates shrinks from about 400 to between 250 and 300 (depending on the number of seats the LDP holds in the lower house).

Second, a candidate for the party presidency must be a senior member of the National Assembly. Prime ministers over the past twenty years (since Tanaka) had served in the National Assembly for well over twenty years and at least ten terms prior to becoming prime minister (see table 5.2). Miyazawa, for instance, has been a legislator for nearly forty years. Even the more junior of the potential leaders have already served more than 15 years in the National Assembly, and most have been there for more than twenty. The LDP currently has a fairly rigid seniority system, at least up to the time one is appointed to a cabinet post for the first time. An LDP member must now serve at least five or six terms in the National

TABLE 5.2
National Assembly Experience of
Prime Ministers

	1st Yr in Kokkai	Age Then	Yrs in Kokkai[a]	Terms in Kokkai[a]
Hatoyama Ichirō	1915	32	25	13
Ishibashi Tanzan	1947	63	9	4
Kishi Nobusuke	1953	59	4	2
Ikeda Hayato	1949	50	12	5
Satō Eisaku	1949	48	16	7
Tanaka Kakuei	1947	29	25	10
Miki Takeo	1937	30	37	14
Fukuda Takeo	1952	47	24	10
Ōhira Masayoshi	1952	42	26	10
Suzuki Zenkō	1947	36	33	14
Nakasone Yasuhiro	1947	29	35	14
Takeshita Noboru	1958	34	29	11
Uno Sōsuke	1960	38	29	10
Kaifu Toshiki	1960	29	29	10
Miyazawa Kiichi	1956	37	36	8 + 2[b]
Mean		41	25	10
Range		29–63	4–37	2–14

a. Years and number of terms in National Assembly at time of inauguration.
b. Miyazawa served two terms in the House of Councillors and then eight terms in the House of Representatives.

Assembly—about fifteen years—before even being considered for a cabinet position. Recent prime ministers were appointed to their first cabinet post between their fourth and sixth terms, and, in addition, they were generally among the youngest of those in the cabinet for the first time (see table 5.3).[12] A potential candidate for the presidency must count on serving another ten years after that—for a total of about ten terms or twenty-five years in the legislature—before having a shot at the party presidency. Fewer than half of a freshman class of LDP members of the House of Representatives can expect to be in the National Assembly after twenty-five or so years, and at any one time there are about fifty LDP members with twenty-five years or more experience in the legislature.[13]

This rules out those who have difficulty holding on to their seats in the legislature. Moreover, a safe seat is a must because potential

TABLE 5.3
First Cabinet Post Occupied by
Prime Ministers

	Age	Term	Post
Hatoyama Ichirō	48	5	MOE
Ishibashi Tanzan	62	1	MOF
Kishi Nobusuke	45	—	MCI
Ikeda Hayato	50	1	MOF
Satō Eisaku	48	1	LP-PARC
Tanaka Kakuei	39	5	MPT
Miki Takeo	39	4	MC
Fukuda Takeo	53	4	LDP-PARC
Ōhira Masayoshi	52	5	MFA
Suzuki Zenkō	49	6	MPT
Nakasone Yasuhiro	41	6	STA
Takeshita Noboru	47	5	CCS
Uno Sōsuke	52	5	DA
Kaifu Toshiki	45	6	MOE
Miyazawa Kiichi	42	UH2[a]	EPA
Mean	48	4.0	
Range	39–62	1–6	

Note:
CCS   Chief cabinet secretary
EPA   Director of Economic Planning Agency
LDP-PARC   LDP, chairman of PARC
LP-PARC   Liberal Party, chairman of PARC
MC   Minister of communications (later became MPT)
MCI   Minister of commerce and industry (prewar)
MFA   Minister of foreign affairs
MOE   Minister of education (prewar)
MOF   Minister of finance
MPT   Minister of posts and telecommunications
STA   Director general of Science and Technology Agency
a. Miyazawa was a second-term member of the upper house when he was first appointed to a Cabinet post and is not included in the calculations for the mean and range.

candidates for the LDP presidency must have the time and energy necessary not only to serve the needs of their constituents but also to rise in the party. Thus, even if LDP politicians who have to struggle to keep their seats manage to stay in the legislature for twenty-five years, they are not likely to be able to get very far ahead in the party.[14] This means that party leaders tend to come from the more rural districts, where voting patterns are generally more stable. No recent prime minister has come from a district that can be considered urban (see table 5.4). The last one was Ikeda Hayato, who represented the city of Hiroshima. The last prime minister who came from a metropolitan area was the first under LDP rule, Hatoyama Ichirō, who represented one of the districts in Tokyo. The coming generation of leaders also tends to be from the more rural districts.

One example of an LDP member of the Kokkai whose highly urban constituency will make advancement in the party difficult is Hatoyama Ichirō's grandson, Hatoyama Kunio, from Tokyo District # 8. If he were from a more rural district, he would likely be considered party presidency material, but the volatility of his constituency may prove to be a major obstacle. He was first elected in 1976 but was defeated in 1979. In the following three elections he finished first or second, but he is likely to remain vulnerable because his district has generally had four strong candidates for only three seats. His vulnerability led him to oppose the party leadership publicly because of strong opposition by his constituents to the imposition of the new indirect tax. Hence, even if he manages

TABLE 5.4
Type of District Represented by
Prime Ministers

	District	Type[a]
Hatoyama Ichirō	Tokyo #1	Type 1: most urban
Ishibashi Tanzan	Shizuoka #2	Type 3: semiurban
Kishi Nobusuke	Yamaguchi #2	Type 5: semirural
Ikeda Hayato	Hiroshima #2	Type 3: semiurban
Satō Eisaku	Yamaguchi #2	Type 5: semirural
Tanaka Kakuei	Niigata #3	Type 6: rural
Miki Takeo	Tokushima	Type 6: rural
Fukuda Takeo	Gunma #3	Type 6: rural
Ōhira Masayoshi	Kagawa #2	Type 6: rural
Suzuki Zenkō	Iwate #1	Type 6: rural
Nakasone Yasuhiro	Gunma #3	Type 6: rural
Takeshita Noboru	Shimane	Type 6: rural
Uno Sōsuke	Shiga	Type 5: semirural
Kaifu Toshiki	Aichi #3	Type 4: medium
Miyazawa Kiichi	Hiroshima #3	Type 4: medium

a. Election district types are based on Kobayashi Yoshiaki's analysis in his *Tenkanki no Seiji Ishiki* (Tokyo: Keiō Tsūshin, 1985). Kobayashi categorizes election districts on a scale from 1 to 7. Type 1 districts are most urban and type 7 are most rural, as of 1980.

to maintain his seat, he is unlikely to rise to the top levels of the party hierarchy.

The third qualification for a candidate for the party presidency is relative youth. Because of the rigors of the job, it is widely believed (by both political insiders and the public) that serious candidates should be no older than their late sixties or very early seventies. Miki Takeo, for instance, believed that a prime minister should be no older than 70 in order to be able to carry out effectively the work of the office.[15] When Uno resigned as prime minister in 1989, the LDP briefly considered three party elders—Fukuda Takeo (then 84), Kanemaru Shin (75), and Kōmoto Toshio (78)—but decided that they were too old and instead turned to a younger candidate (Kaifu, 58). Of the past presidents none was older than 72 (Ishibashi and Miyazawa) and most were in their sixties, the mean age being about 65. The age at which LDP prime ministers assumed office is as follows:

Hatoyama Ichirō	71
Ishibashi Tanzan	72
Kishi Nobusuke	60
Ikeda Hayato	60
Satō Eisaku	64
Tanaka Kakuei	54
Miki Takeo	67
Fukuda Takeo	71
Ōhira Masayoshi	68
Suzuki Zenkō	69
Nakasone Yasuhiro	64
Takeshita Noboru	63
Uno Sōsuke	66
Kaifu Toshiki	58
Miyazawa Kiichi	72
Mean	65
Range	54–72

Counting the number of senior LDP members of the lower house with twenty-five years or more of experience who are under 72, then, the pool shrinks from over fifty to about twenty.

These three qualifications provide an objective profile of possible candidates for the party presidency, one that has a number of implications. First, LDP politicians must start their careers in the National Assembly relatively early. In order to serve twenty-five years and still be younger than 70 means winning a seat no later than one's early- to mid-forties—and starting even earlier would be a distinct advantage. Most of the prime ministers over the past twenty years were elected to the legislature at a relatively young age; the average for those since Tanaka is about 35 (see table 5.2). Tanaka, Nakasone, and Kaifu were actually elected before they were 30. This tendency is even more accentuated among those considered to be likely candidates in the future, many of whom were first elected in their twenties: Hashimoto Ryūtarō, Obuchi Keizō, Ozawa Ichirō, and Yamaguchi Toshio.

Among the earlier presidents were some who started their careers in the National Assembly relatively late. During the first years of the party, the seniority system was much less rigid, and a few, particularly former elite bureaucrats, were able to start their political careers in their late forties and older and still be in the running for the presidency.[16] Over the years, however, the fast track has been eliminated. Virtually all LDP legislators must now take the long route.[17] Even former elite bureaucrats or governors who would have once been given a one-term bonus or more in seniority (i.e., first-termers would have been given second-term status) have largely lost even that advantage. Hence it may now be virtually impossible for those in their late forties to start their first term in the National Assembly with any hope of becoming prime minister.

The emphasis on starting young has had two consequences on the type of LDP legislators who have the best chance of making it to the top. First, they tend to be career politicians. This is a change from the early years of the party. During the first twenty-five years or so, the bureaucracy was the primary recruiting ground for the party leadership. The career background of LDP prime ministers is as follows:

Hatoyama Ichirō	Politician
Ishibashi Tanzan	Journalist
Kishi Nobusuke	Bureaucrat, Commerce and Industry Ministry
Ikeda Hayato	Bureaucrat, Finance Ministry
Satō Eisaku	Bureaucrat, Transportation Ministry
Tanaka Kakuei	Businessman
Miki Takeo	Politician

Fukuda Takeo	Bureaucrat, Finance Ministry
Ōhira Masayoshi	Bureaucrat, Finance Ministry
Suzuki Zenkō	Interest group (fisheries)
Nakasone Yasuhiro	Bureaucrat, Home Ministry
Takeshita Noboru	Prefectural assemblyman
Uno Sōsuke	Prefectural assemblyman
Kaifu Toshiki	Politician's secretary
Miyazawa Kiichi	Bureaucrat, Finance Ministry

Kishi, Ikeda, Satō, Fukuda, and Ōhira all had distinguished careers in the civil service before becoming members of the National Assembly and eventually party president. But the past five presidents can all be considered career politicians. Both Nakasone and Miyazawa are former elite bureaucrats (Nakasone from the prewar Home Ministry, Miyazawa from the Finance Ministry), but both left their ministries early in their bureaucratic careers and can also be considered career politicians. Those considered to be up-and-coming have for the most part spent their entire adult lives in party politics in one way or another (and one, Obuchi, won a seat while still a master's student at Waseda University). The overwhelming majority worked either as personal secretaries to members of the National Assembly or as prefectural assembly members. Only four of the fifteen had much of a career outside party politics before winning a seat in the National Assembly.

The second consequence of starting young is that those who have the best chances to become party president tend to be *nisei giin* (second-generation politicians)—those who inherit their seats from their fathers or fathers-in-law. About half of those on the list of potential prime ministers (see table 5.1) belong to this category.[18] The second-generation politicians have the advantage because it is very difficult to be elected at a young age unless one can inherit an already developed campaign machine. Starting young is important because everyone—politicians, journalist, interest groups—believes it is important. Although this qualification is not carved in stone, it has become a self-fulling prophecy. Those who start their career in the National Assembly at a young age, particularly second-generation politicians, are more likely to receive media attention, political contributions from groups wishing to build a relationship with an up-and-coming politician, and preferential treatment in party and government appointments. Thus they have a significant advantage in acquiring the funds and experience needed to become top party leaders and eventually having a shot at the LDP presidency.

Becoming Leader of a Faction

The LDP members of the House of Representatives, who have served at least ten terms, and are under the age of 70 or so, number about twenty at any one time. Perhaps another fifty or so among current LDP members can expect to meet this profile sometime in the future. It is out of this pool that the leaders of factions—and therefore party presidents—are most likely to come. Although most, if not all, of those in this group are or will become part of the party leadership, only a few will become the head of their own bloc and make serious challenges for the presidency. The process by which a particular individual becomes the leader of a faction, as I mentioned above, is not well understood. Luck and timing—being the right age and having the right qualifications at the right time—have a lot to do with it. But it seems clear that the ones out of this select group who are likely to be in the running are those who have developed experience in three areas: factional and party affairs, policy affairs, and legislative management.

Party and Factional Affairs

The most important factor in becoming party president is to have the backing of a faction. Without it one has virtually no chance regardless of how well qualified one is in other aspects. The importance of this support is shown clearly in two recent cases. The first was in 1980 following Prime Minister Ōhira's death. The party leaders agreed to have a member of the Ōhira bloc serve the remainder of the president's term. The main candidates to succeed were Miyazawa Kiichi and Suzuki Zenkō. Miyazawa had much more experience in government than Suzuki and was well known to the public and well respected abroad. Yet the party leaders decided on Suzuki, a virtual unknown outside the party, as Ōhira's successor, because of his experience in handling factional and party affairs.

The second case was in 1989 following Uno's resignation. The leading candidate to succeed was Hashimoto. He had served in the important post of secretary general of the LDP and had shown his ability in a number of other important party and government positions; moreover, he had considerable public support. But he did not become president because he did not have the backing of the faction of which he was a member (the Takeshita bloc). The post went instead to Kaifu, a much less qualified candidate in terms of government and party experience, but one who had the backing of the Kōmoto faction.

No academic studies have been done on how one gains the support of one's faction. However, a few political journalists, in particular Tahara Sōichirō, suggest that there are two interconnected means. One is developing a good relationship with the leader of the faction early in order to get the backing needed to obtain good posts and connections. And the other is working hard to look after the interests of the bloc's members. The two go together because by doing the latter one is also achieving the former. Hence success requires the ability and willingness to develop relationships and look after the interests of a lot of people.

The LDP is often described by its members as a "village" and the selection of its president as a village mayoral election. In the village, everyone knows everyone else fairly well. An important factor in climbing the ladder to the top of the LDP is one's reputation among its members. "Those who may look good on the surface but not on the inside—those who grandstand, senior members in the National Assembly who don't help new members, those who cannot be trusted, those who gossip about the affairs of the village—are weeded out."[19] Tahara notes that LDP politicians who are relatively well liked by the public are often not very popular within the party.[20] Miyazawa was not one known to help others within the faction or party, and so he was not able to get the support of the Suzuki camp until he worked hard in party and factional affairs. Takeshita was known to be especially tireless in helping others and yet modest about it, as was reflected in his aphorism "Ase wa jibun de kakimashō, tegara wa hito ni agemashō" (Sweat it out yourself and give others the credit).[21]

Aspiring legislators can build a personal base of support within their faction and party by providing support in election campaigns and by helping others obtain appointments to party and government posts. Perhaps the most important resource for these aspiring leaders—but not the only one—is money. Running for a seat in the National Assembly and maintaining and keeping it are expensive. There are no accurate figures on the amount of money raised and spent on election campaigns and other related activities; it is an open secret that the candidates go well beyond the legal limits. Although faction leaders do not monopolize the raising of these political funds, as they once did, the faction still is an important source of funds.[22]

There are other important ways of helping members of one's bloc besides supplying political funds. Nakasone, for example, was able to take over the Kōno faction in part because he was a good public speaker and was willing to go around to members' districts to help them get elected.[23] Tanaka and Takeshita certainly were more than able political fund raisers, but they also built up their following by teaching junior LDP members about getting elected and helping in terms of advice, personnel, and organization. Takeshita, who is especially known for his *kikubari* (helping others), describes some of the services he helped provide to members of the then Tanaka faction:

> Of course, for members of the National Assembly, the most important
> thing is to get elected, so we put a lot of emphasis on helping them out
> with that. For example, we provide good speeches for those who aren't very
> good at giving speeches. For those who aren't very good at setting up orga
> nizations, we help build them. And when constituents come to present a
> petition, we will arrange it so that they are able to give the petition to a
> receptive bureaucrat and make sure that petitioners are not incon
> venienced.[24]

Finally, an aspiring leader can build a personal base of support in the faction by helping its members receive official party recognition as candidates during elections and good party and government posts. This requires having clout with the head of the faction as well as other party leaders, particularly the party president, who appoints the cabinet and the *san'yaku* (the top three party executive positions, i.e., secretary general, chairman of the executive council, and chairman of the PARC), and the secretary general, who controls most of the other appointments in the government and party. Much of this involves the ability to distribute political funds. Hori Shigeru, in talking about the qualities required to become party president, said:

One is the ability to raise money. Relatively speaking, just about all those who try to become prime minister/party president have this ability. But what is important is the other ability, the ability to get people to receive money from you. This ability of course applies to one's own faction, but the question is whether one has the ability to pass on money to members of rival factions. This is the problem. It requires trust. Most of the members of the National Assembly will take the money if they trust the person giving it not to talk about it. The receiver will certainly not take the money if he does not trust the giver. The ability to distribute funds equals trust.[25]

On the party side, the general belief is that it is essential that a party president serve in at least one of the top three party executive posts.[26] The conventional wisdom is that the single most important stepping-stone to the presidency is the position of secretary general.[27] The secretary general is in essence the acting head of the party, because the president, as prime minister, generally concentrates on government affairs.[28] Almost all past party presidents have served at least one term as secretary general, as well as in one or both of the other two posts (see table 5.5)[29] But many of the recent prime ministers—Suzuki, Uno, Kaifu, and Miyazawa—have not.

The secretary general's post, however, may not be as important in the future. On the one hand, the experience gained in the post is considered indispensable, and Suzuki's poor performance as prime minister only reinforced that impression. On the other hand, prime ministers have been very reluctant to appoint rivals to the powerful post. This was particularly true under Nakasone, who resisted appointing any of his main rivals as secretary general until his last year as party president—and then only because Kanemaru Shin would not take the job again. Before 1974 prime ministers generally appointed to the position some-one from their own camp who was typically a candidate to inherit the faction.[30] But since then prime ministers have been forced to choose legislators from outside their own bloc as a result of an agreement to share power more equally among the factions. A prime minister, there-fore, tries to appoint an elder of another group who would not be a serious challenger, although at times he has little choice but to choose a rival in order to establish and maintain a stable party base, as was the case with Kaifu's appointment of Ozawa Ichirō in 1989.

TABLE 5.5
Terms Served by Prime Ministers
in Previous Cabinet and Party Posts

	Cabinet Posts					Party Posts		
	MOF	MITI	MFA	CCS	Other	SG	EC	PARC
Hatoyama Ichirō	—	—	—	—	2	—	—	—
Ishibashi Tanzan	2	3	—	—	—	—	—	—
Kishi Nobusuke	—	—	1	—	2	1	—	—
Ikeda Hayato	5	2	—	—	1	1	—	1
Satō Eisaku	2	1	—	1a	4	2	1	1
Tanaka Kakuei	3	1	—	—	1	4	—	1
Miki Takeo	2	2	—	—	7	2	—	—
Fukuda Takeo	5	—	1	—	4	3	—	2
Ōhira Masayoshi	1	1	1	3a	—	1	—	1
Suzuki Zenkō	—	—	—	1a	4	—	7	—
Nakasone Yasuhiro	—	4	—	—	5	1	2	—
Takeshita Noboru	5	—	—	2	1	1	—	—
Uno Sōsuke	—	—	2	—	3	—	—	—
Kaifu Toshiki	—	—	—	—	2	—	—	—
Miyazawa Kiichi	3	1	1	2	5	—	2	—

Note:
  MOF   Finance Minister
  MITI   International Trade and Industry Minister
  MFA   Foreign Minister
  CCS   Chief cabinet secretary
  SG   LDP secretary general
  EC   Chairman of the LDP executive council
  PARC   Chairman of the LDP PARC
  a. Satō, Ōhira, and Suzuki served as chief cabinet secretary before the position was
made a cabinet-level position.

Partly for this reason, more attention has been focused on the other
two party executive positions, that is, the chairmanships of the executive
council and the PARC. The chairmanship of the executive council has not
generally been considered to be an intermediate post on the way to the
top. The position was generally filled by party heavyweights, but not
necessarily ones considered to be contenders for the party presidency
(much like the vice presidency which will be described below). The
chairman's main function is to serve as coordinator within the party—
generally a role for those who prefer to work behind the scenes. But a
number of recent prime ministers, including Nakasone, Suzuki, and
Miyazawa, have served in the post (as had Abe Shintarō). Even more

attention has been focused on the chair of the PARC. Satō and Matsuzaki write that that council has superseded the executive council as the main decision-making body in the party.[31] There have been four chairmen of the PARC who have become prime ministers: Miki, Tanaka, Fukuda and Ōhira. Of those who were seen to be likely candidates for the party presidency, Abe Shintarō, Watanabe Michio, Mitsuzuka Hiroshi, and Katō Mutsuki have held the position.[32]

While the top party executive posts are considered to be the most important positions from which to advance to the presidency, the party's formal number-two position, the vice presidency, is not.[33] In fact, no vice president has gone on to become president.[34] Over the years, the position has been filled by what political journalists call number-two types of LDP politician. They are those who prefer to remain behind the scenes, and they generally have good negotiating abilities and connections to members of all factions. Thus an important role for the vice president is to act as mediator within the LDP during times of crisis.[35] In the past, he has played a critical part in keeping the party together when it was in danger of splitting apart, for example, when it was in turmoil over whom to select as party president.[36]

Expertise in Policy

Although a potential candidate for the party presidency must rise up through faction and party, the promotion system also emphasizes expertise in policy. Because the president of the party also serves simultaneously as prime minister, a potential candidate must show competence in handling matters of policy. In the past, policy expertise was not emphasized, perhaps because so many of the party leaders had previously been career bureaucrats. But one of the hot topics in the study of the ruling party in the past few years has been the rise of the so-called *zoku-giin*, or *zoku* member. *Zoku* refers to groups of LDP members of the Kokkai who have special influence in a particular area of policy such as agriculture, education, commerce and industry, construction, and taxes. Becoming a *zoku-giin* is important to a rising politician because it means establishing connections with bureaucrats dealing with policy as well as with interest groups affected by the particular ministry.

Most recent prime ministers and virtually all of the next generation of leaders are established *zoku-giin*.[37] To become one, an LDP politician serves in various posts in the PARC, on National Assembly committees, and in the cabinet (as minister or parliamentary vice minister, or both), or by having a bureaucratic background. A potential candidate for the party presidency, however, cannot just remain a specialist in one or two policy areas. Ambitious legislators try to be appointed to cabinet posts outside their area of specialty. Kaifu, a member of the education *zoku*, for instance, was deeply disappointed to be named education minister in 1985 (for the second time) because he felt the post would not advance his career very much.

Recent prime ministers have occupied a number of cabinet positions. They have been in the cabinet at least a few times, with a mean of about nine times (see table 5.5). And there are a few cabinet posts that are considered especially important for those contemplating running for the party presidency. The general view has been that they should serve as at least one of the "big three," namely, finance minister, international trade and industry minister, or foreign minister. The finance and international trade and industry positions are supposed to provide experience in economic affairs, and the foreign affairs post in diplomacy. Virtually all party presidents have served at least a few terms as minister in one or more of these positions. Miyazawa, for instance, has served in each of them at least once. The two exceptions to this rule, Suzuki and Kaifu, both became president under unusual circumstances,[38] Suzuki following the death of Ōhira, and Kaifu after the Recruit scandal tainted most of the top party leaders.

Lately, political analysts have seen the positions of chief cabinet secretary and deputy chief cabinet secretary as important stepping-stones. The former is being grouped with the big three in terms of importance for the experience it gives in running the Cabinet Secretariat.[39] In fact, some political observers now see it as replacing the party secretary generalship as the most important route to the prime ministership. This change may be due in large part to the current practice of preventing prime ministers from appointing someone from their own faction as secretary general. As Jin Ikkō writes, "The factions' heirs apparent are being appointed to the position as a sort of training ground for becoming prime minister."[40] Examples include Takeshita under Satō, Abe under Fukuda, and Miyazawa under Suzuki. The deputy's position is also seen as a training ground for the more promising younger members of the prime minister's bloc. Kaifu was deputy chief cabinet secretary under his mentor, Miki, and a number of the other younger leaders, including Mori, Katō Kōichi, Kajiyama, and Kawara, have also done so very early in their careers in the National Assembly.

Legislative Management

Experience in dealing with opposition parties has also become more important.[41] Part of the experience comes from serving on the LDP's Legislative Affairs Committee or the lower house's Legislative Management Committee, in which members deal directly with the opposition parties and manage legislation.[42] Although such experience in legislative management does not figure prominently in the background of past party presidents, most of the current and next generations of leaders, such as Takeshita and Kaifu, have had considerable experience in dealing with the opposition parties. In addition, the ability to give political funds to members of the opposition parties is important in setting up such "pipelines" to the other side.[43]

Takeshita, in particular, has been well known for his connections to opposition party leaders, such as *Kōmeitō's* secretary general, Ōkubo Naohiko, and the DSP's general secretary, Ōuchi Keigo, who like Takeshita are graduates of Waseda University. These connections played a big part in advancing Takeshita's career, as well as in helping him pass legislation while prime minister.[44]

It should be noted that the speaker of the House of Representatives is not in line for the party presidency. Prime Minister Nakasone, for instance, offered the appointment to Nikaidō Susumu in 1986, but he turned it down for fear that his chances for the presidency would be eliminated. The post is very prestigious—constitutionally it ranks almost with the prime minister's—but those who are appointed are generally party elders who are near the end of their political careers.

In summary, in order for an LDP politician to become a serious candidate for the party's presidency, he must become the head or at least a top leader of an intraparty faction. While no study exists yet that explains how one becomes head of such a group, one can narrow the field of likely legislators. They are most likely to be career politicians with long experience in the National Assembly—usually with twenty-five years and ten terms or more in the lower house—as well as experience in a number of important cabinet and party posts. In addition, the process favors those who work well as party insiders; they develop close relationships not only with members of their own faction but also with other LDP leaders and even opposition party leaders.

The Race for the Presidency of the LDP

At least every two years the LDP holds a convention to choose its president. The convention has not played a major role in recent years in determining the presidency—the outcome has generally already been decided by the time it takes place—but the race is real.[45] There is usually more than one candidate running, and incumbents eligible for another term as president generally face strong challenges. Among recent incumbents only Nakasone has been able to serve more than two full terms—the last one before him was Satō, who won reelection in 1970.

The current LDP rules, revised in September 1989, require candidates to obtain the endorsement of thirty fellow LDP members of the National Assembly. If more than one candidate runs, the rules call for an election in which not only LDP members of the National Assembly participate but also other party members and "LDP supporters" (those who have paid dues to the party for the last three consecutive years without officially joining the party). At the convention, each LDP member of the National Assembly has one vote, and each prefecture is given one to four votes depending on the number of ballots cast (the candidate who places first in the prefecture receives all of the prefecture's votes).[46] If no one candidate receives a majority, then a run-off is held in which only the top two finishers are eligible to run and the voting is limited to LDP members of the National Assembly.

The LDP has tinkered often with the rules and procedures for selecting its president, but two major methods have been used: elections and negotiations. Early in its history, the party tended to hold elections by LDP members of the National Assembly and prefectural party representatives. Elections, however, are seen to have two negative effects. First, candidates often spend huge sums of money to buy votes. Tanaka, for example, was rumored to have spent more than 10 billion yen in 1972 in order to defeat Fukuda.[47] Besides the monetary cost, this use of money costs the LDP in terms of public image. In the words of one political journalist, "In reality, the election corrupts the party, makes money rather than policy or knowledge the important attribute of the party leader, and ultimately poses the danger of enfeebling party authority."[48] Second, elections often divide the party. The 1972 presidential election helped lead to internal strife for more than ten years (the period after 1972 is often referred to as the "civil war" years).

The party, therefore, has tried to determine the presidency through negotiations whenever possible in order to maintain unity. After the 1972 presidential elections, the next two presidents, Miki and Fukuda, were selected through negotiations. And after the bruising primary election in 1978 between Ōhira and Fukuda, Ōhira's successor, Suzuki, was also chosen through negotiations among party leaders. Negotiations also have some drawbacks: when Uno was selected, many, both local politicians and members of the legislature, criticized the process as undemocratic. Many junior LDP members wanted to run their own candidate. Hence when Uno, because of sex scandals, turned out to be a disaster for the LDP, the party decided to hold a formal election for his successor. But even with the election, the presidency was effectively decided through negotiations among faction leaders; Miyazawa already had the backing of three of the five factions beforehand.

The key to winning the LDP presidency is to get the support of a majority of the LDP members of the Kokkai. If a candidate is able to get the backing of a majority, then the remaining members will usually go along without forcing an election. And, of course, if there is one—whether an election by just LDP members of the National Assembly or a primary election by LDP party members and supporters—the candidate is virtually assured of victory. Getting a majority, however, is rarely a small task. First, the leader of the largest faction controls less than 30 percent of the LDP contingent in the National Assembly. Second, an alliance of at least three blocs is needed to obtain a majority; even the two largest together are not enough. But in order to get three factions to ally themselves, two of the three leaders involved will have to step aside to allow the third to become party president. Given that these leaders are ambitious—they strive to become faction leaders precisely in order to become prime minister—such alliances are difficult to hold together.

This was clearly shown in 1987 when the three so-called new leaders, Takeshita, Abe, and Miyazawa, were running for the presidency. Takeshita, Abe, and Kōmoto agreed to ally themselves to determine the selection of the next president after Nakasone's term expired. Their three camps together had more than the required majority of LDP members of the National Assembly; thus, if they had been able to unite behind a single candidate, they would have been able to determine the outcome. Since Kōmoto was not running (his faction was too small and he was considered too old to be prime minister), the alliance depended on Takeshita and Abe deciding who would run and who would step down. But both strongly wanted to be the next president, and, despite their close friendship, neither would back down. In the end the alliance fell apart and all the candidates agreed to let the sitting prime minister, Nakasone, pick his successor.[49]

In recent years, kingmakers have played a major role in determining which of the candidates is selected party president. Tanaka was largely responsible for determining the presidency from Ōhira to Nakasone. Nakasone played a major part in the selection of Takeshita, who in turn influenced the choice of Uno and Kaifu. The Takeshita faction again played kingmaker in 1991, first by withdrawing its support from Kaifu and then endorsing Miyazawa.

Because the competition for the party's presidency is so fierce, there is a strong possibility that any major faction not running a candidate will be able to decide the result. From the late 1970s to the early 1980s, the Tanaka bloc became the largest one in the party by a significant margin, yet it did not run a candidate for the presidency.[50] Tanaka, therefore, was able to play kingmaker in a number of presidential elections. In 1978 he backed Ōhira over Fukuda in the primary. In 1980 he supported Suzuki to be Ōhira's successor after Ōhira's sudden death. In 1982 he (and Suzuki) backed Nakasone. And in 1984 he again backed Nakasone and forced Nikaidō, a lieutenant of his and the choice of Suzuki and Fukuda, out of the race.

In 1987, Nakasone played kingmaker.[51] The other three major factions were running candidates, leaving the Nakasone camp and the minor Kōmoto bloc with a chance to use their leverage. Kōmoto tried to form an alliance with Takeshita and Abe but failed when the two were unable to agree between themselves who should step aside. With no consensus in the party, the three candidates left the decision to Nakasone, who picked Takeshita to be his successor.

In 1989, Takeshita was a key actor in the selection of the two most recent party presidents, Uno and Kaifu. Like Tanaka before him, Takeshita prevented anyone from his own faction from becoming a candidate for fear of losing control of his group. In particular, he prevented Hashimoto, widely regarded to have been the leading candidate in the race to succeed Uno, from entering. Instead, Takeshita supported Kaifu, a member of the Kōmoto faction, with whom Takeshita had close personal ties. When the Takeshita bloc could not field a candidate in 1991 (Ozawa Ichirō declined to run in part because of concerns about his health), by supporting Miyazawa it again determined the winner.

The winning candidate for the presidency of the party, therefore, is indebted to the kingmaker. The Tanaka faction, first under Ōhira, then under Suzuki and the first Nakasone administration, was given choice cabinet and party posts. This was particularly true under the first two Nakasone cabinets, which the press derisively labeled the "Tanakasone cabinets."[52] Nakasone's bloc also received a disproportionate number of important appointments (including foreign, construction, and posts and telecommunications) in the first Takeshita cabinet.

With political factors so dominant in determining the party's presidency, policy proposals and public popularity are generally secondary.[53] In 1980 the LDP picked a relatively unknown insider, Suzuki, over the much better-known and well-respected Miyazawa. In 1987, Takeshita became LDP president even though he was the least popular among the three candidates in public opinion polls. In 1989 the party chose Kaifu rather than the much more popular and experienced Hashimoto. In 1991, Kaifu was forced to step down despite his record-breaking public approval ratings. Perhaps the reason for the relatively minor influence of public image is that party leaders do not believe that the president has much direct impact on the LDP's fortunes in National Assembly elections, except in unusual circumstances such as scandals. The main exception so far is Nakasone, who enjoyed high popular support during most of his five years in office. In particular, it was because of the enormous LDP victory—credited in large part to Nakasone's public popularity—in the 1986 double election that the party rewarded him with a one-year extension of his term in office. But as was shown in subsequent presidential selections, he is an exception rather than part of a trend.

Some political analysts believe this will change. Satō and Matsuzaki predicted that, with the involvement of party members and supporters in the election, presidential candidates would have to present political ideas and policy proposals in order to get their votes.[54] Indeed, some candidates have tried to use policy proposals to help them in their campaigns for the presidency. In the three-way race to succeed Nakasone in 1987, Miyazawa offered ideas to stimulate the domestic economy, but he was given the least chance to win. By contrast, Takeshita, who had the largest faction and had the inside track, offered only vague ideas about *furusato sōsei* (reviving hometowns). Thus the candidates with the smallest chances of winning tend to talk about policies in their campaign in order to improve their public image, while those with the best chances tend to avoid such talk. In other words, despite predictions that policy issues and public image would become important in the presidential elections, the process continues to center on factional considerations.

Nevertheless, the campaigns for the presidency of the party do provide an opportunity to talk about policy; at the very least, candidates are forced to respond to questions about what they would do while in office even if such issues do not determine who wins or loses. Other times, candidates will actively try to latch onto an issue in order to promote their public image. Very often, the winning candidate goes on to use these proposals as some of the central issues of his administration. Examples include Ikeda and his plan for doubling the nation's income; Satō and his proposal to regain Japanese sovereignty of Okinawa; Tanaka and his idea to restructure the Japanese archipelago and his plan to restore relations with China; Miki and his crusade for clean politics; and Nakasone and his push for administrative reform.

Conclusion

How does the process of selecting the prime minister affect his performance in office? In particular, what sort of prime minister does this process tend to produce? How does it affect style, competence, policies, and the manner of operating?

The first point is that the process results in prime ministers who are well experienced in just about all aspects of national politics. While the selection process in the United States is often criticized for producing presidents who are professional campaigners but Washington amateurs, the process of selecting the party president in Japan has quite the opposite result.[55] Japanese prime ministers tend to have more experience in the various aspects of national politics than even those in West European countries. Candidates for the prime ministership must rise through the party hierarchy, and the LDP's promotion ladder is such that the successful must gain experience in virtually all aspects of national politics. By the time a prime minister takes office, he will have spent more than ten terms or about twenty-five to thirty years in the National Assembly and served in a number of important government and party posts. On the government side, he will have served on legislative committees and in a number of cabinet positions, as well as more informally as *zoku-giin*. Hence he will have experience in handling legislation and at least be fairly well versed in important economic and foreign policy issues. On the party side, he will have been a faction leader and a top party executive. Thus he will have had experience both in intraparty and interparty relations.

But although prime ministers are thoroughly experienced, they are unlikely to be agents of major change. They are unlikely to want it and would have trouble accomplishing it even if they did, because they are insiders; they made it to the top by working within the system. The way the process is currently set up, there is no path to the top for mavericks. One must work hard to please others in the party. To rise in the party means that LDP legislators must first establish good relations with their faction leaders in order to be nominated for important party and government posts. And once they themselves become a leader, they have to work within the system and cooperate with other leaders in order to satisfy the needs of members of their own bloc. Cooperation with other party leaders is necessary also to put together a coalition needed to become president. So prime ministers are not likely to press for major changes.

Even if a prime minister wanted to promote major change, the selection process makes it difficult. First, the fact that selection is not based on policy means that a premier rarely receives a mandate for change when he is selected party president. The intraparty alliances of

factions needed to win the presidency are usually built more on promises of party and government posts than on policy considerations, which
are generally secondary factors. This means that the prime minister
generally cannot claim that he was elected to carry out specific changes.

Also, while the process tends to produce prime ministers who are
experienced in government affairs, they tend to be relatively unskilled in
"going public," as Richard Rose would say. The type of person likely to make
it to the top is one who works hard within the organization and keeps a
relatively low public profile. LDP prime ministers, then, are not generally
charismatic public figures who have the skills to communicate and lead the
public. They have the reputation, deserved or not, of having bland personalities. Ōhira, for example, had a tremendous number of policy ideas, but he
was a horrible public speaker. Satō and Takeshita, both powerful figures in
the party, tended to bewilder listeners with their obfuscating statements.
There have been some exceptions: Nakasone and Kaifu were both good
public speakers. But although these skills certainly helped them to some
degree, they are not considered particularly important in making it to the
top. It is perhaps no coincidence that both were from smaller antimainstream factions (although Nakasone eventually turned his into one of
the big four). They might have had much more difficulty in reaching the top
had they belonged to one of the more established factions.

Finally, prime ministers are unlikely to be major initiators of change
because the selection process rules out issues that are time-consuming
and controversial. As will be detailed in chapter 6, the process makes the
incumbent's position very vulnerable.

The selection process, however, does not entirely inhibit policy
change. The LDP prime ministers as a group are very ambitious and
energetic. Most have spent much of their political lives working hard to
get to the top position and have been planning what they want to do
when they finally get there. They want to make an impact. The two main
exceptions, Suzuki and Uno, were compromise selections who were not
considered presidential material and did not actively campaign for the
post. Incidentally, they were the only two LDP presidents who resigned
voluntarily. Most left office unwillingly.[56] Thus, many prime ministers
looked for changes that would be well received by the public, such as
Tanaka with his proposal to restructure the Japanese archipelago. But
many were also willing to pursue potentially controversial policies

anyway. For example, Miki pushed for stronger antimonopoly laws despite strong opposition from the party.

In addition, the selection process encourages policy change in that it offers frequent opportunities to evaluate the performance of the incumbent. Although policy matters are not the primary factors determining the prime ministership, they are not completely irrelevant either. Faction leaders are in competition with one another, and they look for something to advocate as a way to enhance their public image. The party will not select a president who would be a disaster with the public, so that candidates often develop policy ideas to show either that they are competent and worthy to become prime minister (e.g., Nakasone and administrative reform) or that they have alternatives to the prime minister's or other rivals' policy ideas (or lack thereof). For example, Ikeda presented his plan for income doubling as an alternative to Kishi's controversial issues; Satō presented proposals to ease some of the inequitable features of Ikeda's high-growth policies; Tanaka promoted himself as an activist with a grand vision in contrast to Satō's "politics of waiting." More recently, Nakasone's policy of austerity was challenged by Kōmoto and Miyazawa, who advocated more stimulatory fiscal policies.

It should be emphasized that the current system, as outlined here, is not immune to change. Because the Recruit scandal tainted the heads of the four largest factions at the time, the LDP had to turn to those who were not leaders of blocs (although those groups still played the determining role). The system could change much more drastically if those in the party felt that their electoral fortunes were to become dependent on the public image of the LDP president. If the public started voting in general elections on the basis, at least in part, of how they view the party's president, then the LDP could make the public image of a candidate an important factor in the selection process. The LDP has changed its rules at various times to make the process seem more democratic and allow its supporters more say. But presidential elections involving party supporters so far have simply followed along factional lines, so it is not at all certain that the new system will become more responsive to the public as a whole. It should also be pointed out that party members and supporters do not necessarily choose leaders who would be most likely to win general elections. Many have criticized the selection processes of the U.S. Democratic party and the British Labour party for this reason.

6

The Prime Minister and Party Politics:
The LDP and the Opposition

The reactive leadership of the Japanese prime minister, as I observed earlier, presents a puzzle. Japan has a parliamentary system of government that is at least formally similar to that of many European countries, such as Great Britain's. With a parliamentary system controlled by a single majority party, it should be easy to produce policy change because there are few institutional checks and balances on the majority party's power. The prime minister should, theoretically, have considerable power to make an impact on policy. Yet, as was demonstrated in both the education and tax reform cases, change in Japan is not so easy. The Japanese political system, in other words, is quite inertial.

Bert A. Rockman observes that "the exercise of leadership is inevitably conditioned by the strategic environment surrounding it."[1] Part of this environment is determined, but not exclusively, by the formal government structure.[2] From the prime minister's perspective, there are two major forces inhibiting efforts toward major policy change: political party constraints and the fragmentation of the political system into strong subgovernments. Subgovernments will be the focus of chapter 7; this chapter looks at the prime minister's relationship with the political parties.

George Jones, in his analysis of West European prime ministers, argues that the number and nature of parties are the most important variables in determining a prime minister's power.[3] In particular, they determine the ability to get legislation passed. In the Japanese premier's case, legislative management is made difficult for two major reasons. First, while the LDP maintains a majority in the House of Representatives of the National Assembly, it is not a particularly disciplined party, hence the prime minister often has difficulty keeping it in line. Second, even though the opposition parties are in the minority, they nevertheless have significant resources at their disposal to delay and now veto bills that the LDP may want to pass.

The LDP

In systems with a majority party, the prime minister's relationship with it is especially important. The prime minister's impact on the policy process will largely depend on maintaining party support. If he can do that, then he at least has a chance to push for change in policy even over objections by the opposition parties. Without party unity, chances are very slim. Americans sometimes idealize the effectiveness of party discipline in parliamentary systems, but that is not something most party leaders can easily take for granted. The problems in maintaining party unity in Great Britain, for example, have often been underestimated.[4] Doing so in the LDP seems to be particularly difficult—it is not a tightly organized cohesive party.[5]

In his study of Westminster systems, Patrick Weller cites party structure, in a curvilinear fashion, as one of the important factors that determine the majority party's impact on the prime minister's influence. At one end of the spectrum are highly centralized parties, which he argues tend to be ideologically coherent, such as those in Great Britain and New Zealand.[6] Here prime ministers have greater opportunities to control the party machinery. Margaret Thatcher's strong rule, for example, was based in large part on her ability to control the Conservative party. She was adept at undercutting her rivals, to whom she often referred disparagingly as "wets."

At the other end of the spectrum are parties in which power is highly dispersed and the structure is highly decentralized. Weller puts Canadian parties, in particular the Liberals, in this category, and of course American parties are similar. Highly dispersed parties also enhance the chief executive's influence because there are no clear rivals to contend with. John Kingdon, in his study of agenda setting in the U.S. federal government, writes that the president has organizational advantages over Congress because the executive branch is a more unitary decision-making entity than the highly dispersed Congress.[7]

It is parties in the middle of the spectrum that most inhibit the chief executive. Such parties have a number of independent centers of power, "each with its own interests and its own legitimacy."[8] The prime minister in these cases must "cultivate a set of relationships with [other] leaders, each of whom has an independent base."[9] Australian parties, for example, have a number of independent power centers in state political leaders, usually state premiers. Australian prime ministers are accordingly constrained more by their parties than their colleagues in either the centralized parties of Great Britain and New Zealand or the highly decentralized parties of Canada.

The LDP, in this scheme, appears most similar to the Australian model: it is neither tightly organized and cohesive nor highly dispersed. The prime minister faces two types of problem when trying to keep the party in line: the intraparty factions and the relative independence from party discipline of the rank-and-file members in the National Assembly.

Factions

The LDP's highly organized intraparty factions serve as fairly independent bases of power for their leaders. As was shown in the previous chapter, the prime minister depends in large part on a coalition of factions to reach his position, and his effectiveness even thereafter largely depends on his ability to manipulate them.[10] The party is currently divided into four major factions and one smaller one.[11] They are not just loosely organized, informal groups of legislators bound together by ideology. Rather, they are "formal political entities with a headquarters, regular meetings, a known membership, an established structure, and firm discipline" bound together by a reciprocal arrangement between the head of the faction and the members.[12] The members support their leader, particularly in presidential elections, and in return he looks after their interests by providing government and party posts, campaign funds, and other support. The factions, then, give their leaders an institutionalized base of support within the party that the prime minister cannot ignore.

LDP factions constrain the prime minister in a number of ways. First, they make him relatively more vulnerable than prime ministers in other parliamentary systems. Weller says of the Westminster systems that "changes of party leaders or prime ministers are rare and treated as of great significance.... Leaders have considerable resources that can bolster their position. To remove them is not easy."[13] In Japan, prime ministers change quite regularly, usually every two years or so.

There are four ways that a prime minister can leave office: retire voluntarily, lose his party majority in parliament, die in office, or be pushed or nudged out of office by his own party, either through persuasion or by force. In most majoritarian parliamentary systems, the premier is generally secure from internal challenge. In addition to Margaret Thatcher's recent ouster, John Mackintosh noted that there has only been one somewhat marginal case in the twentieth century in which a British prime minister was forced to resign because of the withdrawal of party support.[14] Weller largely agrees, though he adds that the Eden and Macmillan retirements might be placed between the "willing" and "reluctant."[15] Among other Westminster systems, Weller finds that only in Australia have incumbent prime ministers been forced out of office by their party and only two prime ministers, both in New Zealand, have been persuaded to retire.[16] Out of the more than forty prime ministers who have served in the four Westminster systems since 1932, then, only a handful have been forced out involuntarily, and two to four more were persuaded to retire.

In comparison, since 1955, when the LDP became the ruling party, thirteen premiers have left office. Only two seem to have stepped down completely on their own: Ishibashi Tanzan and Ikeda Hayato, both for health reasons. In virtually all the other cases, pressure from within the party was significant, if not always the sole factor. Indeed, it is almost inevitable that a prime minister will face a serious challenge to his position as party president—he can never take it for granted. During the "civil war" years of the 1970s, all of the prime ministers were forced out.[17] Tanaka resigned after Miki Takeo and Fukuda Takeo left the cabinet to protest his "money politics" in the 1974 election campaign for the upper house; Miki fended off several attempts to oust him before finally resigning to take responsibility for the poor LDP showing in the 1976 general election; Fukuda lost the first LDP presidential primary to Ōhira Masayoshi.

Ōhira faced the most serious challenges of all. After the 1979 election he was not able to appoint a cabinet for over a month because of factional strife. Then after a no confidence motion passed the Kokkai in 1980 as a result of the abstention of rival factions, he was forced either to dissolve the lower house or to resign. He decided on dissolution, but he died shortly thereafter, in large part because of exhaustion from campaigning.

The 1980s were not much more placid. Ōhira's successor, Suzuki Zenkō, spent just over two years in office and perhaps could have served longer had he wanted to, but even in this case there were strong undercurrents of disapproval in the party that probably contributed to his decision to step down.[18] Nakasone was in office for five years, longer than any prime minister since Satō Eisaku, but even he faced a surprising challenge from Nikaidō Susumu. He stepped down in 1987 after the maximum number of consecutive years (five) in office allowed by LDP rules. But in a sense he too was nudged out. Before his popularity dropped following the VAT debacle, many had expected that the party would change its rules to allow him at least another year in office. Takeshita Noboru and Uno Sōsuke resigned as a result of scandals: Takeshita because of the Recruit scandal and Uno because of his geisha affair. And the 1990s have already seen the fall of another prime minister, Kaifu Toshiki.

One implication of being so vulnerable is that the Japanese prime minister has to spend more of his time on party affairs than other leaders. Any conflict is likely to become embroiled in factional politics, and most of the serious intraparty conflicts in the past have centered on struggles for power among heads of blocs. Moreover, prime ministers often put themselves in debt to other faction leaders in order to become party president; they have political IOUs that must be paid back.

Almost from the moment of taking office, the prime minister needs to worry about his reelection as president of the party, just two years later. Anything that can be portrayed as poor performance in office, in terms of election results or policy, will almost inevitably lead to a strong challenge. Kishi writes in his memoirs that a party president spends his first year in office healing the wounds left by bitter interfactional competition of the last presidential election and his second year preparing for his reelection at the forthcoming party conference.[19] Haruhiro Fukui notes that the selection process puts the prime minister on a short leash: he "is left with little time to think seriously about general policy problems, much less to cope with controversial issues at the risk of providing the rival factions with an excuse, if not a sound reason, to oppose his leadership and obstruct his reelection."[20]

What makes factional constraints all the more severe is that the rivalries are often intertwined with revolts among the party's rank and file. If the prime minister cannot maintain the support of the heads of the other major factions, other members of the party can take advantage of his weak position to press various policy demands. Miki and Ōhira are the best examples. After the first attempt to oust him, Miki was forced by the hawkish LDP members of the National Assembly to deny public employees the right to strike, even though his personal inclination was to go the other way.[21] Similarly, hawks in the party made the so-called *Gengō* bill (which gave legal backing for the determination and use of names from the imperial era to designate calendar years) a test case of Ōhira's political will vis-à-vis the Socialists and the Communists.[22] Thus, while it is not impossible for the prime minister to take controversial positions that are unpopular with the party members, barriers to doing so are probably higher than elsewhere.

Factions also constrain the prime minister in other ways. Internal politics eventually led to limits on the LDP president's (and therefore the prime minister's) term. Because each leader wants a chance to be prime minister, the LDP's version of the U.S. Constitution's Twenty-Second Amendment was adopted to give more of them a chance.[23] The current LDP rules allow the president only two consecutive two-year terms, extendable by one year with the consent of two-thirds of the LDP members of the National Assembly. The relatively short term allows limited time to make an impact and to put off worrying about reelection.

The importance of an extra year or two can be seen in the cases of Satō and Nakasone. It took two years for Satō to settle the "textile wrangle" and more than that to negotiate the return of Okinawa. Satō's impressive legacy in large part depended on his being in office for over seven years. Likewise, Fukui points out that the achievements of Nakasone's administration during the first term were relatively few, and his legacy is due partly to being in office a relatively long time.[24]

Factions also restrict the prime minister's powers to appoint and dismiss. On paper, the Constitution and the LDP rules give the chief executive significant powers: cabinet ministers on the government side and the top party executives (i.e., the secretary general, the chairmen of the executive council and the PARC, and the vice president) on the party side. However, the prime minister must take into account the number of cabinet posts to give to each faction (the general rule since 1968 is simply divide the number proportionally to factional strength) and often must include influential party leaders.[25] In addition, the factions largely determine who is appointed. The leader of each camp submits a list of members he would like appointed to the cabinet, and the prime minister usually complies.[26] Of course, the new prime minister also often needs to pay back IOUs in return for support. Nakasone, for instance, gave the Tanaka faction a number of important posts; Tanaka was said also to have specified the positions his people should be given. Likewise, Takeshita gave the Nakasone faction preferential treatment after being picked by Nakasone to take over the party.

This type of consideration also means that the prime minister cannot dismiss a cabinet member except under very unusual circumstances. Nakasone's dismissal of Fujio Masayuki in 1986 from his post as education minister was only the third such case, although there have been quite a few examples of ministers resigning under pressure.[27]

These limitations, however, are not so binding that the prime minister cannot use the power of patronage to his advantage. He generally has enough leeway in setting up his cabinet to be able to appoint to specific spots people who will help him with a certain policy. Satō was able to resolve the dispute between the United States and Japan over Japan's textile exports largely through his appointment of Tanaka Kakuei. Nakasone was especially astute in his use of appointments, first to consolidate his base in the party and second to influence certain policies. His appointments of Kanemaru Shin as LDP secretary general and Gotōda Masaharu as chief cabinet secretary, for example, turned into allies powerful LDP legislators who had previously admitted publicly their dislike for Nakasone.

The extent to which factionalism restricts a given prime minister can vary quite a bit. Rivals within the party are always competing among themselves for influence, particularly as they try to position themselves to become the next prime minister. When the level of competition is intense, the prime minister will have to apply most of his energy to trying to keep his mainstream coalition together.

The intensity of feuding within the party seems to depend on several factors. First, a poor election showing will often trigger factional fights. The prime minister is considered responsible for the party's fortunes in the elections, so that, whenever it does poorly, many of the faction leaders will call for his resignation. Given the successive poor showings in the 1970s, it is no surprise that internal strife during that time was particularly high. Fukuda and Miki, for example, left Tanaka's cabinet in July 1974 after the LDP suffered a setback in the upper house elections. In 1976, Miki resigned as prime minister to take responsibility for the poor showing of the LDP in the 1976 election. And Ōhira was blamed for poor results in the 1979 election, which was partly the reason why the Miki and Fukuda camps abstained during a no confidence vote and allowed the motion to pass. The poor showing by the LDP in 1983 might have led to a serious challenge to Nakasone had there been more credible rivals.

Second, internal feuding depends on the existence of leaders of rival factions who are of the same political generation as the prime minister. Satō's long tenure was aided not only by his skillful use of appointments to keep the party in line, but also by the lack of any serious competitors. Three of his most powerful rivals, Ōno Bamboku, Ikeda Hayato, and Kōno Ichirō, had all died during the early years of his tenure. Satō, therefore, was spared the necessity of expending much time and energy in fending off opponents. Nakasone enjoyed a similar situation. Tanaka had been knocked out of the political scene by a stroke, and Fukuda and Suzuki, having already been prime minister and handed over their factions to the next generation, were not serious contenders. As the last of his generation to be head of government, Nakasone had a much easier time dealing with the party. Kishi, Tanaka, Miki, Fukuda, and Ōhira, on the other hand, spent much of their time trying to repel rivals.

Third, the personalities of the leaders also help determine the level of fighting within the party. Until Tanaka Kakuei became prime minister in 1972, coalitions between factions were rather flexible, with few restrictions on their makeup. The composition of the mainstream and the antimainstream alliances changed fairly frequently. In 1959, for example, Kishi was to bring Ikeda's faction into the mainstream while moving Kōno's out. As Michael Leiserson revealed, most of the ruling coalitions of factions during this time could even be predicted mathematically.[28] But from 1972 until Tanaka's stroke in February 1985, coalitions were quite inflexible because of personal rivalry: the LDP was consistently divided into two camps, with Tanaka and Ōhira on one side and Fukuda and Miki on the other.[29]

The prime minister, however, is not without resources to deal with the other factions. For one, he can use his own bloc as leverage against other party leaders, and it can often be very important in determining the succession. Although it turned out that Satō did not manage to swing the presidential election to Fukuda, his preferred successor, he was able to play Tanaka and Fukuda off against each other while he was prime minister. Similarly, Nakasone played his three challengers, Takeshita, Miyazawa, and Abe Shintarō, against one another. None was willing to go against Nakasone for fear of losing his support in the next LDP presidential election.

The prime minister can also call an election for the House of Representatives in the hope that an LDP victory will strengthen his position. Nakasone's overwhelming win in 1986, for example, led the party to extend his term by another year. Similarly, the surprisingly large LDP victory in the 1990 election for the lower house consolidated Kaifu Toshiki's position as the head of the party.

If the prime minister can gain the support of all the heads of the major factions, he has a very good chance to maintain party unity. Daniel Okimoto notes that "although the existence of factions decentralizes and disperses power, it also concentrates power among a small handful of faction bosses. These leaders are capable of making on-the-spot decisions that have a crucial bearing on the country's well-being."[30] Factions, then, can provide at least some capability for the government to achieve direction.

The Rank-and-File

Even if the prime minister can keep the loyalty of the faction leaders, he can still face revolt from the LDP rank and file. Even if the leaders are unified on an issue, the junior and middle-level LDP members in the National Assembly may still not cooperate. Certainly, the extent of party discipline in parliamentary systems can be exaggerated—the problems of maintaining party unity in Great Britain, for example, have often been underestimated, and government bills have failed to pass on occasion because of defections among the rank and file.[31] Although the LDP has never lost a vote in the Kokkai because of such a rebellion, many proposals have been dropped to avoid the danger of losing. The problems in keeping LDP members in line can be perhaps even more severe than in other ruling parties, as was shown when a number them openly defied the leadership in opposing the unpopular VAT proposed by Nakasone.[32]

The rank and file members oppose party leaders because they have to pay attention to their constituents: the multimember district electoral system enhances competition not only between candidates of different parties but also within the LDP. This makes LDP members of the National Assembly unusually vulnerable to grass-roots pressure. Approximately 20 percent of lower house members who run for reelection are defeated, compared to less than 10 percent in the United States and Great Britain and about 15 percent in West Germany.[33]

They are able to defy the party leadership because they generally rely on their own efforts for reelection rather than on the party. They have their own electoral support groups (*kōenkai*), and they have also become more self-sufficient in terms of political funding.[34] While most of the funds needed to run campaigns and *kōenkai* used to come from the head of the faction, today they come from the politician's own ties to businesses.[35] Thus, as Inoguchi Takashi and Iwai Tomoaki observe, members of the rank and file will rally together like "a mob at a fire" to protect some specific interests even if these are contradictory.[36] They also suggest that the rank and file may be becoming more difficult to control, likening its members to "unleashed hunting dogs" who spontaneously create a movement in the party to protect some interest.[37] The revolt over the VAT was the most widespread case in recent years, but LDP members have often also gone against the decisions of their leaders in agricultural issues.[38]

Nevertheless, the rank and filers do not easily defy their leaders, for the prime minister and other leaders have resources to deter them. One is determining promotion: those who revolt will have greater difficulty in rising in the hierarchy of the party and faction. Many who participated in the tax rebellion were reluctant to go against the party, and particularly the leader of their faction. For example, Hatoyama Kunio did not want to hurt Takeshita, the leader of the faction he belonged to, but he felt he had no choice, given the demands of his constituents.[39]

Because of the potential for rebellion, leaders are careful to bring the rank and file at least formally into the decision-making process, so that those who are discontented can at least be heard.[40] In the tax case, for instance, any LDP member of the National Assembly was allowed to attend the general meetings of the LDP Tax Council.

The National Assembly

The usual image of Japan's National Assembly is that it is very weak. In Chalmers Johnson's words, it is the "supreme ratifier," simply legitimating decisions made elsewhere.[41] Given that Japan has a parliamentary system of government with a single majority party, one would assume that it follows the British model of strong majoritarian rule. As long as the LDP can maintain party discipline (which, as was shown above, is not always easy to do), it should theoretically have little difficulty in enacting policy change. Yet there is considerable evidence to suggest that the opposition parties have substantial influence on the legislative process in the National Assembly. As Mike Mochizuki's study of the legislative process shows, the Kokkai has a high capacity to "resist, change, or retard the executive branch's legislative proposals."[42] This section looks at how the legislative process contributes to the inertia of the system and thus constrains the prime minister.

The Power of the Opposition Parties

In most cases, the National Assembly does not seem to play an influential role in policy making. Most bills are passed either with no amendments or quite minor ones.[43] But these numbers are rather misleading. For one thing, the LDP may negotiate with the opposition parties, explicitly or implicitly, even before introducing legislation. The result is that most bills are passed with the support not only of the LDP but also of one or more of the opposition parties.[44]

On the other hand, legislative approval of bills sponsored and approved by the LDP and the cabinet is far from automatic. As was seen in chapter 4, Nakasone's VAT bill was effectively killed in the National Assembly, and the one to eliminate the *maruyū* system of tax-free savings required extensive negotiations with the opposition before it was passed

The opposition, then, has often been able to thwart or amend LDP bills, or to trade their support for other concessions.[45] The LDP and government leaders, therefore, consider the likely opposition reaction to bills when planning the legislative agenda.[46]

The National Assembly, then, is different from the usual model of parliamentary government in that the opposition parties have considerable influence over what legislation is passed. First, there are strong norms of consensus in the legislature, reinforced by general public norms, to include the opposition parties in the legislative process.[47] The public has continued to support the LDP over the other parties in elections, but LDP legislators know that they cannot force legislation through without risking a breakdown in the legislative process as well as a serious public backlash. The opposition parties will often organize demonstrations, rallies, and petitions to demonstrate public support for their position. They will also often boycott deliberations in the National Assembly with little fear that the LDP will continue without them.

This strong norm against the LDP using its majority to ram legislation through over opposition objections makes the Japanese legislature more of a constraint than most parliaments. Of the Westminster parliaments, only Canada seems to have similar norms. In Great Britain, Australia, and New Zealand, the use of the "guillotine" and closure is much more common.[48]

Second, the legislative process consists of a number of stages before a bill becomes law.[49] After cabinet approval, a bill is introduced into the legislature through the House Management Committee, which is run by an executive committee of representatives from the major parties represented in the Kokkai. The executive committee decides to which house committee the bill will be assigned.[50] If there is no agreement the matter is postponed, a practice that gives the major opposition parties an opportunity to delay deliberations on bills they vehemently oppose.

Once a bill is assigned to committee, the opposition parties have another opportunity to delay deliberations. As in the House Management Committee, there is an informal norm among committee directors to delay any controversial measure. Though the government can force a bill out of committee to the floor of the full house, it is generally reluctant to do so for fear of public criticism.[51] Mochizuki concludes that the committee system in the Japanese National Assembly is at least as influential as in the British and Canadian parliaments.[52]

When it has been passed in the House of Representatives, a bill then must go through the House of Councillors, where there is another set of hurdles even if the LDP has a majority there. Although the lower house is the more powerful (it selects the prime minister, controls the budget, and ratifies treaties), the upper house is not impotent. Most legislation must be passed by both houses. With a two-thirds majority the lower house can override rejection of a bill by the upper house, but the LDP has never had enough seats.

There are a number of reasons why the legislative process can be held up in the House of Councillors. First, many conservative members of the upper house try to maintain some independence from the LDP, so maintaining party discipline there is often more difficult than in the lower house.[53] Second, the opposition parties have held the chairmanship of a number of standing committees of the House of Councillors throughout the postwar period, which has allowed them to kill several important bills even though they had been passed by the lower house.[54] In this sense, the Japanese upper house is considerably more powerful than the British House of Lords or the Canadian Senate, which can delay legislation but not stop it (the New Zealand parliament is unicameral).[55] It is also somewhat more of a restraint than the Australian Senate, which formally has similar powers, when the government controls both houses. Note, however, that in recent years the Australian Senate has often been in opposition hands, a possible lesson for the Japanese House of Councillors today.[56]

The upper house has become even more of a constraint since the LDP lost its majority there in 1989. This was apparent when Kaifu had to make many concessions to the Kōmeitō in his attempt to pass a bill to allow unarmed personnel of the Self-Defense Force to participate in United Nations peace-keeping missions. The Kōmeitō not only forced the deletion of parts of the bill it did not like (e.g., allowing SDF transport aircraft to evacuate refugees), but it also had the LDP drop its support for the incumbent Tokyo governor.

The third factor that limits the majority party is the shortness of deliberative sessions, which makes time important. The National Assembly actually sits and conducts parliamentary business for only eighty to one-hundred days a year—one of the shortest sessions of any parliament.[57] In addition, after each of the usual three terms a year, the legislative agenda is wiped clean (except for certain bills that the opposition parties agree should be carried over to the next session). Most often, if a bill does not get passed in one session, it must start from the beginning in the next.

The combination of all these factors—the norms of consensus, the number of stages in the legislative process, and the shortness of sessions—makes the National Assembly more restricting than other parliaments. First, the short sessions limit the number of difficult bills that the government can get through the legislature, because of the time and effort needed to negotiate with the opposition parties. So the opposition parties, with their ability to slow down the process, are often able do so for long enough to prevent bills from coming to a vote before the end of the session.

Second, the opposition parties can effectively hold hostage all other bills before the National Assembly—ones that they do not particularly object to but which are important to the prime minister or the LDP. This strategy was important in killing the VAT bill in 1987. Nakasone finally gave up because he needed to have the budget passed before going on his scheduled trip to the United States, to show Congress and the president that Japan was taking steps to ease the trade imbalance.

Finally, the legislative process can stall for reasons entirely unrelated to the bills themselves, such as a scandal about corruption or even a careless or controversial remark by a cabinet minister. These sorts of controversy can delay legislation enough to threaten its passage, as happened with the bill to establish the National Council on Educational Reform when a scandal delayed a vote virtually until the last minute of the session.

In addition to these static restraints, which are always present, the opposition parties have additional leverage in certain situations, and the legislative process becomes even more limiting for the majority party. First of all, the opposition parties' leverage depends largely on their unity. When the opposition is divided, the prime minister can often make deals to obtain the support of one or more parties, as was the case in the early 1980s, when divisions between centrist parties (the DSP and the Kōmeitō) and the parties of the left (the JSP and the JCP) were deep. Tax reform demonstrates well the difference that opposition unity can make. In the case of the VAT proposed by Nakasone, all of the opposition parties were firmly united in their opposition and were thus able to kill the bill. But in the *maruyū* case, the division between the DSP and the Kōmeitō on the one side and the JSP on the other allowed Nakasone to get the bill passed.

The constraint of the opposition also depends to some degree on the level of LDP support in one or the other house of the National Assembly. In the lower house, the party has on occasion lost its "stable majority." Although it has never failed to maintain a simple majority (now 257 seats), it has sometimes fallen below the level needed to control both the chairmanship and the majority of votes in each of the legislative committees (currently about 272 seats).[58] During these times of *hakuchū* (rough parity between the two sides), the opposition had more leverage in the Kokkai. For example, in the 1977 budget, the opposition parties forced the LDP to incorporate some of their demands to ensure its passage.[59] The opposition held a voting majority in the lower house budget committee and threatened to submit a motion to rewrite the budget or boycott the deliberations if their demands were not taken into consideration. This threat was effective because a delay would have seriously threatened Fukuda's scheduled trip to the United States. In no other parliament does the majority party seem to need a cushion to maintain control of committees (although elsewhere such cushions may give the government more assurance that legislation can be passed despite defections in the majority party).

The level of LDP support in the House of Councillors has proven to be even more volatile. As in the House of Representatives, the party has at times had to operate under *hakuchū* in the upper house, for example, in the early to mid-1970s. More than that, it now faces an opposition majority in the upper house since losing its majority after the 1989 election, and this difficult situation will likely continue at least until 1995. When the LDP controlled both houses, it had at least the potential to ram legislation through, and it was often able to pass bills with just the acquiescence of the opposition parties. In the case of the *maruyū* bill, for example, the opposition parties did not vote for it but they agreed not to block it. With the upper house in opposition hands, however, the LDP will need more than acquiescence; it will need support from at least one or two parties. Among Westminster parliaments, only in Australia has the government party similarly faced an influential upper house not under its control.

The Prime Minister's Resources

The prime minister has a number of resources in dealing with the opposition parties. First, the Constitution gives the premier, with the approval of the cabinet, the authority to dissolve the lower house of the National Assembly (but, as I mentioned above, not the upper house) and call for new elections.[60] This is often referred to as the prime minister's *denka no hōtō* (literally, "heirloom sword," but usually translated as "trump card"). Nakasone used this power to some effect, as both a threat and an inducement, to help him handle the opposition (as well as in controlling the LDP). In the summer of 1983, the opposition parties were unprepared for an election. He was, therefore, able to break their boycott of the National Assembly by threatening to hold elections for the lower and upper houses simultaneously. He also used the tool in reverse. Following Tanaka's conviction in a bribery case later the same year, the opposition parties again boycotted legislative deliberations. This time, because it was much more confident of its electoral chances, Nakasone was able to bring it back into the National Assembly to finish the session by promising to hold elections.[61]

But the prime minister's ability to use this authority is limited. First of all, it is confined to the House of Representatives. He cannot dissolve the House of Councillors, and, given that it is and will be in opposition hands for the foreseeable future (at least until 1995), this is a severe limitation. In this regard, the Japanese prime minister has less leverage than his Australian counterpart, who can dissolve the Senate at the same time as the House if the Senate twice rejects a piece of legislation within three months.[62]

Furthermore, the ability to call elections is not a card that the prime minister can play or even threaten to play very often. For one thing, elections are costly affairs, so the party coffers need to be full. It is therefore difficult to threaten to call another election soon after one has been held. For another, the so-called trump card can be effective only when the chances for LDP success are good. And for yet another, the benefits of dissolving the National Assembly must be balanced against the cost of delaying consideration of bills. Given the difficulty in getting them through the legislature, particularly if they are controversial, the prime minister risks killing important legislation if he delays deliberations on it by dissolving the National Assembly.

Second, some premiers have informal contacts with opposition party leaders, or can use someone else who has them, in order to deal with the opposition. Takeshita and Kanemaru, for example, were both known for their connections to a number of opposition party leaders.[63] Nakasone was able to use both of them in helping to persuade the opposition to cooperate on the bill to eliminate the *maruyū* system.

Third, and perhaps most important, is the prime minister's influence over the legislative agenda. Formally, the agenda and timetable are controlled by the speaker and the House Management Committee of the respective houses. But, in actuality, the prime minister is the one who usually determines which major bills to put forward, when, and how hard to push them. In the tax reform cases, for example, it was Nakasone who kept pushing the legislative process forward. After the debacle over the VAT, tax reform could have easily been laid to rest, but Nakasone managed to keep it alive, so that eventually the bill eliminating *maruyū* was passed.

One reason why the prime minister has so much influence over the legislative agenda is simply that he is head of both government and the majority party. He appoints most of the main LDP actors in the negotiations in the National Assembly, such as the secretary general, the chairman of the LDP Legislative Affairs Committee, and the chairman of the House Management Committee. The LDP Legislative Affairs Committee decides the party's strategy in the National Assembly, while most of the negotiations occur in the House Management Committee, which provides the primary links between the various parties' legislative affairs committees. In major matters, however, the LDP secretary general, under the guidance of the prime minister, generally handles the negotiations with the opposition parties, as Takeshita did with the *maruyū* bill.

Thus, although the Japanese National Assembly does not compare to the U.S. Congress in influence, it probably offers more of a constraint than most other majoritarian parliamentary legislatures. Although many parliaments may share one or two of the attributes of the National Assembly, none seems to allow the parliamentary opposition quite as much leverage against the majority party. According to Weller's analysis, the majority party in most Westminster parliaments can fairly easily override the objections of the minority opposition. Only in Canada does the ruling party have relatively few resources to ram legislation through its parliament, but, unlike Japan, it does not have an influential second house.

Conclusion

Although Japan has a parliamentary system with a single majority party, this has not meant that the prime minister is able to get his way very easily. In practice, the political parties, both the LDP and the opposition parties, limit him and make change rather difficult. First, the LDP is not very disciplined. Rival factions as well as the party's rank and file restrict the prime minister in a number of ways. Factions make his tenure unusually vulnerable compared to that of leaders of most other countries. At least every two years the prime minister must face reelection, and reelection has rarely come easily. Internal politics also limit the number of years that he can serve and his powers of patronage. In addition, LDP members of the National Assembly can revolt and prevent the passage of legislation even if the party leaders are unified.

Second, the opposition parties have more influence than most people believe. Although the Kokkai's influence in no way compares to the power of the U.S. Congress, the opposition parties nevertheless can and often do have a substantial impact on legislation. This is the result of norms supporting consensual decision making and institutional attributes that provide opportunities for the opposition to raise objections and slow down the process—in particular, attributes such as the number of stages that bills must go through and the shortness of legislative sessions. And there are times when the opposition parties have even more leverage, such as when the LDP loses a comfortable majority in one or both of the houses in the National Assembly.

One of the main factors that makes both the partisan and intraparty politics so constraining is that the prime minister faces some sort of major election nearly every year:

Year	Elections for
1979	Local seats, lower house
1980	LDP presidency, lower house, and upper house
1981	
1982	LDP presidency
1983	Local seats, upper house, lower house
1984	LDP presidency

1985
1986   Lower and upper houses (simultaneous), LDP presidency
1987   Local seats, LDP presidency
1988
1989   Upper house, LDP presidency (twice)
1990   Lower house
1991   Local seats, LDP presidency
1992   Upper house

First, the LDP presidential election is held every two years. He has relatively little time after taking office before he starts thinking about his reelection. Next, there are National Assembly elections. The prime minister must call an election for the House of Representatives within four years of the previous one, though it is usually called somewhat sooner.[64] Elections for the House of Councillors are held every three years. Unified local elections are held simultaneously across the country every four years in April. They are important for they involve many of the prefectural assemblies, governorships, and other local offices that are critical in maintaining the LDP's majority at the national level. In addition, by-elections for vacated National Assembly seats often serve as referenda for the LDP.

The relatively high frequency of elections limits the prime minister in two ways. First, it cuts into his time and energy. He must attend to matters related to these elections, such as campaigning and fund-raising, that he otherwise would be able to spend on other matters. Second, the partisan and intraparty environment imposes restrictions on the prime minister. He must consider the short-term effects of his actions more than he would otherwise. In particular, the frequent elections make the LDP and the opposition parties more difficult to control.

The nature of the parliamentary system and political parties, then, contributes to the inertia of the system. The prime minister often has great difficulty in exerting control over the LDP and overcoming resistance by the opposition parties. He does have some leverage over both his own party and the opposition. In particular, if he can keep the factions in line and prevent any controversy from becoming entangled in factional politics, then the prime minister has a good chance of enacting change.

7

The Prime Minister and
Subgovernments

Japan *should have* a relatively strong political "center" not only because of the majority rule of the LDP but also because of its parliamentary system. The U.S. presidential system, with its checks and balances, subdivides political authority; hence no single institution is able to declare the will of the government as a whole. Richard Rose argues that this allows subgovernments to flourish.[1] West European parliamentary systems, on the other hand, "fuse" government and politics in the cabinet; thus "cabinet government provides a strong political counterweight to the particularistic demands of pressure groups."[2]

Japan, given its formal similarity to the parliamentary systems of Europe, should likewise have a strong center to counter the centrifugal forces of subgovernments. Indeed, until quite recently, the prevailing view of Japanese politics was that authority and power were centralized in the hands of "Japan, Inc."—a ruling triad made up of leaders of the bureaucracy, the LDP, and big business, usually with the bureaucracy taking the lead, in promoting high growth above all else.[3] The ruling triad model was reinforced by all the attention given to Japan's industrial policy, in which MITI bureaucrats supposedly play a dominant role.[4]

Recent studies, however, challenge this view. They suggest that policy making in Japan is much more pluralistic than previously thought. Case studies across a number of policy areas reveal that more social interests than just big business and agricultural and other conservative groups have access to and influence in the system.[5] But these studies have also found that government institutions have structured the access of social interests, which leads to the suggestion that Japanese politics can be best described as some sort of limited pluralism. Michio Muramatsu and Ellis Krauss, call it "patterned pluralism." "Policymaking conflicts under patterned pluralism are *pluralist* in that many diverse actors whose alliances may shift participate, but *patterned* in that the shifting coalitions occur within the framework of one-party dominance and of a bureaucracy that procedurally structures the types of possible alliances and policymaking patterns."[6] Others have come up with similar terms, such as Inoguchi Takashi's "bureaucratic-led mass inclusionary pluralism," and Satō Seizaburō and Matsuzaki Tetsuhisa's "canalized pluralism."[7]

Instead of seeing Japanese decision making as highly centralized and unified, then, the tendency now is to emphasize the system's fragmentation, especially because the cleavages caused by the bureaucracy's long-recognized sectionalism are being reinforced with the development of policy specialists among LDP legislators generally known as *zoku-giin*. In particular, attention is shifting to the role and influence of subgovernments. Although strong subgovernments and subgovernmental conflict are hardly unique to Japan, they do seem to be particularly prominent there, as was shown earlier in the cases of education reform and tax reform. Satō and Matsuzaki see subgovernments as being even stronger in Japan than in the United States.[8] This chapter describes the role of bureaucrats and politicians in subgovernments, and how subgovernments and the consequent fragmentation of the system constrain the prime minister's role in the policy process.

Subgovernments

Subgovernments are "small groups of political actors, both governmental and nongovernmental, that specialize in specific issue areas."[9] They generally involve three types of actor: politicians, bureaucrats, and clientele groups. In the United States a subgovernment supposedly consists of a congressional subcommittee, the corresponding bureau, and private groups interested in the policy area.[10] The configuration of subgovernments in Japan is slightly different. In Japan a subgovernment is made up essentially of one ministry or bureau, its corresponding division in the LDP PARC, and a number of interest groups.[11] In particular, there are often alliances between LDP *zoku* politicians, who are specialists in certain policy areas, and the corresponding ministries. It is these alliances that the prime minister must often deal with in the policy process.[12]

The importance of subgovernments from the prime minister's perspective is clear from the two case studies involving Nakasone. In educational reform, he first had to negotiate with LDP legislators who were influential in education policy (the education *zoku*) in setting up the National Council on Educational Reform, and later he was unable to influence the content of proposed reforms, which was dominated by the Education Ministry and the LDP education *zoku*. In tax reform, Nakasone was at odds with the Finance Ministry and the LDP Tax Council over the type of indirect tax. In this case, too, he was unable to determine the content of the most important part of the tax reform package. And in passing legislation to abolish the *maruyū* savings system, only after the members of the postal *zoku* agreed to it was the bill able to move on to the legislative process.

Bureaucratic Sectionalism

There has been considerable debate about the degree of the bureaucracy's influence. Some argue that the Japanese political system is dominated by it, while others see politicians as gaining the upper hand. But the two sides generally agree on two points: the organizational structure of the bureaucracy sets the pattern for the entire system, and the bureaucracy has a strong tendency toward sectionalism.

As Muramatsu and Krauss argue, "the bureaucracy is the pivot around which policymaking alliances are formed on particular issues."[13] Its influence stems from a number of resources. One is prestige. Japan has a strong tradition of bureaucratic rule; the ministries attract the best and the brightest, such as the graduates of the elite Tokyo University's Faculty of Law.[14] Surveys show that civil servants tend to have a much more elite background—higher socioeconomic status, graduates of elite universities—while politicians tend to attend lesser universities and come from poorer family backgrounds.[15]

Compared with politicians, bureaucrats possess more knowledge and expertise. Legislation is almost always drafted by the ministries.[16]

Although LDP politicians are certainly consulted, they do not have their own policy staffs that would provide expertise and information to rival the ministries. By comparison, U.S. members of Congress have large congressional and personal staffs, and German politicians can turn to policy staffs within their party organizations.[17] Thus, politicians in Japan have few alternative sources of information and expertise other than the bureaucracy. According to Destler et al., "If leaders cannot go elsewhere for these resources, they must go to bureaucrats: they will thus tend to see the facts of issues as the officials see them, and their policy decisions will tend to reflect bureaucratic preferences."[18] These advantages make civil servants important actors in the policy-making process and help make the ministry or bureau the key actor in the subgovernment, at least in terms of the formulation of policy.

Although civil servants may be influential, the bureaucracy is far from being unified. The Japanese bureaucracy is divided into twelve ministries (*shō*), plus a number of agencies under the umbrella of the PMO.[19] These formal cleavages are important, because ministries try to cordon off areas over which they have jurisdiction and resist any encroachment on their turf. Chalmers Johnson notes that this sort of sectionalism has long been an important characteristic of Japanese bureaucracy.[20] There are a number of factors that enhance sectionalist tendencies.

First, these organizational cleavages overlay and thus reinforce similar cleavages of competing interests in society at large and in the LDP.[21] Ministries and bureaus often deal with, and become the voice for, quite specific clienteles, and they also develop allies in the LDP. Many believe that the party has gained in this influence particularly through its *zoku-giin*.[22] But this by no means necessarily brings more influence to the prime minister. Some believe just the opposite has happened. Yamamoto Sadao, the chief of the Management and Coordination Agency's administrative inspection bureau, and Hayashi Shūzō, a former director of the Cabinet Legislative Bureau, believe that conflicts between ministries used to be handled at least to some degree through the cabinet or the PMO.[23] But now they see a tendency for ministry officials to run to their supporters in the LDP before even trying to handle the conflicts either by themselves or through the Cabinet Secretariat. The result is that splits between ministries are carried over into the LDP, with no opening for the prime minister to influence the outcome.

Second, Japanese ministries tend to be very cohesive organizations. John Campbell points out that, "in comparison at least with their American counterparts, Japanese ministries appear better able to maintain autonomy by controlling their own organizations."[24] Through recruitment and socialization, they foster strong ministerial loyalty among their members.[25] In addition, they are relatively insulated from outside interference. The prime minister's power of appointment is restricted to the minister and the parliamentary vice minister. The minister could serve as the agent of the prime minister in controlling a particular ministry, but as I already observed, most are not really the prime minister's choice; rather, they are selected by their faction leaders. Moreover, while the minister has strong formal powers, these are rarely used. Most ministers are shuffled out after a year and have little time to make an impact.[26] Meanwhile, the parliamentary vice minister has virtually no influence.[27]

The prime minister has little direct say in appointments to the top career positions, including that of administrative vice minister, who is generally the most influential person in the ministry.[28] All of these are largely decided internally. Thus the ministries are able to keep out virtually all outsiders, who might weaken ministerial loyalty—there are no other political appointees and no mid-career entrants. The result is that the primary focus of bureaucrats tends to be their ministry, rather than a larger entity such as the civil service (as is generally the case in Great Britain), a subministerial group such as the bureau (such as in the United States), or even a professional specialization or association.

Compared to the powers of the U.S. president, who can appoint people to the top several layers in each department, the prime minister's ability to penetrate the ministries is miniscule. While the limitations on the Japanese prime minister's power of appointment are not unique among parliamentary systems (e.g., the German chancellor's are similar), they are much greater than those on many other heads of government. In Great Britain, for instance, the prime minister can make appointments to over a hundred ministerial posts, as well as having a great deal of influence over the appointment of permanent secretaries.[29]

The ministries' autonomy, moreover, is reinforced legally. The prime minister under the Cabinet Law has the authority to control and supervise the administrative branches, decide the jurisdiction of issues, and suspend temporarily ministry orders pending cabinet action. But he does not have the legal authority to give directives to ministry officials unless he has the backing of the full cabinet.[30]

These factors have given the ministries relatively large discretionary powers over their areas of jurisdiction, and they make it difficult for the prime minister to intervene. Legislation is relatively vague, which means that the details of implementation are largely filled in by the bureaucracy through administrative guidance, bureaucratic ordinances, directives, and informal persuasion, as in the case of industrial policy.[31] The strength of the ministries makes it difficult for the prime minister to formulate policies independently of the bureaucracy and to exert control over it. And on broader issues, the sectionalism makes coordination—resolving policy conflict—across ministerial boundaries difficult. Tsuji Kiyoaki, the dean of Japanese public administration scholars, pointed to this as Japan's most serious deficiency in governing.[32]

Fragmentation in the LDP

In a way similar to the bureaucracy, the LDP is also often fragmented along interest lines. When it was founded in 1955, it was a party that received its support mostly from the traditional sectors—farmers and owners of small businesses. But over the years it has been in power, the LDP has expanded its base of support to include virtually all parts of society.[33] Because of the party's longtime rule, interest groups are not able to turn to opposition parties for help and have thus sought to "infiltrate" the LDP to have their interests represented.[34] The LDP, hence, has become a catchall party.[35] In a 1986 survey, it received majority support from every age group, from rural villages to large cities, and all occupation groups, apart from industrial workers—and even among those, it received more support than any other party.[36] The LDP's responsiveness to social interests usually involves the so-called *zoku-giin*.

In the party, these social interests are represented in the PARC, particularly in its divisions and research committees.[37] The PARC did not serve much as a policy-making body in the early days of the party's rule. Satō and Matsuzaki note that LDP legislators were generally not involved in the details of policy; PARC was more a forum for bureaucrats to explain the content of legislation to LDP members of the National Assembly than a body of politicians making decisions.[38] Thus, policy details and decisions were largely left to the civil servants.

Increasingly, LDP legislators particularly certain *zoku-giin*, have gained in influence. Decision making now is a matter of cooperation and interdependence between the LDP and the bureaucracy.[39] Over time, the party's legislators have gained in expertise and become more involved in policy making and have simultaneously developed closer ties to interest groups. A survey by Muramatsu and Krauss, for instance, reveals that in the budget process officials have contacts with the LDP even at an early stage, and their need for LDP cooperation rises as the process continues, particularly with new programs.[40] Many now see *zoku-giin* as rivaling and often exceeding the influence of civil servants, as is reflected in the popular phrase, "tōkō seitei" (party dominant and bureaucracy subordinate). Indeed, the literature on the LDP in recent years has emphasized the role of *zoku-giin* so much that many sometimes feel the need to remind readers that the bureaucracy is still quite influential.[41]

When LDP politicians are elected to the Kokkai, they are assigned to a legislative committee and its corresponding PARC division(s) and generally join two other PARC divisions, which provide them with opportunities to learn about these policy areas.[42] Gradually, after being reelected a number of times and having served in some of the positions in the National Assembly (e.g., as committee chairman), the government (e.g., as the ministry's parliamentary vice minister), or the party's PARC (e.g., as division chairman), they become specialists in one or two of these areas.[43] As a result of self-selection and socialization, these legislators tend to be sympathetic to ministry views. Some were officials of the corresponding ministry before entering politics; most of the others have extensive interactions with bureaucrats while serving in PARC divisions or as parliamentary vice minister. Such politicians sometimes become better acquainted with a specific policy area than government officials because they are at it for so long, whereas civil servants are generally rotated to different bureaus within their ministry (although bureaucrats are still important because they still tend to be the main source of information and are the actual drafters of proposals). And a legislator who becomes particularly influential in a particular area becomes known as a member of that area's *zoku*.

PARC, then, is the place where the various interest groups and public officials converge to make demands on the LDP. Murakawa Ichirō, a staff member of the PARC, writes that, in particular, it is in the divisions of the council that the party's policy is basically formed.[44] The formal meetings of the divisions are used to gather information or make formal decisions, while important items are handled informally among the *zoku* members, including the division chief.[45]

The various *zoku* in the LDP support interests of all kinds. As the two case studies show, there are well-established *zoku* in education, taxes, and posts and telecommunications (which handled the *maruyū* issue). In the past, the "big three" *zoku* were in construction, agriculture, and commerce, all of which provided their members with political funds or votes, or both. More recently, *zoku* have developed around more specialized interests, such as air transportation, tobacco, and telecommunications.[46] Thus the LDP is providing forums for interest groups to talk to its legislators, helping to make it a catchall party. *Zoku* have used their ties to interest groups to obtain political funds and votes, and in return they support the demands of those interest groups.

In addition to their ties to the bureaucracy and to interest groups, *zoku* also derive much of their strength as "masters" who manage and coordinate the actions of ad hoc groups of politicians formed to protect an important constituency interest.[47] In a number of cases, *zoku* "masters" have been able to prevent enactment of change by mobilizing political opposition within the party. Kanemaru Shin, for example, was known as the boss of the postal *zoku*, who played a major role in organizing opposition within the LDP that prevented the implementation of the "green card" system.[48]

The Alliance Between Bureaucrats and Politicians

The sectionalism of the bureaucracy, then, is reinforced by cleavages within the LDP along interest lines into *zoku*. The alliances between divisions of PARC and ministries cut across party and bureaucratic lines to create strong subgovernments. "Policy-making in Japan tends to break down into segmented policy domains, each with its own configuration of political alignments. The welter of interest-group demands are funnelled through the extant structure of political-bureaucratic institutions, where they are sorted into separate and self-contained policy arenas."[49] In other words, fairly consistent and rather stable coalitions of interest groups, ministries, and LDP legislators organize themselves around common issues or policy areas. "Subgovernments constitute a set of interest-based cleavages that divide the entire decision-making system. . . . The relationships *between* subgovernments are the key to understanding most issues that are broader than the jurisdiction of a single ministry."[50]

What makes the subgovernments in many areas of policy so strong is the exceptionally stable relationships between LDP politicians and bureaucrats.[51] Ministries generally have clearly defined areas of jurisdiction, and there is relatively little overlap between them.[52] Also, civil servants tend to stay in their ministry for their entire career, and there is only one political appointment of consequence. On the party side, its long rule has meant that the legislators involved also tend to be long-term actors in specific areas of policy. Thus close ties often develop between bureaucrats and LDP politicians.

The alliances, however, do not mean that there is complete agreement among all the members of the subgovernment. A number of disagreements, for example, often arise within the education subgovernment, particularly between LDP legislators who tend to push issues that will reverse the reforms of the Occupaton (revising the Fundamental Law of Education and using the national flag and anthem in school functions), while education officials tend to be more supportive of the postwar education system. There can also be disagreements because politicians tend to emphasize the demands of their constituents, while bureaucrats tend to emphasize more "rational" policies. Many members of the National Assembly, for instance, have emphasized subsidies to and protection of rice farmers, whereas agricultural officials want to reduce subsidies and narrow the gap between the producers' and consumers' price of rice.[53] According to Curtis, the *zoku* play an autonomous role vis-à-vis the bureaucrats and interest groups, "trying to find areas of compromise between what interest groups want and what the government is prepared to give."[54]

Nevertheless, the members of the subgovernment will often band together—despite their internal disagreements—to resist encroachment from outsiders. An extreme case may be found in the education arena. The Education Ministry and the Japan Teachers' Union have vehemently battled over education issues throughout the postwar period. However, both sides were opposed to Nakasone's efforts to have the issue of educational reform handled by an ad hoc council rather than the Education Ministry's advisory body, the CEC.

A consequence of strong subgovernments is that conflicts tend not to be between the bureaucracy and the party, but rather between subgovernments. "The most common conflict is among supporters of different policy areas. Cross-ministerial battles in the bureaucracy will be paralleled by cross-divisional battles inside the LDP; these struggles are essentially cross-subgovernment conflicts."[55] And compared to the situation in other nations, the Japanese decision-making system "is dominated by subgovernmental conflict: it is more nearly the only game in town."[56]

The Prime Minister and Subgovernments

Subgovernments in Japan, then, constrain the prime minister's influence in the policy process in two major ways. First, they often dominate areas of policy that fall within a single jurisdiction, determining most of the content of change. Hence the prime minister finds it difficult to intervene. Nakasone,for example, had his own ideas of what to do with education but could not overcome resistance from the education subgovernment.

Second, subgovernments structure the conflict over issues that are broader than the jurisdiction of a single ministry or subgovernment.[57] From the prime minister's perspective, it is these disputes that he must usually deal with. Eliminating the *maruyū* tax-free savings system, for instance, required extensive negotiations between the postal and tax subgovernments. The conflicts among subgovernments, then, largely define the premier's options in terms of change. Because these differences are difficult to resolve, the tendency is to maintain the status quo. Most of the cases cited in the literature as evidence of the strength of *zoku*, for instance, concern efforts to prevent change rather than to bring it about.[58] Campbell points out that such conflicts are generally not resolved; rather, they are "ignored, papered over, postponed in hopes that will go away, or arbitrarily settled by imposing some mechanical and therefore acceptable decision-making rule."[59]

The Prime Minister's Resources

The prime minister is not without resources in dealing with particular subgovernments. One is the power of patronage. Although he is rather severely limited, he can still make an impact by appointing powerful politicians as cabinet ministers or to other important positions. According to Yung Park, some cabinet ministers are influential because either they are policy experts as a result of their experience in the party's policy committees or they are powerful LDP politicians.[60] The prime minister can, for example, influence *zoku-giin* to his advantage. Nakasone, in pushing for educational reform and the establishment of the National Council on Educational Reform, was able to overcome resistance from the education *zoku* by using his ties to members of his faction who were also members of the *zoku*, and by appointing an ambitious rising politician, Mori Yoshirō, as education minister. Mori was a relatively young but important member of the LDP education *zoku* who belonged to the then Fukuda faction. This was his first appointment to a cabinet post, and hoping to further his career by identifying himself with a potentially big issue, he agreed to go along with Nakasone's desire to establish the ad hoc council. In the tax reform case, Nakasone appointed Yamanaka Sadanori, a member of his faction who would be an aggressive promoter of tax reform, to the chairmanship of the LDP Tax Council.

Nevertheless, the resources that the prime minister can use as leverage against the subgovernments are quite limited. Nakasone's use of patronage was limited to insiders. Both Mori and Yamanaka were central members of the education and tax *zoku*, respectively. And, though they agreed to support Nakasone in pushing for reform in a general sense, both tended to side with the other members of their subgovernments rather than with the prime minister in substantive matters of policy.

In addition, even though cross-subgovernmental conflicts are a restricting factor, the prime minister can sometimes exploit cleavages between subgovernments. Subgovernments are mainly effective within their own spheres, which may be quite small. Many issues, however, may involve more than one interest and therefore more than one subgovernment. Here the prime minister can either use the divisions that already exist to make his influence felt, or he can mobilize support from other

interests to counteract a subgovernment. Hugh Heclo, writing about the
U.S. system, suggests that chief executives can counteract sabotage by
"strengthening their outside contacts, extending their lines of information and competitive analysis, finding new points of counter-tension."[61]
The Japanese prime minister may also be able to pull an issue out of the
hands of a subgovernment, give it publicity, and mobilize other groups to
participate. Muramatsu, in his analysis of Nakasone's effort at administrative reform, notes that the prime minister was able to put together a
"center structure" of the Finance Ministry, LDP leaders, and business
groups to counteract the demands of the "bureaucracy, the LDP, and
opposition parties."[62]

The prime minister's ability to use outsiders to push his ideas,
however, is likewise limited, as was shown in Nakasone's efforts at both
educational and tax reforms. In both cases, he appointed members of his
informal network of advisers to important committees (i.e., the National
Council on Educational Reform and the Government Tax Council), but
their impact in the end was small. The actors in the subgovernment are
full-time permanent players, while the people the prime minister brings
in are not. The big business groups, for instance, were initially very
interested in education issues, and Nakasone hoped that they would
support him as they had in administrative reform. But their interest in
education waned over time, and in the end they provided little support.
And, as will be described in the next chapter, the prime minister's
institutional resources (e.g., his staff, the Cabinet Secretariat) do not
give him much help.

Variance Among Subgovernments

Subgovernments, however, do not dominate all policy making. As
Inoguchi and Iwai note, the role of *zoku-giin* in policy making varies
considerably. Their influence varies with the cohesiveness of the subgovernment and the strength of their support, and the prime minister's
ability to make an impact will likely vary accordingly. Subgovernments
that are cohesive and have widespread support are likely to be more
resistant to prime ministerial intervention.

Some subgovernments are very cohesive, their members banding
together to protect the interests of an industry or ministry. The *zoku*

members serve as watchdogs looking out for the interests of the subgovernment.[63] Nakasone's difficulty with educational reform, for instance, was in large part due to the cohesiveness of the education subgovernment. Some subgovernments, however, are less cohesive. For example, the commerce *zoku*, which is one of the largest and usually considered to be one of the more influential groups in the LDP, was quite divided over the VAT proposed by Nakasone. MITI, big business groups, and certain industries such as automobile manufacturers were supportive, but the retailers and wholesalers were adamantly opposed. The result of this split was that MITI and the commerce *zoku* played little role in the decision to promote the tax.[64] Another example is medical care, where the *zoku* has long sided with the Japan Medical Association in its often bitter battles with the Health and Welfare Ministry.[65]

Subgovernments also vary in their degree of political support. Okimoto argues that within the LDP's "grand coalition" there are certain interests that give critical support to the party.[66] In particular, the LDP provides political goods and services to certain groups in exchange for electoral and financial support. These are clientelistic linkages with interest groups such as farmers, fishermen, small- and medium-scale businessmen, heads of local postal services, and doctors, as well as "reciprocal patronage" with industries such as construction, housing, real estate, tobacco, and telecommunications. Any effort to hurt these interests is likely to meet fierce resistance in the party. An obvious example is subsidies to rice farmers, seen by many LDP members of the National Assembly as too important a constituency to cross. The prime minister's influence is more constrained with regard to interests that LDP legislators see as critical to their reelection.

Other areas do not much involve subgovernments. One example is diplomacy. Twenty years ago, Aaron Wildavsky wrote that the "United States has one president, but it has two presidencies; one presidency is for domestic affairs and the other one is concerned with foreign and defense policy."[67] Wildavsky's thesis was that presidents have had much greater success in controlling the nation's defense and foreign policies than in dominating its domestic policies. Are there two prime ministerships in Japan?

My impression is that Wildavsky's thesis applies, with some important qualifications, to the Japanese prime minister. There is no question that premiers have had their main influence in foreign policy, particularly with issues of diplomacy. Hatoyama reestablished relations with the Soviet Union, Satō with Korea, and Tanaka with China. Other successes included Kishi's negotiation for a revision of the United States–Japan Security Treaty, Satō's for the reversion of Okinawa, and Fukuda's with China for the Peace and Friendship Treaty. Indeed, most of the prominent accomplishments of postwar prime ministers have been in foreign policy.

It is not hard to see why the prime minister would have the easiest time with these sorts of foreign policy issues. First, there is a tendency to defer to the prime minister, as head of government, in diplomatic issues at least initially in order to present a united front. The three main party rivals to Nakasone, for instance, made public vows not to create problems for him at least until after the Tokyo Summit held in 1986. Also, many matters of foreign policy do not involve legislation.

Moreover, diplomatic questions are rarely intertwined with domestic interests of members of the National Assembly to the extent of, say, agricultural ones. The reestablishment of relations with the Soviet Union and South Korea may have been controversial, but few LDP politicians saw their reelection endangered. In addition, the relative political freedom means that the prime minister is able to limit participation in the negotiations to those who either are loyal to him or view the issue in the same way. Thus, as I mentioned before, Tanaka was able to use several members of the opposition to help set the stage for the normalization of ties with China.[68] And Hatoyama was able to circumvent the Foreign Ministry, which opposed the reestablishment of diplomatic ties with the Soviet Union, and put the negotiations in the hands of trusted lieutenants and allies in the LDP.[69] Diplomatic issues such as reestablishing relations also involve few economic restrictions and are often rather simple conceptually.

The prime minister, of course, does not have such an easy time with all areas of foreign policy. Unlike the U.S. president, who is usually given quite a bit of leeway in security matters as commander-in-chief of the military, the prime minister is severely limited in what he can do to shape security policy. Nakasone's attempts to strengthen Japanese defense capabilities, for instance, were only modestly successful. Constraints work in the other direction, too. Suzuki, a dovish prime minister, wanted to slow down the rate of increase in the defense budget but was forced to reverse himself because of pressure from the United States (which might be seen as a member of the defense subgovernment) and the more hawkish members of the LDP. As a result, despite their sharply contrasting attitudes, the defense budget continued to grow at a relatively constant rate under these two prime ministers.

The premier also has difficulty with foreign policy issues that directly affect the economic interests of important constituents of the LDP. Satō, for example, successfully negotiated the reversion of Okinawa but ran into severe trouble on textile exports to the United States.[70] Only after changing the MITI minister twice and severely straining relations was he able to resolve the problem. It also seems that domestic and international issues have become much more intertwined. As T. J. Pempel argues, there is far more division in Japan today over foreign, economic, and defense policy than during the high-growth period.[71]

Conclusion

One of the main characteristics of the Japanese system is the strength of subgovernments. Bert Rockman notes that "subgovernments are a widespread phenomenon," and what differs across political systems is not whether subgovernments exist but "how and in what form, if at all, [they] are assimilated (or forced) into broader national decision-making structures."[72] In European countries, Rockman argues, there are central organs (e.g., the cabinet, corporatist bodies) that can handle and aggregate the demands of the subgovernments, which consequently do not dominate decision making.[73]

From the Japanese prime minister's point of view, however, subgovernments seem to be particularly strong. They constrain his influence in the policy process in a number of ways. First, they are a major contributor to the inertia of the system. On issues involving a single subgovernment, the alliance between the ministries, the party's PARC divisions, and clientele groups are capable of resisting most attempts by outsiders to intervene in their policy domain. On broader questions that span subgovernments, the prime minister must negotiate the conflicts that arises between subgovernments. These disputes, especially those that concern strong interests of the rank and file, are difficult to resolve, and the tendency is to maintain the status quo for quite long periods.

In addition, subgovernments also limit the prime minister's policy options. The ministries possess most of the information and expertise; hence, in consultation with and with the support of their allies in the LDP, they largely determine the content of change. If the prime minister wants to bring about some sort of change, then, he generally has to develop cooperation with the subgovernment. He has little chance of going against them.

8

The Prime Minister's Staff

L*eaders of democratic countries* inevitably face strong constraints on their ability to influence policy, but they are usually not without significant resources of their own. The rise in the prominence of presidents and prime ministers in the government and politics of many countries is the result, at least in part, of the increased level of staff supporting them. In the United States, the rise of presidential government has led to and been stimulated by the growth of the modern White House staff and other organs of the Executive Office.[1] In Great Britain, a similar, if smaller, growth in staff now assists the British prime minister. Margaret Thatcher made use of a personal policy unit in the Cabinet Office, as well as having on hand personal advisers on economics, foreign affairs, and defense to give her independent advice. In Canada the staff of the Prime Minister's Office (PMO) has become an increasingly important power center.[2] The Japanese prime minister's staff has also become more prominent. Nakasone worked on developing a personal staff by making use of private advisory committees and government commissions in pushing his policy goals, and he reorganized the Cabinet Secretariat and other administrative organizations.[3]

A head of government's staff can be helpful in a number of ways. Journalists in Japan often describe the prime minister's support system as extensions of his body: his arms, legs, eyes, ears, and even brain. This is in fact a rather useful way to describe it. It can act as his "arms" by supplying services such as clerical work; as his "legs" in carrying messages between him and others; as his "ears" and "eyes" by providing information (e.g., monitoring activities in the bureaucracy); as his "brain" through policy expertise and advice; and as "muscle" in helping in the control of governmental affairs.

One of the main products of the administrative reform effort of the 1980s was a revamped staff for both the prime minister and the cabinet, a reform that was intended to give them more effective coordination and control of policy making in domestic and international affairs. The prime minister's staff is made up of two main parts: the "inner staff," which serves him in the Kantei (the prime minister's official residence); and the Cabinet Secretariat, which serves the cabinet as well as the prime minister. In addition, two other types of support have been prominent in recent years: the Management and Coordination Agency, which was established in 1984 to help in the general coordination of government administration; and advisory committees and commissions. Despite the changes, however, the Japanese prime minister's support system is still much weaker both in terms of numbers and in its capabilities than those of the heads of government of other countries.

The Inner Staff

One thing that was not directly affected by the reforms, at least immediately, is the prime minister's so-called inner staff. Largely because of the lack of space in the Kantei, no more members can be added to the prime minister's most immediate staff, although this will likely change if the new Kantei is built as planned, sometime in the next ten years. The inner staff is made up of eight people: five private secretaries, the chief cabinet secretary, and the two deputy cabinet secretaries. According to Morita Hajime, Ōhira Masayoshi's chief private secretary, the decisions that Ōhira made were based on the information and advice of these eight.[4]

Chief secretary
Administrative secretary for finance
Administrative secretary for foreign affairs
Administrative secretary for international trade and industry
Administrative secretary for national police

Chief cabinet secretary
Parliamentary deputy chief cabinet secretary
Administrative deputy chief cabinet secretary

The Private Secretaries

Packed together in the room adjoining the prime minister's office are his five private secretaries: one political, more generally referred to as the chief secretary (*shusseki hishokan*), and four administrative, who are on secondment from career positions in government ministries.[5] They are often described as his "hands and feet." The specific duties of the political secretary and the administrative secretaries differ somewhat, but essentially they carry messages, handle much of the prime minister's clerical work, give advice, and brief him on various matters.[6] Miki Takeo often told his secretaries, "The prime minister moves Japan by playing catch with the secretaries."[7]

The chief secretary is the prime minister's most trusted aide and closest confidant. Of the eight members of the inner staff, it is the chief secretary whom the prime minister talks with most.[8] He is the last person, except perhaps members of his household, to whom the prime minister talks at night. When many party leaders were trying to oust him from the LDP presidency, Miki listened to briefs about factional movements from his chief secretary while he readied himself for bed.[9]

The chief secretary acts behind the scenes, sometimes handling the political dirty work, such as the gathering and distribution of political funds. He often acts in the prime minister's stead in party and factional matters, such as attending banquets when the premier is too busy. He is also expected to gather information about goings-on in the political world, in the way that Nakamura Keiichirō did for Miki by using his connections with his former colleagues at the *Yomiuri Shimbun*.[10] According-ing to a former secretary, "one-third of our job is to associate with reporters. Exchanging information is important. It also helps to be on good terms with them, for they may prove useful at some point. In any case, almost every night, we have to go out with reporters to a club or a restaurant. It's quite common to be out until two or three in the morning."[11] These sorts of duty necessarily require the chief secretary to spend much of his time away from the Kantei.

The chief secretary is generally the prime minister's longtime parliamentary secretary. Kamiwada Yoshihiko was Nakasone's secretary for over thirty years. The importance of trust in the relationship is reflected in the fact that, very often, the chief secretary will also be the prime minister's son or son-in-law. Fukuda Takeo's secretary was his first son, Yasuo. Sons-in-law include Abe Shintarō (son-in-law of Kishi Nobusuke), Takahashi Wataru (Miki), and Morita (Ōhira). Prime ministers have also often picked journalists, such as Nakamura under Miki, as their chief secretaries for their ability to get information on political machinations and other activities in the political world, as well as to offer political advice.[12]

There are currently four administrative secretaries, one each from the Foreign, Finance, and International Trade and Industry ministries, and the NPA.[13] They are generally in their mid-forties and on the elite course within their own organizations. When they return, they can expect promotion to the rank of bureau chief or councillor (*shingikan*) and eventually become a candidate for the top career post of administrative vice minister. They are usually assigned by the ministry, though sometimes the prime minister will have a particular person in mind, such as when Fukuda ignored the Foreign Ministry's recommendation and instead pulled in Owada Wataru, who had served him as administrative secretary while he was foreign minister.[14]

But as an official from the Foreign Ministry noted, the ministries resist sending someone who is too close to the prime minister (e.g., a relative), feeling that such personal ties would affect performance.[15] The implication seems to be that the official would not have as much loyalty to the home ministry.[16] Thus the loyalty of the administrative secretaries to the prime minister is in some doubt, as was revealed in the journalist Tahara Sōichirō's interviews with former members of the Cabinet Secretariat. One interviewee said, "A secretary is the operations man sent by the ministry to be at the side of the nation's most powerful man. In that sense, he is very dangerous."[17] Another admitted that secretaries often receive directives from their home ministries that are to be kept secret from the prime minister or the chief cabinet secretary.[18]

The administrative secretaries, according to one former secretary, "do not touch the political jobs."[19] Rather, they serve as administrative aides and sometimes as policy advisers. One of them accompanies the prime minister throughout the day—a job known as *kaban-mochi* [briefcase holder], which is rotated daily among the four. The *kaban-mochi* goes to meet the prime minister at his private residence about an hour before he leaves for the office.

> We walk with the prime minister from morning to night as his *kaban-mochi*. It was easy with Nakasone since he lived at the *Kōtei* [the prime minister's official residence], but when a prime minister resides at home, we would arrive there at about 6:30 in the morning, about the time he gets out of bed. Moreover, by that time, we would have had to look through all the newspapers and have in our heads the important articles so that we could report the important points to him.[20]

Besides offering briefings on the latest news, the *kaban-mochi* also goes over the day's schedule and arranges any changes that may need to be made. He stays with the prime minister throughout the day and carries all of the necessary documents, memos, materials, and so on that are needed for the prime minister to carry out his work.[21] At the end of the day, he accompanies the premier back to his private residence, where the chief secretary takes over. Administrative secretaries will also accompany him on weekends and holidays when he goes on retreat so that he will be ready to handle any emergency that may arise.

The administrative secretaries are responsible for keeping the prime minister informed about what is being covered in the media. Besides reading the morning newspapers, they watch the news on television and talk with the reporters assigned to the prime minister's beat. In particular, the secretaries are looking to find out the sorts of issue the media are interested in and the sorts of thing they want to know, as well as reporters' critical opinions of the administration. Information that the secretaries feel is important is then passed on to the prime minister in briefs and used to prepare him for any of the questions that may come from reporters. They try to keep him as informed as possible without taking up much of his time: "So that we can have the prime minister see only the necessary items when he has a free moment, we must do things such as wait for him in an anteroom during the evening banquets or parties and take turns recording television broadcasts."[22]

One of the main duties of the administrative secretaries is to serve as the prime minister's liaison with the ministries. Each administrative secretary acts as the conduit for his home ministry, as well as others, summarizing information received. The secretary from the Foreign Ministry receives top-secret cables from the ministry every day, which he then summarizes. On the day that President Reagan was shot, it was this secretary who telephoned the prime minister early in the morning. Information about domestic incidents is similarly channeled through the secretary from the NPA.

The administrative secretaries also transmit the prime minister's directives and requests to the ministries. In the summer of 1987, when Nakasone directed the Finance Ministry to drop its proposal for a cut in corporate taxes (and an "outline" for an indirect tax), he did so through his secretary.[23] However, the prime minister will also telephone ministry officials directly. Nakasone talked at least once a week with the administrative vice minister for foreign affairs.[24] In addition, the secretaries give policy advice and sometimes ideas for policies based on their experience and the information they gather. Suzuki Zenkō wanted his secretaries to gather and present to him ideas from the bureaucracy. And Tanaka Kakuei brought with him his administrative secretary from the MITI to help him with his plan to restructure the Japanese archipelago.

One of the constant themes that comes up in interviews with the secretaries is the physical demands of the job.

> It is quite an honor to be named a secretary. And because it speeds up advancement in the ministry, everyone is happy to be appointed. But when one actually does the work, the load is just overwhelming. This is no ordinary job. . . . The amount of work is unimaginable. All the care needed to avoid making mistakes itself is enough to make one's head hurt. During the time one is a secretary, there is absolutely no time for "privacy." One must banish any thoughts about home life; otherwise, one cannot handle the job.[25]

An example is the secretaries' task of preparing the prime minister's answers to the official questioning session in the National Assembly.

> First, the various ministries and agencies hand in drafts of hypothetical questions with the appropriate replies. The Cabinet Councillors' Office and the Cabinet Legislative Bureau then carefully check the drafts. The papers then come to us. We check them again and refine the style of the answers to fit the prime minister's. The prime minister then sees them. Before a regular session of the legislature, the stack of papers is more than one full meter in height.[26]

The work is physically demanding because, as Morita notes, the secretaries get little support themselves.

> I wish the personal secretaries also had a staff. The drafts of the questions and answers come at night and we then start to correct them. That's okay. But even the printing of the final clean copies is done by the personal secretaries. The secretaries in the ministries [who do similar work for the minister] have a number of people under them. While a cabinet minister is supported by the entire ministry's staff, the prime minister has but the Cabinet Secretariat and the private secretaries. The difference is like that between the president of a major corporation and the president of a small enterprise.[27]

Indeed, this comment suggests one of the big differences between the Japanese prime minister's personal staff and those of other chief executives. The Japanese prime minister's five private secretaries are similar to the British prime minister's both in number and in function. But the Japanese secretaries have virtually no supporting staff, while No. 10 Downing Street has a total staff of about 70.[28]

The Chief Cabinet Secretary

The most important person on the inner staff, much higher in status than those mentioned above, is the chief cabinet secretary. The post is a cabinet-level one and is generally given to a trusted, fairly senior member of the prime minister's faction.[29] The chief cabinet secretary works more closely with the prime minister than any other politician and is often referred to as the prime minister's "political wife" or "chief clerk." His office is in the Kantei, very close to the prime minister's.[30]

The chief cabinet secretary has one of the most demanding jobs in government. He presides over the affairs of the Cabinet Secretariat (Cabinet Law, Article 13-3). And, while the prime minister presides over cabinet meetings, it is the chief cabinet secretary who conducts them; he also serves as liaison between the party and the cabinet and ensures that the party has a voice in the cabinet. He is also the cabinet's spokesman. Most of the formal comments about the cabinet and the prime minister that go to the press come from the chief cabinet secretary. He announces the names of members after a new cabinet has been formed, and after each cabinet meeting—regularly scheduled twice a week on Tuesdays and Fridays—he holds a press conference to report on it. In addition, the secretary gives two or three regular press conferences every day, and at any other time when it is deemed necessary, such as to indicate a government reaction to an international incident.[31] The chief cabinet secretary is like the U.S. president's White House chief of staff, press secretary, and top political adviser all in one.

Three types of politicians are appointed to the position of chief cabinet secretary: (1) policy experts, (2) influential LDP legislators, and (3) trusted friends.[32] Policy experts include Ōhira in the Ikeda cabinet and Kimura Toshio under Satō. A former Finance Ministry official, Ōhira played an important part in promoting Ikeda's income-doubling plan, and Kimura in Satō's efforts to return Okinawa to Japanese sovereignty. Influential LDP members of the Kokkai are put into the post to help the prime minister keep control over the party. Shiina Etsusaburō helped Kishi keep the party from getting out of hand during the controversy surrounding the police bill and the revision of the United States–Japan Security Treaty. Hori Shigeru helped stabilize the Satō administration. Trusted friends include Nikaidō Susumu, Tanaka's chief cabinet secretary (who boasted that his hobby was Tanaka); Miki's longtime friend Ide Ichitarō; and one of Nakasone's protégés, Fujinami Takao.

The post is also now seen as an important stepping-stone to the LDP presidency. Prime ministers who have also held the position include Satō (under Yoshida Shigeru), Ōhira and Suzuki (both under Ikeda), Takeshita Noboru (under Satō and Tanaka), and Miyazawa Kiichi (under Suzuki).[33] Some of the next generation of leaders have also served in the post, including Fujinami (under Nakasone) and Obuchi Keizō (under Takeshita).

Nakasone's selection of Gotōda Masaharu for three out of the administration's five years was virtually unprecedented in that he was not a member of the prime minister's faction.[34] Nakasone picked him for a number of reasons. First, the Nakasone faction did not have anyone who had much experience in handling the bureaucracy. In particular, Nakasone wanted someone capable of keeping it in line so that he could pursue administrative reform.[35] Gotōda, often known as "the Razor" (*Kamisori*), was a former director of the NPA and served under Tanaka as an administrative deputy chief cabinet secretary. Thus he had ample experience on the bureaucratic side. He was reportedly also able to keep politicians in line. Through the connections he built up while in the NPA, he is said to have had a better intelligence network than anyone. It was his ability to gather information about politicians that made him powerful. Most politicians, from both the ruling and opposition parties, break campaign laws in raising political funds and have reason to be afraid.

One other unofficial role is to handle the Cabinet Secretariat's coordination fund (*naikaku kanbō chōseihi*), also known as the prime minister's secret fund, which has a yearly budget of about 1.5 billion yen.[36] The chief cabinet secretary distributes the funds according to the prime minister's instructions.[37] The money is used for a variety of purposes, such as to deal with members of the opposition parties and political journalists.[38] One former cabinet member comments on the giving of money to journalists: "I don't know how effective this sort of use of money is. It's also very difficult to say how much of a role it plays in running the country. But unless the money is paid, they will not speak well of the chief cabinet secretary or the prime minister, and they may exaggerate rumors. We have had instances when we have been the targets of such attacks. Thus, it is true that we pay."[39]

In addition, the money is given as bon voyage presents for members of the National Assembly taking trips overseas and buys gifts for foreign dignitaries either when they visit Japan or when the prime minister goes abroad.[40] One prime minister is said to have used money from the fund for factional campaign funds and to buy presents for cabinet ministers, the speaker of the lower house, and the president of the upper house.

The chief cabinet secretary is assisted by four private secretaries.[41] One is his political secretary, and the others are on loan from the NPA, the Finance Ministry, and the Foreign Ministry. The secretary from the NPA is considered the head administrative secretary and also serves simultaneously as a cabinet research officer in the Cabinet Information Research Office.

The Parliamentary Deputy Chief Cabinet Secretary

Under the chief cabinet secretary are two deputies: the parliamentary deputy chief cabinet secretary and the administrative deputy chief cabinet secretary. The parliamentary post is usually given to a promising junior or middle-level LDP member of the Kokkai from the prime minister's faction to give him some experience in dealing with cabinet matters. Typically it is filled by a three- or four-term member in his forties who has not yet served in a cabinet position. Usually the parliamentary deputy is replaced during each cabinet shuffle, or about every year or so. Many of the younger generation of party leaders have held the position, including Kaifu Toshiki (Kōmoto faction), Mori Yoshirō (Abe), Katō Kōichi (Miyazawa), and Fujinami (Nakasone). Occasionally, the prime minister may ask a fairly senior member of his faction, one who has been a cabinet member before, to take the post. Satō asked Kimura to take the lesser position of deputy secretary just after serving as the chief cabinet secretary so that he would be nearby during the negotiations with the United States for the return of Okinawa. Fujinami and Ozawa Ichirō are other examples.

The Administrative Deputy Chief Cabinet Secretary

The administrative deputy is responsible for handling the administrative affairs of the cabinet and attends the cabinet meetings, where he explains items before the cabinet at the direction of the chief cabinet secretary. Because he needs to be experienced in bureaucratic affairs, the administrative deputy is a top-ranking civil servant. In fact, he is often referred to as the head bureaucrat because he chairs the administrative vice ministers' conference.[42] As such, he is responsible for coordinating matters among the ministries and agencies before they go to the cabinet. According to Gotōda: "The administrative deputy chief cabinet secretary controls the administrative affairs of the cabinet; thus he is selected from the bureaucracy. And since he must handle the administrative vice ministers, he must be a person higher than they are."[43]

The administrative deputy also works to coordinate policy through the Cabinet Secretariat. Kusuda Minoru, Satō's chief secretary, notes:

Prime Minister Tanaka appointed Gotōda [as deputy secretary], who dealt forcefully in rapid succession with a number of deadlocked problems, such as the land tax system. With Gotōda's pull and large network of acquaintances in the bureaucracy, Tanaka was able to break up deadlocks in the bureaucracy. Gotōda had at his beck and call the people in the Cabinet Councillors' Office whose loyalties until then were to their home ministries.[44]

The prime minister has the power to appoint the administrative deputy, who is generally a former administrative vice minister from either the Health and Welfare Ministry, the Labor Ministry, or a former director of the NPA.[45] Unlike the parliamentary deputy and all other cabinet ministers and vice ministers, the administrative deputy usually remains in the post as long as the prime minister who made the appointment, in order to provide the cabinet with some continuity.

Much has been made of the fact that the administrative deputy comes from a ministry or agency that was part of the powerful prewar Home Ministry.[46] A former administrative deputy, Fujimori Shōichi, claims that the reason is that they are relatively "neutral": "What I mean by 'neutral' is not doing something for one's own ministry. It means being able to make decisions from a broad perspective."[47] According to Ōkina Hisajirō, another former administrative deputy:

Because the cabinet is sort of the administrative bureau of all the ministries and agencies, it's best to have someone from an internal affairs related ministry or agency who can coordinate the workings of the whole system. The Foreign, Finance, and International Trade and Industry ministries each have their own independent work, so there would be a problem with them. Moreover, the ministries and agencies of the old Home Ministry are related. A person from one of these ministries or agencies would be better able to coordinate matters.[48]

Ōkina believes that the reorganization of the Cabinet Secretariat will increase the importance of the administrative deputy in trying to integrate cabinet policies.[49] He points out that because the former Cabinet Councillors' Office has split into two—one for internal and one for external affairs—a number of items could be handled by either. In addition, he believes that the number of matters requiring coordination by the offices will increase, and that some of these will require quick action. Hence Ōkina believes that these changes will make the responsibilities of the administrative deputy, who will be handling them, increasingly important. Even if this comes about, however, there is little prospect of the administrative deputy becoming as powerful as the British cabinet secretary.

The Cabinet Secretariat

In the attempt to strengthen the government's ability to exercise central coordination, much of the focus was on the Cabinet Secretariat. In 1986 much of it was reorganized: some of its offices were expanded and their responsibilities increased. The secretariat now has a total staff of 176 in six offices:[50]

> Cabinet Advisers' Office
> Cabinet Councillors' Office on Internal Affairs
> Cabinet Councillors' Office on External Affairs
> Cabinet Security Affairs Office
> Cabinet Information Research Office
> Cabinet Office of the Director General of Public Relations

It should be pointed out that the prime minister is also supported by the PMO, which is formally a separate institution from the Cabinet Secretariat. The PMO is supposed to serve the prime minister directly, whereas the Cabinet Secretariat is supposed to serve the cabinet.[51] In reality, the two overlap almost completely.[52] Not only are the members and staff of the Cabinet Secretariat located in the PMO building (which is across the street from the Kantei), but the two institutions also share most of their personnel. In particular, all of the top officials in the PMO secretariat serve concurrently in the Cabinet Secretariat. This section, therefore, focuses primarily on the Cabinet Secretariat.

The Cabinet Advisers' Office[53]

One office that was not directly affected by the 1986 reorganization was the Cabinet Advisers' Office (naikaku sanjikan shitsu), which handles the staff work for the cabinet meetings. Under the direction of the chief cabinet secretary and the two deputy secretaries, the office handles the administrative matters for cabinet meetings, such as the arrangement of the agenda, coordination of important matters necessary for cabinet decisions, and the collection of information and materials.

In addition, the office is in charge of putting together the policy speeches that the prime minister gives to the National Assembly, and it acts as the liaison between the cabinet and the Imperial Household. The emperor, with the advice and approval of the cabinet, performs certain acts in matters of state, as defined by the Constitution (Article 7), such as promulgating new laws, cabinet orders, and treaties; convening legislative sessions; dissolving the lower house of the legislature; and proclaiming general elections of members of the National Assembly. The office receives requests for these from the cabinet and transmits them to the Imperial Household Agency, then receives, on behalf of the chief cabinet secretary, the documents with the imperial seal. The exact timing of lower house elections was often in the past a closely held secret. When reporters felt that an election might be called, they would closely follow the movements of the head of the office to see when he would depart for the Imperial Household.

The office is staffed by four cabinet advisers (*naikaku sanjikan*).[54] The chief *naikaku sanjikan* is the only person in the Cabinet Secretariat, other than the chief cabinet secretary and his deputies, who works in the Kantei, and he is sometimes regarded as a ninth member of the inner staff.[55] In fact, he has a residence on the grounds of the Kantei, and unlike the prime minister and the chief cabinet secretary, who have similar residences but do not generally use them, he is expected to be there to handle any unexpected matters that may come up at the Kantei even when the prime minister and chief cabinet secretary are away from Tokyo.[56] He is generally a former administrative vice minister of the Health and Welfare Ministry, and four of the ten chief *naikaku sanjikan* in the postwar period previously served as administrative deputy chief cabinet secretaries. Hence the position is considered to be a very high one for bureaucrats.

The Cabinet Councillors' Offices on Internal Affairs and External Affairs

One of the main goals of the 1986 reorganization was to strengthen the general coordinating function of the Cabinet Secretariat. The feeling was that the ministries were turning to their allies in the LDP for help rather than trying to work out problems between themselves, and that thus conflicts were being resolved politically. The reorganization was meant to provide the Cabinet Secretariat with better machinery to work out problems more rationally.[57] Not incidentally, it would also give the prime minister more leverage over policy should he choose to use it.

One of the main targets of reform in the Cabinet Secretariat was the Cabinet Councillors' Office, which was supposed to coordinate policy among the ministries. The reorganization, based on the recommendations made in July 1985 by the Administrative Reform Promotion Council (*Gyōkakushin*), changed the former Cabinet Councillors' Office into the Cabinet Councillors' Office on Internal Affairs (*naikaku naisei shingi shitsu*) and established alongside it a new office, the Cabinet Councillors' Office on External Affairs (*naikaku gaisei shingi shitsu*).[58]

The Cabinet Councillors' Office on Internal Affairs is formally responsible for "providing overall coordination on important items engaging the Cabinet and for providing the overall coordination needed to preserve the unity related to policies of each administrative part" (Cabinet Law). In the office are ten cabinet councillors (*naikaku shingikan*) and forty others are also on the list for the office but work elsewhere. The ten cabinet councillors represent most of the ministries and agencies dealing with domestic policy.[59]

The head of the office is seconded from the Finance Ministry. Matoba Junzō, before becoming the chief of the office under Nakasone, was the deputy chief of the Finance Ministry's budget bureau. The internal affairs office staffs the cabinet councils and other similar groups that are established by the cabinet, in addition to the parliamentary vice ministers' conference. In 1987 the internal affairs office served as the staff for the Japan National Railways Reform Commission, the Headquarters for the Employment of JNR Workers, and the Cabinet Council on the Aging of Society. The office also dealt with labor issues, pension issues, and public corporations.[60]

The Cabinet Councillors' Office on External Affairs is formally responsible for "providing overall coordination on important items engaging the cabinet and for providing the overall coordination needed to preserve the unity related to policies of each administrative part, with particular emphasis on items related to foreign relations" (Cabinet Law). These items include those that also affect domestic affairs. The head of the office is seconded from the Foreign Ministry. Kunihiro Michihiko, who occupied the position under Nakasone, was an experienced trade negotiator with the United States. In addition, six other *naikaku shingikan* are also on secondment, one each from the PMO, the Economic Planning Agency, and the Foreign, Finance, Agriculture, and International Trade and Industry ministries.[61]

The report by the Administrative Reform Promotion Council noted that the Cabinet Secretariat did not enable the prime minister and the cabinet to manage the bureaucracy effectively when trying to deal with the rising number of urgent foreign policy issues, such as trade friction.[62] The main responsibilities of the old Cabinet Councillors' Office focused on the coordination of domestic and economic policies. Although the coordination of some foreign affairs matters in the Cabinet Secretariat was handled by staff offices for the cabinet councils, the Comprehensive Security Cabinet Council, and the Cabinet Council on Indochinese Refugess, there was no office for foreign affairs in general. The report noted that because these issues tend to cut across the boundaries of ministries and agencies, the general coordinating functions of the cabinet had to be strengthened.

The Foreign Ministry was opposed to the establishment of the external affairs office. The foreign minister at the time the proposal was released, Abe Shintarō, said that he feared that the new office would make the Foreign Ministry unnecessary, or at least split Japan's foreign policy between two competing voices.[63] Because the head of the office is on secondment from the Foreign Ministry, many have expressed doubts that the office will be able to do very much. One official from the Management and Coordination Agency remarked that the Foreign Ministry sends someone to the office as a "saboteur" to make sure that the ministry retains control over the coordination in policy.[64]

Many doubt, however, that the reorganization of the councillors' offices will increase the Cabinet Secretariat's ability to coordinate policy. As Kataoka Hiromitsu notes, the staff of the offices was increased, but the increase is made up of more seconded officials.[65] The seconded officials are supposed to overcome their tendency simply to represent their own ministries,[66] but the general view is that they do not succeed, with the result that it is difficult for the office to be actively involved in coordination.[67] Kusuda Minoru, who was a private secretary to Satō, believes that only an exceptional chief cabinet secretary or administrative deputy chief cabinet secretary—someone like Gotōda—can overcome this sectionalism in the office.[68]

The Cabinet Security Affairs Office

Besides the reorganization of the Cabinet Councillors' Office, the other focus of the 1986 reorganization was the establishment of the Cabinet Security Affairs Office (*naikaku anzen hoshō shitsu*). The office was established on July 1, 1986 to staff the new Security Council of Japan, which replaced the National Defense Council.[69] Whereas the National Defense Council concentrated on national defense matters, the new council handles issues involving security in a broader sense. The new council and office are supposed not only to deal with questions of national defense, but also to serve as a center to handle crises such as those involving terrorism, hijackings, and natural disasters such as earthquakes. If an emergency situation should arise, the prime minister or the chief cabinet secretary would direct the Cabinet Security Affairs Office to carry out the necessary work to open the Security Council of Japan.

Its staff of twenty-four is made up of officials on loan from various ministries.[70] The director of the office is from the Defense Agency. The director under Nakasone, Sasa Atsuyuki, served as the director of the Defense Agency's secretariat and director of the Defense Facilities Administration Agency. He is also said to have done the initial research for setting up a crisis center by studying the system in the United States. Besides the director, four other officials are in the office, plus seven others who are serving concurrently elsewhere.[71] The four are on loan from the Defense Agency, the Foreign Ministry, the Finance Ministry, and the NPA.

The main impetus for the new cabinet council and Cabinet Secretariat office is said to have been Gotōda's belief that the Cabinet Secretariat was not serving the prime minister and the chief cabinet secretary adequately during crises. This was based on his experiences as chief cabinet secretary during the KAL 007 incident in 1983, which he details in his memoirs.[72] He believed that the government as a whole dealt with the incident fairly well, but he had strong doubts as to whether the Cabinet Secretariat could always cope with such emergency situations appropriately. He is critical, for instance, of the government's handling of the 1977 hijacking of a Japan Airlines jet by the Japan Red Army. His main concern is information. "If an emergency situation comes up, the final decision about how to handle it must be made by the prime minister. The problem is that, in order for him to make the decision, he needs information, and the organization of the present Cabinet Secretariat is not fully able to deliver that information."[73] During an emergency, he believes, ministries and agencies have a tendency to withhold information.

> The Defense Agency, the Foreign Ministry, the National Police Agency, the National Land Agency, the MITI, the Agriculture Ministry, the Fire Defense Board, and others have each prepared a system to handle emergency situations. The problem is that information about which the ministries and agencies have some worries will not reach the Kantei. This is the habit of officials. The information is withheld not only from the Kantei but also from the minister in charge. Sometimes, the information is stopped at the bureau level and is not even reported to the administrative vice minister. The information just disappears inside the government agencies.[74]

He was able to get the information he needed during the KAL 007 incident because he knew where to get it.

> I knew from my experience as a bureaucrat what sort of information each government agency had. Instead of waiting for information, I asked them to deliver it. I would say, "Deliver information about 'x' to the Kantei and at the same time notify 'y.'" It is, however, very doubtful that information can always be gathered this way. The position of chief cabinet secretary is not limited, of course, to those who are able to do this all the time.[75]

The Japanese government's inability to formulate a timely response to the 1990 Iraqi invasion of Kuwait, however, suggests that the new office has not lived up to expectations. One problem is that it suffers from lack of experience and continuity because its members rotate positions about every two years.[76] According to Sasa, the government still lacks the unified, centralized management that is needed to organize a coherent, prompt response to international crises.[77]

The Cabinet Information Research Office

The Cabinet Information Research Office (*naikaku jōhō chōsa shitsu*) is the center for information gathering and is often referred to as the prime minister's "eyes and ears."[78] Its responsibility is to coordinate the gathering of intelligence from the information organizations in the government.[79] Before the reorganization in 1986, the office was known simply as the Cabinet Research Office. The 1986 reorganization added *information* to its name and analysis to its responsibilities. The office chief at the time of the reform, Taniguchi Morimasa, said that although the fundamental work of the office had not changed, the result of the reform has been to emphasize the importance of information. "The issue is how to analyze quickly and reliably the information that pours in not just from inside the country but also from around the world."[80]

The office was originally established in April 1952 as the Research Office and was part of the secretariat in the PMO. This was the year that Japan regained its sovereignty with the signing of the San Francisco Treaty. Yoshida, then prime minister, directed Murai Jun, the chief of the Security Division of the National Police Headquarters, to make the preparations for the establishment of the office.[81] Murai's main concern was the activity of left-wing groups. And because of the need to gather intelligence about communist countries, the Foreign Ministry's cooperation was necessary. In 1957 the office was incorporated into the Cabinet Secretariat and became known as the Cabinet Research Office.

The pertinent results of the office's research and analysis are reported to the chief cabinet secretary regularly and at any other time when the need arises. One day every week, the head of the office arrives at the Kantei and reports to the chief cabinet secretary on domestic and international intelligence that has been collected and analyzed. Other information from the office is sent to the chief cabinet secretary via his NPA private secretary.

The director of the office is on loan from the NPA, and many have gone on from the post to become administrative deputy chief cabinet secretaries.[82] The vice director is on loan from the Foreign Ministry and serves simultaneously as an official in the ministry's Public Information and Cultural Affairs Bureau. The general practice of appointing the director of the office from the NPA and the vice director from the Foreign Ministry dates back to the time of the office's establishment in 1952 when information from both sides was considered necessary to counter left-wing activities.

In addition, the office officially includes fourteen other cabinet research officers (*naikaku chōsakan*) (and thirteen more listed as serving elsewhere) and three research officers.[83] The office is located on the fifth floor of the PMO. Its work is generally secret: reporters are not allowed the access they might have in other ministries and agencies and are allowed to see only the chief, the deputy, and heads of sections.

The JCP often refers to the office as "Japan's CIA" and accuses it of being the government's agency for covert activities. The party's suspicions, of course, date back to the early 1950s, when the office's primary purpose was to counter left-wing activities. But much of its reputation as "Japan's CIA" stems from a case in 1967, when Uchikawa Masatomi was arrested in the Soviet Union for taking pictures of a military installation and was accused of being a spy for the U.S. Central Intelligence Agency and the Japanese Cabinet Research Office.[84] It turned out that he was sent by the Research Council on World Politics and Economics (*sekai seikei chōsakai*), which was commissioned by the office to do research on countries around the world. The directors of this council were formerly from the prewar thought police (*tokkō-keisatsu*), and its members were postwar elite police officials who dealt with security and public order.

The Cabinet Information Research Office generally gets most of its information from outside groups, which, besides the already mentioned Research Council on World Politics and Economics, include organizations such as NHK (Japan's state-owned broadcasting corporation); Radio Press, and Kyōdō and Jiji news services.[85] It is also rumored that research fees are given to some scholars who visit communist countries.[86] The office has a budget of 1.8 billion yen, well over half of which goes to outside groups commissioned to do research. The sort of intelligence these groups supply, as well as the amount of money given to them, is not publicly known, but the JCP accuses the office of pouring huge sums into groups that are used to subvert communists.[87]

Researchers from the office also often go abroad—usually on "private trips"—to gather information. The wish among those in the office, however, is to be able to station people overseas, particularly in major countries such as the United States, the former Soviet Union, and China and in Europe, so that they can directly control the collection of information. Another wish is to increase the number of personnel in the office by another twenty members or so to increase the office's ability to put together and analyze intelligence.

The office does have the reputation of being able to obtain information more quickly than any other public agency in Japan. It is said to have found out before the United States that South Korean President Chun would commute the death sentence of Kim Dae-Jung.[88] It also seems to have especially good intelligence on China. It reportedly received information more quickly and reliably than the Foreign Ministry and the MITI on important items regarding Japanese interests in China, such as the Sentaku Islands incident in 1977 and the cancellation of the Baoshan steel plan project.[89] Mori Kishio also writes that he was given a very detailed account of the battles along the Sino-Soviet border by a researcher for the office while the battles were going on.[90]

One of the main activities of the Cabinet Information Research Office is said to be to analyze electoral trends, particularly for the two houses of the National Assembly. It reports to the prime minister through the chief cabinet secretary and gives election forecasts that are independent of the LDP and the factions. The office is also said to make forecasts of local elections and those abroad, such as the U.S. presidential election.

Many, however, question the quality of the office's information. Gotōda does not have a very high opinion of the office, saying that it is "very incomplete."[91] Tahara's interviews with other officials who have served in the Kantei are also highly critical. "Those guys stamp the information 'secret' and bring it in as if it's really important. But it's little more than newspaper clippings. Not only that, the information gives only the police's perspective."[92] A research officer in the office did not deny these remarks: "Unfortunately, the current office is very weak. The Japan Communist party advertises us as Japan's CIA; I wish we could somehow keep up that image. Thanks to the JCP's big campaign, people overseas look upon us much too highly. This is a big plus in international politics, so I think we need to give thanks to the Communist party."[93] One problem the office faces, according to Morita Yūji, its head during the Persian Gulf War, is a lack of analysts, rather than a lack of information.[94] Another is that ministries and agencies are still reluctant to share intelligence with one another. Sectionalism in the bureaucracy is carried over into the Cabinet Secretariat. The Cabinet Information Research Office is known for its ties to the NPA, while the Foreign Ministry has its closest ties within the Cabinet Secretariat to the Councillor's Office on External Affairs, and the Defense Agency has ties to the Cabinet Security Affairs Office.[95]

The Cabinet Office of the Director General of Public Relations

The Cabinet Office of the Director General of Public Relations (*naikaku kōhōkan shitsu*) is in charge of supplying information about the government to the nation and abroad, and in particular to provide public relations for government policies; hence it is often referred to as the prime minister's "mouth." Before the 1986 reforms the office was known simply as the Cabinet Public Relations Office (*naikaku kōhō shitsu*). The current office, besides coordinating matters related to public relations, now prepares for the prime minister's and the chief cabinet secretary's press conferences and press releases, which were previously handled by the Cabinet Advisers' Office. Ōkina writes that this change is one step toward the position of the press secretary vis-à-vis the U.S. president.[96]

Technically, two separate offices, one a part of the Cabinet Secretariat and the other a part of the PMO, take care of these duties. In reality, the two overlap completely. They have the same staff (the PMO is considered its home office), and the head of the office, usually an official from the NPA, serves simultaneously as the head of the office in the PMO. The staff consists of forty-eight members, including eight who have concurrent positions in the Cabinet Secretariat and in the PMO. Of the eight, six come from the PMO itself, and one each from the Agriculture Ministry and the NPA.

The Management and Coordination Agency

In addition to the Cabinet Secretariat, the other main focus of the reorganization was the establishment of the Management and Coordination Agency.[97] The agency was inaugurated on July 1, 1984 as an external organ of the PMO to provide "the national government with a new structure for vigorous and effective central management and coordination to ensure that government operations are efficient, well coordinated, and responsive to the social and economic changes."[98]

Although the inauguration of the new agency was a central part of the attempt to centralize government authority, its current configuration is a greatly watered down version of the type of agency that many wanted to see.[99] During the deliberations of the Second Ad Hoc Council on Administrative Reform (Rinchō), Sejima Ryūzō, a central member of the commission, proposed that there be a central coordination agency that would have authority over the personnel, organization, and budget of the ministries and also absorb the Economic Planning Agency and National Land Agency.[100] Because of opposition from bureaucrats and others, Rinchō in the end proposed something much more modest: a "comprehensive management agency" that combined the Administrative Management Agency and parts of the PMO.[101]

The new Management and Coordination Agency was involved in a number of Nakasone's priorities, including administrative reform, opening domestic markets to trade, and the promotion of private sector activity. At first, the general view was that the creation of the agency would not change very much; it was after all a merger of two relatively minor agencies. But according to a top official in the MITI, the passage of various proposals for administrative reform shows that the agency can serve as an effective coordinator.[102]

The leverage of the Management and Coordination Agency to coordinate policy depends primarily on the resources of three bureaus: personnel, administrative management, and administrative inspection. Its influence over personnel management derives from the personnel bureau's authority to draft legislation that determines the pay, hours of work, and other working conditions of national public employees, and the administrative management bureau's review of requests for changes in the number of staff submitted by each ministry and agency at the end of August every year as a part of the annual budgetary request.[103] The agency's authority over personnel policy is limited because the National Personnel Authority, an independent agency, has the power to approve and enforce the distribution of fixed numbers of staff by the classes of position within each ministry and agency, and the Finance Ministry has the authority to prepare the salary budget. And, most importantly, the Management and Coordination Agency has no say in how each ministry and agency determines the movement and promotion of its staff.[104]

The agency's influence over personnel management nevertheless has been used a number of times. To help gain the opposition parties' acceptance of the bill to establish a new administrative reform council in 1986, Tamaki Kazuo, the agency's director, threatened that, if it did not pass, he would withhold submission of a bill to raise wages of national employees.[105] In addition, he used the agency's control over staff numbers to overcome Foreign Ministry opposition to his idea of importing American rice to use as aid to less developed countries as part of the effort to reduce trade frictions between Japan and the United States.[106] As part of a strategy to pressure the Foreign Ministry, Tamaki threatened to withhold the agency's approval of the ministry's request for more regular staff.[107]

The administrative management bureau is responsible for the planning and implementation of administrative reform.[108] The agency provided most of the staff for the Administrative Reform Promotion Council and played an important role in the development and enactment of the proposals of the Administrative Reform Outline adopted by the cabinet in September 1985, which included the reorganization of the Cabinet Secretariat, the development of a crisis center (and the establishment of the Security Council of Japan), the easing of licensing and standards to widen access to Japan's domestic market, and the easing of regulations to expand domestic demand.[109]

Tahara believes that the crisis management system will be used to set up the infrastructure for stronger central control. He reports that Gotōda, the director at the time, wanted to set up an information network as part of a crisis management system that could also be used to help overcome the sectionalism of the bureaucracy. Gotōda believed that, as I mentioned above, the ministries tend to withhold information, hence as director he beefed up its intelligence-gathering capability by establishing an "administrative data network" and a "comprehensive personnel information system."[110] According to Senda Hisashi, a former expert member of Rinchō, Gotōda's aim was to crack open the bureaucracy.

> If you think of how the idea for an agency like the *naikaku-fu* [cabinet office] of the first Rinchō was shot down, the whole bureaucracy will necessarily rise up in protest and squash [any such proposal]. It is impossible to strengthen the authority over personnel, not to mention the authority to compile the budget. Even the idea for comprehensive planning was squashed. Gotōda, as a former bureaucrat, knows this full well. Thus . . . he is cracking open the [bureaucracy] with information. By possessing an information system—by possessing the information of all the ministries— [the agency] will have authority over personnel, organization, and in essence function as a comprehensive planning agency. This is the starting

point of Mr. Gotōda's crisis management system. The Management and Co-ordination Agency is acting as the engineering corps to build the infra-structure for this.[111]

The third bureau, the administrative inspection bureau, monitors activity in government agencies, and many regard it as the main focus of the agency's efforts to keep ministries in line.[112] An agency official described the inspection authority as "sort of an FBI power over the administration."[113] Nakasone asked Tamaki to use this authority to encourage ministries to support the Maekawa report on liberalization.[114] Tamaki had the agency inspect the Foreign Ministry as part of his effort to have it accept his plan for rice imports.[115] In addition, Gotōda used the inspection authority on the JNR to investigate suspicions that its offi-cials were withholding information that would help in the JNR's privatiz-ation. The resulting investigation confirmed the suspicions, finding that the JNR still had over a thousand hectares of land that it could sell.[116] The bureau also has carried out policy evaluations of welfare and the Labor Ministry's programs for the elderly.

Personal Advisers and Advisory Committees

One of the problems with the prime minister's institutional support is that it furnishes virtually no policy advice or expertise apart from what the bureaucracy provides. There have been a number of attempts to give the prime minister policy aides, but they have all failed because of opposition from the bureaucracy and many members of the LDP. The bureaucracy has been adamantly opposed; it prefers that the prime minister not have the organization to make decisions by himself so that it can continue to draw up the drafts for policy. LDP members are afraid that a system of prime ministerial aides would allow the prime minister to act independently of the party.

The premier, if he is to develop proposals independently of the bureaucracy, must rely on outside help. Hence one of the main strategies employed by Nakasone to exert control over policy making was to use advisory committees staffed for the most part by his personal advisers, his "brain." This was most evident in the development of proposals for administrative reform, which was handled first by Rinchō and its suc-cessors.[117] Nakasone also used a similar commission to develop proposals for educational reform (see chapter 3), in an attempt to bypass the Education Ministry, and he tried to influence the debate on tax reform by appointing members of his brain trust to the Government Tax Council.

A number of other prime ministers have also used personal advisers. Usually they have developed this network prior to becoming prime minister, and the network can include scholars, businessmen, journalists, and bureaucrats (both retired and active). Yoshida recruited top civil servants (who included future prime ministers Ikeda and Satō) into his administration. Satō had his Research Group in Military Bases to deliberate on the issue of the status of U.S. military bases upon the return of Okinawa to Japanese sovereignty. Then there were Tanaka's Restructuring the Japanese Archipelago Consultation Group and Miki's Life Cycle Consultation Group. Tanaka also regularly invited civil servants from the level of section chief to his private residence to hear their opinions.

Ōhira went further than any of his predecessors and set up an ad hoc cabinet staff office and nine advisory groups made up of 176 scholars who were entrusted to make recommendations on a variety of policy issues.[118] Ōhira, however, died in office before the groups were able to present the results of their research, and his successor, Suzuki, did not have any policy research groups of his own and soon abolished the ad hoc cabinet staff office.

Nakasone revived the advisory committees and used them much more aggressively than any of his predecessors to establish a "top-down presidential-style prime ministership."[119] He placed on the various commissions scholars, businessmen, and others who were close to him personally and philosophically. The basic conclusions of the recommendations were largely formed from the very beginning. The commissions, in other words, were used deliberately to change policy rather than just to study issues.

The use of commissions, however, is clearly limited. Although they played a big part in Nakasone's successes in administrative reform,[120] there were a number of other commissions and advisory groups that had little effect. Nakasone tried to use one to legitimize his visits to Yasukuni Shrine, but the strategy backfired when it raised the ire of countries in East and Southeast Asia. Clearly, the proposals set forth by commissions must have wide support if they are to have an effect. Another problem was that many, particularly opposition party members, questioned the legitimacy of the commissions, arguing that they undermined or by-passed the democratic process because they did not explicitly involve the political parties in the National Assembly. Members of the LDP, particularly members of *zoku*, also often opposed them because they too were being bypassed, as was seen in Nakasone's efforts at educational and tax reform.

Conclusion

Presidents and prime ministers are usually not without significant resources of their own to provide them with support. Their staff can be helpful in furnishing services such as clerical work; carrying messages between them and others; supplying information (e.g., monitoring activities in the bureaucracy), policy expertise and advice; and helping in the control of governmental affairs. The Japanese prime minister is no exception. Supporting the prime minister is an inner staff in the Kantei, the Cabinet Secretariat, and most recently, the Management and Coordination Agency. The 1986 reorganization of the Cabinet Secretariat and the establishment of the Management and Coordination Agency was meant to increase the cabinet's, particularly the prime minister's, ability to coordinate and control functions centrally. In addition, some prime ministers have set up commissions and used a network of private advisers.

The prime minister's support system, however, is still relatively modest, and it is weak in three areas. First, the prime minister has but a small staff: in the Kantei, the total staff is eleven. By contrast, the White House staff numbers in the hundreds, while the British prime minister's office at No. 10 Downing Street has a total staff of about seventy.[121] Even the Cabinet Secretariat, which has a total staff of fewer than two hundred, is less than half the size of Britain's Cabinet Office, which has a total of about four hundred.

Second, the prime minister's staff does not give him the resources to penetrate the bureaucracy very effectively. The premier appoints the ministers and parliamentary vice ministers, but, as was detailed in the previous chapter, their influence is generally limited. In reality, the bureaucracy penetrates the prime minister's staff in the Kantei more than the prime minister penetrates the bureaucracy. Almost all of those who directly serve the premier and in the institutions supporting him and the cabinet are on loan from the ministries. Only a handful owe their primary loyalty to the prime minister. By contrast, most heads of government elsewhere have a staff that works primarily either for them personally or for the institutions serving them. They either have an independent institutional or personal staff, as in the case of the United States and Germany, or are at least able to control the appointments from the bureaucracy, as in the case of the French president and prime minister.[122]

Perhaps as a result of this lack of personal staff, the Japanese prime minister is quite isolated. A number of those who have worked in the Kantei believe so. A former chief private secretary to Ōhira explains: "While the prime minister is at the center of authority, the Kantei is like the president's office of a small enterprise. The Cabinet Secretariat has a number of offices within it and a number of people in those offices, but information that comes up from these offices is filtered by the chief cabinet secretary and his deputies. Thus the prime minister is isolated from information."[123]

Third, the Japanese prime minister, as compared to other chief executives, lacks any real staff for formulating and analyzing policy. He has no institutionalized staff and must rely almost entirely on the bureaucracy for information and expertise unless he has a strong network of personal advisers. The U.S. president, by contrast, has a number of agencies, such as the Council of Economic Advisers, which offer policy advice and expertise. The British prime minister has a personal policy unit in the Cabinet Office, and Thatcher had personal advisers on economics, foreign affairs, and defense at No. 10 Downing Street to give her independent advice. As I. M. Destler et al. write, "If leaders cannot go elsewhere for these resources, they must go to bureaucrats; they will thus tend to see the facts of issues as bureaucrats see them and their policy decisions will tend to reflect bureaucratic preference."[124]

Thus, despite the recent attempt to strengthen the prime minister's support system, many believe that it is still inadequate, as Gotōda makes clear: "When the prime minister has to hand down a decision, there really is no one who helps him. . . . That there should be support systems to help him is self-evident. Unfortunately, the present Cabinet Secretariat has a very difficult time doing that."[125]

9

The Prime Minister and Public Policy

The *leadership of* the prime minister in Japan seems quite different from that generally seen elsewhere, either in the West or in Asia. Leaders are often expected to be policy activists. They are supposed to be involved in a wide variety of issues and to be proactive, participating in the process of the issues by setting the agenda or determining the solutions, or both. That is, leadership is usually either technocratic or political. The Japanese premier, however, seems relatively passive and reactive by comparison. He does not get involved in very many issues, and when he does, he generally does not either set the agenda or have much of an impact on the proposals for policy change. As the previous chapters have shown, the prime minister's reactive leadership is shaped by a number of broad forces: the selection process, an undisciplined ruling party, relatively strong opposition parties in the National Assembly, strong subgovernments, and a weak supporting staff. The system is quite inertial; the prime minister effects major change only with great difficulty.

Because of the various limitations, the prime minister is now generally viewed as a weak leader. Karel van Wolferen, for instance, argues that Japan's government has no top and that the Japanese premier is weaker than the head of government of any Western country.[1] Certainly, the system is not particularly coherent. It is fragmented, and the prime minister does not have many resources to influence the policy process. But the inertia of the system and the constraints on the prime minister do not necessarily mean that his impact is small or insignificant. The purpose of this chapter is to bring together what has been learned up to this point to obtain a fuller understanding of the prime minister and the policy process. This chapter analyzes how the limitations and resources affect first the number of issues in which he is involved and then his ability to influence the process of them. It argues that although there are political constraints on the prime minister's participation in the policy process, particularly in the number of issues in which he is involved, he nevertheless is able to play an important part in bringing about policy change.

The Size of the Prime Minister's Agenda

One measure of the prime minister's effect on the policy process is the size of his agenda—whether he is involved in many issues or only a very few. The lists of prime ministerial issues developed in chapter 1 suggest that the premier does not participate actively in many. There are a number of reasons for this. One is that he is a busy person. He must attend meetings with his cabinet, LDP groups, interest groups, and foreign dignitaries—meetings that very often have little to do directly with policy. Thus, he may have little energy to spend on policy goals that he may think are important.

Such factors will affect any leader, whose time is always in demand, but it is perhaps especially true in the Japanese prime minister's case, because his position as president of the ruling party is less secure than, say, that of his British counterpart, who, while certainly having to consider the views of the party, does not need to be obsessively preoccupied with keeping the party in line. By contrast, the Japanese prime minister must be constantly on his guard to prevent movements within the party to dump him. He has, therefore, correspondingly less time to devote to policy.

In particular, factions put the prime minister on a short leash. In extreme cases, political troubles drive everything else off the agenda. Miki's second year was dominated by the Lockheed scandal and the numerous attempts to force him out of office. And because of the LDP's poor showing in the 1979 election, Ōhira had to endure calls for resignation by many members of the party. The only issues he dealt with to any substantial degree for the rest of his term were those that were forced upon him: near crises in relations with the United States over defense expenditures, Iran, Afghanistan, and trade.

The short leash also means that the premier is inhibited from taking on controversial issues that rivals may use against him. This does not necessarily mean that he will not be able to handle them, but rather that he must consider the political consequences of such a move more carefully than other leaders, and he is likely to stay behind the scenes.

Another reason why the prime minister is not more involved is that he lacks positive incentives. Issues play but a marginal role in the election of party presidents (except perhaps negatively by offending someone). Hence it is quite possible to be elected party president, and therefore prime minister, with no platform whatsoever. And because prime ministers often rely on shaky coalitions of factions for support, there may be strong disincentives for them to push anything controversial. Candidates for the U.S. presidency, on the other hand, are expected to campaign on a number of issues; the president, therefore, has much more motivation to be active in matters of policy.

The Prime Minister and the Policy Process

The policy-making process, in simplified form, consists of three general processes: agenda setting, determining the content of change, and the enactment of change.[2] Correspondingly, the prime minister can play three types of leadership roles: political, in which leaders determine the agenda; technocratic, in which they determine the content of change; and reactive, in which they determine neither the items on the agenda nor the alternatives but instead have their greatest impact in the enactment process. This section analyzes the prime minister's ability to exert each type of leadership. It suggests that the chief executive has few incentives to set the agenda and little influence over the content of policy and that his main impact comes in the enactment process. His participation in the policy process generally comes after an issue is already on the agenda. The prime minister's leadership, then, tends to be reactive.

Political Leadership: Agenda Setting

Agenda setting means bringing serious attention to an issue in a general way. In political models of change, leaders have their main effect in this aspect of the policy process. They have clear goals and pursue them using the resources at their disposal to overcome opposition. As I showed in chapter 1, however, this type of leadership does not describe recent Japanese prime ministers very well. Rather than setting the agenda, they have tended to be most involved in questions already on the agenda.

The prime minister faces a number of limitations in this part of the process, mostly related to the nature of the ruling LDP. One important difference between Japan and other countries is that Japan is characterized by a dominant political party. Whereas other industrialized democracies regularly experience some form of alternation of party power, the LDP has been in power continuously since 1955. In systems that experience alternations, the top political leader, the president or prime minister, tends to be the focus of agenda setting, especially at the beginning of his or her term in office.[3] During its time out of power, the party develops ideas and proposals, which the leader is able to use.[4]

In Japan, the LDP's dominance has lessened the prime minister's role in agenda setting in two ways. First, there is less reason to change priorities because of a change in leaders. In other countries, a change in the head of government often accompanies a change in party power, which brings about a change in priorities.[5] In Japan, because there is no change in party rule, a new premier is less likely to make a sharp break with past policies. Thus there is less of a tendency to change basic priorities, and one would expect much more continuity in policy from administration to administration than one would see in other countries.

Second, dominance over time has meant that the LDP no longer has much of an agenda of its own to push, which has meant there are fewer incentives for the prime minister to push for something. Certainly, in the beginning the conservatives had their own agenda, largely in reaction to the reforms of the Occupation and in terms of setting a direction for Japan for the postwar period.[6] But the LDP no longer has much of a distinct program. In expanding its base of support, it has become a catchall party in which interests across a broad spectrum are represented.[7] These interests include those of big business, small businesses (retailers, mom-and-pop type stores), farmers, white-collar workers, and to a large extent blue-collar workers, especially those who do not belong to the large labor unions. In Tanaka Zen'ichirō's view, the LDP's main interest since the early 1960s has been to maintain stability and the status quo.[8] Given the wide range of interests within the party, the LDP is less interested in advocating an agenda than it is in maintaining its majority by not making too many waves.

Thus, since the 1960s, the LDP has largely been reacting to outside pressures, rather than advancing an agenda of its own. Since then, other actors have been more important in the placing of most of the major items on the policy agenda. For example, citizen movements led the way for environmental protection, and the United States for opening Japan's market to imports. At a lower level, the bureaucracy is always active.[9] At other times the agenda is set by outside events, such as the two oil shocks and economic stagflation of the 1970s. For this reason, issues have been of only marginal importance in the selection of party presidents. It is quite possible to be elected party president (and therefore prime minister) without much of a platform.

Finally, the prime minister is not likely to be active because forceful leadership violates Japanese norms of style, which emphasize consensus and harmony.[10] He is expected to be the articulator for a consensus. Nakasone, for instance, was constantly being criticized by other party leaders for trying to be too much of an activist leader; they claimed that he did not consider the views of the party enough and tried to garner too much publicity for himself. More typical is Takeshita and his view of leadership: "It is the role of the leader today not to pull people along, it is to get the consensus of the people."[11]

Technocratic Leadership: Policy Proposals

The second part of the process is determining policy proposals. In the technocratic style of leadership, leaders have their main influence here. They rarely are able to exert such leadership in its pure form; they generally are not the only participants. Nevertheless, in many political systems, the top political leader often at least attempts to define problems and advance proposals, often in great detail. While negotiations with specialized bureaucrats and politicians are often necessary, the head of government is expected to have a point of view and actively press it. In the United States, presidents present their legislative programs to Congress in great detail and so have a fairly extensive policy staff, such as the Office of Management and Budget, to help draft bills.[12]

The Japanese prime minister will on occasion affect the content of proposed changes. But most often his influence is at best indirect. One resource is his ability to appoint people to certain posts. As was seen in the two case studies, Nakasone was able to affect the debate on both tax reform and education reform by adding some of his personal advisers to the government councils responsible for developing proposals. The premier is also able to influence what is discussed by making public commitments, usually negative ones, such as Nakasone's promise not to introduce a "large-scale indirect tax that is opposed by the people" during the campaign for the double elections in 1986.

But Nakasone's attempts to influence the debate also show the prime minister's limitations. Despite his efforts, neither the National Council on Educational Reform nor the Government Tax Council ended up with reports that supported him. Part of the problem is that the prime minister cannot easily develop proposals without some expertise. Some have made an impact because they were relatively expert in the issues they were advocating. Ikeda, for instance, who pushed his income-doubling plan, was a former top Finance Ministry official. Miki, who pressed for clean politics, had been working for a long time on his ideas for party reform, which would make the LDP less prone to corruption and factional divisions. Fukuda, known for his knowledge of economic policy, was very active in deciding what sort of measures were to be taken in fighting recession. In most cases, however, the prime minister will be an outsider to the subgovernment that handles legislation in a particular policy area, such as taxes and education.

Another constraint is that prime minister does not have an institutionalized policy staff that can help him develop proposals independently of the party and particularly the bureaucracy. He must rely on informal contacts for such advice. Tanaka, for instance, had regular discussions with middle-level officials in his search for ideas, and he brought along a MITI official to the Kantei to help develop the plan to restructure the Japanese archipelago. Miki turned to a group of friendly academics to draw up his "life-cycle" welfare plan. Ōhira and Nakasone developed a brain trust of scholars, businessmen, and journalists, which they used to staff formal and informal advisory committees.

Prime ministers face some difficulties, however, in using nonregular mechanisms such as advisory committees to develop independent proposals. First, many question the legitimacy of such committees, arguing that they undermine or bypass the democratic process. Nakasone, in fact, was unique among Japanese prime ministers in his use of these groups. His successors so far have not followed suit.[13] Second, even formal advisory committees still tend to be heavily dependent on the bureaucracy, for it often provides much of the staff and most of the expertise.

Perhaps the main limitation is the strength of the subgovernments, particularly the ministries. How an issue is shaped—what problems are addressed and what is to be done—is largely determined by the subgovernments. The bureaucracy still more or less monopolizes the actual drafting of legislation in cooperation with the corresponding policy experts in the party and perhaps interest groups. Thus, even if the prime minister makes an impact on which items are deliberated—for example, through an advisory committee—the proposals must still be handled by the bureaucracy and the party. As was seen with education reform, the civil service and the LDP tend to pick the proposals they like and ignore the others.

Reactive Leadership: Enactment

The third type of leadership is reactive. Leaders in this case do not take the initiative for change and are not involved directly in its content. The main characteristic of reactive leaders is that they are not strongly attached to issues, problems, or solutions; they are more pragmatic than ideological. Their main impact is on the enactment process, such as reaching a cabinet decision or passing legislation in the National Assembly. They take up issues that are at hand and apply their energy to them: their role is mainly to try to resolve them in some way.

In Japan, once an issue that is not controversial has reached the stage where it has been passed by the party organs (i.e., the PARC and the executive council), the rest is usually relatively easy. If a matter is controversial, however, the process can be very slow and difficult, given both the relative lack of party discipline in the LDP and the leverage of the opposition parties over the legislative process. Especially given the strong norms of consensus in the legislature, such bills tend to be tabled.

The prime minister, then, has few incentives to set the agenda and few resources to participate in the details of policy, and the enactment process erects a number of obstacles that can make progress very slow and difficult. Nevertheless, he does have a significant impact on the enactment process. As was shown in the tax reform case, he can have a great deal of influence over the legislative agenda. He is the one who usually determines which major bills to put forward, and when and how hard to push them. He will also often have the most influential voice in whether and how much a proposal will be compromised to win opposition assent. And it is the inertia of the system that makes his role in this part of the process so important. For one thing, if the premier is opposed to a proposed change, he has the ability to stop the movement for change at any stage—his power to veto change is in this sense stronger than the U.S. president's. He can also often do it unobtrusively and therefore not pay the political costs of a U.S. presidential veto.

Moreover, as previous chapters show, the prime minister does have more power than any single actor in the system. He has levers granted to him by the Constitution and the party, such as the power to appoint important government and party officials, and informal levers such as his faction. Without the active support of the premier, the inertia of the system would likely prevent change, for he is one of the few who can persistently apply the energy necessary for it to be enacted. The prime minister's role, then, is largely reactive. He generally becomes involved in issues after they are on the agenda and their content already determined. The prime minister's major impact is influencing whether such issues are enacted.

Three Types of Role

Within the general framework of reactive leadership, the prime minister can be a force for policy change in three ways. First, he can act as a broker in mediating conflict. Some issues are thrust in front of him because of policy conflicts that only he as party president and head of government can resolve. In these cases, the prime minister serves as sort of a court of last resort. Rather than choosing, he might often split the difference at some point. These disputes usually are between two subgovernments: each side brings in all its guns and the result is a stalemate, which only the prime minister can resolve. In many cases, of course, he will not intervene; such stalemates can persist for years.

Second is his role as process manager. This is a matter of setting deadlines, establishing ad hoc committees and deciding who should be appointed, making sure that things are moving and that problems are resolved. The prime minister may have more interest in ending the conflict by passing something—anything—than in the substance of the outcome; he may devote his energy to enforcing rules, procedures, and schedules to force the disputing parties into some sort of resolution that is at least tolerable to all sides. Very often, he will affect the process not by promoting proposals but by forcing the actors to settle their disputes so that the item is taken off the agenda. John Campbell's analysis of reform in government employee pensions in the 1980s is an example: without playing a substantive role, Prime Minister Nakasone devised and publicly announced a detailed schedule of committee meetings and reports aimed at bringing diverse interests into compromise.[14]

And finally, the prime minister can take an issue behind which there is already quite a bit of support and give it enough of a boost to get it enacted. If a proposal already has considerable energy behind it, he can mobilize and focus the energy of the support to press for change. Only the prime minister can set up the machinery by putting people in favor of change in critical spots and persuading others to go along.

The Choice of Issues

If the prime minister has some discretion over the issues in which he becomes involved, what determines his choice? His motives may fall into any of three categories: political advancement or security, historical achievement, and personal interest.[15]

Political Advancement or Security   Prime ministers sometimes decide to deal with a question for political reasons. That is, they use issues as part of their bid to become prime minister, to maintain their position, or to become reelected. Although policy matters are not decisive in determining the presidency of the party, they may play a part. Candidates often propose a centerpiece for their administration, hoping the idea will catch the imagination of the people and those in the party and boost their chances. Examples include Tanaka's plans for restructuring the Japanese archipelago and for normalizing relations with China, Miki's promotion of clean politics, Nakasone's administrative reform, and Takeshita's idea for *furusato sōsei* (hometown revival).

In addition, most prime ministers seek reelection, which is mainly dependent on factional strength and the intraparty coalition. This was true for Nakasone, who, as a supposedly lame-duck party president, worked to abolish the two-term limit and continue for a third term.[16] Issues probably affect the prime minister's chances only marginally, but they may be important for two reasons: they are one of the few variables he can manipulate; and he may raise them during election campaigns in the hopes that the party will do well and he will thus increase his strength within it. One example is Fukuda's efforts to negotiate and sign a peace treaty with China, in his second year, to burnish his image prior to the presidential primaries (which he lost anyway to Ōhira). Another is the way Satō managed the internal process to get pollution control laws passed in the legislature.[17]

Sometimes the prime minister promotes an issue to help maintain his intraparty support. Miki's efforts to pass the revenue and finance bills to ease the government deficit were due to the insistence of then Finance Minister Ōhira, a major rival to Miki.[18] Miki had to push these bills through the National Assembly in order to keep Ōhira in the cabinet. Another case was Kishi's endorsement of Ikeda's income-doubling plan in order to lure Ikeda back into the cabinet.[19] Party support for Kishi was wavering in 1959 because of the controversy over the revision of the United States—Japan Security Treaty, and he was able to strengthen it for a time by bringing Ikeda into the cabinet.

Historical Achievement   Another goal may be the desire to be remembered in history for a solid policy achievement. Paul Light writes that U.S. presidents are "generally aware of the historical rankings of past executives; they are interested in the paths to greatness," and thus they often single out issues that will "mark" their administrations.[20] There is evidence to suggest that this is also the case for Japanese prime ministers. Hatoyama Ichirō, for example, committed himself to reestablishing Japan's relations with the Soviet Union when he became prime minister and resisted efforts to oust him until he had accomplished his goal.[21]

This suggests that the premier will pick proposals that will produce visible achievements during his tenure for which he can claim credit. This motive favors matters over which he has considerable authority, one reason why so many of those most identified with prime ministers have been diplomatic ones. Besides the Hatoyama case, these include: Kishi and the revised security treaty; Tanaka and China; Satō and South Korea and the return of Okinawa to Japanese sovereignty; Fukuda and the signing of the peace treaty with China and the Fukuda Doctrine; and Suzuki and Takeshita and foreign aid.

Personal Interest   Finally, the prime minister may take up an issue simply because of personal interest. Despite resistance from the public, the opposition parties, and even his own party, he may feel so strongly about a proposal that he is willing to push it despite the problems it may bring. One might view Nakasone's efforts to raise defense spending above the 1-percent-of-GNP ceiling in this way. Despite opposition from the public, the opposition parties, and most notably, three former prime ministers (Miki, Fukuda, and Suzuki), Nakasone spent quite a bit of his energy on the issue and after four years in office was finally able to have the ceiling removed.

If a prime minister chooses to be involved in an issue because of personal beliefs, then it is likely to be one on which he has worked before, as Light has noted in the case of U.S. presidents.[22] Similarly, Miki's proposals for party reform were based on his long-held interest in that area; and it is no surprise that Nakasone was pressing for educational reform and higher defense spending given his long interest in the two areas.

The Prime Minister and Policy Change

Although no person can bring about change alone, the Japanese prime minister seems particularly constrained, given the inertia of the system and his limited resources. Yet he can make a difference. To explain how this is possible, one can liken the country's political system to a structure that has certain resonant frequencies.[23] If energy is applied at one of these frequencies, the whole system can vibrate, even if the level of energy is relatively low. At nonresonant frequencies, even at much higher levels of energy, there is little movement in the system. The prime minister's ability to effect change depends on whether he applies his limited energy to an issue that has resonance, that is, one that elicits "sympathetic vibrations" from other actors in the system. The prime minister adds his energy to that which is already being applied by other actors, which in turn elicits more energy from still others. When resonance occurs, then, it requires two forces: ideas and issues being pushed from below at the same time as they are being pulled up from above.

Resonant Frequencies: Pushing from Below

Most major changes result from ideas that have been worked on for a number of years. Advocates of change often spend much of their time trying to "soften up" the process to make their ideas more acceptable.[24] Issues may be promoted by bureaucrats, interest groups, opposition parties, and the public, as well as from abroad, especially the United States. Bureaucrats in particular are always studying problems, making proposals, and trying to manipulate assistance from politicians to have them enacted.[25] Finance Ministry officials, for example, had been trying to convince LDP leaders of the need for a VAT for years. By the time Nakasone had taken up tax reform, the idea for the new tax had already gained a number of important supporters in the party, including Takeshita, Kanemaru, and Fujio.

The "frequencies" of resonance, then, are determined by these demands for change from below. And as the two case studies indicate, the content of policy change is largely set by the subgovernment. The educational reforms that were enacted were determined by the Education Ministry along with members of the LDP education *zoku*. Likewise, the content of tax reform, particularly the form of the indirect tax, was determined by the Finance Ministry and the LDP tax *zoku*. In neither case did the prime minister play a major role in determining the content of change. Hence the premier can add energy to an issue, but he may have little influence over the frequency at which it "vibrates." As with a tuning fork, whether it vibrates or not depends on whether someone hits it, but the frequency at which it vibrates is predetermined.

The Prime Minister's Role: Pulling from Above

The prime minister needs to add his energy to a resonant issue if he expects to see any response; otherwise, very likely nothing will happen.

Nakasone, for example, considered two other problems besides juvenile delinquency: cancer research and the need for greenery in urban areas. He made public references to all three. Whereas the politicians, interest groups, and the public in general responded to the matter of juvenile delinquency, there was little reaction to his tentative espousal of the two other issues. Nakasone, therefore, abandoned them and concentrated his energy on education.

The problem for the prime minister is that far more time and energy is needed to develop a program not already being advocated. This is true perhaps for any leader, as Light writes of the U.S. president. "Presidents do not have the resources to generate new ideas. . . . The President simply does not have enough time, energy, information, or expertise to move into vastly new endeavors."[26] The prime minister can try to promote something new, by setting up a task force or directing his staff to study it and make recommendations. But he has few incentives to do this; the limitations seem particularly critical in Japan.

The process leading to enactment, in addition, is time-consuming even if there is relatively little active opposition. Legislation has to be drafted (probably by a ministry) and approved by the party before being presented to the legislature and passed into law. Even if the prime minister tries to press the issue throughout his term, there may not be enough time to get anything enacted, given that he will be up for reelection in only two years. And if the issue is not taken up by his successor, nothing will happen. Little came out of Ōhira's numerous study groups established to advance his ideas about Japanese style welfare, garden cities, and the Pacific Basin. He died too soon, and his successor, Suzuki, did not follow up on the reports of the study groups.

Rather than pursuing his own ideas to the end, a prime minister will often give up after a proposal meets resistance or even apathy, or when other more pressing or appealing ones intervene. Several issues initiated by the prime minister, such as Miki's Life Cycle Plan, Fukuda's administrative reform, Nakasone's visits to Yasukuni Shrine, and Takeshita's plan for hometown revival, died rather quickly.

Thus, certain ideas are attractive because they already have a constituency; the prime minister can accomplish something more easily by providing the added energy needed to propel them through to enactment. Even the discretionary issues identified in chapter 1 were quite active at a lower level at the time the premier took them up. These include negotiations for a peace treaty with China (Miki, Fukuda); revision of the antimonopoly law (Miki); introduction of a large-scale indirect tax (Ōhira); administrative reform (Suzuki); tax reform (Nakasone); land reform (Takeshita); and foreign aid (Suzuki, Takeshita).

The Process of Change

Policy change is most likely to occur, then, when the prime minister is pulling from above what is being pushed from below. One important opportunity to do this occurs at least every two years with the race for the LDP presidency. Candidates, both incumbents and challengers, look for something that will catch the imagination of the people and those in the party and thus boost their chances in the election. In addition, opportunities arise with elections to the lower and upper houses of the Kokkai, the local unified elections, the annual cabinet reshuffles, the numerous policy speeches to the National Assembly, and the inevitable two or three trips abroad that the prime minister makes every year. These all provide opportunities—or what John Kingdon refers to as "policy windows"—for the prime minister (and often other ambitious politicians) to look for issues and for issues to look for the prime minister.[27]

When he does look for an issue, the prime minister is provided with a *menu* of possibilities.[28] At any one time there are a number of proposals being pushed from below. The items on the menu change over time. Some may be there for a long time either because a condition is chronic (e.g., budget deficits) or because the idea's sponsor is well organized and influential, or both. The probability that these will at some point be picked up by a prime minister (or perhaps some other leader) is high. An example of this is the indirect tax, which had been advocated by the Finance Ministry for fifteen years before it was enacted.

Other items may be on the menu for a short time, perhaps because the problems that energize them recede from view after a short while. The chances that a prime minister will pick up such an issue are small, but that may happen if it makes it onto the menu when he is looking for one. Nakasone's choice of educational reform was very much like that. Education happened to be in the news because of several successive incidents of juvenile violence at about the time Nakasone was looking for an attractive domestic political issue to use for an upcoming election campaign for the upper house. Certainly, Nakasone's interest in education helps explain his involvement—another prime minister in a similar situation might have taken up something else—but had the timing been other than in early 1983, very likely Nakasone would not have made education one of his major priorities.

Whether the prime minister picks up a certain issue, then, can be largely a matter of timing. The timing was right for tax reform and education reform. A possible example of an active issue that was not adopted because of timing was the question of land prices. Prices of land particularly in and around Tokyo were almost doubling yearly during 1986 and 1987. The subject was receiving a lot of press and there was certainly considerable public clamor for the government to do something. But Nakasone never gave it much attention. The timing was not right because he was already preoccupied (with privatizing the JNR and tax reform). But the matter made the agenda of his successor, Takeshita, because it was active at the start of his term when his agenda was being determined.

Sustaining Resonance

Applying energy at a resonant frequency alone, however, does not ensure that change will occur. The "vibrations" may die out before anything happens. Indeed, most efforts at change lose their impetus well before the matter is actually brought to a vote. So sustaining resonance is important. Three factors are important in determining whether vibrations continue to resonate or are damped out: the prime minister, the political environment, and the issue itself.

The Prime Minister

The prime minister's ability to sustain resonance depends on factors such as his personality and style, his political skill, his competence in the area of policy, and his personal inclinations. Skill, for example, is important in aligning and focusing political forces. Nakasone was able to sustain the effort at educational reform by establishing a relatively high-profile national council, whose reports ensured that the issue would be in the news regularly. He was also skillful in using the race for the presidency of the LDP to help promote the elimination of the *maruyū* system of tax-free savings, when the race easily could have diverted attention away from the issue.

Much also depends on whether the prime minister is persistent in his efforts. Some prime ministers are more activist than others, as can be seen with Nakasone and his predecessor, Suzuki. Whereas Nakasone was very active on a number of policies in his top-down presidential style, Suzuki was an advocate of the politics of *wa*, or harmony, and tended to be quite passive. A passive leader may allow an issue to fade away, whereas a more activist one may be able to keep it going. Nakasone's persistence was crucial in keeping tax reform alive after the debacle over the VAT and in passing legislation that eliminated the *maruyū* savings system.

The Political Environment

The influence of the prime minister on policy depends not only on the degree to which he uses his resources and the degree of skill with which he uses them, but also on the political climate. Some conditions may dampen resonance. Political infighting in the LDP can foil efforts at change, as energy flows out of policy issues and into political affairs. Both Miki and Ōhira were particularly affected in this way. Opposition strength in the National Assembly can also dampen resonance. Especially during the *hakuchū* period in the 1970s, the LDP had to negotiate with the opposition parties in order to pass the budget and other legislation. It may be even more difficult to sustain effort now that the LDP has lost its control of the upper house. Instead of needing just the acquiescence of at least some of the opposition parties, the LDP now needs their active support in order to obtain the majority of votes needed to pass legislation.

The environment can also enhance the resonance of the system. If the prime minister has the support of the major factions, then resonance is much more likely to be sustained. Factions concentrate power among a few party leaders. Therefore, contrary to the situation in the United States, where the parties in Congress are so atomized that energy for change can be quickly dissipated, the factions give the LDP the capability of maintaining discipline.[29] In particular, crises can bring the party together.[30] Kent Calder's study of conservative rule in postwar Japan suggests that political crises prompt the LDP to take quick action in a number of areas of policy to forestall erosion of its electoral support.[31] In this sort of situation, the system is in a "superconductive state," in which efforts at change meet little or no resistance to enactment: "Japanese conservative elites have not typically been too discriminating about the content of policy responses or their price tags during crisis periods."[32] The prime minister can play an important role in taking these programs through the legislature, as with Tanaka and the "First Year of Welfare" in 1973.

The Issue

A third important influence on the premier's ability to sustain resonance is the specific issue. A number of studies of the U.S. presidency suggest that the president has greater influence in certain matters than on others. Robert Spitzer, using Theodore Lowi's typology, suggests that the president generally faces the least opposition politically in constituent (administrative, overhead) issues, followed in declining order by redistributive (fiscal, monetary, social welfare), distributive (pork barrel and other concrete, discrete benefits), and regulatory (manipulation of individual conduct through sanctions) ones.[33] Though a similar analysis is beyond the scope of this study, it is easy to see that some types of proposal require less energy for change. On the one hand, those that adversely affect important interest groups supporting the LDP would be difficult. These groups include a number of traditional supporters of the party, such as agriculture, small-scale enterprises, heads of local postal services.[34] On the other hand, matters that do not involve domestic interests very much, such as foreign policy issues, are more likely to be easier to influence. As I mentioned previously, prime ministers have had most of their successes with diplomatic policies.

Conclusion

The Japanese prime minister's impact on the policy process is largely shaped by the Japanese system, which is characterized more by a dispersion than by a concentration of power. Change is difficult. "The Japanese government seems to change direction rather infrequently, certainly compared with the United States and probably other nations as well."[35] The premier has some resources, including the power of appointment and informal levers such as his faction, but he has few incentives to become more actively involved. He has a lot to struggle against—the party, the subgovernments, the National Assembly. His resources to push for change are limited, and one or more of these actors can easily frustrate most attempts. Thus the prime minister does not play a particularly activist role in the policy process: he participates in only a few issues at a time and is not a major actor in initiating change in policy or in determining its content. The Japanese prime minister appears relatively weak and passive when compared to other heads of government.

Nevertheless, the prime minister can make an important impact on the policy process. His ability to effect change depends on whether he applies his limited energy to an issue that has resonance in the political system. That is, if he takes an issue that already has considerable support, his efforts can often be enough, added to those of others, to lead to the enactment of change. In other cases, he may try to put his energies into an issue that does not resonate, and nothing happens. The prime minister, then, can play a critical role in bringing about policy change by taking a well-defined issue that is already on the agenda and giving it enough energy to reach a resolution.

One of the main factors determining resonance is the factions of the LDP. Largely through its factions, the party has mechanisms to enforce the discipline needed to exploit the opportunities for change. If the prime minister can obtain the support of most of the major factions, then the chances for change are good. In this sense he serves as an articulator of consensus, and, if necessary, as an enforcer.[36] Nakasone used his position as kingmaker to persuade the three candidates for the presidency of the LDP, particularly Takeshita, to push for the abolition of the *maruyū* system of tax-free savings. All of the major faction leaders supported the idea. Had one or more of them opposed the bill, Nakasone would not have been able to obtain the party consensus needed to pass it. But although these rival leaders supported it, their main concern was not the bill; rather, it was the race for the party's presidency. Hence, without pressure from Nakasone, they would have diverted their attention from the issue. The prime minister, in other words, provided the crucial energy needed to propel the issue through to enactment.

10

Conclusion

I _n virtually all countries_ around the world, the focus of the political system is on the top political leader. In both descriptive and prescriptive models of government leadership, these leaders are expected to play strong, forceful roles in the policy process. Japan, however, offers a distinct contrast to this view. The Japanese prime minister, by the standards of most other countries, is seen to be a weak and passive leader.

As is shown throughout this book, the prime minister is subject to severe limitations. The selection process makes his position highly vulnerable to challenges from his own party. The political system is extremely inertial: the party, the National Assembly, and subgovernments are all significant constraints. His staff is small and its loyalties are at best mixed, since so many of its members are on loan from various ministries. All these factors limit the number of issues in which the prime minister is involved, as well as his ability to initiate change in policy and influence the development of alternatives. His leadership, therefore, is neither political (he does not set the agenda) nor technocratic (he does not determine solutions). Instead, he generally takes up well-defined issues after they are already on the agenda, that is, in the enactment process. His involvement in the policy process is, therefore, reactive.

Given the conventional wisdom that good and powerful leaders are needed to prevent drift and stagnation of the system, the Japanese prime minister's reactive leadership seems to contradict what many consider to be important to good government. Japan provides an interesting case in which a system has been able to function and adapt without a powerful head of government. This concluding chapter concentrates on two arguments. First, strong leadership is not without its perils, and second, good government is not necessarily inconsistent with weak leadership.

The Perils Of Strong Leadership

The assumption generally is that good and powerful leaders are needed to prevent drift and stagnation of the political system. Harvey C. Mansfield, Jr., writes: "No modern state is considered a going concern unless it is equipped with a strong executive, and every state without one is held to be courting disaster, and regarded with pity and contempt by those more fortunate."[1] Alexander Hamilton, in his famous essay in the Federalist Papers, defended the need for a strong presidency. "Energy in the executive is a leading character in the definition of good government. . . . A feeble executive implies a feeble execution of the government. A feeble execution is but another phrase for a bad execution; and a government ill executed, whatever it may be in theory, must be, in practice, a bad government."[2] Such advocates view government as a positive, directing force with a strong, forceful leader at the helm. When a country faces a new and difficult set of demands, the usual prescription is to look to the top leader, and, if need be, to strengthen his or her position. This has been the story of the U.S. presidency in the twentieth century. Presidential government has reached the point where "the whole system revolves around an activist, persuasive president who knows how to avoid the pitfalls and the sand traps of the Washington obstacle course."[3] A "great" president, such as Franklin Roosevelt, is one who dominates the agenda and creates change by political skill and force of personality.[4] Even in parliamentary systems, such as the Westminister systems of Great Britain, Canada, and Australia, many see a trend toward "presidentialized" prime ministerships.[5]

Given the problems that Japan faces, such as trade frictions with the United States and other countries and an aging society at home, many argue that it needs a stronger prime minister. Nakasone, who pushed for reforms to strengthen the prime minister's position, was explicit in his desire to make it more "presidential." Despite the recent reorganization of the Cabinet Secretariat, Gotōda Masaharu, chief cabinet secretary in the Nakasone administration, believes that the prime minister needs still more help.[6] On the face of it, especially given Japan's fragmented system, the argument for a stronger premiership sounds plausible.

But the solution to problems of governability does not necessarily lie in building up the head of government's position. In the United States, for instance, many scholars are convinced that increased presidential power is not the answer. According to Theodore Lowi, for example, because the demands now being made on the presidency are impossible for anyone to meet, perhaps, "nothing is enough" in terms of presidential power.[7] The solution for Lowi and others is to "build down" the presidency, in order to lessen the emphasis on the president's capacity to govern.[8]

Indeed, there are a number of good reasons not to rely on a strong head of government. First, heavy demands fall on the individual who occupies the office. The organization or system will be dependent on the skill, competence, and morals of a single person, which makes finding and electing the right individual critical. The question is what happens when the leader is deficient in one or more of these areas. Paul Light's analysis suggests that U.S. presidents tend to be more influential at the beginning of their term, when their level of personal expertise is at its lowest.[9] In the rush to advance programs before the honeymoon is over, presidents often have little time to consider the alternatives or the details.[10] Light, therefore, supports Richard Neustadt's contention that the presidency is no place for amateurs.[11] Then there must be concern over the abuse of power. In the United States, we have had the Vietnam War, the Watergate scandal, and more recently the Iran-Contra affair.[12] Given the number of recent corruption scandals in Japan, that problem could become even more acute if power becomes more centralized.

The second reason is that, in the long run, strong leadership can decrease the system's ability to adapt. Strong leadership generally implies providing more coherence to the management and policies of government; conversely, incoherence is usually associated with weak leadership. More coherence, however, may make the system less adaptive and more rigid. This loss of appreciation for contradictions and complexity can occur at all levels. Individuals are limited in their ability to face complexity, as John D. Steinbruner notes in his study of cognition. "Under complexity, the mind does not match the uncertain structure of the environment in which events might take a number of alternative courses. Rather, it imposes an image and works to preserve that image."[13] Inevitably, new leaders become old leaders who become less interested in change and more rigid in their thinking.[14] It also happens to those around the leader. Light's study of the White House suggests that, after the first year, domination by the internal staff "may be an inevitable outcome of the White House decision process."[15] Presidents, he finds, tend to remove internal conflict within their staff, making multiple advocacy impossible. Joel Aberbach and Bert Rockman argue that such centralization is harmful to the president and undermines the political system because they are deprived of valuable sources of expertise and advice that could help in keeping clear of trouble.[16]

Third, political systems must balance the values of direction with legitimacy. As Rockman argues, governing inevitably involves the balancing of desirable but contradictory goals: "Political systems need not only rudders but stabilizers. They need leadership, but if they are to remain constitutionalist they also need limits on leadership. They require direction, but also consent. And while there are demands for effectiveness, there also is insistence on accountability and responsiveness. These are the central paradoxes of constitutional government."[17] And, as Lowi notes, "problems in any institution are likely to grow in importance and danger whenever people lose their appreciation for the contradictions inherent in an institution and proceed to maximize one side of a contradiction at the expense of the other."[18] Strengthening the effectiveness of government by strengthening the prime ministership risks a loss of legitimacy of the political system as a whole.

The Prime Minister and the Japanese Political System

If strong leadership brings its own type of perils, then one must also be concerned about effectiveness and direction under weak leadership. Japan, however, is an interesting case in which a system has been able to function and adapt without a powerful head of government. John Campbell notes that Japan has been successful in achieving its two most important national goals, peace and prosperity, and suggests two possible explanations: either Japan has been lucky, or rational policy making and good coordination are not as important as we have been led to believe.[19]

Luck certainly has played a part. The Japanese government has benefited from a rather benevolent environment in the postwar years, including help from the United States in providing its security and an open world market for its goods.[20] But this explanation is insufficient. Some changes in the world environment have created problems for Japan; but it has adjusted remarkably well to two oil shocks, as well as the recent doubling in the value of the yen against the dollar. It has also weathered enormous social changes: urbanization, industrialization, postindustrialization. Even without a powerful head, the government has been able to adapt. Reactive leadership seems to work in Japan because of two main factors: first, the development of diverse ideas and proposals for change; and second, the capability to enact change.

Diversity of Proposals for Change

In the biological world, a species cannot survive a new environment unless it already has within it the genes that give at least some of its members the capability to meet the new environment; otherwise, natural selection does not work, for there is nothing to be selected. In a similar way, an organization has to maintain sufficient internal diversity to sense accurately the variety present in its environment. This is the concept of requisite variety.[21] As Karl Weick puts it, "No one is ever free to do something he can't think of. That's why requisite variety produces adaptation."[22]

Largely because of its fragmenation, the Japanese system displays considerable diversity, in both the LDP and the bureaucracy. First of all, as was noted earlier, the ruling LDP is not a particularly coherent or disciplined party.[23] It is a loose structure of factions and *zoku* that contribute to the diversity within the party. LDP factions, Daniel Okimoto argues, "have helped to infuse the party with a healthy dose of pluralism, which has helped the party escape the extremes of iron-handed rule or stultifying stagnancy."[24] Leaders of factions are in competition with one another for the presidency of the LDP and thus often promote policy alternatives or new ideas as a way of promoting themselves for the top post. They often present, for example, competing views on fiscal policy, with some advocating stimulating the economy while others emphasize fiscal conservatism, and this has allowed for flexibility on macroeconomic policies.[25] "Once the political need for policy change has become evident, factionalism in the LDP has actually hastened change by stimulating rivalries among competing policy proposals. Factions compete to introduce, put their stamp on, and claim credit for the compensation measures that help bring crisis to an end.[26]

Another factor is the catchall nature of the LDP. Through the *zoku* and the rank and file, the party represents, other than organized labor, virtually all aspects of Japanese society: "The coalition is so encompassing that the party can hardly be considered the puppet of any single interest group," so that the "interests of some sectors . . . are bound to clash with those of others.[27] In addition, Okimoto argues that the LDP's flexibility on policy is safeguarded by the multiseat constituency system, which tends to inhibit campaigning based on a clear delineation and differentiation of policy positions.[28] LDP legislators, therefore, are generally not locked into campaign promises that may constrain their flexibility. Certainly, one main reason why the party has been able to stay in power so long is its pragmatic, responsive "creative conservatism."[29]

The bureaucracy likewise has within it many competing interests. In an analysis of the influence of interest groups on policy making, Michio Muramatsu and Ellis Krauss found that interest groups of all kinds had frequent or regular contact with the middle levels of the bureaucracy, as well as some contact with the upper levels.[30] Their survey revealed that even groups relatively excluded from the LDP's coalition, such as labor and citizen/political groups, had a fair amount of access to the bureaucracy. Thus, ministries often become the voice for competing clientele groups, which "provide both stimulus and resources for conflict within and between ministries."[31] Throughout the civil service is an intense "territorial consciousness," punctuated by "gangster like struggles over jurisdiction.[32] During major international negotiations, the Foreign, International Trade and Industry, and Finance ministries are often in contention with one another. The three have different interests, and policy is a result of compromises among their positions.[33] Moreover, each of the individual ministries is active in advocating proposals, and together they initiate a high proportion of important policy change.[34]

The system contains within it, then, many inconsistencies, within both the LDP and the bureaucracy. People from below, particularly bureaucrats, are active in pushing up their ideas for change. Although these struggles over jurisdiction between subgovernments are often derided as part of the problem with Japan's political system, these diverse ideas nevertheless provide the system with the variety needed for adaptation. Hence the subgovernments play the important roles of agenda setting and policy formulation that are often considered elsewhere to be the role of the head of government. But in Japan, the prime minister does not need to set the agenda or to be intimately involved in the formulation of policy, because the system as a whole is capable of doing so.

Maintaining the requisite variety, however, is not without its difficulties. One is inefficiency. It requires considerable organizational slack, that is, a lot of resources and energy, to develop proposals and ideas for change that are ultimately not used. The other is inertia and the potential for paralysis. Simply having the ideas is not enough. Opportunities and the mechanisms to enact change must exist as well.

Capability of Enacting Change

The Japanese system has often been maligned as immobilist. Certainly, the government has on occasion suffered from paralysis. It has not, for example, responded very quickly to resolve trade frictions with the United States, and it was especially slow in responding to the crisis prompted by the Iraqi invasion and occupation of Kuwait in 1990–91. Indeed, the Japanese system may have particular difficulty in dealing with sudden, intense, and unforeseen crises. But the inertia of the process does not mean that the system, and particularly the prime minister, is unable to bring about change.

Even though the prime minister's reactive leadership is relatively passive by the standards of most other countries, his role in the process is not unimportant. Ironically, one of the factors that makes his role important is the inertia of the process. The prime minister has the main say in what is to be pushed and how hard. Without his active support, a controversial bill, one that requires keeping the LDP in line as well as dealing with the opposition parties, will have virtually no chance of passage. James March, in talking about organizational management, noted, "Management may be extremely important even though managers are indistinguishable. It is hard to tell the difference between two different light bulbs also; but if you take all the light bulbs away, it is difficult to read in the dark."[35] In a similar way, who the Japanese prime minister is may be relatively unimportant in terms of the agenda or proposals, but he nevertheless is important, even critical, in bringing about policy change in the enactment process. In particular, the system has both the opportunities and the mechanisms that enable the premier to promote the enactment of change.

Opportunities for change occur frequently. Although one of the main limitations on the prime minister is the insecurity of the position—Japan has had ten prime ministers in the past twenty years—the revolving prime ministership has also contributed to the flexibility of the political system. Even though the biennial elections for the LDP presidency rarely turn on matters of policy, they nevertheless force candidates to debate the issues of the time and present proposals for change. New prime ministers often bring new factional alignments that "tend to create opportunities for major changes in policy."[36] Examples include Tanaka and the recognition of China, Miki and his program for clean politics, and Takeshita and the introduction of the VAT.

Moreover, the prime minister has the mechanisms to effect change despite limited resources. By advancing an issue that has resonance in the political system, that is, one that already has considerable support, either latent or active, the prime minister has enough energy, if it is added to that of others, to have the measure enacted. In other cases, he may try to put his energies into an issue that does not resonate, and nothing happens. The prime minister, then, can be crucial in bringing about change in policy by taking a well-defined problem that is already on the agenda and giving it enough energy to reach a resolution. One main factor determining resonance is the LDP factions. Although they limit the premier's power, they also provide one of the main mechanisms for pulling the ruling party together. If the prime minister can obtain the support of most of the major factions in the party, then he has a good chance to bring about policy change.

Thus, while calls for a more powerful prime ministership have grown stronger, one must doubt the need for this. The system has the requisite variety for adaptation, so that there is no need for the prime minister to set the agenda or to be intimately involved in the formulation of policy. The system as a whole is capable of handling these tasks. A stronger head of government might in fact make the system more rigid and therefore less adaptable. At the same time, the system does not suffer from an unusual degree of paralysis. Because it has the mechanisms for the prime minister to provide the energy needed to push an issue through to enactment, the government has usually managed to cope with the changes in its environment. Japan's system is one that has been able to function and adapt without a powerful head of government.

Appendixes
Notes
Bibliography
Index

Appendix A

Lists of Prime Ministerial Issues

In developing the lists of prime ministerial issues in chapter 1 (see table 1.1), I relied on two main souces of data. The first is newspaper coverage. By counting the number of articles linking prime ministers and particular issues, one can develop a measure of their involvement. *Nihon Keizai Shimbun* (Japan's equivalent to the *Wall Street Journal*, hereafter referred to as *Nikkei*) has indices of its headlines in its monthly bound volume—none of the other major newspapers has this feature. But these indices did not start to appear until 1973 (the middle of Tanaka Kakuei's tenure); hence full coverage begins with the term of Miki Takeo.

The advantage of the *Nikkei* index is that it is current rather than retrospective and thus is more objective than, say, interviews with participants recalling events a number of years afterward. In addition, it provides a quantitative measure of involvement that allows the issues to be ranked in order. The index, however, may not reflect the participation of premiers accurately because the newspaper either does not cover some of his activities or has a bias in its coverage. It is possible that what a prime minister does is behind the scenes and therefore not picked up by journalists. Or newspaper coverage may be biased toward spectacular rather than lower-key issues. The index also has a bias against short-lived issues, and if a prime minister accomplishes a policy goal quickly, that issue will not make the list. One such example was Nakasone's goal to improve relations with Korea. After taking office, Nakasone decided to make an early trip to Korea and had the matter of aid to Korea settled by the time he got there.

The second source of data is the major policy statements the prime minister makes, which he does a number of times a year. First, he gives policy speeches before both houses of the Kokkai at the beginning of each regular legislative session (generally in late January) and most extraordinary ones (usually in the summer or fall, or both). These speeches, similar to the State of the Union addresses the U.S. president makes to Congress, outline the prime minister's major policy goals for the coming session and political year. Many of the issues mentioned actually have little to do with his goals since the speech is usually produced more by the bureaucracy than by the prime minister himself. The points most emphasized in a speech, however, can be taken as a formal statement of his main priorities. In addition to the National Assembly policy speeches, the prime minister has regular press conferences during which he outlines his views on policy and his objectives. He holds them after being formally selected president of the party and after being formally selected prime minister by the National Assembly. He also gives press conferences after the formation of each new cabinet and cabinet reshuffle (generally in November or December of each year), and during the New Year's holidays (one held at the Kantei and published in newspapers on January 1, and one held at the Ise Shrine on January 4 or 5).

The main advantage of this method over the *Nikkei* index is that it can be used for prime ministers before Miki. Also, distortion due to bias in newspaper coverage is less likely. Transcripts of the press conferences are published in all the major newspapers. Thus, I checked both the *Asahi Shimbun* and the *Yomiuri Shimbun* for coverage. One problem with this method is that issues may come up between statements. Most of the public statements occur during December and January. An issue that suddenly comes up in February is not counted very heavily. An example is the Lockheed scandal, which surfaced in February 1974, in Miki's second year in office. Even though it was the top issue on the *Nikkei* index, it is near the bottom of the index based on statements. Another problem with this index is that statements may not reflect involvement. Prime ministers may tend to say a lot about a particular issue but not do very much about it. This often seems to be the case with political ethics and party reform. Fukuda, Ōhira, and Suzuki listed party reform frequently in their public statements, but the *Nikkei* index suggests that their involvement was relatively low.

Despite some problems with both methods, there is substantial agreement between them in measuring the questions that have most concerned prime ministers (see tables in this appendix for detailed breakdowns of issues by prime minister and by method). The top issues on the *Nikkei* index (arbitrarily defined as those rating at least 50 on the 24-month normalized index) were, with one exception, also always on the public statements index. The notable exception, as I mentioned above, was the Lockheed scandal under Miki. Apart from this, the short list of top issues also makes subjective sense. The lists would not differ substantially on the basis of impressions of accounts of the respective administrations. There are some questions not listed that one might argue should be on the extended list of secondary issues (e.g., Miki and the ratification of the Nonproliferation Treaty; Fukuda and omnidirectional diplomacy; Ōhira and Japanese-style welfare and comprehensive security). But none of these can be plausibly argued to be of top priority.

TABLE A-1
Miki Takeo

Nikkei *Index*		Public *Statements*
	12/74–12/75	
Clean politics	68 (63)	Economy
Economy	61 (56)	Clean politics
Antimonopoly law	58 (54)	Welfare
China peace treaty	41 (38)	China peace treaty
Right to strike	36 (33)	Antimonopoly bill
Welfare/life cycle	25 (23)	Taiwan airline treaty
Revenue bills	22 (20)	
	01/76–12/76	
Lockheed scandal	133 (133)	Revenue bills
Clean politics	24 (24)	Economy
Revenue bills	16 (16)	Clean politics
Economy	14 (14)	China peace treaty
China peace treaty	11 (11)	Right to strike
		Lockheed scandal
		Antimonopoly bill
	Total	
Lockheed scandal	133 |133|	Economy
Clean politics	92 |92|	Clean politics
Economy	75 |75|	China peace treaty
Antimonopoly law	60 |60|	Antimonopoly law
China peace treaty	52 |52|	Welfare
Right to strike	39 |39|	
Revenue bills	38 |38|	
Welfare/life cycle	28 |28|	

Note: ( ) 12-month normalized value
      \| \| 24-month normalized value

TABLE A-2
Fukuda Takeo

Nikkei *Index*		*Public Statements*
	12/76–11/77	
Economy	138 (151)	Economy
Trade	61 (67)	Lockheed scandal
China peace treaty	47 (51)	Party reform
ASEAN/Fukuda Doctrine	47 (51)	China peace treaty
Administrative reform	32 (35)	Administrative reform
USSR fishing treaty	31 (34)	Education
Party reform	23 (25)	Territorial waters
Energy	17 (19)	Energy
Antimonopoly bill	11 (12)	South East Asia
	12/77–11/78	
China peace treaty	108 (108)	China peace treaty
Trade frictions	55 (55)	Economy
Economy	53 (53)	Trade frictions
Energy	26 (26)	Upper house reform
Narita Airport	12 (12)	Education
	Total	
Economy	191 |191|	Economy
China peace treaty	155 |155|	China peace treaty
Trade frictions	117 |117|	Trade frictions
ASEAN/Fukuda Doctrine	54 |54|	Lockheed scandal
Energy/Energy diplomacy	43 |43|	Party reform
Administrative reform	32 |32|	Education
USSR fishing treaty	31 |31|	
Party reform	29 |29|	

Note: ( ) 12-month normalized value
| | 24-month normalized value

TABLE A-3
Ōhira Masayoshi

Nikkei *Index*		*Public Statements*
12/78–10/79		
Fiscal reform	54 (59)	Fiscal reform
Trade frictions	35 (38)	Economy
Energy	35 (38)	Grumman scandal
Government procurements	15 (16)	Welfare
Economy	13 (14)	Energy
		Political ethics
11/79–5/80		
Defense expenditures	40 (69)	Fiscal reform
Iran	37 (63)	Energy
Fiscal/administrative reform	24 (41)	U.S. relations
Afghanistan	21 (36)	Political ethics
Economy	16 (27)	
Energy	14 (24)	
Trade frictions	11 (19)	
Political ethics	10 (17)	
Total		
Fiscal reform	78 |104|	Fiscal reform
Energy	49 |65|	Energy
Trade frictions	46 |61|	Political ethics
Defense	40 |53|	Economy
Iran	37 |49|	U.S. relations
Economy	29 |39|	
Afghanistan	21 |28|	
U.S. Relations	139 |185|[a]	

Note: ( ) 12-month normalized value
\| \| 24-month normalized value
  a. Number of *Nikkei* headlines involving Japan's relations to the United States over a number of different issues (e.g., defense, trade, Iran, Afghanistan).

TABLE A-4
Suzuki Zenkō

Nikkei *Index*		*Public Statements*
	7/80–11/81	
Administrative reform	98 (69)	Fiscal reform
Defense expenditures	84 (59)	Party reform
Foreign aid	63 (44)	Defense expenses
Trade frictions	60 (42)	Administrative reform
Fiscal reform	52 (37)	ASEAN/foreign aid
Economy	30 (21)	Economy
Political ethics/reform	26 (18)	
	12/81–11/82	
Fiscal reform	74 (74)	Fiscal reform
Trade frictions	59 (59)	Administrative reform
Administrative reform	47 (47)	Trade frictions
Textbook controversy	46 (46)	Defense expenditures
Defense expenditures	41 (41)	Economy
Economy	27 (27)	Aid to Korea
Foreign aid	18 (18)	
Aid to Korea	13 (13)	
	Total	
Administrative reform	145 |120|	Fiscal reform
Fiscal reform	126 |104|	Administrative reform
Defense expenditures	125 |103|	Defense expenditure
Trade frictions	119 |98|	Party reform
Foreign aid	81 |67|	Trade frictions
Economy	57 |47|	
Textbooks	46 |38|	
Ethics/party reform	26 |21|	

Note: ( ) 12-month normalized value
  | | 24-month normalized value

TABLE A-5
Nakasone Yasuhiro

Nikkei *Index*		*Public Statements*

11/82–12/83

Defense	86 (79)	Fiscal reform
Administrative reform	79 (73)	Administrative reform
Trade frictions	74 (68)	Defense
Economy	54 (50)	Trade frictions
Fiscal reform	34 (31)	Constitution reform
Education reform	16 (15)	

01/84–10/84

Education reform	58 (70)	Administrative reform
Trade frictions	51 (61)	Education reform
Administrative reform	41 (49)	Economy
Fiscal reform	27 (32)	Fiscal reform
Defense	23 (28)	Trade frictions
Kokkai representation	12 (14)	

11/84–12/85

Trade Frictions	180 (154)	Administrative reform
Defense	85 (73)	Trade frictions
Tax reform	53 (45)	Kokkai representation
Kokkai representation	42 (36)	Education reform
Administrative reform	36 (31)	Tax reform
Fiscal reform	17 (15)	Fiscal reform
Education reform	16 (15)	Defense

01/86–11/86

Economy	99 (108)	Administrative reform
Trade frictions	60 (65)	Tax reform
Tax reform	58 (63)	Kokkai representation
Administrative reform	30 (33)	Education reform
Defense	25 (27)	Economy
Kokkai representation	23 (25)	Trade frictions
Yasukuni Shrine	21 (23)	

12/86–10/87

Tax reform	122 (133)	Tax reform
Trade frictions	66 (72)	Defense
Economy	52 (57)	Kokkai representation
Defense	24 (26)	Agricultural reform
Administrative reform	8 (9)	Education reform

TABLE A-5 *continued*

Nikkei *Index*		Public *Statements*
Total (11/82–10/84)		
Administrative reform	130	Administrative reform
Trade frictions	125	Fiscal reform
Defense	109	Trade frictions
Education reform	74	Defense
Fiscal reform	61	Economy
Economy	60	Education reform
Total (01/84–12/85)		
Trade frictions	238	
Defense	108	
Administrative reform	77	
Education reform	74	
Kokkai representation	54	
Tax reform	53	
Fiscal reform	44	
Total (11/84–11/86)		
Trade frictions	240 |230|	Administrative reform
Tax reform	113 |108|	Kokkai representation
Defense	110 |106|	Tax reform
Economy	105 |101|	Trade frictions
Administrative reform	66 |63|	Education reform
Kokkai representation	65 |62|	Economy
Total (01/86–10/87)		
Tax reform	180 |196|	
Economy	155 |165|	
Trade frictions	126 |137|	
Defense	49 |53|	
Administrative reform	38 |41|	
Five Year Total		
Trade frictions	431 |172|	Administrative reform
Defense	243 |97|	Defense
Tax reform	234 |94|	Fiscal reform
Economy	217 |87|	Trade frictions
Administrative reform	194 |78|	Tax reform
Education reform	110 |44|	Education reform
Fiscal reform	89 |36|	Kokkai representation
Kokkai representation	80 |32|	
Yasukuni Shrine	52 |21|	

Note: ( ) 12-month normalized value
 \| \| 24-month normalized value

TABLE A-6
Takeshita Noboru

Nikkei *Index*		Public Statements
	11/87–12/88	
Tax reform	189 (162)	Tax reform
Trade frictions	94 (81)	Trade frictions
Foreign aid	52 (45)	Land reform
Land reform	36 (31)	Hometown revival
Recruit scandal	32 (27)	
Political reform	22 (19)	
	01/89–5/89	
Recruit scandal	77 (185)	Political reform
Tax reform	37 (89)	Hometown revival
Political reform	34 (82)	Tax reform
Foreign aid	12 (29)	
Trade frictions	10 (24)	
Hometown revival	6 (14)	
	Total	
Tax reform	226 |301|	Tax reform
Recruit scandal	109 |145|	Trade frictions
Trade frictions	104 |139|	Political reform
Foreign aid	64 |85|	Land reform
Political reform	56 |75|	Hometown revival
Land reform	39 |52|	
Hometown revival	17 |23|	

Note: ( ) 12-month normalized value
| | 24-month normalized value

Appendix B

The Constitution of Japan

Promulgated on November 3, 1946
Came into effect on May 3, 1947

We, the Japanese people, acting through our duly elected representatives in the National Assembly, determined that we shall secure for ourselves and our posterity the fruits of peaceful cooperation with all nations and the blessings of liberty throughout this land, and resolved that never again shall we be visited with the horrors of war through the action of government, do proclaim that sovereign power resides with the people and do firmly establish this Constitution. Government is a sacred trust of the people, the authority for which is derived from the people, the powers of which are exercised by the representatives of the people, and the benefits of which are enjoyed by the people. This is a universal principle of mankind upon which this Constitution is founded. We reject and revoke all constitutions, laws, ordinances, and rescripts in conflict herewith.

We, the Japanese people, desire peace for all time and are deeply conscious of the high ideals controlling human relationship, and we have determined to preserve our security and existence, trusting in the justice and faith of the peace-loving peoples of the world. We desire to occupy an honored place in an international society striving for the preservation of peace and the banishment of tyranny and slavery, oppression and intolerance for all time from the earth. We recognize that all peoples of the world have the right to live in peace, free from fear and want.

223

We believe that no nation is responsible to itself alone, but that laws of political morality are universal; and that obedience to such laws is incumbent upon all nations who would sustain their own sovereignty and justify their sovereign relationship with other nations.

We, the Japanese people, pledge our national honor to accomplish these high ideals and purposes with all our resources.

Chapter I: The Emperor

Art. 1   The Emperor shall be the symbol of the State and of the unity of the people, deriving his position from the will of the people, with whom resides sovereign power.

Art. 2   The Imperial Throne shall be dynastic and succeeded to in accordance with the Imperial House Law passed by the National Assembly.

Art. 3   The advice and approval of the Cabinet shall be required for all acts of the Emperor in matters of state, and the Cabinet shall be responsible therefor.

Art. 4   The Emperor shall perform only such acts in matters of state as are provided for in this Constitution and he shall not have powers related to government.

The Emperor may delegate the performance of his acts in matters of state as may be provided by law.

Art. 5   When, in accordance with the Imperial House Law, a Regency is established, the Regent shall perform his acts in matters of state in the Emperor's name. In this case, paragraph one of the preceding article will be applicable.

Art. 6   The Emperor shall appoint the Prime Minister as designated by the National Assembly.

The Emperor shall appoint the Chief Judge of the Supreme Court as designated by the Cabinet.

Art. 7   The Emperor, with the advice and approval of the Cabinet, shall perform the following acts in matters of state on behalf of the people:

Promulgation of amendments of the constitution, laws, cabinet orders and treaties.

Convocation of the National Assembly.

Dissolution of the House of Representatives.

Proclamation of general election of members of the National Assembly.

Attestation of the appointment and dismissal of Ministers of State and other officials as provided for by law, and of full powers and credentials of Ambassadors and Ministers.

Attestation of general and special amnesty, commutation of punishment, reprieve, and restoration of rights.

Awarding of honors.

Attestation of instruments of ratification and other diplomatic documents as provided for by law.

Receiving foreign ambassadors and ministers.

Performance of ceremonial functions.

Art. 8   No property can be given to, or received by, the Imperial House, nor can any gifts be made therefrom, without the authorization of the National Assembly.

Chapter II: Renunciation of War

Art. 9   Aspiring sincerely to an international peace based on justice and order, the Japanese people forever renounce war as a sovereign right of the nation and the threat or use of force as means of settling international disputes.

In order to accomplish the aim of the preceding paragraph, land, sea, and air forces, as well as other war potential, will never be maintained. The right of belligerency of the state will not be recognized.

Chapter III: Rights and Duties of the People

Art. 10   The conditions necessary for being a Japanese national shall be determined by law.

Art. 11   The people shall not be prevented from enjoying any of the fundamental human rights. These fundamental human rights guaranteed to the people by this Constitution shall be conferred upon the people of this and future generations as eternal and inviolate rights.

Art. 12   The freedoms and rights guaranteed to the people by this Constitution shall be maintained by the constant endeavor of the people, who shall refrain from any abuse of these freedoms and rights and shall always be responsible for utilizing them for the public welfare.

Art. 13   All of the people shall be respected as individuals. Their right to life, liberty, and the pursuit of happiness shall, to the extent that it does not interfere with the public welfare, be the supreme consideration in legislation and in other governmental affairs.

Art. 14   All of the people are equal under the law and there shall be no discrimination in political, economic or social relations because of race, creed, sex, social status or family origin.

        Peers and peerage shall not be recognized.

        No privilege shall accompany any award of honor, decoration, or any distinction, nor shall any such award be valid beyond the lifetime of the individual who now holds or hereafter may receive it.

Art. 15   The people have the inalienable right to choose their public officials and to dismiss them.

        All public officials are servants of the whole community and not of any group thereof.

        Universal adult suffrage is guaranteed with regard to the election of public officials.

        In all elections, secrecy of the ballot shall not be violated. A voter shall not be answerable, publicly or privately, for the choice he has made.

Art. 16   Every person shall have the right of peaceful petition for the redress of damage, for the removal of public officials, for the enactment, repeal or amendment of laws, ordinances or regulations and for other matters; nor shall any person be in any way discriminated against for sponsoring such a petition.

Art. 17　Every person may sue for redress as provided for by law from the State or a public entity, in case he has suffered damage through illegal act of any public official.

Art. 18　No person shall be held in bondage of any kind. Involuntary servitude, except as punishment for crime, is prohibited.

Art. 19　Freedom of thought and conscience shall not be violated.

Art. 20　Freedom of religion is guaranteed to all. No religious organization shall receive any privileges from the State, nor exercise any political authority.

No person shall be compelled to take part in any religious act, celebration, rite or practice.

The State and its organs shall refrain from religious education or any other religious activity.

Art. 21　Freedom of assembly and association as well as speech, press and all other forms of expression are guaranteed.

No censorship shall be maintained, nor shall the secrecy of any means or communication be violated.

Art. 22　Every person shall have freedom to choose and change his residence and to choose his occupation to the extent that it does not interfere with the public welfare.

Freedom of all persons to move to a foreign country and to divest themselves of their nationality shall be inviolate.

Art. 23　Academic freedom is guaranteed.

Art. 24　Marriage shall be based only on the mutual consent of both sexes and it shall be maintained through mutual cooperation with the equal rights of husband and wife as a basis.

With regard to choice of spouse, property rights, inheritance, choice of domicile, divorce and other matters pertaining to marriage and the family, laws shall be enacted from the standpoint of individual dignity and the essential equality of the sexes.

Art. 25   All people shall have the right to maintain the minimum standards of wholesome and cultured living.
In all spheres of life, the State shall use its endeavors for the promotion and extension of social welfare and security, and of public health.

Art. 26   All people shall have the right to receive an equal education correspondent to their ability, as provided for by law.
All people shall be obligated to have all boys and girls under their protection receive ordinary education as provided for by law. Such compulsory education shall be free.

Art. 27   All people shall have the right and the obligation to work.
Standards for wages, hours, rest and other working conditions shall be fixed by law.
Children shall not be exploited.

Art. 28   The right of workers to organize and to bargain and act collectively is guaranteed.

Art. 29   The right to own or to hold property is inviolable.
Property rights shall be defined by law, in conformity with the public welfare.
Private property may be taken for public use upon just compensation therefore.

Art. 30   The people shall be liable to taxation as provided by law.

Art. 31   No person shall be deprived of life or liberty, nor shall any other criminal penalty be imposed, except according to procedure established by law.

Art. 32   No person shall be denied the right of access to the courts.

Art. 33   No person shall be apprehended except upon warrant issued by a competent judicial officer which specifies the offense with which the person is charged, unless he is apprehended, the offense being committed.

Art. 34   No person shall be arrested or detained without being at once informed of the charges against him or without the immediate privilege of counsel; nor shall he be detained without adequate cause; and upon demand of any person such cause must be immediately shown in open court in his presence and the presence of his counsel.

Art. 35   The right of all persons to be secure in their homes, papers and effects against entries, searches and seizures shall not be impaired except upon warrant issued for adequate cause and particularly describing the place to be searched and things to be seized, or except as provided by for Article 33.

Each search or seizure shall be made upon separate warrant issued by a competent judicial officer.

Art. 36   The infliction of torture by any public officer and cruel punishments are absolutely forbidden.

Art. 37   In all criminal cases the accused shall enjoy the right to a speedy and public trial by an impartial tribunal.

He shall be permitted full opportunity to examine all witnesses, and he shall have the right of compulsory process for obtaining witnesses on his behalf at public expense.

At all times the accused shall have the assistance of competent counsel who shall, if the accused is unable to secure the same by his own efforts, be assigned to his use by the State.

Art. 38   No person shall be compelled to testify against himself.

Confession made under compulsion, torture or threat, or after prolonged arrest or detention shall not be admitted in evidence.

No person shall be convicted or punished in cases where the only proof against him is his own confession.

Art. 39   No person shall be held criminally liable for an act which was lawful at the time it was committed, or of which he has been acquitted, nor shall he be placed in double jeopardy.

Art. 40   Any person, in case he is acquitted after he has been arrested or detained, may sue the State for redress as provided by law.

Chapter IV: The National Assembly

Art. 41   The National Assembly shall be the highest organ of state power, and shall be the sole law-making organ of the State.

Art. 42   The National Assembly shall consist of two Houses, namely the House of Representatives and the House of Councillors.

Art. 43   Both Houses shall consist of elected members, representatives of all the people.
           The number of the members of each House shall be fixed by law.

Art. 44   The qualifications of members of both Houses and their electors shall be fixed by law. However, there shall be no discrimination because of race, creed, sex, social status, family origin, education, property, or income.

Art. 45   The term of office of members of the House of Representatives shall be four years. However, the term shall be terminated before the full term is up in case the House of Representatives is dissolved.

Art. 46   The term of office of the members of the House of Councillors shall be six years, and election for half the members shall take place every three years.

Art. 47   Electoral districts, method of voting, and other matters pertaining to the method of election of members of both Houses shall be fixed by law.

Art. 48   No person shall be permitted to be a member of both Houses simultaneously.

Art. 49   Members of both Houses shall receive appropriate annual payment from the national treasury in accordance with the law.

Art. 50   Except in cases provided by law, members of both Houses shall be exempt from apprehension while the National Assembly is in session, and any members apprehended before the opening of the session shall be freed during the term of the session upon demand of the House.

Art. 51   Members of both Houses shall not be held liable outside the House for speeches, debates or votes cast inside the House.

Art. 52   An ordinary session of the National Assembly shall be convoked once per year.

Art. 53   The Cabinet may determine to convoke extraordinary sessions of the National Assembly. When a quarter or more of the total members of either House makes the demand, the Cabinet must determine on such convocation.

Art. 54   When the House of Representatives is dissolved, there must be a general election of members of the House of Representatives within forty (40) days from the date of dissolution, and the National Assembly must be convoked within thirty (30) days from the date of the election.

When the House of Representatives is dissolved, the House of Councillors is closed at the same time. However, the Cabinet may in time of national emergency convoke the House of Councillors in emergency session.

Measures taken at such session as mentioned in the proviso of the preceding paragraph shall become null and void unless agreed to by the House of Representatives within a period of ten (10) days after the opening of the next session of the National Assembly.

Art. 55   Each House shall judge disputes related to qualifications of its members. However, in order to deny a seat to any member, it is necessary to pass a resolution by a majority of two-thirds or more of the members present.

Art. 56   Business cannot be transacted in either House unless one-third or more of its total membership is present.

All matters shall be decided, in each House, by a majority of those present, except as elsewhere provided in the Constitution, and in case of a tie, the presiding officer shall decide the issue.

Art. 57   Deliberation in each House shall be public. However, a secret meeting may be held where a majority of two-thirds or more of those members present passes a resolution therefor.

Each House shall keep a record of its proceedings. This record shall be published and given general circulation, excepting such parts of proceedings of secret session as may be deemed to require secrecy.

Upon demand of one-fifth or more of the members present, votes of the members on any matter shall be recorded in the minutes.

Art. 58   Each House shall select its own president and other officials.

Each House shall establish its rules pertaining to meetings, proceedings and internal discipline, and may punish members for disorderly conduct. However, in order to expel a member, a majority of two-thirds or more of those members present must pass a resolution thereon.

Art. 59   A bill becomes a law on passage by both Houses, except as otherwise provided by the Constitution.

A bill which is passed by the House of Representatives, and upon which the House of Councillors makes a decision different from that of the House of Representatives, becomes a law when passed a second time by the House of Representatives by a majority of two-thirds or more of the members present.

The provision of the preceding paragraph does not preclude the House of Representatives from calling for the meeting of a joint committee of both Houses, provided for by law.

Failure by the House of Councillors to take final action within sixty (60) days after receipt of a bill passed by the House of Representatives, time in recess excepted, may be determined by the House of Representatives to constitute a rejection of the said bill by the House of Councillors.

Art. 60   The budget must first be submitted to the House of Representatives.

Upon consideration of the budget, when the House of Councillors makes a decision different from that of the House of Representatives, and when no agreement can be reached even through a joint committee of both Houses, provided for by law, or in the case of failure by the House of Councillors to take final action within thirty (30) days, the period of recess excluded, after the receipt of the budget passed by the House of Representatives, the decision of the House of Representatives shall be the decision of the National Assembly.

Art. 61   The second paragraph of the preceding article applies also to the National Assembly approval required for the conclusion of treaties.

Art. 62   Each House may conduct investigations in relation to government, and may demand the presence and testimony of witnesses, and the production of records.

Art. 63   The Prime Minister and other Ministers of State may, at any time, appear in either House for the purpose of speaking on bills, regardless of whether they are members of the House or not. They must appear when their presence is required in order to give answers or explanations.

Art. 64   The National Assembly shall set up an impeachment court from among the members of both Houses for the purpose of trying those judges against whom removal proceedings have been instituted.

Matters relating to impeachment shall be provided by law.

Chapter V: The Cabinet

Art. 65   Executive power shall be vested in the Cabinet.

Art. 66   The Cabinet shall consist of the Prime Minister, who shall be its head, and other Ministers of State, as provided for by law.

The Prime Minister and other Ministers of State must be civilians.

The Cabinet, in the exercise of executive power, shall be collectively responsible to the National Assembly.

Art. 67   The Prime Minister shall be designated from among the members of the National Assembly by a resolution of the National Assembly. This designation shall precede all other business.

If the House of Representatives and the House of Councillors disagree and if no agreement can be reached even through a joint committee of both Houses, provided for by law, or the House of Councillors fails to make a designation within ten (10) days, exclusive of the period of recess, after the House of Representatives has made designation, the decision of the House of Representatives shall be the decision of the National Assembly.

Art. 68   The Prime Minister shall appoint the Ministers of State. However, a majority of their number must be chosen from among the members of the National Assembly.

The Prime Minister may remove the Ministers of State as he chooses.

Art. 69   If the House of Representatives passes a non-confidence resolution, or rejects a confidence resolution, the Cabinet shall resign en masse, unless the House of Representatives is dissolved within ten (10) days.

Art. 70   When there is a vacancy in the post of Prime Minister, or upon the first convocation of the National Assembly after a general election of members of the House of Representatives, the Cabinet shall resign en masse.

Art. 71   In the cases mentioned in the two preceding articles, the Cabinet shall continue its function until the time when a new Prime Minister is appointed.

Art. 72   The Prime Minister, representing the Cabinet, submits bills, reports on general national affairs and foreign relations to the National Assembly and exercises control and supervision over various administrative branches.

Art. 73   The Cabinet, in addition to other general administrative functions, shall perform the following functions:
Administer the law faithfully; conduct affairs of state.
Manage foreign affairs.
Conclude treaties. However, it shall obtain prior or, depending on circumstances, subsequent approval of the National Assembly.
Administer the civil service, in accordance with standards established by law.
Prepare the budget, and present it to the National Assembly.
Enact cabinet order to execute the provisions of this Constitution and of the law. However, it cannot include penal provisions in such cabinet orders unless authorized by such law.
Decide on general amnesty, special amnesty, commutation of punishment, reprieve, and restoration of rights.

Art. 74   All laws and cabinet orders shall be signed by the competent Minister of State and countersigned by the Prime Minister.

Art. 75   The Ministers of State, during their tenure in office, shall not be subject to legal action without the consent of the Prime Minister. However, the right to take that action is not impaired hereby.

Chapter VI: Judiciary

Art. 76   The whole judicial power is vested in a Supreme Court and in such inferior courts as are established by law.

No extraordinary tribunal shall be established, nor shall any organ or agency of the Executive be given final judicial power.

All judges shall be independent in the exercise of their conscience and shall be bound only by this Constitution and the laws.

Art. 77   The Supreme Court is vested with the rule-making power under which it determines the rules of procedure and of practice, and of matters relating to attorneys, the internal discipline of the courts and the administration of judicial affairs.

Public procurators shall be subject to the rule-making power of the Supreme Court.

The Supreme Court may delegate the power to make rules for inferior courts to such courts.

Art. 78   Judges shall not be removed except by public impeachment unless judicially declared mentally or physically incompetent to perform official duties. No disciplinary action against judges shall be administered by any executive organ or agency.

Art. 79   The Supreme Court shall consist of a Chief Judge and such number of judges as may be determined by law; all such judges excepting the Chief Judge shall be appointed by the Cabinet.

The appointment of the judges of the Supreme Court shall be reviewed by the people at the first general election of members of the House of Representatives following their appointment, and shall be reviewed again at the first general election of members of the House of Representatives after a lapse of ten (10) years, and in the same manner thereafter.

In cases mentioned in the foregoing paragraph, when the majority of the votes favors the dismissal of a judge, he shall be dismissed.

Matters pertaining to review shall be prescribed by law.

The judges of the Supreme Court shall be retired upon the attainment of the age as fixed by law.

All such judges shall receive, at regular stated intervals, adequate compensation which shall not be decreased during their terms in office.

Art. 80 The judges of the inferior courts shall be appointed by the Cabinet from a list of persons nominated by the Supreme Court. All such judges shall hold office for a term of ten (10) years with privilege of reappointment, provided that they shall be retired upon the attainment of the age as fixed by law.

The judges of the inferior court shall receive, at regular stated intervals, adequate compensation which shall not be decreased during their terms of office.

Art. 81 The Supreme Court is the court of last resort with power to determine the constitutionality of any law, order, regulation or official act.

Art. 82 Trials shall be conducted and judgment declared publicly.

Where a court unanimously determines publicity to be dangerous to public order and morals, a trial may be conducted privately, but trials of political offenses, offenses involving the press or cases wherein the rights of people as guaranteed in Chapter III of this Constitution are in question shall always be conducted publicly.

Chapter VII: Finance

Art. 83 The power to administer national finances shall be exercised as the National Assembly shall determine.

Art. 84 No new taxes shall be imposed or existing one modified except by law or under such conditions as the law may prescribe.

Art. 85 No money shall be expended, nor shall the State obligate itself, except as authorized by the National Assembly.

Art. 86   The Cabinet shall prepare and submit to the National Assembly for its consideration and decision a budget for each fiscal year.

Art. 87   In order to provide for unforeseen deficiencies in the budget, a reserve fund may be authorized by the National Assembly to be expended upon the responsibility of the Cabinet.

The Cabinet must get subsequent approval of the National Assembly for all payments from the reserve fund.

Art. 88   All property of the Imperial Household shall belong to the State. All expenses of the Imperial Household shall be appropriated by the National Assembly in the budget.

Art. 89   No public money or other property shall be expended or appropriated for the use, benefit or maintenance of any religious institution or association, or for any charitable, educational or benevolent enterprises not under the control of public authority.

Art. 90   Final accounts of the expenditures and revenues of the State shall be audited annually by a Board of Audit and submitted by the Cabinet to the National Assembly, together with the statement of audit, during the fiscal year immediately following the period covered.

The organization and competency of the Board of Audit shall be determined by law.

Art. 91   At regular intervals and at least annually the Cabinet shall report to the National Assembly and the people on the state of national finances.

Chapter VIII: Local Self-Government

Art. 92   Regulations concerning organization and operations of local public entities shall be fixed by law in accordance with the principle of local autonomy.

Art. 93   The local public entities shall establish assemblies as their deliberative organs, in accordance with the law.

The chief executive officers of all local public entities, the members of their assemblies, and such other local officials as may be determined by law shall be elected by direct popular vote within their several communities.

Art. 94 Local public entities shall have the right to manage their property, affairs and administration and to enact their own regulations within the law.

Art. 95 A special law, applicable only to one local public entity, cannot be enacted by the National Assembly without the consent of the majority of the voters of the local public entity concerned, obtained in accordance with law.

Chapter IX: Amendments

Art. 96 Amendments to this Constitution shall be initiated by the National Assembly, through a concurring vote of two-thirds or more of all the members of each House and shall thereupon be submitted to the people for ratification, which shall require the affirmative vote of a majority of all votes cast thereupon, at a special referendum or at such election as the National Assembly shall specify.

Amendment when so ratified shall immediately be promulgated by the Emperor in the name of the people, as an integral part of this Constitution.

Chapter X: Supreme Law

Art. 97 The fundamental human rights by this Constitution guaranteed to the people of Japan are fruits of the age-old struggle of man to be free; they have survived the many exacting tests for durability and are conferred upon this and future generations in trust, to be held for all time inviolate.

Art. 98 This Constitution shall be the supreme law of the nation and no law, ordinance, imperial rescript or other act of government, or part thereof, contrary to the provisions hereof shall have legal force or validity.

The treaties concluded by Japan and established laws of nations shall be faithfully observed.

Art. 99   The Emperor or the Regent as well as Ministers of State, members of the National Assembly, judges, and all other public officials have the obligation to respect and uphold this Constitution.

Chapter XI: Supplementary Provisions

Art. 100   This Constitution shall be enforced as from the day when

the period of six months will have elapsed counting from the day of its promulgation.

The enactment of laws necessary for the enforcement of this Constitution, the election of members of the House of Councillors and the procedure for the convocation of the National Assembly and other preparatory procedures necessary for the enforcement of this Constitution may be executed before the day prescribed in the preceding paragraph.

Art. 101   If the House of Councillors is not constituted before the effective date of this Constitution, the House of Representatives shall function as the National Assembly until such time as the House of Councillors may be constituted.

Art. 102   The term of office for half the members of the House of Councillors serving in the first term under this Constitution shall be three years. Members falling under this category shall be determined in accordance with the law.

Art. 103   The Ministers of State, members of the House of Representatives and judges in office on the effective date of this Constitution, and all other public officials who occupy positions corresponding to such positions as are recognized by this Constitution shall not forfeit their positions automatically on account of the enforcement of this Constitution unless otherwise specified by law. When, however, successors are elected or appointed under the provisions of this Constitution, they shall forfeit their position as a matter of course.

Appendix C

Data on Potential Prime Ministers

TABLE C-1
First Cabinet Post

	Age	Term	Post
Mitsuzuka Faction			
Mitsuzuka Hiroshi	58	5	MOT
Abe Shintarō	50	6	MAFF[a]
Katō Mutsuki	56	6	NLA
Mori Yoshirō	46	6	MOE
Miyazawa Faction			
Katō Kōichi	45	5	DA
Kawara Tsutomu	50	6	DA
Kōno Yōhei	48	7	STA
Watanabe Faction			
Fujinami Takao	46	5	MOL
Watanabe Michio	53	5	MHW
Yamaguchi Toshio	44	7	MOL
Takeshita Faction			
Hashimoto Ryūtarō	41	5	MHW
Hata Tsutomu	50	6	MAFF
Kajiyama Seiroku	61	6	MHA
Obuchi Keizō	42	6	PMO
Ozawa Ichirō	43	6	MHA
Watanabe Kōzō	51	6	MHW
Mean	45	5.8[b]	
Range	41–61	5–7[b]	

Note: DA Director general of Defense Agency
MAFF Minister of agriculture
MHA Minister of home affairs
MHW Minister of health and welfare
MOE Minister of Education
MOL Minister of labor
MOT Minister of transportation
NLA Director general of National Land Agency
PMO Director general of PMO
STA Director general of Science and Technology Agency

a. Abe headed the faction until his death in 1991.

b. Miyazawa was a second-term member of the upper house when he was first appointed to a cabinet post and is not included in the calculations for the mean and range.

TABLE C-2
National Assembly Experience

	1st Year in Kokkai	Age then	Years in Kokkai[a]	Terms in Kokkai[a]
Mitsuzuka Faction				
Mitsuzuka Hiroshi	1972	45	20	6
Abe Shintarō	1958	34	30	10[b]
Katō Mutsuki	1972	33	20	8
Mori Yoshirō	1969	32	23	7
Miyazawa Faction				
Katō Kōichi	1972	35	20	6
Kawara Tsutomu	1972	35	20	6
Kōno Yōhei	1967	30	25	8
Watanabe Faction				
Fujinami Takao	1967	34	25	8
Watanabe Michio	1963	40	29	10
Yamaguchi Toshio	1967	26	25	8
Takeshita Faction				
Hashimoto Ryūtarō	1963	26	29	9
Hata Tsutomu	1969	33	23	7
Kajiyama Seiroku	1969	42	19	6
Obuchi Keizō	1963	26	29	9
Ozawa Ichirō	1969	27	23	7
Watanabe Kōzō	1969	37	23	7
Mean Age		34		
Range		26–45		

a. Years and number of terms in National Assembly as of 1992.

b. Abe lost one election, which is why he is one term and three years junior to others elected in 1958 (e.g., Takeshita). Abe headed the faction until his death in 1991.

TABLE C-3
District Type

	District	Type[a]
Mitsuzuka Faction		
Mitsuzuka Hiroshi	Miyagi #1	Type 3: semiurban
Abe Shintarō	Yamaguchi #1	Type 4: medium[b]
Katō Mutsuki	Okayama #1	Type 5: semirural
Mori Yoshirō	Ishikawa #1	Type 4: medium
Miyazawa Faction		
Katō Kōichi	Yamagata #2	Type 7: most rural
Kawara Tsutomu	Ishikawa #2	Type 6: rural
Kōno Yōhei	Kanagawa #5	Type 3: semiurban
Watanabe Faction		
Watanabe Michio	Tochigi #1	Type 6: rural
Fujinami Takao	Mie #2	Type 6: rural
Yamaguchi Toshio	Saitama #2	Type 3: semiurban
Takeshita Faction		
Hashimoto Ryūtarō	Okayama #2	Type 4: medium
Hata Tsutomu	Nagano #2	Type 6: rural
Kajiyama Seiroku	Ibaragi #2	Type 4: medium
Obuchi Keizō	Gunma #3	Type 6: rural
Ozawa Ichirō	Iwate #2	Type 7: most rural
Watanabe Kōzō	Fukushima #2	Type 6: rural

a. Election district types are based on Kobayashi Yoshiaki's analysis in his *Tenkanki no Seiji Ishiki* (Tokyo: Keiō Tsūshin, 1985). He categorizes election districts on a scale from 1 to 7. Type 1 districts are most urban and type 7 are most rural, as of 1980.
b. Abe headed the faction until his death in 1991.

TABLE C-4
Career Background

	Position Before Entering National Assembly
Mitsuzuka Faction	
Mitsuzuka Hiroshi	Kokkai secretary, prefectural assembly-man
Abe Shintarō	Journalist (Kishi's son-in-law)[a]
Katō Mutsuki	Kokkai secretary
Mori Yoshirō	Kokkai secretary
Miyazawa Faction	
Katō Kōichi	Diplomat (2nd generation)
Kawara Tsutomu	Kokkai secretary
Kōno Yōhei	Radio Kantō manager (2nd generation)
Takeshita Faction	
Hashimoto Ryūtarō	Kokkai secretary (2nd generation)
Hata Tsutomu	Salaried worker (2nd generation)
Kajiyama Seiroku	Prefectural assembly chairman
Obuchi Keizō	Graduate student (2nd generation)
Ozawa Ichirō	Kokkai secretary (2nd generation)
Watanabe Kōzō	Prefectural assemblyman
Watanabe Faction	
Watanabe Michio	Prefectural assemblyman
Fujinami Takao	Prefectural assemblyman
Yamaguchi Toshio	Kokkai secretary (2nd generation)

a. Abe headed the faction until his death in 1991.

Appendix D

Results of Elections for President of the LDP

Date	Winner	Method of Selection
4/5/56	Hatoyama Ichirō	Uncontested election

The LDP was formed in November 1955 through the merger of the Democratic party, headed by Hatoyama, and the Liberal party, headed by Ogata Taketora. The two were expected to be the main contenders for the presidency of the new party, but Ogata died unexpectedly and no other candidate emerged to challenge Hatoyama. Hatoyama won on the first ballot (Hatoyama 394; Other 19; Invalid 76). Still, there were 95 electors who decided not to vote for Hatoyama and either cast their ballots for other members or left them blank.

Date	Winner	Method of Selection
12/14/56	Ishibashi Tanzan	Election

When Hatoyama resigned, there were three main contenders to succeed him, Ishibashi, Ishii Mitsujirō, and Kishi Nobusuke. Although Kishi had the most support on the first ballot, he did not have a majority (Kishi 223; Ishibashi 151; Ishii 137). In the runoff, Ishii threw his support to Ishibashi, who was able to defeat Kishi by seven votes (Ishibashi 258; Kishi 251; Invalid 1).

246

Date	Winner	Method of Selection
3/21/57	Kishi Nobusuke	Uncontested election

Soon after becoming prime minister, Ishibashi became seriously ill, and he stepped down in February 1957. Kishi had been serving as acting prime minister during Ishibashi's illness and was immediately named the new prime minister. At the special party convention in March, he was elected president (Kishi 471; Other 4; Invalid 1).

Date	Winner	Method of Selection
1/24/59	Kishi Nobusuke	Election

Kishi was under fire within the party because of his attempt to pass a controversial bill to strengthen the power of the police, but he managed to keep most of the party behind him by promising to pass the presidency to Ōno Bamboku when his next term expired. He won easily on the first ballot (Kishi 320; Matsumura Kenzō 166; Other 5; Invalid 1).

Date	Winner	Method of Selection
7/14/60	Ikeda Hayato	Election

Kishi resigned following the Ampo crisis. There were five main contenders: Ikeda, Ōno, Ishii, Matsumura, and Fujiyama Aiichirō. The party was divided into two camps, the factions headed by career politicians (i.e., Ōno, Ishii, Kōno, Matsumura-Miki, and Ishii) and the ones headed by former bureaucrats (i.e., Kishi, Satō, and Ikeda). In the election for Kishi's successor, the politicians' camp supported Ishii and the bureaucrats' camp supported Ikeda. Ikeda placed first on the first ballot but did not receive a majority (Ikeda 246; Ishii 196; Fujiyama 49; Other 7; Invalid 3). In the runoff, Ikeda won with the support of the Fujiyama faction (Ikeda 302; Ishii 194; Invalid 5).

Date	Winner	Method of Selection
7/14/62	Ikeda Hayato	Uncontested election

Ikeda won on the first ballot with minor opposition (Ikeda, 391; Other 37; Invalid 38).

Date	Winner	Method of Selection
7/10/64	Ikeda Hayato	Election

Satō, with support from the Kishi and Ishii factions, tried to prevent Ikeda from winning a third term as party president. Ikeda was able to overcome the challenge from his former allies with support from a number of the factions that opposed him in 1960, namely those of Kōno, Ōno, and Miki, and won on the first ballot (Ikeda 242; Satō 160; Fujiyama 72; Other 1; Invalid 3).

Date	Winner	Method of Selection
12/1/64	Satō Eisaku	Negotiations

Ikeda resigned from office because of illness. The party leadership decided to select the successor through negotiations. The major candidates were Satō, Fujiyama, and Kōno Ichirō. Vice President Kawashima Shōjirō and Secretary General Miki Takeo, on the basis of discussions with other party leaders, recommended that Satō, who had been Ikeda's main challenger in the previous election, become the new LDP president.

Date	Winner	Method of Selection
12/1/66	Satō Eisaku	Election

Satō faced no major challengers because most of them had died, Ōno in May 1964, Kōno in July 1965, and Ikeda in August 1965. Satō won on the first ballot (Satō 289; Fujiyama 94; Maeo 47; Other 25; Invalid 9).

Date	Winner	Method of Selection
11/27/68	Satō Eisaku	Election

Satō won on the first ballot (Satō 249; Miki 107; Maeo 95; Fujiyama 1; Invalid 2). Because Maeo Shigesaburō did unexpectedly poorly, he was forced to step down as leader of his faction and was replaced by Ōhira.

Date	Winner	Method of Selection
10/29/70	Satō Eisaku	Election

Satō was able to win a fourth term as party president by playing Fukuda Takeo and Tanaka Kakuei off against each other. Neither wanted the other to become president first, so both agreed to support Satō (Satō 353; Miki 111; Other 3; Invalid 14).

Date	Winner	Method of Selection
7/5/72	Tanaka Kakuei	Election

Satō resigned before serving his full two-year term largely because of the Nixon "shocks." The two main contenders were Tanaka and Fukuda. Satō's preferred successor was Fukuda, but because Tanaka had widespread support within the Satō faction, Satō was forced to remain neutral. In the first round, Tanaka received the support of the Fukada, Ishii, Mizuta, Nakasone, and Shiina factions and placed first (Tanaka 156; Fukuda 150; Ōhira 101; Miki 69). Tanaka was able to win the runoff with the addition support of the Ōhira and Miki factions (Tanaka 282; Fukuda 190; Invalid 4). Tanaka was rumored to have spent more than 10 billion yen in his campaign to win the election.

Date	Winner	Method of Selection
12/4/74	Miki Takeo	Negotiations

Tanaka announced his resignation on November 26, 1974. The candidates to succeed him were Fukuda, Ōhira, Miki, and Nakasone, with

Fukuda and Ōhira considered the main contenders. There was no agreement within the party over who should select Tanaka's replacement or
how. The decision was left to Vice President Shiina Etsusaburō, who
picked Miki.

Date	Winner	Method of Selection
12/23/76	Fukuda Takeo	Negotiations

Miki gradually lost the support of the other factions for pursuing
policies opposed by the party and for aggressively investigating the
Lockheed scandal. After the lower house election in December 1976, Miki
announced his resignation to take responsibility for the poor showing.
Through negotiations, Fukuda was chosen to succeed.

Date	Winner	Method of Selection
11/27/78	Ōhira Masayoshi	Primary election

Fukuda was able to introduce a new system of selecting the LDP
president that involved a primary election by all party members to
choose two candidates, and then a runoff election by LDP members of the
Kokkai. Fukuda had been expected to place first in the primary, but Ōhira
pulled off an upset with Tanaka's help (Ōhira 748; Fukuda 638; Nakasone
93; Kōmoto 46). Fukuda then conceded the election to Ōhira.

Date	Winner	Method of Selection
11/6/79	Ōhira Masayoshi	National Assembly vote

Because of the LDP's poor showing in the lower house election,
Fukuda and others demanded that Ōhira take responsibility and resign.
When Ōhira refused, the party split in the National Assembly vote for the
prime minister. No one received a majority on the first ballot in both
houses of the Kokkai, although Ōhira received the most votes (Ōhira had
the support of the New Liberal Club in the lower house). In the runoff,
Ōhira won a majority of the valid votes (the opposition parties for the

most part purposely cast invalid ballots) and was elected prime minister (House of Representatives, first round: Ōhira (LDP) 135; Fukuda (LDP) 125; Asukata (JSP) 107; Takeiri (Kōmeitō) 58; Miyamoto (JCP) 41; Sasaki (DSP) 36; Den (SDL) 2; Invalid 7; second round: Ōhira 138; Fukuda 121; Invalid 251; Blank 1. House of Councillors, first round: Ōhira 78; Asukata 51; Fukuda 38; Takeiri 27; Miyamoto 16; Sasaki 10; Den 3; Kōno (New Liberal Club) 2; Blank 10; second round; Ōhira 97; Asukata 52; Invalid 1; Blank 87).

Date	Winner	Method of Selection
7/15/80	Suzuki Zenkō	Negotiations

Ōhira died suddenly on June 12, 1980 during the campaign for the double election for both houses of the National Assembly. After that election, Vice President Nishimura Eiichi was delegated to select the new president. Among the candidates considered were Miyazawa, Suzuki, Nakasone, and Kōmoto Toshio. Tanaka suggested that an Ōhira faction member be selected to take over the remainder of Ōhira's term, so the field was narrowed to his two lieutenants, Miyazawa and Suzuki. Although Miyazawa was better known to the public and abroad, Suzuki became president on the basis of his party experience and the support of the Ōhira faction.

Date	Winner	Method of Selection
11/27/80	Suzuki Zenkō	No contest

Suzuki, after finishing the remainder of Ōhira's term, faced no opposition in the election and was given a two-year term.

Date	Winner	Method of Selection
11/25/82	Nakasone Yasuhiro	Primary election

Suzuki most likely would have been able to win another two-year term, but he decided to pull out of the race. There were four official candidates to succeed him: Nakasone, Kōmoto, Abe Shintarō, and Nakagawa Ichirō. Party leaders at first tried negotiations to select a consensus candidate. Fukuda proposed a compromise in which he would become party president but Nakasone would become prime minister. Nakasone turned this down, and when there was no consensus, the party went ahead with a primary election. The party rules had been changed since the last primary. Under the new system, the top three vote-getters would be eligible for the runoff election by National Assembly members. Nakasone, with the support of the Tanaka and Suzuki factions, was able to garner a majority of the votes in the primary (Nakasone 559,673 [57.6 percent]; Kōmoto 265,078 [27.2]; Abe 80,443 [8.2]; Nakagawa 66,041] [6.8]). Kōmoto and Abe, who both were eligible for the runoff, conceded the election to Nakasone.

Date	Winner	Method of Selection
10/31/84	Nakasone Yasuhiro	No contest

Nikaidō Susumu briefly challenged Nakasone, but pulled out of the race before the party convention.

Date	Winner	Method of Selection
10/31/86	Nakasone Yasuhiro	No contest

The party rules had stipulated that presidents could not serve more than two consecutive terms. But the rules were amended after the overwhelming LDP victory in the 1986 double election, and Nakasone was given a one-year extension to his term.

Date	Winner	Method of Selection
10/31/87	Takeshita Noboru	Nakasone's recommendation

There were three formal candidates to succeed Nakasone: Takeshita, Abe, and Miyazawa. Nikaidō Susumu also wanted to run but was unable to gather the fifty signatures required to file for candidacy. Takeshita and

Abe, along with Kōmoto Toshio, tried to form an alliance to determine the next president, but it fell apart when neither Takeshita nor Abe was willing to drop out of the race and support the other. The three candidates then decided to let Nakasone make the choice, and his choice was Takeshita.

Date	Winner	Method of Selection
6/2/89	Uno Sōsuke	Negotiations

Takeshita announced his intention to resign as party president on April 25 because of his involvement in the Recruit scandal. Itō Masayoshi was offered the post but turned it down because of his suspicion that the LDP leaders were not really interested in political reform. Takeshita then obtained a consensus for Uno, who was then foreign minister. Some of the LDP members, including Fukuda and Suzuki, were absent from the convention in protest of the choice. Also, many junior LDP members tried to propose Yamashita Ganri as a formal candidate, but the majority voted against the proposition.

Date	Winner	Method of Selection
8/8/89	Kaifu Toshiki	Election

Uno resigned after the LDP lost its majority in the upper house election. The party decided to have an "open election" following criticism of the way Uno was selected. The restrictions on formal candidacy were eased somewhat; instead of fifty signatures, the number needed to file for candidacy was reduced, for this election only, to twenty. At first, the electors were limited to the 408 LDP members of the Kokkai, but when local politicians protested, 47 local delegates, one from each prefecture (usually the secretary general of the prefectural party organization), were also allowed to vote. Kaifu was elected on the first ballot (Kaifu, 279; Hayashi Yoshirō, 120; Ishihara Shintarō, 48; Invalid, 4), receiving the support of four of the five factions (Takeshita, Abe, Nakasone, and Kōmoto). Hayashi received the support of the Miyazawa and Nikaidō blocs. Ishihara received support from a group of younger LDP members.

Date	Winner	Method of Selection
10/27/91	Miyazawa Kiichi	Election

Kaifu decided not to run for reelection after the Takeshita faction abruptly withdrew its endorsement of his candidacy in early October. It tried to field its own candidate, but it could not turn to either of its two leading contenders, Ozawa Ichirō and Hashimoto Ryūtarō. Ozawa resisted requests to run because of both his health—he had suffered a mild heart attack earlier in the year—and his lack of government experience. Hashimoto, as finance minister, was tainted by the securities scandals. The faction then decided to support Miyazawa Kiichi over the other two declared candidates, Mitsuzuka Hiroshi and Watanabe Michio. With the support of the Miyazawa, Takeshita, and Kōmoto blocs, Miyazawa easily won the three-way race on the first ballot (Miyazawa, 285; Watanabe, 120; Mitsuzuka, 87).

Sources: Nathaniel B. Thayer, *How the Conservatives Rule Japan* (Princeton, N.J.: Princeton University Press, 1969); Uchida Kenzō, *Habatsu* (Tokyo: Kōdansha, 1983); Iijima Kiyoshi, Miyazaka Yoshimasa, and Watanabe Tsuneo, eds., *Seiji no Jōshiki Daihyakka* (Tokyo: Kōdansha, 1983); Itō Masaya, *Saisō Tori* (Tokyo: PHP Kenkyūjo, 1986); Tanaka Zen'ichirō, *Jimintō no Doramatsurugī* (Tokyo: Tokyo Daigaku Shuppankai, 1987); Yomiuri Research Institute, "The Making of an LDP President," *Japan Echo* 14 (1987): 77–84; *Asahi Shimbun*; *Japan Times*.

Appendix E

Summary of Changes in Rules Governing Elections for President of the LDP

November 1955 The president is selected by a vote of all LDP National Assembly members and two delegates from each of the prefectural federations. The president's term is two years.

January 1962 The number of delegates from each of the prefectural federations who are eligible to vote is reduced from two to one.

January 1971 Candidates for the presidency must receive the endorsement of at least ten LDP members of the Kokkai. Incumbent presidents are required to gain the consent of two-thirds of the LDP members of the Kokkai in order to be elected for more than two consecutive terms. The two-term restriction was instituted because of dissatisfaction among many in the party with Satō's reelection to a fourth term. The president's term was extended from two to three years with the expectation that the longer term would reduce the constant turmoil in the party over the presidency.

January 1977 The president's term is reduced to two years. The change was rumored to be the result of a secret deal between Fukuda and Ōhira in which Fukuda was to pass the presidency on to Ōhira at the end of his term.

April 1977 The LDP introduces a two-stage selection process consisting of a primary election open to all party members and a presidential election by National Assembly party members only. The primary election system was originally one of Miki's proposals to increase grassroots support for the party and to reduce factional influence in presidential elections. The primary election is based on prefectural results. The top two finishers in each prefecture receive points based on the number of ballots cast and the relative number of votes that the two candidates receive. The two who win the most points overall are eligible to run in the presidential election. The number of endorsements from LDP National Assembly members required for presidential candidates is raised from ten to twenty.

January 1980   The LDP abolishes the point system used in the primary election. Instead, the two candidates with the largest number of absolute votes in the primary election are eligible to run in the presidential election. Eligible to vote in the primary election are party members and party supporters who have paid two years' dues. Presidents are not eligible to serve more than two consecutive terms.

September 1986   Incumbent presidents who have served two consecutive terms can be given a one year nonrenewable extension if they receive the consent of two-thirds of the LDP members of the Kokkai. The change was made to reward Nakasone for the overwhelming LDP victory in the 1986 double election.

August 1989   Because of the debacle with Uno as prime minister, there were calls to have an open election instead of the back-room negotiations that led to Uno's appointment. To ensure that a number of candidates would actually run, the number of required endorsements was reduced, for this one time, to twenty LDP Kokkai members. In addition, the local politicians demanded a voice, so one delegate from each prefectural federation forty-seven altogether) was allowed to vote in the presidential election.

September 1989   The minimum number of required endorsements was reduced from fifty to thirty LDP members of the National Assembly. The primary election was eliminated, but the prefectural party organizations were given a say. Each LDP member of the Kokkai continued to have one vote in the presidential election, but in addition each prefectural party federation was given one to four votes depending on the number of ballots cast by party members and party supporters who had paid dues for the past three consecutive years. The top finisher in the balloting in each prefecture receives all of that prefecture's votes. If no candidate receives a majority of the vote, the two who win the most votes face each other in a run-off election in which only LDP members of the National Assembly vote.

Sources: Nathaniel B. Thayer, *How the Conservatives Rule Japan* (Princeton, N.J.: Princeton University Press, 1969); Tanaka Zen'ichirō, *Jimintō no Doramatsurugī* (Tokyo: Tokyo Daigaku Shuppankai, 1987); Yomiuri Research Institute, "The Making of an LDP President," *Japan Echo* 14 (1987): 77–84; *Asahi Shimbun*, October 4, 1989.

Notes

Preface

1. Hugh Heclo, *Studying the Presidency: A Report to the Ford Foundation* (New York: Ford Foundation, 1977), cited in Stephen J. Wayne, "An Introduction to Research on the Presidency," in *Studying the Presidency*, ed. George C. Edwards III and Stephen J. Wayne (Knoxville: University of Tennessee Press, 1983), 3.

2. Anthony King, "Executives," in *Handbook of Political Science*, vol. 5, *Governmental Institutions and Process*, ed. Fred I. Greenstein and Nelson W. Polsby (Reading, Mass.: Addison-Wesley, 1975), 173.

3. Paul C. Light, *The President's Agenda: Domestic Policy Choice from Kennedy to Carter* (Baltimore: Johns Hopkins University Press, 1983); Mark A. Peterson, *Legislating Together: The White House and Capitol Hill from Eisenhower to Reagan* (Cambridge, Mass.: Harvard University Press, 1990).

4. Bert A. Rockman, *The Leadership Question: The Presidency and the American System* (New York: Praeger, 1984); Rockman, "The American Presidency in Comparative Perspective: Systems, Situations, and Leaders," in *The Presidency and the Political System*, 2d ed., ed. Michael Nelson (Washington, D.C.: Congressional Quarterly Press, 1988); Richard Rose, *The Postmodern President: George Bush Meets the World*, 2d ed. (Chatham, N.J.: Chatham House, 1991); Rose, "The Job at the Top: The Presidency in Comparative Perspective," in *The Presidency and Public Policy Making*, ed. George C. Edwards III, Steven A. Shull, and Norman C. Thomas (Pittsburgh: University of Pittsburgh Press, 1985), 3–21; David F. Prindle, "Toward a Comparative Science of the Presidency," *Presidential Studies Quarterly* 16 (Summer 1986): 467–80.

5. Richard Rose and Ezra N. Suleiman, eds., *Presidents and Prime Ministers* (Washington, D.C.: American Enterprise Institute, 1980); Patrick Weller, *First among Equals: Prime Ministers in Westminster Systems* (Sydney: Allen and Unwin, 1985); George W. Jones, ed., *West European Prime Ministers*, special issue of *West European Politics* 14 (April 1991): 1–182.

6. Haruhiro Fukui, "Studies in Policymaking: A Review of the Literature," *Policymaking in Contemporary Japan*, ed. T. J. Pempel (Ithaca, N.Y.: Cornell University Press, 1977), 22–59.

7. For chronicles of the terms of individual prime ministers, see Hayashi Shigeru and Tsuji Kiyoaki, eds., *Nihon Naikakushi-roku*, 6 vols. (Tokyo: Daiichi Hōki, 1981); Shiratori Rei, ed., *Nihon no Naikaku*, 3 vols. (Tokyo: Shinhyōron, 1981); Masumi Junnosuke, *Gendai no Seiji*, 2 vols. (Tokyo: Tokyo Daigaku Shuppankai, 1985). For chronicles of individual administrations, see Yoshimura Katsuri, *Ikeda Seiken: 1575 Nichi* (Tokyo: Gyōseimondai Kenkyūjo, 1985); Kusuda Minoru, *Satō Seiken: 2797 Nichi*, 2 vols. (Tokyo: Gyōseimondai Kenkyūjo, 1983); Nakano Shirō, *Tanaka Seiken: 886 Nichi* (Tokyo: Gyōseimondai Kenkyūjo, 1982); Nakamura Kei-ichirō, *Miki Seiken: 747 Nichi* (Tokyo: Gyōseimondai Kenkyūjo, 1981); Kiyomiya Ryū, *Fukuda Seiken: 714 Nichi* (Tokyo: Gyōseimondai Kenkyūjo, 1984); Arai Shunzō and Morita Hajime, *Ōhira Masayoshi: Bunjin Saisō* (Tokyo: Shunjūsha, 1982); Kawauchi Issei, *Ōhira Seiken: 554 Nichi* (Tokyo: Gyōseimondai Kenkyūjo, 1982); Yoshida Masanobu, *Ōhira Masayoshi no Seijiteki Jinkaku* (Tokyo: Tōkai Daigaku Shuppankai, 1986); Uji Toshihiko, *Suzuki Seiken: 863 Nichi* (Tokyo: Gyōseimondai Kenkyūjo, 1983); Maki Tarō, *Nakasone Seiken: 1806 Nichi*, 2 vols. (Tokyo: Gyōseimondai Kenkyūjo, 1988). Among journalistic analyses, four have been useful: Jin Ikkō, *Sōridaijin no Isu no Nedan* (Tokyo: KK Besutoserāzu, 1987); Mori Kishio, *Shushō Kantei no Himitsu* (Tokyo: Ushiobunsha, 1981); Tahara Sōichirō, *Abe, Takeshita ni Sun'nari Seiken ga Ikanai Riyū* (Tokyo: Kōbunsha, 1986); Onda Mitsugu, *Naze Sōridaijin Nanoka* (Tokyo: Pīpurusha, 1988). For studies in English, see Robert C. Angel, "Prime Ministerial Leadership in Japan: Recent Changes in Personal Style and Administrative Organization," *Pacific Affairs* 61 (Winter 1988–89): 583–602; Kent E. Calder, "*Kanryō* vs. *Shomin*: Contrasting Dynamics of Conservative Leadership in Postwar Japan," in *Political Leadership in Contemporary Japan*, ed. Terry Edward MacDougall, Michigan Papers in Japanese Studies, no. 1 (Ann Arbor: Center for Japanese Studies, University of Michigan, 1982), 1–28; Sun Ryang Key, "Postwar Japanese Political Leadership—A Study of Prime Ministers," *Asian Survey* 13 (November 1973): 1010–20; Michio Muramatsu, "In Search of National Identity: The Politics and Policies of the Nakasone Administration," *Journal of Japanese Studies* 13 (Summer 1987): 307–42.

8. The most serious example of this is Nixon's threat in 1971 to use the Trading with the Enemy Act against Japan over the so-called textile wrangle. See I. M.

Destler et al., *Managing an Alliance: The Politics of* U.S.-*Japanese Relations* (Washington, D.C.: Brookings Institution, 1976); I. M. Destler, Haruhiro Fukui, and Hideo Sato, *The Textile Wrangle: Conflict in Japanese-American Relations, 1969–1971* (Washington, D.C.: Brookings Institution, 1976).

9. For an analysis of basic forces shaping the U.S. Presidency, see Ryan J. Barrileaux, "The Presidency: Levels of Analysis," *Presidential Studies Quarterly* 14 (Winter 1984): 73–77; and Barrileaux, "Toward an Institutionalist Framework for Presidency Studies," *Presidential Studies Quarterly* 12 (Spring 1982): 154–58.

10. The LDP lost its majority in the other house of the National Assembly, the House of Councillors, in 1989. But the Constitution (Article 67) gives the House of Representatives the controlling power to select the prime minister.

11. Hans H. Baerwald, *Party Politics in Japan* (Boston: Allen and Unwin, 1986).

Chapter 1
The Japanese Prime Minister: Reactive Leadership

1. Richard Rose and Ezra N. Suleiman, preface, in *Presidents and Prime Ministers*, ed. Richard Rose and Ezra Suleiman (Washington, D.C.: American Enterprise Institute, 1980).

2. See Lucian W. Pye, *Asian Power and Politics: The Cultural Dimensions of Authority* (Cambridge, Mass.: Belknap Press of Harvard University Press, 1985).

3. Edwin O. Reischauer, *The Japanese Today: Change and Continuity* (Cambridge, Mass.: Belknap Press of Harvard University Press, 1988), 291. See also Pye, *Asian Power and Politics*, 63.

4. Steve Lohr, *New York Times*, July 11, 1990.

5. Joseph A. Massey, *Youth and Politics in Japan* (Lexington, Mass.: Lexington Books, 1976), 37.

6. The conservative control of the government has been broken only twice, and that for only a year and a half early in the U.S. occupation. Socialists, in a coalition with one of the conservative parties, headed the government under Katayama Tetsu from May 1947 to March 1948 and took part in a coalition government headed by Ashida Hitoshi from March to October 1948.

7. See John W. Dower, *Empire and Aftermath: Yoshida Shigeru and the Japanese Experience, 1878–1954*, Harvard East Asian Monographs, no. 84 (Cambridge, Mass.: Council on East Asian Studies, Harvard University, 1988).

8. John Creighton Campbell, "Policy Conflict and Its Resolution within the Governmental System," in *Conflict in Japan*, ed. Ellis S. Krauss, Thomas P. Rohlen, and Patricia G. Steinhoff (Honolulu: University of Hawaii Press, 1984), 294–334. See also Ellis S. Krauss, "Japanese Parties and Parliament: Changing Leadership

Roles and Role Conflicts"; and Terry Edward MacDougall, "Asukata Ichio and Some Dilemmas of Socialist Leadership in Japan," both in *Political Leadership in Contemporary Japan*, ed. Terry Edward MacDougall, Michigan Papers in Japanese Studies, no. 1 (Ann Arbor: Center for Japanese Studies, University of Michigan, 1982).

9. See, for instance, Kiyoaki Tsuji's analysis of bureaucratic decision making in "Decision-Making in the Japanese Government: A Study of Ringisei," in *Political Development in Modern Japan*, ed. Robert E. Ward (Princeton, N.J.: Princeton University Press, 1968), 457–75.

10. Chie Nakane, *Japanese Society* (Berkeley and Los Angeles: University of California Press, 1970), 65.

11. Ibid., 69.

12. Bradley M. Richardson and Scott C. Flanagan, *Politics in Japan* (Boston: Little, Brown, 1984), 159. See also Richard J. Samuels, "Power behind the Throne," in *Political Leadership in Contemporary Japan*, ed. Terry Edward MacDougall, Michigan Papers in Japanese Studies, no. 1 (Ann Arbor: Center for Japanese Studies, University of Michigan, 1982), 127–44.

13. *Business Week*, October 14, 1985, 39.

14. For a review of the various models of Japanese democracy, see Haruhiro Fukui, "Studies in Policymaking: A Review of the Literature," in *Policymaking in Contemporary Japan*, ed. T. J. Pempel (Ithaca, N.Y.: Cornell University Press, 1977), 385–435.

15. Of the top-level officials (division chief and above), approximately 80 percent graduated from Tokyo University and 8 percent from Kyoto University. Paul S. Kim, *Japan's Civil Service System: Its Structure, Personnel, and Politics* (New York: Greenwood Press, 1988), 42–43. See also B. C. Koh, *Japan's Administrative Elite* (Berkeley and Los Angeles: University of California Press, 1989), 91–92.

16. Chalmers Johnson, *MITI and the Japanese Miracle: The Growth of Industrial Policy, 1925–1975* (Stanford, Calif.: Stanford University Press, 1982), 71.

17. See Taketsugu Tsurutani, *Political Change in Japan: Response to Postindustrial Change* (New York: David McKay, 1977), 70–116.

18. The one major exception was the dismantling of the Home Ministry, which was divided into a number of new ministries and agencies.

19. Ōkubo Shōzō, *Hadaka no Sekai* (Tokyo: Saimaru Shuppankai, 1975), cited in Johnson, MITI, 45.

20. Johnson, MITI, 71.

21. Ibid., 50.

22. Gerald L. Curtis, *The Japanese Way of Politics* (New York: Columbia University Press, 1988), 120–21.

23. Tsurutani, *Political Change in Japan*, 95.

24. Donald C. Hellmann, "Japanese Politics and Foreign Policy: Elitist Democ-

racy within an American Greenhouse," in *The Political Economy of Japan*, vol. 2, *The Changing International Context*, ed. Takashi Inoguchi and Daniel I. Okimoto (Stanford, Calif.: Stanford University Press, 1988), 345–78.

25. Michio Muramatsu and Ellis S. Krauss, "The Conservative Policy Line and the Development of Patterned Pluralism," in *The Political Economy of Japan*, vol. 1, *The Domestic Transformation*, ed. Kozo Yamamura and Yasukichi Yasuba (Stanford, Calif.: Stanford University Press, 1987); Inoguchi Takashi, *Gendai Nihon Seiji Keizai no Kōzu: Seifu to Shijo* (Tokyo: Tōyō Keizai Shimpōsha, 1983); Satō Seizaburō and Matsuzaki Tetsuhisa, *Jimintō Seiken* (Tokyo: Chūō Kōron, 1986); Ōtake Hideo, *Gendai Nihon no Seiji Kenryoku Keizai Kenryoku* (Tokyo: San'ichi Shobō, 1979); Sone Yasunori, "Tagen Minshushugi-ron to Gendai Kokka," *Nenpō Seijigaku* (1982), 117–49.

26. T. J. Pempel, "Unbundling 'Japan, Inc.': The Changing Dynamics of Japanese Policy Formation," *Journal of Japanese Studies* 13 (Summer 1987): 271–306.

27. See I. M. Destler et al., *Managing an Alliance: The Politics of U.S.-Japanese Relations* (Washington, D.C.: Brookings Institution, 1976); I. M. Destler, Haruhiro Fukui, and Hideo Sato, *The Textile Wrangle: Conflict in Japanese-American Relations, 1969–1971* (Washington, D.C.: Brookings Institution, 1976).

28. Pempel, "Unbundling Japan, Inc.," 304.

29. Most writers on *zoku-giin* (members of *zoku*) believe that the rise of the influence of the LDP members of the National Assembly in policy making started in the 1970s. John Creighton Campbell, however, argues that the change occurred in the late 1950s and early 1960s. See J. C. Campbell "Fragmentation and Power: Politicians and Bureaucrats in the Japanese Decision-Making System," paper presented to the Midwest Seminar on Japan, Ann Arbor, Mich., 1988.

30. Curtis, *Japanese Way of Politics*. See also Michio Muramatsu and Ellis S. Krauss, "The Dominant Party and Social Coalitions in Japan," in *Uncommon Democracies: The One-Party Dominant Regimes*, ed. T. J. Pempel (Ithaca, N.Y.: Cornell University Press, 1990), 282–305; Daniel I. Okimoto, *Between MITI and the Market: Japanese Industrial Policy for High Technology* (Stanford, Calif.: Stanford University Press, 1989).

31. For more details on *zoku-giin* see chap. 7; see also Nihon Keizai Shimbunsha, ed., *Jimintō Seichō* (Tokyo: Nihon Keizai Shimbunsha, 1983); Satō and Matsuzaki, *Jimintō Seiken*; Inoguchi Takashi and Iwai Tomoaki, *"Zoku-Giin" no Kenkyū* (Tokyo: Nihon Keizai Shimbunsha, 1987).

32. For a discussion of subgovernments in the United States, see Randall B. Ripley and Grace A. Franklin, *Congress, the Bureaucracy, and Public Policy*, 3d ed. (Homewood, Ill.: Dorsey Press, 1984); Rose, "Government against Sub-Governments," 284–347. For France, see Frank Baumgartner, *Conflict and Rhetoric in French Policymaking* (Pittsburgh: University of Pittsburgh Press, 1989).

33. Satō and Matsuzaki, *Jimintō Seiken*, 84.

34. Muramatsu and Krauss, "Conservative Policy Line," 542–43. Other scholars

have come up with similar terms, such as Inoguchi Takashi's "bureaucratic-led mass inclusionary pluralism" (*Gendai Nihon Seiji Keizai no Kōzu*); Satō and Matsuzaki's "canalized pluralism" (*Jimintō Seiken*).

35. Murakawa Ichirō, "Jiyūminshutō no Seisaku Kettei Kikō," *Jurisuto* 805 (January 1–15, 1984): 216.

36. Karel G. van Wolferen, "The Japan Problem," *Foreign Affairs* 65 (Winter 1987): 289. See also van Wolferen, *The Enigma of Japanese Power: People and Politics in a Stateless Nation* (New York: Alfred A. Knopf, 1989).

37. Van Wolferen, "Japan Problem."

38. Ibid.

39. Kent E. Calder, *Crisis and Compensation: Public Policy and Political Stability in Japan, 1949–1986* (Princeton, N.J.: Princeton University Press, 1988).

40. For studies of these cases, see Donald C. Hellmann, *Japanese Foreign Policy and Domestic Politics: The Peace Agreement with the Soviet Union* (Berkeley and Los Angeles: University of California Press, 1969); George R. Packard III, *Protest in Tokyo: The Security Treaty Crisis of 1960* (Princeton, N.J.: Princeton University Press, 1966); I. M. Destler et al., *Managing an Alliance.*

41. Haruhiro Fukui, "Tanaka Goes to Peking: A Case Study in Foreign Policymaking," in *Policymaking in Contemporary Japan*, ed. T. J. Pempel (Ithaca, N.Y.: Cornell University Press, 1977), 100. See also Gene T. Hsiao, "The Sino-Japanese Rapprochement: A Relationship of Ambivalence," *China Quarterly* (January-March 1974): 103–44.

42. Muramatsu and Krauss, "Conservative Policy Line."

43. Ibid., 522.

44. John Creighton Campbell, *Contemporary Japanese Budget Politics* (Berkeley and Los Angeles: University of California Press, 1977), 233–34.

45. J. C. Campbell, *Budget Politics*, 241–51. See also Yutaka Kosai, "The Politics of Economic Management," in *The Political Economy of Japan*, vol. 1, *The Domestic Transformation*, ed. Kozo Yamamura and Yasukichi Yasuba (Stanford, Calif.: Stanford University Press, 1987).

46. Daniel I. Okimoto, "Political Inclusivity: The Domestic Structure of Trade," in *The Political Economy of Japan*, vol. 2, *The Changing International Context*, ed. Takashi Inoguchi and Daniel I. Okimoto (Stanford, Calif.: Stanford University Press, 1988).

47. See Mark A. Peterson's critique of what he calls the "presidency-centered perspective" in the literature on American politics in his *Legislating Together: The White House and Capitol Hill from Eisenhower to Reagan* (Cambridge, Mass.: Harvard University Press, 1990).

48. John W. Kingdon, *Agendas, Alternatives, and Public Policy* (Boston: Little, Brown, 1984).

49. For outlines of various models, see Graham T. Allison, *Essence of Decision: Explaining the Cuban Missile Crisis* (Boston: Little, Brown, 1971); John Creighton

Campbell, "Aging Society," chap. 2 of his *How Policies Change: The Japanese Government and the Aging Society* (Princeton, N.J.: Princeton University Press, 1992); Jeffrey Pfeffer, *Organizations and Organization Theory* (Boston: Pitman, 1982).

50. Herbert A. Simon, *The Models of Man* (New York: John Wiley and Sons, 1957); Charles E. Lindblom, "The Science of 'Muddling Through,'" *Public Administration Review* 14 (Spring 1959): 79–88.

51. Joel D. Aberbach, Robert D. Putnam, and Bert A. Rockman, *Bureaucrats and Politicians in Western Democracies* (Cambridge, Mass.: Harvard University Press, 1981), 257.

52. Ibid., 252–62.

53. See Calder, *Crisis and Compensation*, 137–49; Johnson, MITI.

54. Calder, *Crisis and Compensation*, 133.

55. Aberbach, Putnam, and Rockman, *Bureaucrats and Politicians in Western Democracies*, 257, 262.

56. David McKay, *Domestic Policy and Ideology: Presidents and the American State, 1964–1987* (Cambridge: Cambridge University Press, 1989).

57. See Steven A. Shull, *Domestic Policy Formation: Presidential-Congressional Partnership?* (Westport, Conn.: Greenwood Press, 1983); Kingdon, *Agendas, Alternatives, and Public Policy,* 25–28.

58. Richard Rose, *Do Political Parties Matter?* (Chatham, N.J.: Chatham House, 1984), 152.

59. Richard Rose, "Organizing Issues In and Organizing Problems Out," in *The Managerial Presidency*, ed. James P. Pfiffner (Pacific Grove, Calif.: Brooks/Cole Publishing, 1991), 116.

60. Rose, *Do Political Parties Matter?* 52–73.

61. See Jeffrey Pfeffer's critique of individual-level rational-actor models in his *Organizations and Organization Theory*. See also James G. March, "Bounded Rationality, Ambiguity, and the Engineering of Choice," *Bell Journal of Economics* 9 (Autumn 1978) 587–608; March, "The Power of Power," in *Varieties of Political Theory*, ed. David Easton (Englewood Cliffs, N.J.: Prentice-Hall 1966); March and Herbert A. Simon, *Organizations* (New York: John Wiley and Sons, 1958), chap. 6; Robert A. Dahl, "Power," in *International Encyclopedia of the Social Sciences*, ed. David L. Sills (New York: Macmillan and Free Press, 1968), 12:405–15.

62. Michael D. Cohen, James G. March, and Johan P. Olsen, "People, Problems, Solutions, and the Ambiguity of Relevance," in *Ambiguity and Choice in Organizations*, ed. James G. March and Johan P. Olsen (Bergen: Universitetsforlaget, 1976), 25.

63. Michael D. Cohen, James G. March, and Johan P. Olsen, "A Garbage Can Model of Organizational Choice," *Administrative Science Quarterly* 17 (March 1972): 1–25.

64. Michael D. Cohen and James G. March, *Leadership and Ambiguity: The American College President*, 2d ed. (Boston: Harvard Business School Press, 1986), 203.

65. Renate Mayntz, "Executive Leadership in Germany: Dispersion of Power or *Kanzlerdemokratie?*" in *Presidents and Prime Ministers*, ed. Richard Rose and Ezra N. Suleiman (Washington D.C.: American Enterprise Institute, 1980), 169–70, cited in Bert A. Rockman, *The Leadership Question: The Presidency and American System* (New York: Praeger, 1984).

66. Sabino Cassese, "Is There a Government in Italy? Politics and Administration at the Top," in *Presidents and Prime Ministers*, ed. Richard Rose and Ezra N. Suleiman, 201–02, cited in Rockman, *Leadership Question*. For a similar analysis of leadership in Sweden, see Thomas J. Anton, *Administered Politics: Elite Political Culture in Sweden* (Boston: Martinus Nijhoff Publishing, 1980).

67. Anthony King, "The American Policy in the Late 1970s: Building Coalitions in the Sand," in *The New American Political System*, 1st ed., ed. Anthony King (Washington, D.C.: American Enterprise Institute, 1978), 371–95. See also Charles O. Jones, "Presidents and Agendas: Who Defines What for Whom?" in *The Managerial Presidency*, ed. James P. Pfiffner (Pacific Grove, Calif.: Brooks/Cole Publishing, 1991), 197–213.

68. Hedrick Smith, *The Power Game: How Washington Works* (New York: Random House, 1988), 9–19.

69. Hugh Heclo, "The Presidential Illusion," in *The Illusion of Presidential Government*, ed. Hugh Heclo and Lester M. Salamon (Boulder, Colo.: Westview Press, 1981), 1–17.

70. Kerry Mullins and Aaron Wildavsky, "The Procedural Presidency of George Bush," *Society* 28 (January/February 1991): 49–59.

71. For a similar analysis in the United States, see Jack L. Walker, "Setting the Agenda in the U.S. Senate," *British Journal of Political Science* 7 (October 1977): 423–45.

72. The Lockheed and the Recruit scandals both shook the political world. In 1976 Tanaka Kakuei, the previous prime minister, was arrested for accepting bribes from the Lockheed Corporation. The Recruit scandal dominated politics in 1988–89, during the Takeshita administration. The president of Recruit, Ezoe Hiromasa, gave huge amounts of contributions to politicians and other officials to help gain favorable treatment for his relatively new set of companies. Among those tainted by the scandal included not only virtually all of the top LDP leaders but also many of the top opposition party leaders.

73. The numbers show a month-to-month increase from January to May: January, 0; February, 3; March, 8; April, 14; May, 19; June, 4.

74. See chap. 3, n. 11.

75. Energy and economic problems also topped the agenda of U.S. presidents during this time. See Paul C. Light, *The President's Agenda: Domestic Policy Choice from Kennedy to Carter* (Baltimore: Johns Hopkins University Press, 1983), 70.

76. Fukuda and Ōhira were also former Finance Ministry officials.

Chapter 2
The Japanese Prime Minister in
Comparative Perspective

1. Richard Rose, "Prime Ministers in Parliamentary Democracies," *West European Politics* 14 (April 1991): 9.

2. Arend Lijphart, *Democracies: Patterns of Majoritarian and Consensus Government in Twenty-One Countries* (New Haven, Conn.: Yale University Press, 1984).

3. Bert A. Rockman, *The Leadership Question: The Presidency and the American System* (New York: Praeger, 1984), 225–29.

4. See Philip Norton, " 'The Lady's Not for Turning' but What about the Rest? Margaret Thatcher and the Conservative Party 1979–89," *Parliamentary Affairs* 43 (January 1990): 41–76.

5. Jürg Steiner and Robert H. Dorff, "Decision by Interpretation," *British Journal of Politics* 10 (January 1980): 1–13, cited in Rose, "Prime Ministers in Parliamentary Democracies," 19.

6. Rose, "Prime Ministers in Parliamentary Democracies," 18.

7. The only other countries among the industrialized democracies with federal systems are Switzerland and Austria. See Lijphart, *Democracies*, 68.

8. Richard P. Nathan, "Federalism—The Great 'Composition,'" in *The New American Political System*, 2d ed., ed. Anthony King (Washington, D.C.: AEI Press, 1990), 233–41.

9. Thomas A. Hockin, "The Prime Minister and Political Leadership: An Introduction to Some Restraints and Imperatives," in *Apex of Power: The Prime Minister and Political Leadership in Canada*, 2d ed., ed. Thomas A. Hockin (Scarborough, Ont.: Prentice-Hall, 1977), 16–18.

10. This does not mean that local governments are entirely passive. They have, for instance, been important forces in pollution control and health care. See Terry Edward MacDougall, "Democracy and Local Government in Postwar Japan," in *Democracy in Japan*, ed. Takeshi Ishida and Ellis S. Krauss (Pittsburgh: University of Pittsburgh Press, 1989), 139–69.

11. Steven R. Reed, *Japanese Prefectures and Policymaking* (Pittsburgh: University of Pittsburgh Press, 1986), 26.

12. Richard E. Neustadt, *Presidential Power: The Politics of Leadership from FDR to Carter* (New York: John Wiley and Sons, 1980), 26.

13. Leon D. Epstein, "Parliamentary Government," in *International Encyclopedia of the Social Sciences*, ed. David L. Sills (New York: Macmillan and Free Press, 1968), 11: 419–23. Switzerland, however, has a system where the members of the Federal Council are elected by the legislature, but the council is subsequently invulnerable to legislative attacks. See Jürg Steiner, *Amicable Agreement versus Majority Rule:*

Conflict Resolution in Switzerland (Chapel Hill: University of North Carolina Press, 1974), 43.

14. Yves Mény, *Government and Politics in Western Europe: Britain, France, Italy, West Germany*, trans. Janet Lloyd (Oxford: Oxford University Press, 1990), 182–85.

15. Richard Rose, "Government against Sub-Governments: A European Perspective on Washington," in *Presidents and Prime Ministers*, ed. Richard Rose and Ezra N. Suleiman (Washington, D.C.: American Enterprise Institute, 1980), 292.

16. The first two occurred in 1947 and 1954, before the LDP was formed. The third was in 1980, when the LDP was effectively divided in two. When the opposition parties presented a no confidence resolution in the National Assembly, half of the party abstained, allowing the resolution to pass.

17. Mike Masato Mochizuki, "Managing and Influencing the Japanese Legislative Process: The Role of Parties and the National Diet" (Ph. D. diss., Harvard University, 1982), 110.

18. Johan P. Olsen, "Governing Norway: Segmentation, Anticipation, and Consensus Formation," in *Presidents and Prime Ministers*, ed. Richard Rose and Ezra N. Suleiman (Washington, D.C.: American Enterprise Institute, 1980), 209; Rudy B. Andeweg, "The Dutch Prime Minister: Not Just Chairman, Not Yet Chief?" *West European Politics* 14 (April 1991): 117.

19. Lawrence C. Mayer and John H. Burnett, *Politics in Industrial Societies: A Comparative Perspective* (New York: John Wiley and Sons, 1977), 204.

20. Lijphart, *Democracies*, 187.

21. Other countries with flexible constitutions include Iceland, Israel, and Sweden. Ibid., 191.

22. Countries whose constitutions can be amended by national referendum include Denmark, France, Ireland, and Italy. Ibid., 189–90.

23. See Haruhiro Fukui, "Constitutional Revision," *Party in Power: The Japanese Liberal-Democrats and Policymaking* (Berkeley and Los Angeles: University of California Press, 1970), chap. 8.

24. The exceptions are Denmark, Finland, Sweden, Israel, Luxembourg, and New Zealand. Lijphart argues that Iceland and Norway also essentially have unicameral parliaments. *Democracies*, 91–92.

25. When Thomas Jefferson asked George Washington why a second legislative chamber had been created, Washington asked, "Why did you pour your coffee into your saucer?" "To cool it," Jefferson answered. "Even so," said Washington, "we pour legislation into the senatorial saucer to cool it." Max Farrand, ed., *The Records of the Federal Convention of 1787*, 1937 rev. ed. (Yale University Press, 1966), 359, as quoted in James Sundquist, *Constitutional Reform and Effective Government* (Washignton, D.C.: Brookings Institution, 1986), 22. See also James Madison, "No. 51" and "No. 62," in *The Federalist Papers*, by Alexander Hamilton, James Madison, and

John Jay (New York: Mentor Books, 1963).

26. Patrick Weller, *First among Equals: Prime Ministers in Westminster Systems* (Sydney: George Allen and Unwin, 1985), 176.

27. The government has controlled the Senate for only six years during the last twenty—between 1975 and 1981. From 1972 to 1975 the opposition controlled the Senate. Since 1981 a minor third party, the Democrats, has held the balance of power. Ibid., 175.

28. See Jürg Steiner, *European Democracies*, 2d ed. (New York: Longmans, 1991), 149–53.

29. For a brief description of the judicial systems of Germany, France, and Italy, see Mény, *Western Europe*, 296–327; Steiner, *European Democracies*, 153–54. For Ireland, see Brian Thompson, "Living with a Supreme Court in Ireland," *Parliamentary Affairs* 44 (January 1991): 33–49.

30. Hiroshi Itoh, *The Supreme Court: Constitutional Practices* (New York: M. Wiener, 1989), 212.

31. Ibid., 186.

32. Ibid., 203.

33. At the time of the ruling, many depopulated rural districts were vastly overrepresented, particularly compared to some of the rapidly growing districts just outside Tokyo. In 1985, Kagoshima's District # 3, with less than 260,000 eligible voters and three seats, was the most overrepresented district. The most underrepresented was Chiba's District # 4, which also had three seats but over 1 million eligible voters. That is, a vote in Kagoshima's # 3 was worth four times a vote in Chiba's # 4. The bill alleviated the most egregious cases, but the disparity in the two most extreme cases today is still over three to one.

34. In some developing democracies, the monarch sometimes has personal prestige that transcends any limitations in formal power he or she may have. Two such examples include King Juan Carlos, whose personal prestige has played an important part in supporting Spain's developing democracy following the death of Francisco Franco in 1975, and the king of Thailand whose personal popularity among the people allowed him to limit the military's control on the government in May 1992.

35. Bert A. Rockman, "The American Presidency in Comparative Perspective: Systems, Situations, and Leaders," in *The Presidency and the Political System*, 2d ed., ed. Michael Nelson (Washington, D.C.: Congressional Quarterly Press, 1988), 61. See also Bradley H. Patterson, Jr., *The Ring of Power: The White House Staff and Its Expanding Role in Government* (New York: Basic Books, 1988); and James P. Pfiffner, ed., *The Managerial Presidency* (Pacific Grove, Calif.: Brooks/Cole Publishing, 1991).

36. Richard P. Nathan, *The Administrative Presidency* (New York: John Wiley and Sons, 1983).

37. Compared to the prewar system, the cabinet's position has improved dramatically. Under the Meiji constitution, executive power was theoretically controlled by the emperor. But, because he did not actually exercise that power, it was in practice extremely fragmented, with several autonomous bodies operating on their own without accountability to either the cabinet or the National Assembly. The ministers were not collectively responsible to the National Assembly; rather, they were theoretically responsible only to the emperor. The military and the Imperial Household Agency, in particular, were not responsible to the cabinet. Moreover, the prime minister was not given the power to select and dismiss the other cabinet ministers. Under the Meiji constitution, the cabinet ministers were direct appointees of the emperor.

38. Summarized in Weller, *First among Equals*, 4.

39. Sabino Cassese, "Is There a Government in Italy? Politics and Administration at the Top," in *Presidents and Prime Ministers*, ed. Richard Rose and Ezra N. Suleiman (Washington, D.C.: American Enterprise Institute, 1980), 186; Andeweg, "Dutch Prime Minister."

40. Anthony King, "The British Prime Ministership in the Age of the Career Politician," *West European Politics* 14 (April 1991): 35.

41. Ibid., 36.

42. Peter Hennessy, *Whitehall* (New York: Free Press, 1989), 681.

43. Paul C. Light, *The President's Agenda: Domestic Policy Choice from Kennedy to Carter* (Baltimore: Johns Hopkins University Press, 1983), 27. See also George C. Edwards III, *At the Margins: Presidential Leadership of Congress* (New Haven, Conn.: Yale University Press, 1989); Edwards, "Director or Facilitator? Presidential Policy Control of Congress," in *The Managerial Presidency*, ed. James P. Pfiffner (Pacific Grove, Calif.: Brooks/Cole Publishing, 1991), 214–23; Jon R. Bond and Richard Fleisher, *The President in the Legislative Arena* (Chicago: University of Chicago Press, 1990); Mark A. Peterson, *Legislating Together: The White House and Capitol Hill from Eisenhower to Reagan* (Cambridge, Mass.: Harvard University Press, 1990).

44. Light, *President's Agenda*, 26.

45. George W. Jones, "West European Prime Ministers in Perspective," *West European Politics* 14 (April 1991): 163–78. See also Mény, *Western Europe*, 218–23.

46. Rose, "Prime Ministers in Parliamentary Democracies," 17.

47. King, "British Prime Ministership," 25–47.

48. According to Michael Laver and Norman Schofield's analysis of West European cabinets between 1945 and 1987, one party has controlled more than 50 percent of the legislative seats under only 10 percent of the total number of cabinets. Laver and Schofield, *Multiparty Government: The Politics of Coalition in Europe* (Oxford: Oxford University Press, 1990), 70–71.

49. David Hine and Renato Finocchi, "The Italian Prime Minister"; Paul

Heywood, "Governing a New Democracy: The Power of the Prime Minister in Spain"; Andeweg, "Dutch Prime Minister"; all in *West European Politics* 14 (April 1991).

50. Rose, "Prime Ministers in Parliamentary Democracies," 19.

51. Only Sweden's Social Democratic Party approaches the longevity of the LDP. It has dominated Swedish politics since 1932. But it was out of power from 1976 to 1982, and it rarely had a majority of the seats of the legislature even while in power. For a comparison of long-term ruling parties, see T. J. Pempel, ed., *Uncommon Democracies: The One-Party Dominant Regimes* (Ithaca, N.Y.: Cornell University Press, 1990); Giovanni Sartori, *Parties and Party Systems: A Framework for Analysis* (Cambridge: Cambridge University Press, 1976), 197–200.

52. Renate Mayntz, "Executive Leadership in Germany: Dispersion of Power or *Kanzlerdemokratie?*" in *Presidents and Prime Ministers*, ed. Richard Rose and Ezra N. Suleiman (Washington, D.C.: American Enterprise Institute, 1980), 145; Mény, *Western Europe*, 220–21.

53. Weller, *First among Equals*, 74–76; Cassese, "Government in Italy," 175.

54. Weller, *First among Equals*, 74.

55. Lester B. Seligman, "Leadership: Political Aspects," in *International Encyclopedia of the Social Sciences*, ed. David L. Sills (New York: Macmillan and Free Press, 1968), 9:107–13. See also Roy C. Macridis, "Political Executive," in *International Encyclopedia of the Social Sciences*, ed. David L. Sills (New York: Macmillan and Free Press, 1968), 12:228–35.

56. Edward S. Corwin, *The President: Office and Powers 1787–1957*, 4th ed. (New York: New York University Press, 1957), 310–13.

57. John P. Mackintosh, *The British Cabinet*, 3d ed. (London: Stevens, 1977); Mackintosh, *The Government and Politics of Britain*, 3d ed. (London: Hutchinson, 1974); Richard H. S. Crossman, "Prime Ministerial Government," in *The British Prime Minister*, 24th ed., ed. Anthony King (Durham, N.C.: Duke University Press, 1985), 175–94; and Crossman, *Inside View: Three Lectures on Prime Ministerial Government* (London: Jonathan Cape, 1972).

58. Denis Smith, "President and Parliament: The Transformation of Parliamentary Government in Canada," in *Apex of Power: The Prime Minister and Political Leadership in Canada*, 2d ed., ed. Thomas A. Hockin (Scarborough, Ont.: Prentice-Hall, 1977); James C. Simeon, "Prime Minister's Office and White House Office: Political Administration in Canada and the United States," *Presidential Studies Quarterly* 21 (Summer 1991): 559–80.

59. Weller, *First among Equals*, 8.

60. See Cassese, in "Government in Italy," 181; Mény, *Western Europe*, 236.

61. Seligman, "Leadership: Political Aspects," 107.

62. See Rockman, *Leadership Question*, esp. 134–46. For Great Britain see Crossman, *Inside View.*

63. Rockman, *Leadership Question*, 168. See also Corwin, *President*; Theodore J. Lowi, *The Personal President: Power Invested, Promise Unfulfilled* (Ithaca, N.Y.: Cornell University Press, 1985); Jeffrey K. Tulis, *The Rhetorical Presidency* (Princeton, N.J.: Princeton University Press, 1987); William M. Lunch, *The Nationalization of American Politics* (Berkeley and Los Angeles: University of California Press, 1987).

64. James P. Pfiffner, introduction, in Pfiffner, *Managerial Presidency*. For further details see, in the same volume, Samuel Kernell, "The Evolution of the White House Staff," 43–59; Bruce Buchanan, "Constrained Diversity: The Organizational Demands of the Presidency," 78–103; Francis Rourke, "Presidentializing the Bureaucracy," 123–33; and Terry M. Moe, "The Politicized Presidency," 135–57.

65. Hennessy, *Whitehall*, 623–82.

66. See Colin Campbell, *Governments under Stress: Political Executives and Key Bureaucrats in Washington, London, and Ottawa* (Toronto: University of Toronto Press, 1983); Simeon, "Prime Minister's Office and White House Office"; Weller, *First among Equals*; Hine and Finocchi, "The Italian Prime Minister"; Mayntz, "Executive Leadership in Germany," 139–70.

67. See John Creighton Campbell, *How Policies Change: The Japanese Government and the Aging Society* (Princeton, N.J.: Princeton University Press, 1992).

68. Yasusuke Murakami, "The Japanese Model of Political Economy," in *The Political Economy of Japan*, vol. 1, *The Domestic Transformation*, ed. Kozo Yamamura and Yasukichi Yasuba (Stanford, Calif.: Stanford University Press, 1987), 33–92; *Shin Chūma Taishū no Jidai* (Tokyo: Chūō Kōronsha, 1984).

69. See Nakasone Yasuhiro, "Reflections of a Presidential Prime Minister," *Japan Echo* 15 (Spring 1988): 8–16; trans. from "Sōri kantei o saru ni saishite," *Bungei Shunjū* (December 1987): 94–109. See also Robert C. Angel, "Prime Ministerial Leadership in Japan: Recent Changes in Personal Style and Administrative Organization," *Pacific Affairs* 61 (Winter 1988–89): 583–602; Gerald L. Curtis, *The Japanese Way of Politics* (New York: Columbia University Press, 1988), 98–106.

70. Michio Muramatsu, "In Search of National Identity: The Politics and Policies of the Nakasone Administration," *Journal of Japanese Studies* 13 (Summer 1987): 307–42. For further details about Nakasone's use of advisory committees, see chap. 8.

Chapter 3
Nakasone and Educational Reform

1. This rise is often referred to as the "third wave" of postwar juvenile delinquency. The number of juveniles arrested for major crimes had crested twice before, according to NPA statistics, in 1951 and 1964. The third wave peaked in

1984, but at a level 50 percent higher than the previous two. NPA, *Police White Paper* 1985.

2. Ibid.

3. Fifty-one percent expressed some level of dissatisfaction with schools as opposed to 46 percent who expressed some level of satisfaction. *Mainichi Shimbun,* January 4, 1983.

4. According to an *Asahi Shimbun* poll published February 19, support for the Nakasone cabinet dropped from 37 percent in December 1982 to 29 percent in February 1983. Another *Asahi Shimbun* poll, published February 21, 1983, showed widespread opposition to a number of Nakasone's statements on defense and the Constitution.

5. Suzuki Zenkō, Nakasone's predecessor, was especially critical of Nakasone for making "irresponsible" statements and asked him to change the course of his policies. Two other party leaders, Kōmoto Toshio and Fukuda Takeo, as well as members of the Tanaka faction (which was Nakasone's main source of support within the party apart from his own faction) made similar criticisms.

6. *Asahi Shimbun*, February 19, 1983.

7. The first incident involving the gang was reported on February 12, 1983, and the second on February 16. On February 21, 1983, Nakasone announced that he intended to have the cabinet as a whole, not just the Education Ministry, tackle the problem, and he referred to the two incidents of juvenile delinquency as part of a continuing series of "heartbreaking" incidents.

8. According to Gotōda, the government's intention was to concentrate on broader family and youth problems, as well as women's problems. In particular, he noted Nakasone's interest in the policy proposals developed by one of Ōhira Masayoshi's many private advisory groups on strengthening the family system and encouraging three-generation households.

9. Nakasone did not give the PMO officials specific directions about what to do to counter juvenile delinquency. They turned to his earlier statements, in which he emphasized the role of the family in preventing delinquency, but they were doubtful how far politics could interfere with the privacy of the family. *Yomiuri Shimbun*, February 22, 1983. The PMO then formed the Conference to Promote Measures to Prevent Juvenile Delinquency, gathering together all the relevant personnel from the various ministries to study many different kinds of measures, which included setting up a national conference on raising children and strengthening cooperation among organizations such as police and schools to prevent delinquency.

10. For more background on the politics of education policy in the postwar period, see Leonard James Schoppa, *Education Reform in Japan: A Case of Immobilist Politics* (London: Routledge, 1991).

11. The Education Ministry in 1982 softened a history textbook's account of the Japanese involvement in the China war. The original text stated that the Japanese "invaded" China. The revised text stated, instead, that the Japanese "advanced" into China. When this change became public, it exploded into a major diplomatic issue. China and South Korea, in particular, made clear their opposition to the revision both through diplomatic channels and through massive public demonstrations. Only after long negotiations between the Education Ministry and the Foreign Ministry was a compromise reached where the former retained the right to screen textbooks but would on its own revert to the previous account of the war.

12. The U.S. occupation installed a one-track, 6-3-3 system: six years of primary education, three years of middle school, and three years of high school. For more on the background of the multitrack proposal as a partisan issue, see Steven R. Reed, *Japanese Prefectures and Policymaking* (Pittsburgh: University of Pittsburgh Press, 1986), chap. 6.

13. Nikkeiren's special committee on school violence published its proposals on July 6, 1983. They included a review of the 6-3-3 system, the revival of moral education, and a reform of the teacher training system.

14. This seven-point proposal was based on a twelve-point one drafted by Nishioka Takeo, a leading member of the LDP education *zoku*. Nakasone was said to have liked the ideas listed in it and asked bureaucrats from the Education Ministry to draft a plan to present during a campaign speech. See Hara Masahiko and Kawanabe Masahiro, *Kyōiku Rinchō* (Tokyo: Tōken, 1984), 20.

15. Of the 97.4 percent of those who responded, 17 percent replied that education was the issue they wanted to raise most during the campaign. This compares with social welfare, 19 percent; political ethics, 15 percent; the economy, 14 percent; and administrative reform, 13 percent. *Mainichi Shimbun*, June 20, 1983.

16. The three were Inaba Osamu, Sunada Shigetami, and Fujinami Takao. Inaba and Sunada were both former ministers of education, while Fujinami was at the time chief cabinet secretary. Yagi Atsushi, *Monbu Daijin no Sengoshi* (Tokyo: Bijinesusha, 1984), 214.

17. The Fundamental Law of Education, which outlines the principles of education, was passed by the National Assembly in 1947 during the Occupation. The purpose of education was defined as "the creation of independent-minded citizens capable of building a peaceful state and society." Article 10 of the law states that "education should not be subject to improper control," which has been interpreted to mean that it should be politically neutral. The controversy over the law centers on the fact that it is largely based on a report made in 1946 by a U.S. educational mission to Japan. Conservative critics who want to revise it say that it

was imposed by the Occupation. See Nagai Michio, "Educational Reform: Developments in the Postwar Years," *Japan Quarterly* 30 (January–March 1985): 14–17; Benjamin Duke, *Japan's Militant Teachers: A History of the Left-Wing Teachers' Movement* (Honolulu: University of Hawaii Press, 1973); Donald R. Thurston, *Teachers and Politics in Japan* (Princeton, N.J.: Princeton University Press, 1973).

18. The total time given to questioning the bill was about forty-one hours in the lower house Cabinet Committee and about forty-two hours in the upper house Cabinet Committee. Of these totals, only two hours in the lower house and ten hours in the upper house were taken up by the LDP, the Kōmeitō, and the DSP combined. The rest was taken up by the JSP and JCP. Yagi, *Monbu Daijin*, 219.

19. The Rinkyōshin's four reports were released on June 26, 1985; April 23, 1986; April 1, 1987; and August 8, 1987.

20. The Rinkyōshin called for the promotion of sports at all levels, including competitive sports, which was added after the poor performance by Japanese athletes in the Seoul Asia Games in September 1986.

21. Dokō Toshio was the chairman of the second Ad Hoc Council on Administrative Reform (Rinchō). He was a former chairman of the Federation of Economic Organizations (Keidanren), who was a highly respected figure among businessmen and politicians, and his simple lifestyle made him a popular symbolic figure for the government's attempts to streamline government.

22. Those on the main council who were in the Nakasone camp included Amaya Naohiro, Ishii Takemochi, Ishikawa Tadao, Kōyama Ken'ichi, Miura Chizuko, Miyata Yoshiji, Nakayama Sōhei, and Sejima Ryuzō. Among those appointed as specialists were Kumon Shumpei, Tawara Kōtarō, Yamamoto Shichihei, Yayama Tarō, and Watanabe Shōichi. Kōyama, Kumon, and Sejima were central figures in Nakasone's brain trust who served on one or more of the administrative reform councils; Ishikawa, Miura, and were members of Yamamoto Nakasone's private advisory group on education and culture; Nakayama Sejima and Miyata served on Nakasone's Research Group on Peace Issues. In addition, Amaya, Ishii, and Watanabe the Kyoto were members of Study Group on Global Issues, a group that proposed that education be liberalized—an idea supported by Nakasone.

The Education Ministry's choices included Arita Kazuhisa, Iijima Sōichi, Minakami Tadashi, Okano Shun'ichirō, Saitō Sei, Tamaru Akiyo, and Tobari Atsuo. The specialist members were Kida Hiroshi, Kōno Shigeo, Kuroha Ryōichi, Onuma Sunao, Sengoku Tamotsu, and Shimogawara Gorō. Arita was a former school principal and member of the upper house *zoku* where he was considered a member of the education *zoku* of the New Liberal Club. Saitō and Kida were former administrative education vice ministers. Shimogawara and Tobari were principals of secondary schools; Minakami was superintendent of the Tokyo Metropolitan Board of Education. Kōno, Kuroha, Okano, Onuma, and Sengoku served on one or more of the Education Ministry's advisory bodies.

Both lists drawn from Harada Saburō, *Rinkyōshin to Kyōiku Kaikaku* (Tokyo: San'ichi Shobō, 1988), 135–36; Ōmori Kazuo, *Rinji Kyōiku: Shingikai Sannenkan no Kiroku* (Tokyo: Hikari Shobō, 1987), 68–69, 96–98; Aoki Satoshi, *Rinkyōshin Kaitai* (Tokyo: Akebi Shobō, 1986).

23. These included teachers; bureaucratic interests such as the Finance, Health and Welfare, and Foreign ministries; and interest groups, such as labor, mass media, culture, and sports.

24. The report, entitled, "Seven Recommendations for the Activation of School Education," included the following proposals: (1) relaxing rules on the establishment of new schools; (2) relaxing the school zone system; (3) revising the teaching license system to allow unlicensed people to teach if they had the ability, aptitude, and interest in education; (4) allowing greater flexibility in the length, content, and methods of education (to allow students to jump grades or be held back according to ability); (5) allowing schools to choose a system besides the 6-3-3 system; (6) abolishing the *hensachi* [deviation value] system, in which test scores are used to determine the schools that students enter; and (7) enforcing moral education that teaches responsibility and respect for social norms.

25. These included Amaya Naohiro, Ishii Takemochi, Yamamoto Shichihei (specialist member), and Watanabe Shōichi (specialist). Yamamoto Shichihei also served in Nakasone's private advisory group on education and culture. Yamamoto, in his personal comments attached to the Nakasone advisory group report, proposed that parents be given the right of choice in regard to their children's education. Watanabe had written an article printed in *Bungei Shunjū* that proposed that cram schools be recognized as regular schools.

26. Under the present system, a publisher must submit textbook manuscripts to the Education Ministry for prepublication screening. Textbooks in use must be rescreened every three years.

27. The belief is that publishers would likely become much more cautious about the contents of their textbooks with the knowledge that if a book was not approved, they would incur a substantial financial loss. See Harada, *Rinkyōshin to Kyōiku Kaikaku*, 148–69; *Japan Times*, April 3, 1987.

28. The existing system does allow parents to petition the local board of education to allow their children to move to a different school (e.g., for children who are victims of bullying).

29. See Ishiyama Morio, *Monbu Kanryō no Gyakushū* (Tokyo: Kōdansha, 1986), 216.

30. Ibid., 211.

31. *Mainichi Shimbun*, August 8, 1987.

32. On July 1, 1987, Education Minister Shiokawa met with the steering committee of the Rinkyōshin and told members that he thought it necessary to emphasize the national flag and the national anthem more. At first the recommendation included the word *tadashiku* [correctly]: "so that people can *correctly* understand and respect the meaning of the national flag and national anthem." The word was dropped when the members of the council could not agree on what "correct understanding" meant. Some members pointed out that the so-called national anthem "Kimigayo" is not officially recognized in law. *Asahi Shimbun*, August 8, 1987; *Mainichi Shimbun*, August 8, 1987. See also Uchida Kenzō, *Rinkyōshin no Kiseki* (Tokyo: Daiichi Hōki, 1987), 196–201.

33. Ishiyama, *Monbu Kanryō no Gyakushū*, 210.

34. *Asahi Shimbun*, August 8, 1987.

35. *Yomiuri Shimbun*, August 8, 1987.

36. See "Immediate Policies of the Implementation of Educational Reform," approved by the cabinet on October 6, 1987, printed in Monbushō, *Outline of Education in Japan* 1989 (Tokyo: Asian Cultural Centre for UNESCO, 1989), 135.

37. *Asahi Shimbun* (evening edition), March 10, 1988.

38. Legislation passed on May 25, 1988.

39. Supplemental textbooks on moral education will be used in primary and middle schools. The new system being studied would allow schools to choose from among ministry-approved supplemental readers. In addition to special classes for moral education, the new guidelines call for more emphasis on moral education in other classes such as Japanese language.

40. A group of Kyoto parents and teachers filed a lawsuit in February 1986 challenging the authority of the Kyoto board of education and school principals to force schools to display the flag and sing the anthem.

41. A recent court ruling, however, may limit some of the ministry's discretionary authority. The Tokyo District Court ruled on October 2, 1989 that the Education Ministry's authority to screen textbooks was constitutional, but it defined certain instances in which it considered the ministry's discretion would become abusive and illegal. This was a result of a case brought by Ienaga Saburō, a textbook author, who claimed that the ministry's strict screening practices were unconstitutional. Yamazumi Masami, "Kyōiku," in *imidas* 1989 (Tokyo: Shūeisha, 1989), 804.

42. Gyōsei, ed., *Rinkyōshin to Kyōiku Kaikaku* (Tokyo: Gyōsei, 1987), 5:65. The Education Ministry also did not pursue a similar proposal to revise the 6-3-3 system in the 1971 CEC report. According to an internal Education Ministry memo, the public wants to maintain the 6-3-3 system and is reluctant to experiment with the lives of children. *Asahi Shimbun*, "Daitan na shian mo chū ni," April 13, 1984.

43. Legislation passed on May 18, 1988.

44. Gyōsei, *Rinkyōshin to Kyōiku Kaikaku*, 70.

45. Yamazumi Masami, "Kyōiku," in *imidas* 1990 (Tokyo: Shūeisha, 1990), 1089.

46. Ibid., 1089–90.

47. Interview with Kōyama Ken'ichi, *Asahi Shimbun*, August 8, 1987.

48. Michio Muramatsu, "In Search of National Identity: The Politics and Policies of the Nakasone Administration," *Journal of Japanese Studies* 13 (Summer 1987): 328–38.

49. *Asahi Shimbun*, April 4, 1987.

50. Ibid., August 8, 1987.

51. Ibid., April 4, 1987.

Chapter 4
Nakasone and Tax Reform

1. Top finance officials first worked to persuade Miki Takeo in 1975 that an indirect tax would be needed to finance welfare programs—knowing that Miki wanted to expand welfare programs. Kishiro Yasuyuki, *Jimintō Zeiseichōsakai* (Tokyo: Tōyō Keizai Shimpōsha, 1985), 181.

2. The 1978 budget ran a big deficit in order to stimulate the domestic economy. At the time leaders of other advanced industrial countries, particularly U.S. President Jimmy Carter, were urging Japan to act as one of the international economic "locomotives." Murayama Tatsuo, the finance minister, decided that in order to get the budget deficit under control, the government needed to implement a VAT by 1980. Soon after Ōhira became prime minister in December 1978, both the LDP Tax Council and Government Tax Council called for the introduction of the tax (called the general excise tax), which the cabinet approved on December 28.

3. Over two hundred LDP members of the National Assembly formed a group to oppose the tax. The stimulus for the movement was the opposition by small- and medium-sized businesses, retailers, self-employed businessmen,and other groups. As the election approached, Kōmoto Toshio and Nakasone Yasuhiro, both heads of factions, also joined in the opposition.

4. Suzuki's promise was against the advice of the Finance Ministry, which felt that it was not possible to solve the deficit problem through spending cuts alone. See Takanashi Akira, *Gyōsei Kaikaku wa Seikō Suruka* (Tokyo: Sōgo Rōdō Kenkyūjo, 1982), 17–24.

5. The *maruyū* system actually refers to three types of tax-exempt savings: *maruyū* (small-lot savings accounts in banks), special *maruyū* (small-lot public

bonds), and postal savings. Each person was legally entitled to keep deposits of up to 3 million yen in each of the three types of savings account, for a total of 9 million yen without having the interest taxed. The interest on deposits over the limit was supposed to be assessed at a tax rate of at least 20 percent. The law, however, was never enforced. The system was widely abused because people could easily open more than three accounts without being found out. The National Tax Agency estimated that, in 1985, more than 10 trillion yen were in deposits that should have been taxed—a loss in revenue of more than 2 trillion yen. *Asahi Nenkan,* 1987, 156.

6. The manufacturers of office automation equipment mounted an intense campaign to block the tax by pressuring its allies in the LDP. The campaign worked. The LDP Tax Council, although sympathetic to the Finance Ministry's proposal, decided in December 1984 against the tax because of its feeling that the opposition to the tax was so intense that implementation would be difficult. See Kishiro, *Jimintō Zeiseichōsakai,* 1–13.

7. The postwar tax system was set up during the Occupation according to recommendations of a mission headed by Dr. Carl S. Shoup. The prewar system was centered on indirect taxes, and the Shoup plan emphasized a highly progressive structure centered on income taxes. See Joseph A. Pechman and Keimei Kaizuka, "Taxation," in *Asia's New Giant: How the Japanese Economy Works,* ed. Hugh Patrick and Henry Rosovsky (Washington, D.C.: Brookings Institution, 1976).

8. For a brief discussion of the changes in the tax structure since 1950, see Kuribayashi Yoshimitsu's interview with Ozaki Mamoru, the deputy chief of the Finance Ministry's tax bureau and head of the section handling indirect taxes, Kuribayashi, *Ōkura Shuzeikyoku* (Tokyo: Kōdansha, 1987), 197–99.

9. VAT of the type in effect in the European Community would be a tax levied at each stage of a transaction through the use of vouchers. As a product moves from one stage to the next, the producer, wholesaler, or retailer pays tax on the value of the product minus the tax that has already been paid at the previous stage. The amount of taxes paid at each stage is recorded on the voucher, which is passed on along with the product. The tax that Ōhira tried to introduce in 1979 and the current tax introduced by Takeshita are also assessed at each stage, but they are different from most other types of VAT in that the tax is not recorded through vouchers. Instead, it is simply recorded through bookkeeping.

10. Murayama was considered perhaps the LDP's most knowledgeable expert on taxes. He had been a top Finance Ministry official before becoming a politician and had served as chief of the ministry's tax bureau. He had also served as finance minister in the Fukuda administration and helped develop the proposals for the VAT that were picked up under the Ōhira administration. For more on Murayama Tatsuo, see Kishiro, *Jimintō Zeseichōsakai,* 98–106; Kuribayashi, *Ōkura Shuzeikyoku,* 74–80.

11. On November 27, 1984, Takeshita and Fujio agreed that a VAT, the same tax that Ōhira had advocated in 1979, should be introduced in the near future. The next day, Kanemaru also called for increased taxes, either the introduction of a new indirect tax or a review of the tax breaks for income accrued from interest and dividends. Kanemaru's goal, at the time, seemed to be to stimulate domestic demand through increased public works spending.

12. The Government Tax Council, in addition, proposed that *maruyū* accounts be taxed separately at a low rate. The LDP Tax Council had also considered reviewing the *maruyū* system, but after fierce resistance by LDP members of the posts and telecommunications *zoku*, the National Association of Postmasters, and the Posts and Telecommunications Ministry, the council was forced to abandon the plan.

13. U.S. tax reforms, particularly the 1986 Tax Reform Act, helped stimulate debates on tax reform in a number of other countries. See John Whalley, "Foreign Responses to U.S. Tax Reform," in *Do Taxes Matter? The Impact of the Tax Reform Act of 1986*, ed. Joel Slemrod (Cambridge, Mass.: MIT Press, 1990), 286–314.

14. The Tanaka faction's New Comprehensive Research Group released its tax reform proposals for fiscal 1986 on July 9.

15. Fujio reinaugurated the Murayama Research Council to study ideas for tax reform. During his term as chairman, he had been continually concerned with asserting the LDP's control over policy making. Thus he moved in on tax reform in order to retain the party's preeminence in the issue and prevent Nakasone from establishing his own advisory council.

16. In March 1980 the National Assembly passed a law requiring depositors to use a green card to identify themselves when making deposits. This was intended to end the use of multiple *maruyū* and postal accounts, but the system was never implemented. Led by Kanemaru, the LDP postal *zoku* pressured the Finance Ministry not to implement the law. See Chalmers Johnson, "MITI, MPT, and the Telecom Wars: How Japan Makes Policy for High Technology," BRIE Working Paper # 21 (Berkeley: Berkeley Roundtable on the International Economy, University of California, Berkeley, 1986), 47–48.

17. In September 1985, Nakasone appointed ten people from the private sector, most of whom were members of his brain trust of businessmen and academicians. In interviews with the *Asahi Shimbun* (September 14, 1985), the ten said that they all agreed with Nakasone that the goals of the tax reform should be fairness, simplicity, and choice, and they supported the prime minister in calling for the easing of the tax burden on middle-income earners. Some also wanted to implement tax cuts by fiscal 1986 (which would start on April 1, 1986), even though the final report was not due until the end of 1986. The ten were split over the introduction of a large indirect tax. Some supported an indirect tax to correct the ratio between direct and indirect taxes. Others said that emphasis

should be placed on cutting government expenditures. All ten, however, supported Nakasone in calling for no overall tax increases. They did not see tax reform as a means to raise revenue for social welfare or easing the national debt.

18. The two reports recommended that the highest rate for income and residential tax of 88 percent be lowered to the 60–70 percent range and that the rate for corporate taxes be lowered from 52.92 percent to the 40–50 percent range. The reports, however, did not mention how much the total amount of the tax cuts would be.

19. Although the Constitution grants the prime minister the right to dissolve the National Assembly and call elections with the approval of the cabinet, Nakasone's legal ability to call elections at that time was unclear because of the Supreme Court's ruling that the imbalance in the representation of districts in the lower house was unconstitutional. The legislature, however, passed the bill alleviating some of the imbalance.

20. See brief biographies of Yamanaka: Kishiro, *Jimintō Zeseichōsakai;* Kishiro Yasuyuki, "Yamanaka Sadanori: Jimintō no Seisaku Keiseiryoku wa Kanryō Soshiki o Koetaka?" in *Jimintō toiu Chie: Nihonteki Seiji Ryoku no Kenkyū* (Tokyo: JICC, 1987).

21. According to Mike Mochizuki, Yamanaka can be seen "more as Nakasone's rival rather than his follower." Mike Masato Mochizuki, "Managing and Influencing the Japanese Legislative Process: The Role of Parties and the National Diet" (Ph. D. diss., Harvard University, 1982), 177–78.

22. On September 29 aides to Nakasone leaked to the press that the manufacturer sales tax would not violate his election promise.

23. On November 3, Nakasone testified before the lower house's Budget Committee that, if the procedure and coverage of the tax were limited, then it would not be a large indirect tax. *Asahi Evening News,* November 8, 1986.

24. Sano Kazuyuki, "Kokumin no Teki 'Uriagezei' o Hineridashita Misshitsu no Genkyōtachi," *Gekkan Gendai* 21 (April 1987): 84–90.

25. The income tax cuts, according to the council, were designed to lighten the burden of taxpayers in the middle-income brackets. The report recommended that the cuts benefit chiefly the middle-income brackets (3–10 million yen); that the maximum income tax rate be reduced from 70 percent to 50 percent; that the residential tax be reduced from 18 percent to 15 percent; and that the number of tax brackets be reduced from sixteen to six for income taxes and from fourteen to four for residential taxes. The Finance Ministry estimated that the total cut in income and residential taxes would be 2.7 trillion yen a year.

The report also proposed that the effective corporate tax rate (local and national taxes combined) be reduced from 52.92 percent to under 50 percent. If it were set at 49.98 percent, the Finance Ministry estimated that the cut would mean an overall reduction of about 1.8 trillion yen. Finally, the council recommended that the *maruyū* tax exemptions be eliminated for all except old people and households headed by single mothers. It estimated that the elimination would produce 1 trillion yen.

26. The new tax was labeled a "sales tax" (*uriagezei*) rather than an "indirect tax" (*kansetsuzei*) because many felt that the public reaction would be less strong.

27. See Iwai Tomoaki and Inoguchi Takashi's analysis of the relative strength of the LDP commerce and industry *zoku* and the postal *zoku* in influencing the debate on tax reform, in their "Zeiseizoku no Seiji Rikigaku," *Chūō Kōron*, March 1987, 99–102. See also Gerald L. Curtis, "Big Business and Political Influence," in *Modern Japanese Organizations and Decision-Making*, ed. Ezra F. Vogel (Berkeley and Los Angeles: University of California Press, 1975), 33–70.

28 Sano, "Kokumin no Teki," 88.

29. By contrast, the countries of the European Community have a much lower ceiling. Britain's is 20,500 pounds (about 5 million yen) and West Germany's is 20,000 marks (about 1.7 million yen). *Japan Times*, March 18, 1987.

30. *Asahi Shimbun*, November 28, 1986.

31. The initial proposal allowed exemptions for nine items: food and drink, medical care covered by public health insurance, school-related goods and services, social welfare services, sales of land and other negotiable securities, interest earned from financial transactions, items already covered by the current commodities tax system, public-chartered entities and other organizations serving the public interest that did not compete with private enterprises, and exports.

32. For a full list see Fujita Sei, *Zeisei Kaikaku, Sono Kiseki to Tenbō* (Tokyo: Zeimu Keiri Kyōkai, 1987), 78.

33. See Johnson, "MITI, MPT, and the Telecom Wars," 47–48.

34. Kishiro, "Yamanaka," 127.

35. The compromise plan had four main points. First, the MPT would be allowed to use some of the funds in postal savings, which were previously under the control of the Finance Ministry. The ministry would be allowed to invest 2 trillion yen of postal savings in fiscal 1987 in securities, which had higher returns and thus could help cover the expected loss in funds deposited. The amount of discretionary funds would be increased by 500 billion yen a year from fiscal 1988 through 1991, with the total reaching 15 trillion yen in five years. Second, the ceiling on the amount an individual would be allowed to deposit would be raised from 3 million to 5 million yen. Third, the law regarding deposit interest would be revised. And fourth, post office branches would be allowed to sell government bonds.

36. The addendum to the policy speech that brought the opposition parties back to the National Assembly took all of ten seconds.

37. Mochizuki, "Japanese Legislative Process."

38. Many of the group's leaders were also leaders in the personal support groups (*kōenkai*) of the LDP politicians.

39. Iwai and Inoguchi, "Zeiseizoku."

40. The survey is quoted in both the *Japan Times* and the *Asahi Evening News*, February 2, 1987.

41. *Asahi Shimbun*, March 9, 1987.

42. Twelve of the forty-seven prefectures adopted resolutions opposing the VAT or calling for the withdrawal of the proposed tax plan. In seventeen others in which the LDP and other conservative groups constituted the majority, the assemblies turned down resolutions calling for the withdrawal of the plan but passed instead resolutions asking Nakasone to deal cautiously with it. Two assemblies, those of Gifu and Kōchi, passed resolutions proposing that the tax plan be amended. Tokushima and Kagawa were the only two that voted to support the new tax. *Asahi Evening News*, March 16, 1987.

43. The final compromise offered by Speaker Hara is as follows (translation and summary from *Japan Times*, April 26, 1987):

> To break the present deadlock, I am using my good offices. Since there is no agreement on how to deal with the [VAT] bills, the speaker will place them in his custody. But, (1) It goes without saying, the problem with the taxation system is one of the most important issues today in view of the need to cope with the problems of an aging society and others as well as in the light of observing our nation's fiscal policies in the future. Thus, there is urgency to the issue of adjusting the ratio between direct and indirect taxes and all parties must cooperate and devote their full efforts. (2) For this purpose, as soon as the 1987 budget is approved by this House, a deliberative organ devoted to the reform of the taxation system should be set up. All parties should immediately confer on its composition and management. (3) How to deal with the bills related to the [VAT] will be decided after the result of the deliberative organ is known. If a conclusion cannot be obtained in the present legislative session, further efforts will be made to seek an agreement among all parties.
>
> (Question-and-Answer Section): *Question* (opposition parties): "What will be done if no agreement can be reached among all parties?" *Answer* (Speaker): "Naturally, every effort must be made to seek agreement. But if it failed, ordinarily, it would either be unfinished or continued business. However, in this case, it would be an unfinished matter." *Question*: "By unfinished matter is generally meant the rejection of the bills. Is that correct?" *Answer*: "This is so. It means this [National Assembly] has rejected them. Please do not forget to establish the deliberative organ mentioned in the 2nd item." *Answer* (opposition parties): "We will comply."

44. *Asahi Shimbun*, April 26, 1987.

45. The length of the extraordinary session was well above the average for extraordinary sessions of twenty-six days. The longest session ran one hundred days and the shortest only one day. See Mochizuki, "Japanese Legislative Process," 57.

46. On May 21 the five parties agreed on the composition of the lower house

council, the LDP having a majority with seven of the thirteen members. Originally the LDP had planned to nominate Yamanaka to be the chairman,but the opposition parties strongly opposed this because he had been one of the main supporters of the VAT. Instead the party nominated Itō. The opposition parties consented to let the LDP have a majority after the LDP agreed not to use its majority to force its own policies through.

47. *Asahi Shimbun*, May 25, 1987.

48. The elimination of the tax-free savings system was supposed to induce Japanese to save less and consume more. For an explanation of why Japan's high savings rate is one of the main factors contributing to its trade surplus, see Ed Lincoln, *Japan: Reaching Economic Maturity* (Washington, D.C.: Brookings Institution, 1985).

49. On August 4, Ichikawa Yūichi, chairman of the Kōmeitō's Legislative Affairs Committee, said that the party would be willing to support *maruyū*'s elimination if it were part of a move to a comprehensive progressive system that included both earned income and interest income. On August 5, Tsukamoto Saburō, the chairman of the DSP, announced that his party would be willing to be flexible on the *maruyū* issue if the tax cut was increased to over 2 trillion yen.

50. With the agreement, the National Assembly could resume as scheduled on August 18, when the LDP would explain the tax reform bills to the lower house plenary session, and then on about August 25 the bills would move to the Finance Committee for deliberations, and be passed in the lower house on September 8, the last day of the scheduled legislative session.

51. *Yomiuri Shimbun*, August 8, 1987.

52. *Asahi Shimbun*, August 20, 1987. Kanemaru, along with Takeshita, is known to have excellent connections to the leadership of the DSP and the Kōmeitō, and these connections probably played a part in preventing them from boycotting the deliberations and getting them to agree to a compromise on the size of the tax cut.

53. The main contents of the bills were: (1) The number of income tax brackets was reduced from fifteen to twelve, with tax rates from 10.5–60 percent; the top rate was lowered from 70 to 60 percent. The minimum taxable income was raised from 500,000 yen a year to 1.5 million yen. Most of the decreases, however, such as an income tax deduction for nonworking spouses, were aimed at the middle-class wage earners. The changes went into effect for fiscal 1987. (2) The number of brackets for the local residential tax was reduced from 14 to 7, while the range of tax rates was changed from 4.5–18 percent to 5–16 percent. The changes would go into effect at the start of fiscal 1988. (3) The *maruyū* system was abolished and a uniform 20 percent separate tax imposed on all types of interest earned, with exceptions for fatherless families, the physically handicapped, and people aged 65 and over. The changes were to go into effect on April 1, 1988.

54. The rates and the number of tax brackets for income, resident, and

corporate taxes were reduced. In particular, the biggest income tax cuts were given to middle-income earners, the salaried workers who were regarded as having the heaviest tax burdens.

55. The exemptions were certain financial transactions, and medical, education, and welfare services.

56. The LDP passed the tax package with its majority in both houses. The DSP and the Kōmeitō voted against the bills, and the JSP and the JCP boycotted the vote.

57. The LDP won 275 seats, and, with conservative independents, it now had a total strength in the lower house of 286 (out of 512).

Chapter 5
The Process of Selecting a Prime Minister

1. Japanese Constitution, Article 67.

2. On two occasions, the party seriously considered splitting the two positions. In 1982, Fukuda Takeo offered a compromise to Nakasone whereby he would take the party presidency and Nakasone would become prime minister; but Nakasone refused and went on to win the presidency and become prime minister. In 1979 the LDP could not decide between Ōhira Masayoshi and Fukuda Takeo, so both became formal candidates for the prime ministership (along with the head of each of the opposition parties). With the LDP split, the opposition parties could have changed the result by either throwing their support behind Fukuda or uniting behind a single opposition candidate. They did neither, allowing Ōhira to win.

3. The LDP held 286 seats in the lower house after the 1990 election and 109 seats in the upper house after the 1989 election.

4. Nathaniel B. Thayer, *How the Conservatives Rule Japan* (Princeton, N.J.: Princeton University Press, 1969), 21.

5. Technically, during the first half-year after the party was formed in November 1955, it was headed by a group of leaders from the former Liberal and Democratic parties, which included Hatoyama Ichirō, the incumbent prime minister and head of the former Democratic party; Ogata Taketora, the head of the former Liberal party; Miki Bukichi; and Ōno Bamboku. Hatoyama became the first formal president of the LDP in April 1956.

6. Suzuki Zenkō, who became prime minister upon Ōhira's death in 1980, might also be considered an exception. But, as will be explained later in this chapter, he was chosen because he had the support of the Ōhira faction. In this sense he too was the head of a faction.

7. On two occasions, during intense intraparty rivalries, a leader of a major faction proposed that a party elder who was not the head of a major faction be allowed to take over the party presidency. In 1974, Tanaka resigned the prime ministership and tried to install someone who would serve only as a temporary replacement so that he could have a chance of regaining the post. He asked Shiina Etsusaburō, then the party's vice president, to consider taking over, but Shiina declined to run. In 1979, Fukuda and Ōhira were battling over control of the party in the so-called Forty-Day War. Fukuda, at one point, suggested that Nadao Hirokichi, a party elder, become president and prime minister. Ōhira refused to go along. Both Ōhira and Fukuda then ran as candidates for the prime ministership in the National Assembly, an election which Ōhira won.

8. There was no such restriction before 1971; any LDP member of the National Assembly was eligible, and candidates were not required to file petitions. Starting in 1971, a formal petition was required. At first, a candidate needed only ten signatures. The number was increased to twenty in 1977 and to fifty in 1981. It was set temporarily at twenty in August 1989 prior to Kaifu's selection for the presidency; and in October 1989 it was reset at thirty signatures. For a summary of the changes, see app. E.

9. Haruhiro Fukui, "The Liberal Democratic Party Revisited: Continuity and Change in the Party's Structure and Performance," *Journal of Japanese Studies* 10 (Summer 1984): 385–435. For an earlier study, see Sun Ryang Key, "Postwar Japanese Political Leadership—A Study of Prime Ministers," *Asian Survey* 13 (November 1973): 1010–200.

10. Abe Shintarō, until his death in 1991, was widely expected to be the successor to Kaifu Toshiki.

11. Most of the leaders of the major opposition parties are also members of the lower house. The exceptions are the DSP's secretary, Ōuchi Keigo, who lost his seat in the lower house in the 1986 election, and the JCP's chairman, Miyamoto Kenji, who is a member of the upper house.

12. See Satō Seizaburō and Matsuzaki Tetsuhisa, *Jimintō Seiken* (Tokyo: Chūō Kōron, 1986). The mean age is about 46 years; most were in their forties, and two, Tanaka Kakuei (fifth term) and Miki Takeo (fourth term), were only 39. The exceptions who were in their early 50s (Fukuda Takeo and Ōhira) were top bureaucrats before being elected to the National Assembly.

13. Satō and Matsuzaki, *Jimintō Seiken*, 47, 215.

14. Tahara Sōichirō, *Abe, Takeshita ni Sun'nari Seiken ga Ikanai Riyū* (Tokyo: Kōbunsha, 1986), 26–27.

15. Nakamura Keiichirō, *Miki Seiken: 747 Nichi* (Tokyo: Gyōseimondai Kenkyūjo, 1981). 43.

16. In particular, top bureaucrats were often appointed to top cabinet and

party posts soon after being elected to the National Assembly. Prime Minister Yoshida Shigeru, who was originally a diplomat, appointed Ikeda Hayato (Finance Ministry) and Satō Eisaku (Transportation Ministry) to important posts during the first year after their election. Fukuda Takeo, a former Finance Ministry official, in only his fourth term in the National Assembly was appointed by Kishi Nobusuke to the LDP executive post of chairman of the PARC. Ikeda also appointed a number of former bureaucrats from the Finance Ministry to important posts in his cabinet. Ōhira was chief cabinet secretary (during his fourth term) and foreign minister (during his fifth term); and Miyazawa served twice as chief of the Economic Planning Agency (during his second term in the upper house).

17. The only top bureaucrat in recent years to be elected to the House of Representatives and not be confined by the seniority system is Gotōda Masaharu, a former commissioner general of the NPA. Even in his case, he himself admits, he was probably too old to make a serious run for the presidency. Gotōda Masaharu, *Seiji towa Nanika* (Tokyo: Kōdansha, 1988).

18. Second-generation politicians include Hashimoto Ryūtarō, Hata Tsutomu, Katō Kōichi, Kōno Yōhei, Obuchi Keizō, Ozawa Ichirō, Watanabe Michio, and Yamaguchi Toshio. See app. C. Gerald L. Curtis notes that the second-generation phenomenon has become a predominant feature of LDP recruitment patterns in the 1970s and 1980s. Curtis, *The Japanese Way of Politics* (New York: Columbia University Press, 1988), 96. He believes that the second-generation politicians give the party a more modern look because of their greater diversity in career backgrounds and life experience compared to other LDP politicians. In particular, they are supposedly more "international" in outlook because of their work experience in banks, trading companies, and other corporations involved in international business. Among the next generation of leaders, however, only Katō Kōichi and Kōno Yōhei have had much international experience. Katō was in the Foreign Ministry and speaks excellent English and Chinese. Kōno studied at Stanford University. But a number of older party leaders also had similar experiences.

19. Tahara, *Abe, Takeshita*, 25.

20. Politicians cited by Tahara include Utsunomiya Tokuma, Ishida Hirohide, Sonoda Tsunao, Ishihara Shintarō, Kimura Toshio, and Ide Ichitarō. Ibid., 30.

21. Ibid., 32–33. See also Hanta Kensuke, *Kikubari Mekubari Shusse Jutsu* (Tokyo: Tokyo Shuppan, 1988).

22. According to Curtis, most of the political funds for members of the faction until the mid-1970s were raised by its head. The 1976 revision of the law regulating political funds made it impossible for these leaders to continue their monopoly on funding channels and helped encourage the individual politicians to set up their own independent channels. Curtis, *Japanese Way of Politics*, 84.

23. Tahara, Abe, Takeshita, 77.

24. Ibid., 141.

25. Interview with Hori Shigeru in Tahara, Abe, Takeshita, 62–63.

26. Of the party posts, Fukui lists the top party executive positions (i.e., the san'yaku posts plus the vice presidency) as the most important stepping-stones to the presidency. Next in importance is the chairmanship of the Legislative Affairs Committee, followed by the chairmanship of the Finance Committee. Of lesser importance are the chairmanships of the national organization, public information, and party discipline committees and the assembly of the members of both houses and the assembly of the House of Representatives, Fukui, "Liberal Democratic Party," 409–11.

27. One political journalist uses a five-point system to rank the importance of positions for becoming party president. The secretary general's post ranks the full five points. The two cabinet posts, foreign and finance, rank in the second tier with four points; the chief cabinet secretaryship, the two other san'yaku posts, the chairs of the executive council and the PARC, rate three points; the chair of the party's National Assembly strategy committee and the MITI post are two points; and all the other cabinet and executive party posts bring just one point. The vice presidency brings no points in this system, because no vice president has ever become party president. Kikuchi Hisashi, Jimintō Habatsu (Tokyo: Pīpurusha, 1987), 95–96.

28. See Thayer, Conservatives, 272–75.

29. There have been three exceptions, two of whom were Hatoyama and Ishibashi Tanzan, the first two party presidents. The only recent example is Suzuki Zenkō.

30. Kishi appointed Kawashima Shōjirō and Fukuda Takeo; Ikeda appointed Maeo Shigesaburō; Satō appointed Tanaka and Fukuda Takeo.

31. Satō and Matsuzaki, Jimintō Seiken, 99.

32. Itō Masoya and Fukuoka Masayuki write that if the value of the secretary general's post is 100, then that of the chairmanship of the PARC has risen from below 50 to well above 50. Itō and Fukuoka, Korekara 10-nen Sengoku Jimintō (Tokyo: Daiichi Kikaku Shuppan, 1988), 38.

33. Ibid. See also Kikuchi, Jimintō Habatsu, 83–85.

34. There have been only six vice presidents since the founding of the party in 1955: Kawashima Shōjirō, Ōno, Shiina Estusaburō, Funada Naka, Nishimura Eiichi, and Nikaidō Susumu. Of these, only Ōno was a serious candidate for the presidency while serving as vice president. Nikaidō also tried in 1984 and 1987, but his candidacy was relatively weak.

35. For a discussion of number-two types, see Itō and Fukuoka, Korekara 10-Nen, 38, 83, 93–98.

36. There have been three cases where the vice president has played an important part in selecting the successor to the presidency. In 1964, when Prime Minister Ikeda announced his resignation because of health problems, Kawashima Shōjirō, along with Secretary General Miki Takeo, handled the negotiations with the factions that led to the selection of Satō. In 1974, after Tanaka resigned, Shiina Etsusaburō took the lead in having Miki Takeo succeed to the presidency. And in 1980, when Ōhira died suddenly, Nishimura Eiichi helped in the meditations that led to the selection of Suzuki.

37. See Satō and Matsuzaki, *Jimintō Seiken*; Inoguchi Takashi and Iwai Tomoaki, *"Zoku-Giin" no Kenkyū* (Tokyo: Nihon Keizai Shimbunsha, 1987). Of the next generation of leaders, only Kawara Tsutomu is not considered a *zoku-giin* in any area, and policy expertise is one area that political observers say he must develop to rise in the party. See information on Kawara in *Gendai Seiji Jōhō*, 1987, 4th ed. (Tokyo: Sekai Nipōsha, 1986), 148.

38. The only other LDP president who did not occupy any of these posts was the first, Hatoyama Ichirō.

39. Fukui's study of career patterns of top party leaders suggests that cabinet appointments can be ranked into four categories. Of critical importance are the four mentioned so far, plus posts and telecommunications. Next in importance are agriculture, defense, construction, labor, and science and technology. And below them are transportation and administrative management, with all other posts ranked as only marginal. Fukui admits that he has no ready explanation why the posts and telecommunications positions are ranked as high as the other four in the top group or why the director general of either the Science and Technology Agency or the Administrative Management Agency should be more important than the director general of the Economic Planning Agency. Fukui, "Liberal Democratic Party," 409–11.

40. Jin Ikkō, *Sōridaijin no Isu no Nedan* (Tokyo: KK Besutoserāzu, 1987), 162.

41. See Ellis S. Krauss, "Conflict in the Diet: Toward Conflict Management in Parliamentary Politics," in *Conflict in Japan*, ed. Ellis S. Krauss, Thomas P. Rohlen, and Patricia G. Steinhoff (Honolulu: University of Hawaii Press, 1984), 243–93.

42. Fukui's study suggests that the House of Representatives Management Committee and Budget Committee, plus the LDP Legislative Affairs Committee, rank highest among legislative posts as rungs on the ladder to the top. On the next rung are the lower house committees on commerce and industry, finance, education, cabinet, construction, local administration, and foreign affairs. All others are of "marginal importance." Fukui, "Liberal Democratic Party," 409–10. See also Krauss, "Conflict in the Diet," 272.

43. Tahara lists four people in particular with this ability: Satō, Tanaka, Kanemaru Shin, and Takeshita. See Tahara *Abe, Takeshita*, 66–69. According to

Tahara, Satō and Tanaka were the first to give money to rival factions or to opposition members. The earlier practice was to give funds to opposition party members only during difficult legislative negotiations. With Tanaka, first as Satō's secretary general and then as prime minister, money was given out regularly to everyone. Tanaka would make a gift of money when he visited someone who was sick. When an opposition member or his wife entered a hospital, he or she would receive an envelope from an influential member of the LDP. Money was also given during gift-giving seasons. Tanaka also started the practice of giving *senbetsu* (bon voyage gifts) to members of the National Assembly—both LDP and opposition— going abroad for an inspection or study tour.

44. One example of Takeshita's influence with the opposition came in 1975 under the Miki administration. The opposition parties were demanding the resignation of Kariya Tadao, then construction minister, for making remarks that the opposition claimed belittled the Constitution and the National Assembly. Takeshita went to the aid of his fellow faction member. He talked with members of the opposition and worked it out so that they would drop their demands for Kariya's resignation in return for an apology. Takeshita also helped save Miki from facing a legislative crisis. Miki commented, "It's frightening how much influence Takeshita has with them." Miki rewarded Takeshita by appointing him construction minister soon after, when Kariya died suddenly in office. Nakamura, *Miki Seiken*, 170–71.

45. The party convention in July 1989 had a choice of candidates for the first time in over fifteen years, although the outcome was already a foregone conclusion, with Kaifu receiving support from four of the five major factions. The last time the LDP members of the Kokkai actually voted in a party convention that meant anything was in 1972 when Tanaka beat Fukuda Takeo for the presidency.

46. The number of votes given to the prefectures under the new system is as follows: under 20,000 ballots, 1 vote; 20,000–49,999 ballots, 2 votes; 50,000– 99,999 ballots, 3 votes; 100,000 or more ballots, 4 votes. In 1991 prefectures had a total of 101 votes.

47. See Iijima Kiyoshi, Miyazaki Yoshimasa, and Watanabe Tsuneo, eds., *Seiji no Jōshiki Daihyakka* (Tokyo: Kōdansha, 1983), 101. According to insiders, during the 1972 presidential election the going rate for a LDP member's vote was 10 million yen. See also Thayer's description of the 1957 and 1960 presidential elections, *Conservatives*, 163–73.

48. Watanabe Tsuneo, *Tōshu to Seitō* (Tokyo: Kōbundō, 1961), 1, quoted in Thayer, *Conservatives*, 174.

49. Ōno is one exception of a faction head stepping aside to give another candidate a better shot at the presidency. Ōno was one of the "party politicians,"

who included Ishii Mitsujirō, Kōno Ichirō, Ishibashi, Matsumura Kenzō, and Kawashima Shōjirō. Ōno pulled out of the race in order to give Ishii a better chance of defeating Ikeda, who was supported by the "career bureaucrats," who included Satō and Kishi. Ōno's efforts, however, were in vain: Ikeda won. See Thayer's account of the 1960 presidential election, *Conservatives*, 170–73.

50. Tanaka, the head of the faction, was not able to compete himself because he was on trial for taking bribes from Lockheed, and he was not willing to allow anyone else from his camp to compete. He was convinced that he would be acquitted of all charges, and his intent was to become party president once again.

51. Tanaka had left the political scene by then, having suffered a stroke in 1985.

52. The Tanaka faction received six cabinet posts and the secretary general's position. One of the six cabinet appointments was that of chief cabinet secretary. When Nakasone appointed Gotōda Masaharu to it, this was seen as further proof of Tanaka's influence over Nakasone. Both Nakasone and Gotōda, however, revealed later that the assignment was made over Tanaka's objection.

53. Curtis writes that public image does matter, as Nakasone was able to show during his five-year tenure. See Curtis, *Japanese Way of Politics*, 100–106. Aside from the resignation of Tanaka, the selection of Miki as his successor, and the case of Nakasone, however, I find it difficult to see how public opinion played a part. The impact of public opinion has been more in tinkering with the selection process to make it seem more democratic rather than in the selection of president itself.

54. Satō and Matsuzaki, *Jimintō Seiken*, 75–76.

55. Richard Rose, "Learning to Campaign or Learning to Govern?" chap. 6 of his *Postmodern President: George Bush Meets the World*, 2d ed. (Chatham, N.J.: Chatham House, 1991), 93–1115. Rose sees three areas in which U.S. presidents need experience: campaigning (going public), the politics of government (going Washington), and managing the economy and national security (going international). His critique of the U.S. system is that the president is a professional in going public but an amateur in dealing with the politics of government or the important issues facing the country.

56. Had he wanted to, Suzuki very likely would have been able to win a second full term as LDP president in 1982. Uno would have had to resign whether he wanted to or not following the LDP's loss of its majority in the upper house in the 1989 election. But he showed his willingness just before the election when he told his aides that he wanted to resign because of the scandal surrounding his affair with a geisha. Party leaders dissuaded him despite the scandal because there was no time to select another person to replace him.

Chapter 6
The Prime Minister and Party Politics

1. Bert A. Rockman, *The Leadership Question: The Presidency and the American System* (New York: Praeger, 1984), 223.

2. Ibid.

3. George W. Jones, "West European Prime Ministers in Perspective," *West European Politics* 14 (April 1991): 163–78. See also Yves Mény, *Government and Politics in Western Europe: Britain, France, Italy, West Germany,* trans. Janet Lloyd (Oxford: Oxford University, 1990), 218–23.

4. For problems of party discipline in the British House of Commons, see Leon D. Epstein, "What Happened to the British Party Model?" *American Political Science Review* 74 (March 1980): 9–22; John E. Schwarz, "Exploring a New Role in Policy Making: The British House of Commons in the 1970s," *American Political Science Review* 74 (March 1980): 23–27; R. K. Alderman and Neil Carter, "A Very Tory Coup: The Ousting of Mrs. Thatcher," *Parliamentary Affairs* 44 (April 1991): 125–39; R. K. Alderman and Martin J. Smith, "Can British Prime Ministers Be Given the Push by Their Parties?" *Parliamentary Affairs* 43 (July 1990): 260–76.

5. See Tanaka Zen'ichirō, *Jimintō Taisei no Seiji Shidō* (Tokyo: Daiichi Hōki, 1981).

6. Patrick Weller, *First among Equals: Prime Ministers in Westminster Systems* (Sydney: George Allen and Unwin, 1985), 20.

7. John W. Kingdon, *Agendas, Alternatives, and Public Policies* (Boston: Little, Brown, 1984), 26–27.

8. Weller, *First among Equals,* 20.

9. Ibid., 24.

10. See Itō Masaya, *Jimintō no Sengokushi: Kenryoku no Kenkyū* (Tokyo: Asahi Sonorama, 1982); *Shin Jimintō no Sengokushi* (Tokyo: Asahi Sonorama, 1983).

11. The four major factions are headed by Takeshita Noboru, Mitsuzuka Hiroshi, Miyazawa Kiichi, and Watanabe Michio, and the smaller one by Kōmoto Toshio.

12. Nathaniel B. Thayer, *How the Conservatives Rule Japan* (Princeton, N.J.: Princeton University Press, 1969), 15.

13. Weller, *First among Equals,* 45.

14. The one case is Neville Chamberlain. But Mackintosh argues that even in this case, the prime minister lost his position largely because the Labour party refused to join in a coalition with him. Mackintosh, *The Government and Politics of Britain,* 3d rev. edition (London: Hutchinson, 1974).

15. Weller, *First among Equals,* 47.

16. Ibid.

17. See Itō, *Jimintō no Sengokushi.*

18. Karel G. van Wolferen claims that Suzuki was actually forced out because of his poor handling of Japan's relationship with the United States: former prime minister Kishi Nobusuke persuaded Suzuki to step down. Van Wolferen, *The Enigma of Japanese Power: People and Politics in a Stateless Nation* (New York: Alfred A. Knopf, 1989), 149–59.

19. Kishi Nobusuke, "Jikyoku Shokan: Naze Tōkakai o Kaisan Shitaka," *KSK Report* (November 20, 1962): 52, quoted in Haruhiro Fukui, *Party in Power: The Japanese Liberal Democrats and Policymaking* (Berkeley and Los Angeles: University of California Press, 1970), 97–98.

20. Fukui, *Party in Power*, 98.

21. Nakamura Kiichirō, *Miki Seiken:747 nichi* (Tokyo: Gyōseimondai Kenkyūjo, 1981).

22. Mike Masato Mochizuki, "Managing and Influencing the Japanese Legislative Process: The Role of Parties and the National Diet," (Ph. D. diss. Harvard University, 1982), 248.

23. See Tanaka Zen'ichirō, *Jimintō no Doramatsurugi* (Tokyo: Tōkyō Daigaku Shuppankai, 1987). As I pointed out in the previous chapter, there has not always been a limit on the LDP president's tenure. Before 1972 there were no restrictions as to the number of consecutive terms: Satō Eisaku was elected four times and Ikeda Hayato three.

24. Haruhiro Fukui, "The Liberal Democratic Party Revisited: Continuity and Change in the Party's Structure and Performance," *Journal of Japanese Studies* 10 (Summer 1984): 421–23.

25. The practice of dividing the posts proportionately started following Satō Eisaku's third term as party president. Before then, the mainstream factions (the coalition of those supporting the president) tended to benefit more. See Satō Seizaburō and Matsuzaki Tetsuhisa, *Jimintō Seiken* (Tokyo: Chūō Kōron, 1986), 63–73.

26. See Thayer, *Conservatives*, 180–206.

27. The other two cases involved Hirano Rikizō, agriculture minister in the Katayama cabinet, dismissed in November 1947; and Hirokawa Hiroyoshi, agriculture minister in the fourth Yoshida cabinet, dismissed in March 1953.

28. Michael Leiserson, "Factions and Coalitions in One-Party Japan: An Interpretation Based on the Theory of Games," *American Political Science Review* 62 (September 1968): 770–87.

29. See Itō, *Jimintō no Sengokushi* and *Shin Jimintō no Sengokushi*.

30. Daniel I. Okimoto, *Between MITI and the Market: Japanese Industrial Policy for High Technology* (Stanford, Calif.: Stanford University Press, 1989), 209.

31. Epstein, "British Party Model," 9–22.

32. Other cases have included back-bench revolts over proposed cuts in

agricultural supports. See Inoguchi Takashi and Iwai Tomoaki, "Zoku-Giin" no Ken kyū (Tokyo: Nihon Keizai Shimbunsha, 1987), esp. chap. 6. See also Susan J. Pharr, "Liberal Democrats in Disarray: Intergenerational Conflict in the Conservative Camp," in Political Leadership in Japan, ed. Terry Edward MacDougall, Michigan Papers in Japanese Studies, no. 1 (Ann Arbor: Center for Japanese Studies, the University of Michigan, 1982), 29–50.

33. Kent E. Calder, Crisis and Compensation: Public Policy and Political Stability in Japan, 1949–1986 (Princeton, N.J.: Princeton University Press, 1988), 66–70.

34. For information on kōenkai see Gerald L. Curtis, Election Campaigning Japanese Style (New York: Columbia University Press, 1971).

35. For sources of funding see Gerald L. Curtis, The Japanese Way of Politics (New York: Columbia University Press, 1988), 84.

36. Inoguchi and Iwai, "Zoku-giin" no Kenkyū.

37. Iwai Tomoaki and Inoguchi Takashi, "Zeiseizoku no Seiji Rikigaku," Chūō Kōron (March 1987): 96–106; Inoguchi and Iwai, "Zoku-Giin" no Kenkyū, 260–72.

38. Inoguchi and Iwai, "Zoku-giin" no Kenkyū, 270–71.

39. Hatoyama Kunio, "Interview: Hatoyama Kunio," Gekkan Gendai 21 (April 1987): 80–83.

40. Thayer, Conservatives.

41. Chalmers Johnson, MITI and the Japanese Miracle: The Growth of Industrial Policy, 1925–1975 (Stanford, Calif.: Stanford University Press, 1982), 49.

42. Mochizuki, "Japanese Legislative Process," 45.

43. During the period from 1967 to 1979, only 13 percent of the cabinet bills passed had substantive amendments. See Ibid., 101.

44. About 60–80 percent of the bills have the support of the DSP, the Kōmeitō, and the JSP, as well as the LDP. Moreover, the DSP and the Kōmeitō join the LDP in 90 percent of the votes. Ibid., 291–96.

45. For examples of such bills during 1970–74, see Bradley M. Richardson and Scott C. Flanagan, Politics in Japan (Boston: Little, Brown, 1984), 355. See also Mochizuki, "Japanese Legislative Process."

46. See Mochizuki's analysis of two separate National Assembly sessions under Prime Minister Satō. Mochizuki, "Japanese Legislative Process," 224–43.

47. Mochizuki believes that the norms of consensus developed after 1960 when Ikeda Hayato became prime minister and the LDP took a more accommodative attitude toward the opposition parties. Ibid., 423–29. Ellis S. Krauss believes that the norms developed somewhat later, when the gains made by the opposition parties in the 1970s forced the LDP to deal with them on a more equal basis. Krauss, "Conflict in the Diet: Toward Conflict Management in Parliamentary Politics," in Conflict in Japan, ed. Ellis S. Krauss, Thomas P. Rohlen, and Patricia G. Steinhoff, (Honolulu: University of Hawaii Press, 1984), 243–93; Krauss, "Japanese

Parties and Parliament: Changing Leadership Roles and Role Conflict," in *Political Leadership in Japan*, ed. Terry Edward MacDougall, Michigan Papers in Japanese Studies, no. 1 (Ann Arbor: Center for Japanese Studies, University of Michigan, 1982), 93–114.

48. Weller, *First among Equals*, 173–76.

49. Mochizuki, "Japanese Legislative Process"; Iwai Tomoaki, *Rippō Katei* (Tokyo: Tokyo Daigaku Shuppankai, 1988); Sone Yasunori and Iwai Tomoaki "Seisaku Katei ni Okeru Gikai no Yakuwari," *Nenpō Seijigaku* (1987): 149–74.

50. Formally, the speaker of the house has the authority to refer bills to the appropriate committee, but in practice it is the House Management Committee that makes the decision. Mochizuki, "Japanese Legislative Process," 50.

51. Ibid., 78.

52. Ibid.

53. See ibid.; Hans H. Baerwald, *Party Politics in Japan* (Boston: Allen and Unwin, 1986), 94–96.

54. A 1975 bill to revise the antimonopoly law, for example, passed the lower house, but was tabled in the upper house. See Mochizuki, "Japanese Legislative Process," 166–97.

55. Under Labour governments, however, the British House of Lords has sometimes used its powers to delay legislation.

56. Weller, *First among Equals*, 176. In addition, Mochizuki notes that the upper house has stronger formal powers than the West German Bundestag or the French Senate, although weaker powers than the Italian Senate. Mochizuki, "Japanese Legislative Process," 82–85.

57. The Interparliamentary Union's comparative survey of parliaments in fifty-five countries states that the number of days when the Japanese National Assembly actually sits in session is among the lowest. Other such legislatures are those of Belgium, Ireland, New Zealand, and Switzerland. Cited in Mochizuki, "Japanese Legislative Process," 55–63. However, Weller indicates that the Australian parliament sits about 70–80 days a year and the New Zealand parliament, 95–110 days, while those of Britain and Canada sit 160–200 days a year. Weller, *First among Equals*, 170.

58. The reason why the LDP needs approximately fifteen seats more than a simple majority for a stable majority is that the chairman is a nonvoting member of the committee. This means that in order for the party to control all of the committees, it must have a voting majority plus one in each. When the number of seats falls below this level, the LDP loses either the chair of some of the committees or its voting majority.

59. For an analysis of the changes in the National Assembly under *hakuchū*, see Krauss, "Japanese Parties and Parliament."

60. The Constitution is vague on the cabinet's authority to call elections. Clearly, according to Article 69, the cabinet can call elections when it loses the confidence of the House of Representatives. The issue of whether elections can be called at other times was settled in 1952 when the Supreme Court upheld Yoshida's decision to call an election under Article 7, which states that the Emperor, with the advice and approval of the cabinet, shall perform a number of acts "in matters of state on behalf of the people," one of which is the dissolution of the House of Representatives.

61. Nakasone was also pressured to hold an election by Tanaka himself, who wanted to be able to claim a mandate from his constituents.

62. Weller, First among Equals, 176.

63. See chap. 5.

64. Elections have been held anywhere from about six months to the full four years after the previous House of Representatives election, but almost all have been called within two and a half to three and a half years.

Chapter 7
The Prime Minister and Subgovernments

1. Richard Rose, "Government against Sub-Governments: A European Perspective on Washington," in *Presidents and Prime Ministers*, ed. Richard Rose and Ezra N. Suleiman (Washington, D.C.: American Enterprise Institute, 1980): 289.

2. Ibid., 292.

3. For a review of the various models of Japanese democracy, see Haruhiro Fukui, "Studies in Policymaking: A Review of the Literature," in *Policymaking in Contemporary Japan*, ed. T. J. Pempel (Ithaca, N.Y.: Cornell University Press, 1977).

4. Chalmers Johnson, MITI *and the Japanese Miracle: The Growth of Industrial Policy, 1925–1975* (Stanford, Calif.: Stanford University Press, 1982). For a view challenging Johnson's, see Richard J. Samuels, *The Business of the Japanese State: Energy Markets in Comparative and Historical Perspective* (Ithaca, N.Y.: Cornell University Press, 1987).

5. Michio Muramatsu and Ellis S. Krauss, "The Conservative Policy Line and the Development of Patterned Pluralism," in *The Political Economy of Japan*, vol. 1, *The Domestic Transformation*, ed. Kozo Yamamura and Yasukichi Yasuba (Stanford, Calif.: Stanford University Press, 1987); Inoguchi Takashi, *Gendai Nihon Seiji Keizai no Kōzu: Seifu to Shijo* (Tokyo: Tōkyō Keizai Shimpō sha, 1983); Satō Seizaburō and Matsuzaki Tetsuhisa, *Jimintō Seiken* (Tokyo: Chūō Kōron, 1986); Ōtake Hideo, *Gendai Nihon no Seiji Kenryoku Keizai Kenryoku* (Tokyo: San'ichi Shobō, 1979); Sone Yasunori, "Tagen Minshushugi-ron to Gendai Kokka," *Nenpō Seijigaku* (1982), 117–49.

6. Muramatsu and Krauss, "Conservative Policy Line," 542–43.

7. Inoguchi, *Gendai Nihon Seiji*; Satō and Matsuzaki, *Jimintō Seiken*.

8. Satō and Matsuzaki, *Jimintō Seiken*, 84.

9. Randall B. Ripley and Grace A. Franklin, *Congress, the Bureaucracy, and Public Policy*, 3d. ed. (Homewood, Ill.: Dorsey Press, 1984).

10. For a study of American subgovernments, see ibid. For an example of how subgovernments can restrict the U.S. president, see Joel D. Aberbach and Bert A. Rockman, "Clashing Beliefs within the Executive Branch: The Nixon Administration Bureaucracy," *American Political Science Review* 70 (1976): 456–68; Hugh Heclo, A *Government of Strangers: Executive Politics in Washington* (Washington, D.C.: Brookings Institution, 1977).

11. John Creighton Campbell, *Contemporary Japanese Budget Politics* (Berkeley and Los Angeles: University of California Press, 1977), 40.

12. John Creighton Campbell, "Policy Conflict and Its Resolution within the Governmental System," in *Conflict in Japan*, ed. Ellis S. Krauss, Thomas P. Rohlen, and Patricia G. Steinhoff (Honolulu: University of Hawaii Press, 1984), 294–334.

13. See, for example, Muramatsu and Krauss, "Conservative Policy Line," 516–54. See also J. C. Campbell, *Budget Politics*, 40; Inoguchi, *Gendai Nihon Seiji*.

14. The examinations to enter the higher civil service, for example, are very competitive. According to B. C. Koh, in most years less than 5 percent of those who take the examinations pass. See Koh, *Japan's Administrative Elite* (Berkeley and Los Angeles: University of California Press, 1989), 79. Historically, the bureaucracy has been considered more "legitimate" than the National Assembly. It predates the parliament. One of the first things that the Meiji oligarchs did in trying to modernize the system of government was to set up a bureaucracy. The parliament did not come until twenty years later. Even after the Kokkai was set up, government officials were still not responsible to it and tended to run the government as servants of the emperor. Politicians, meanwhile, had to fight to become involved in government. There was no institutionalized party control over government. The U.S. occupation of Japan changed the structure of government to make the bureaucracy more responsive to the National Assembly, but it left the civil service largely intact while stripping rivals (e.g., prewar politicians, the military) of power, thus giving it even more influence at least in the short term. See Johnson, *MITI*, 35–82; John Creighton Campbell, "Democracy and Bureaucracy in Japan," in *Democracy in Japan*, ed. Takeshi Ishida and Ellis S. Krauss (Pittsburgh: University of Pittsburgh Press, 1989), 113–38.

15. See Akira Kubota, *Higher Civil Servants in Japan: Their Social Origins, Educational Backgrounds, and Career Patterns* (Princeton, N.J.: Princeton University Press, 1969); Koh, *Japan's Administrative Elite*. Japanese bureaucrats, however, are not unique in

this regard. Officials in many European countries also tend to have more elite backgrounds. See Joel D. Aberbach, Robert D. Putnam, and Bert A. Rockman, *Bureaucrats and Politicians in Western Democracies* (Cambridge, Mass.: Harvard University Press, 1981).

16. In a survey of LDP politicians and bureaucrats, Muramatsu and Krauss show that in the budget process the latter often have contacts with the former even at an early stage. Muramatsu and Krauss, "Conservative Policy Line," 539–41.

17. Satō and Matsuzaki, *Jimintō Seiken* (Tokyo: Chūō Kōron, 1986), 83.

18. I. M. Destler et al., *Managing an Alliance: The Politics of U.S.-Japanese Relations* (Washington, D.C.: Brookings Institution, 1976), 71.

19. The twelve are the Finance, Foreign, Justice, Agriculture, International Trade and Industry, Health and Welfare, Transportation, Posts and Telecommunications, Construction, Labor, Education, and Home Affairs ministries. The main agencies are Defense, Economic Planning, Science and Technology, Environment, National Land, Management and Coordination, Hokkaido Development, and Okinawa Development.

20. Sectionalism, according to Johnson, is the result of tradition (the prewar constitutional setup continued in large part under the postwar Constitutional setup) and circumstances (ministries need clients and captive organizations to provide positions for their officials after retirement). Johnson, MITI, 73–75.

21. Ibid., 300.

22. See Satō and Matsuzai, *Jimintō Seiken*; Nihon Keizai Shimbun, ed., *Jimintō Seichōkai* (Tokyo: Nihon Keizai Shimbunsha, 1983); and Inoguchi Takashi and Iwai Tomoaki, *"Zoku-Giin" no Kenkyū* (Tokyo: Nihon Keizai Shimbunsha, 1987).

23. Ōmori Wataru, Hayashi Shūzō, Kiyomizu Hiroshi, and Yamamoto Sadao. "Konnichi no Naikaku Kinō o Megutte," *Gyōsei Kanri Kenkyū* 35 (September 1986): 7–9.

24. J. C. Campbell, "Democracy and Bureaucracy in Japan," 117.

25. Bureaucrats join the ministry straight out of college (mostly from Tokyo University) and stay with it until they retire; there are no mid-career entrants. By contrast, U.S. departments include many outsiders, such as political appointees and in-and-outers such as professors, businessmen, and scholars. Outside people have less loyalty, and they bring in more diverse views and values, and thus their presence creates a less cohesive bureaucracy. The ministries further foster loyalty by rotating their members from bureau to bureau and giving preference to generalists rather than specialists.

26. Occasionally ministers have actually used their powers to influence personnel decisions, mainly in picking the administrative vice minister, but this is rare. Even in these cases, the ministries reasserted themselves after the ministers left. See the case of Kōno Ichirō and his effort to control the personal

decisions in the Agriculture Ministry. Johnson, MITI, 53–54. Yung H. Park argues that many LDP politicians do have influence over personnel decisions, but usually they are *zoku* politicians whose involvement is generally separate from that of the prime minister's. Park, *Bureaucrats and Ministers in Contemporary Japanese Government* (Berkeley: Institute of East Asian Studies, University of California, 1986), 55–77.

27. The parliamentary vice minister's position is used as a training ground for junior members of the National Assembly.

28. The appointee to the administrative vice ministership, the highest career post, is generally made through consultations among current and past ministry officials.

29. The British prime minister appoints about twenty members of Parliament to cabinet posts, sixty to subcabinet positions, and another three dozen as parliamentary private secretaries. Richard Rose, "British Government: The Job at the Top," in *Presidents and Prime Ministers*, ed. Richard Rose and Ezra N. Suleiman (Washington, D.C.: American Enterprise Institute, 1980), 5.

30. See Cabinet Law, Article 3-1: "The ministers shall divide among themselves administrative affairs and be in charge of their respective share thereof as the competent minister, as provided for by other law." This limitation, however, is one shared by most prime ministers of other countries, and even to some extent the U.S. president. For the president, see Richard A. Watson and Norman C. Thomas, *The Politics of the Presidency* (New York: John Wiley and Sons, 1983), 291–92.

31. T. J. Pempel, "The Bureaucratization of Policy Making in Postwar Japan," *American Journal of Political Science* 18 (November 1974): 647–64; Johnson, MITI.

32. Kiyoaki Tsuji, "Public Administration in Japan: History and Problems," in *Public Administration in Japan*, ed. Kiyoaki Tsuji (Tokyo: Administrative Management Agency, 1982), 10–11.

33. Most writers on *zoku-giin* believe that the rise of the LDP members of the *Kokkai* in policy started in the 1970s. John Campbell, however, argues that the change occurred in the late 1950s and early 1960s. J. C. Campbell, "Fragmentation and Power: Politicians and Bureaucrats in the Japanese Decision-Making System," paper presented to the Midwest Seminar on Japan, Ann Arbor, Mich., 1988.

34. J. A. A. Stockwin, "Dynamic and Immobilist Aspects of Japanese Politics," in *Dynamic and Immobilist Politics in Japan*, ed. J. A. A. Stockwin (London: Macmillan Press, 1988), 16–17; J. C. Campbell, *Budget Politics*, 40–41.

35. See Muramatsu and Krauss, "Conservative Policy Line"; Gerald L. Curtis, *The Japanese Way of Politics* (New York: Columbia University Press, 1988).

36. Curtis, *Japanese Way of Politics*, 204–05.

37. The PARC is divided into divisions along lines corresponding to the ministries and legislative committees. It consists of seventeen divisions, thirty-

one research councils, and forty-eight committees. In addition, there are a number of task forces, formed as subcommittees to study important issues. For a history of the development of the PARC, see Murakawa Ichirō, *Jimintō no Seisaku Kettei Shisutemu*, (Tokyo: Kyōikusha, 1989), 131–40; Murakawa, *Nihon no Seisaku Kettei Katei* (Tokyo: Gyōsei, 1985), 90–95; Murakawa, "Jiyūminshutō Seimuchōsakai," *Jurisuto* 805 (January 1–15, 1984): 46–52.

38. Satō and Matsuzaki, *Jimintō Seiken*, 90.

39. See Nihon Keizai Shimbun sha, *Jimintō Seichōkai*; Satō and Matsuzaki, *Jimintō Seiken*; Inoguchi and Iwai, "*Zoku-Giin*" *no Kenkyū*.

40. Muramatsu and Krauss, "Conservative Policy Line," 539–40.

41. "Indeed it has become so much the fashion to emphasize the LDP's recently expanded policy role that there is some danger of forgetting that . . . the bureaucracy continues to be an extraordinarily powerful player in the policy process." Curtis, *Japanese Way of Politics*, 106.

42. Membership in the PARC divisions is not limited. Murakawa Ichirō, "Jiyūminshutō no Seisaku Kettei Kikō," *Jurisuto* 805 (January 1–15, 1984): 216. Politicians' choice of divisions usually depend on the interests of their constituents. Hence the agriculture, commerce, and construction divisions are the most popular. Inoguchi and Iwai, "*Zoku-Giin*" *no Kenkyū*, 103–104, 132–41.

43. See case studies of individual *zoku-giin*, such as Hashimoto Ryūtarō (social policy), Katō Mutsuki (transportation), Nishioka Takeo (education), and others, in Inoguchi and Iwai, "*Zoku-Giin*" *no Kenkyū*, 105–20.

44. Murakawa, "Jiyūminshutō no Seisaku," 215.

45. Satō and Matsuzaki, *Jimintō Seiken*, 93.

46. Curtis, *Japanese Way of Politics*, 115.

47. Iwai and Inoguchi liken the LDP rank-and-file legislators to "hunting dogs." They see two types of "hunting dog" decision: one where the dogs are leashed and one where they are unleashed. Unleashed hunting dogs are politicians who on their own initiative move to protect some interest and form a large group within the party. Leashed hunting dogs are those who are managed and whose actions are coordinated by *zoku* masters. Iwai Tomoaki and Inoguchi Takashi, "Zeiseizoku no Seiji Rikigaku," *Chūō Kōron*, March 1987, 96–106; Inoguchi and Iwai, "*Zoku-Giin*" *no Kenkyū*, 260–72.

48. On the "green card" system see chap. 4. Inoguchi and Iwai list the green card case and one other, the banking law revision case as examples involving "leashed hunting dogs." Inoguchi and Iwai, "*Zoku-Giin*" *no Kenkyū*, 237–42.

49. Okimoto, *Between MITI and the Market: Japanese Industrial Policy for High Technology* (Stanford University Press, 1989), 202.

50. Campbell, "Policy Conflict," 301.

51. See Satō and Matsuzaki, *Jimintō Seiken*, 84.

52. Ōtake Hideo argues that in Japan there is more agreement over the areas of responsibility of bureaucratic agencies than there is in the United States. Ōtake, *Gendai Nihon no Seiji Kenryoku*, cited in Satō and Matsuzaki, *Jimintō Seiken*, 84.

53. Curtis, *Japanese Way of Politics*, 49–61.

54. Ibid. 116.

55. J. C. Campbell, "Policy Conflict," 301.

56. Ibid., 308.

57. Ibid., 301.

58. See J. C. Campbell's analysis in his "Fragmentation and Power."

59. J. C. Campbell, "Policy Conflict," 320.

60. Park, *Bureaucrats and Ministers*.

61. Heclo, *Government of Strangers*, 228.

62. Michio Muramatsu, "In Search of National Identity: The Politics and Policies of the Nakasone Administration," *Journal of Japanese Studies* 13 (Summer 1987): 328.

63. Inoguchi and Iwai believe that the postal, welfare, transportation, education, and defense *zoku* are particularly cohesive. Inoguchi and Iwai, *"Zoku-Giin" no Kenkyū*, 257–60. See also John Creighton Campbell, "Bureaucratic Primacy: Japanese Policy Communities in an American Perspective," *Governance* 2 (January 1989): 2–22.

64. Iwai and Inoguchi, "Zeisei zoku," 98.

65. John Creighton Campbell, *How Policies Change: The Japanese Government and the Aging Society* (Princeton, N.J.: Princeton University Press, 1992), chap. 9.

66. Okimoto, *MITI and the Market*, 193–202.

67. Aaron Wildavsky, "The Two Presidencies," in *The Presidency*, ed. Aaron Wildavsky (Boston: Little, Brown, 1969), 230–43. See also Donald A. Peppers's critique. Peppers, "The Two Presidencies: Eight Years Later," in *The Presidency*, ed. Aaron Wildavsky (Boston: Little Brown, 1975), 462–71.

68. Haruhiro Fukui, "Tanaka Goes to Peking: A Case Study in Foreign Policymaking," in *Policymaking in Contemporary Japan*, ed. T. J. Pempel (Ithaca, N.Y.: Cornell University Press, 1977); Gene T. Hsiao, "The Sino-Japanese Rapproachment: A Relationship of Ambivalence," *China Quarterly* (January-March 1974): 103–44.

69. See Donald C. Hellmann, *Japanese Foreign Policy and Domestic Politics: The Peace Agreement with the Soviet Union* (Berkeley and Los Angeles: University of California Press, 1969).

70. For studies of the Okinawa reversion see I. M. Destler et al., *Managing an Alliance*, 23–35. For a study on the textile wrangle, see I. M. Destler, Haruhiro Fukui, and Hideo Satō, *The Textile Wrangle: Conflict in Japanese-American Relations, 1969–1971* (Ithaca, N.Y.: Cornell University Press, 1979).

71. T. J. Pempel, "Unbundling 'Japan, Inc.': The Changing Dynamics of Japanese Policy Formation," *Journal of Japanese Studies* 13 (Summer 1987): 271–306.

72. Bert A. Rockman, *The Leadership Question: The Presidency and the American*

System (New York: Praeger Publishers, 1984), 227.

73. Ibid. See also Rose, "Government against Sub-Governments."

Chapter 8
The Prime Minister's Staff

1. Bert A. Rockman, "The American Presidency in Comparative Perspective: Systems, Situations, and Leaders," in *The Presidency and the Political System*, 2d ed., ed. Michael Nelson (Washington, D.C.: Congressional Quarterly Press, 1988), 61; Bradley H. Patterson, Jr., *The Ring of Power: The White House Staff and Its Expanding Role in Government* (New York: Basic Books, 1988).

2. For Great Britain, see George W. Jones, "The Prime Minister's Aides," in *The British Prime Minister*, 2d ed., ed. Anthony King (Durham N.C.: Duke University Press, 1985): 72–95; Colin Campbell, *Governments under Stress: Political Executives and Key Bureaucrats in Washington, London, and Ottawa*, (Toronto: University of Toronto Press, 1983), 50–76. For Canada, see Denis Smith, "President and Parliament: The Transformation of Parliamentary Government in Canada," in *Apex of Power: The Prime Minister and Political Leadership in Canada*, 2d ed., ed. Thomas A. Hockin (Scarborough, Ont.: Prentice-Hall, 1977), 308–25; James C. Simeon, "Prime Minister's Office and White House Office: Political Administration in Canada and the United States," *Presidential Studies Quarterly* 21 (Summer 1991): 559–80; C. Campbell, *Governments under Stress*, 77–99.

3. See, for instance, Michio Muramatsu, "In Search of National Identity: The Politics and Policies of the Nakasone Administration," *Journal of Japanese Studies* 13 (Summer 1987): 307–42.

4. Jin Ikkō, *Sōridaijin no Isu no Nedan* (Tokyo: KK Besutoserāzu, 1987), 142. Another former secretary listed the chief cabinet adviser of the Cabinet Advisers' Office as the ninth member of the inner staff. Tahara Sōichirō, *Nihon no Kanryō* (Tokyo: Bungei Shunjū, 1984), 17.

5. Not all prime ministers have relied on just one political secretary. Miki Takeo, at the start of his administration, had three. Two of them handled the normal political affairs of the prime minister and one handled matters related to the media. Nakamura Keiichirō, *Miki Seiken: 747 Nichi* (Tokyo: Gyōseimondai Kenkyūjo, 1981), 40–41. Note that the Cabinet Law (Article 15-1) provides for only three secretaries. The official title of two of the administrative secretaries is "acting prime ministerial secretaries" (*naikaku sōri daijin hishokan jimu atsukai*). The salaries of the two are paid by their home ministries.

6. The Cabinet Law says that the secretaries "shall, by order of the prime minister . . . take charge of confidential matters or shall assist temporarily in the

affairs of the administrative organs concerned including the Cabinet Secretariat" (Article 15-2).

7. Tahara, *Nihon no Kanryō*, 17.

8. Jin, *Sōridaijin no Isu*, 142.

9. *Mainichi Shimbun* Seiji-bu, ed., *Shushō Kantei* (Tokyo: Asahi Sonorama, 1988), 130–31.

10. See Nakamura Keiichirō's account of the first attempt by the party to oust Mikio Nakamura, *Miki Seiken*, 196–202.

11. Onda Mitsugu, *Naza Sōridaijin Nanoka* (Tokyo: Pīpuru sha, 1988), 32.

12. Mori Kishio, *Shushō Kantei no Himitsu* (Tokyo: Ushiobun sha, 1981), 154. Abe Shintarō was also a reporter for *Mainichi Shimbun*. Others include Hatoyama Ichirō's secretary, Wakamiya Kotarō, from *Asahi Shimbun*; Ikeda's, Itō Masaya, from *Nishi-Nihon Shimbun*; Satō's, Kusuda Minoru, from *Sankei Shimbun*; Tanaka's, Hayasaka Shigezō, from the *Tokyo Times*; and Miki's, Nakamura Keiichirō, from *Yomiuri Shimbun*.

13. It was not until Ikeda became prime minister that the positions for administrative secretaries became institutionalized. The prime ministers from Yoshida to Kishi generally had one or two administrative secretaries on loan from the Foreign, Finance, or International Trade and Industry ministries. With Ikeda, it became standard to have three secretaries, one each from the Foreign and Finance ministries, and, perhaps because of the riots and demonstrations over the United States–Japan Security Treaty, the NPA. Tanaka added a fourth, from the MITI, to help in promoting his plan "Restructuring the Japanese Archipelago." Miki, Tanaka's successor, decided that he did not want a secretary from the MITI, so he had only three. But the post was added again under Fukuda, and the four positions have since become the general rule.

14. During negotiations for a peace treaty with China, Fukuda asked Owada for his opinions on the way to deal with the Foreign Ministry and on the briefs given by it. Tahara, *Nihon no Kanryō*, 20.

15. Interview with Yanagiya Kensuke, a former administrative vice minister, October 1987.

16. The major exception to this rule was Morita Hajime, who was Ōhira's son-in-law. Morita, as I mentioned above, was Ōhira's political secretary, but he also served concurrently as the administrative secretary from the Finance Ministry.

17. Tahara, *Nihon no Kanryō*, 17.

18. Ibid.

19. Onda, *Naze Sōridaijin*, 99.

20. Ibid., 99–100.

21. A former secretary to Nakasone describes the experience of being *kaban-mochi*: "When I was a private secretary, my suit was very heavy. I had in my pockets

every conceivable note so that I could reply immediately to any of the prime minister's questions or requests. Since I've left the post, the load on my body has really gotten lighter." Quoted in *Mainichi Shimbun* Seiji-bu, *Shushō Kantei*, 128.

22. Onda, *Naze Sōridaijin*, 99–100.

23. He felt that the proposal would endanger the other tax reform bills to cut income taxes and to abolish the tax-exempt small-lot savings system. See *Mainichi Shimbun* Seiji-bu, *Shushō Kantei*, 130.

24. Interview with Yanagiya Kensuke.

25. Onda Mitsugu, *Naze Sōridaijin*, 98–100.

26. Mori, *Shushō Kantei no Himitsu*, 145–46.

27. Jin, *Sōridaijin no Isu*, 146.

28. C. Campbell, *Governments under Stress*, 52–55.

29. Although there has been a post for a chief cabinet secretary since soon after the cabinet system was established in 1884, it was not made a cabinet-level position until 1966.

30. Gotōda complains that, while chief cabinet secretary, he could not go to the prime minister's office without running into reporters. While the contents of the meetings are confidential, he says that the better reporters are able to pick up on stories when they know that the chief cabinet secretary is meeting with the prime minister. Gotōda Masaharu, *Seiji towa Nanika* (Tokyo: Kōdansha, 1988), 94.

31. The chief cabinet secretary holds his press conferences in the building next to the Kantei (but still on the Kantei grounds) that houses the Nagata-chō Reporters Club at either 11 A.M. and 4 P.M., or 10 A.M., 12 noon, and 4 P.M.

32. Mori, *Shushō Kantei*, 116–17.

33. The post of chief cabinet secretary was not a cabinet-level position at the time Satō, Ōhira, and Suzuki occupied it.

34. Gotōda was a member of the Tanaka faction. When Nakasone first appointed him chief cabinet secretary, the press saw the appointment as evidence of Tanaka's political influence. In reality, Nakasone made his choice over Tanaka's opposition. When Nakasone went ahead with his decision, Tanaka insisted that the spot not count toward the Tanaka faction's allotment of cabinet positions. See Jin, *Sōridaijin no Isu*, 113–14.

35. Gotōda, *Seiji towa Nanika*, 20–21.

36. Onda, *Naze Sōridaijin*, 26; Mori, *Shushō Kantei*, 112. Jin estimates the annual budget of the fund to be about 2 billion yen (*Sōridaijin no Isu*, 117).

37. The safe containing the fund is in the chief cabinet secretary's office, not in the prime minister's. Onda writes that the chief cabinet secretary often makes the decisions regarding the use of the money, but he reports these in detail to the prime minister (ibid., 28). The amount reported to be in the safe ranges from 5 million yen (Jin and Mori) to 100 million yen (Onda). The prime minister is also

said to keep some money—several million yen—in his desk. When the safe runs low, the secretary himself calls the accounting section chief in the PMO, who manages the entire fund, and within an hour the safe is replenished. See Mori, *Shushō Kantei*, 114; and Onda, *Naze Sōridaijin*, 28.

38. When LDP and opposition diet members go to a restaurant or hotel to discuss informally the passage of an important bill, the government or LDP side will pick up the tab for the drinks and food as well as pass money to the opposition members. Mori says that he has seen such use of money many times by aides of the chairman of the LDP Legislative Affairs Committee or the deputy chief cabinet secretary (Mori, *Shushō Kantei*, 113). Some of the money from the fund is used to entertain reporters and journalists, and some is given during the gift-giving seasons. The amount reportedly ranges from about 10 million yen to about 50 thousand yen. Onda, *Naze Sōridaijin*, 29–30.

39. Ibid., 32.

40. Every year, some five hundred members of the legislature go on trips overseas. Before they leave, they generally visit the Kantei to greet the prime minister and on the way out go into the chief cabinet secretary's office to receive a bon voyage present from the fund. According to a reporter, "The size of the present is on average 300 thousand yen for first- or second-term members of the National Assembly. But I understand that if a member of the kokkai is especially close to the prime minister, he may receive 500 thousand or 1 million yen. Middle-ranking members receive on average a half-million to 1 million yen. This, too, depends on the person. Money is also given to members of the opposition" (Jin, *Sōridaijin no Isu*, 118). A former chief cabinet secretary gives the same information in Mori, *Shushō Kantei*, 113.

41. The Cabinet Law provides for only one secretary. The other three are known officially as "acting secretaries."

42. The administrative vice ministers' conference meets the day before cabinet meetings. Formally, the chief cabinet secretary is the chairman, but because he rarely attends, it is generally run by the administrative deputy. As Tahara notes in *Nihon no Kanryō* (12–15), people sharply disagree over the importance of the vice ministers' conference. On one hand are those who, like Kakizawa Kōji, a former secretary to the chief cabinet secretary, believe that it is the real decision-making body in Japan: "In actuality, it is the government's real decision-making body. The cabinet simply confirms the decisions made at the vice ministers' conference" (ibid., 12). Tahara himself takes the opposite view: that it is largely a rubber-stamp body because the work of preparing for the cabinet meeting is generally already done by that time. In an interview with a former deputy secretary, he got this description of a typical meeting: "The vice ministers get together at about 12:20 P.M., and, as they eat their lunch, the deputy secretary goes through each item on

the agenda one by one asking if anyone has questions. There are none. About 1
P.M., after they have finished lunch, the meeting is over" (Ibid., 15).

43. Jin, *Sōridaijin no Isu*, 122.

44. Tahara, *Nihon no Kanryō*, 19.

45. The list of administrative deputies (and their former positions) since the
Tanaka cabinet is as follows: Gotōda (Tanaka; director of the NPA); Kawashima
Horimori (Tanaka and Miki; NPA, director of the former Cabinet Research Office);
Umemoto Junzō (Miki; vice minister of health and welfare and director of environment); Michimasa Kunihiko (Fukuda, vice minister of labor); Ōkina Hisajirō (Ōhira
and Suzuki; vice minister of labor); Fujimori Shōichi (Nakasone; director of environment); and Ishihara Nobuo (Takeshita; vice minister of home affairs).

46. The prewar Home Ministry was dismantled during the occupation on
December 31, 1947. Agencies that have roots in the Home Ministry include the
ministries of Health and Welfare, Labor, Construction, and Home Affairs, and the
Environment Agency and the NPA. Fujimori Shōichi, Nakasone's administrative
deputy, was a former administrative deputy director of environment, but much of
the Environment Agency was originally part of the Health and Welfare Ministry.

47. Jin, *Sōridaijin no Isu*, 127.

48. Ibid.

49. Ōkina Hisajirō, "Naikaku Kanbō Sōgo Chōsei Kikan ni Tsuite," in *Naikaku
Seido no Kenkyū*, ed. Nihon Gyōsei Gakkai (Tokyo: Gyōsei, 1987), 103–04.

50. *Organization of the Government of Japan* (Tokyo: Institute of Administrative
Management, 1987), 3. The current composition of the Cabinet Secretariat is
based on the reorganization made in 1986. Prior to that date it consisted of four
offices: the Cabinet Advisers' Office, the Cabinet Councillors' Office, the Cabinet
Public Relations Office, and the Cabinet Research Office.

51. Cabinet Law, Article 12-2: The Cabinet Secretariat shall be in charge of
general affairs such as arrangement of the agenda of cabinet meetings, be in
charge of the coordination necessary for keeping integration of the policies of
administrative offices such as the coordination of important matters for decision
by cabinet meetings, and be in charge of the collection of information concerning
important policies of the cabinet.

52. This ambiguity as to whether a staff serves the prime minister or the
cabinet is not unique to Japan. In Great Britain, many consider the Cabinet Office
as the prime minister's department. The office officially serves the cabinet, but
most of its work is for the prime minister. Australia has apparently dealt with the
problem by setting up a single central agency, the Department of the Prime
Minister and Cabinet.

53. The official English name is Cabinet Counsellors' Office. I refer to it as the Cabinet Advisers' Office to avoid possible confusion with the Cabinet Councillor's offices.

54. The chief *naikaku sanjikan* is also the chief of general affairs division in the secretariat of the PMO. Two of the three other *naikaku sanjikan* are division chiefs in the PMO and generally are located in the building housing the PMO, across the road from the *Kantei*. One heads the personnel division and comes from the Transportation Ministry; the other heads the accounting division and comes from the Construction Ministry. The remaining *naikaku sanjikan* covers the legislature and has his office at the National Assembly.

55. Tahara's interview with an anonymous former secretary, in *Nihon no Kan-ryō*, 17.

56. Nakasone was an exception; he was one of the few prime ministers who actually lived in the official residence.

57. Ōmori Wataru, Hayoshi Shūzo, Kiyomizu Hiroshi, and Yamamoto Sadao, "Konnichi no Naikaku Kinō o Megutte," *Gyōsei Kanri Kenkyū* 35 (September 1986): 7–9.

58. For a brief history of the office up to 1979, see Kyōikusha, *Binran: Naikaku/Sōrifu* (Tokyo: Kyōikusha, 1979), 63–66. Currently, at least on the organizational chart, both the Cabinet Secretariat and the PMO have internal and external affairs offices, but the offices in the two agencies are not really distinct entities. The personnel of the two internal affairs offices and of the two external affairs offices are the same, and the directors of the cabinet offices serve simultaneously as the directors of the corresponding office in the PMO.

59. The agencies represented are as follows: the ministries of Finance, Health and Welfare, Labor, Construction, Agriculture, International Trade and Industry, Posts and Telecommunications, and Education, and the NPA. The MPT, which was not represented in the former office, reportedly worked hard to be in the new office. A top official in the ministry said, "The Finance Ministry, the MITI, and others have access to the information in the *Kantei*, which had put us at a disadvantage." *Nihon Keizai Shimbun*, November 15, 1986, quoted in Itō Daiichi, "Naikaku Seido no Soshikironteki Kentō," in *Naikaku Seido no Kenkyū*, ed. Nihon Gyōsei Gakkai (Tokyo: Gyōsei, 1987), 58–59.

60. *Seiji Handobukku*, February 1987.

61. *Seikan Yōran* 6(1988): 505.

62. See Ōkina Hisajirō's summary of the report by the Administrative Reform Promotion Council regarding the reorganization of the Cabinet Councillors' Office in his "Naikaku Kanbō," 99–101.

63. Kaminishi Akio, *Burēn Seiji* (Tokyo: Kōdansha, 1985), 185. Abe is alluding to the independent foreign policy of the military in the 1930s.

64. Interview with an official in the secretariat of the Management and Coordination Agency. May, 1987.

65. Kataoka Hiromitsu, "Naikaku to Gyōsei," in *Naikaku Seido no Kenkyū*, ed. Nihon Gyōsei Gakkai (Tokyo, Gyō sei, 1987), 15.

66. John Creighton Campbell, "Policy Conflict and Its Resolution within the Governmental System," in *Conflict in Japan*, ed. Ellis S. Krauss, Thomas P. Rohlen, and Patricia G. Steinhoff (Honolulu: University of Hawaii Press, 1984), 315.

67. Kataoka, "Naikaku to Gyōsei," 16.

68. Interview in Tahara, *Nihon no Kanryō*, 19.

69. The Security Council of Japan is a cabinet council chaired by the prime minister. Members include foreign and finance ministers, of the chief cabinet secretary, the directors of defense and economic planning, and the chairman of the National Public Safety Commission. The old National Defense Council did not include the chief cabinet secretary or the chairman of the National Public Safety Commission. Whereas the staff of the National Defense Council was separate from the Cabinet Secretariat, the current Cabinet Security Affairs Office is part of it.

70. Of its budget of 200 million yen, 90 percent goes toward personnel expenses. Takahiko Ueda, "Governing in a Crisis, Part 1," *Japan Times Weekly*, May 13–19, 1991.

71. *Seikan Yōran*, 5(1988): 506. The four, like many of the other members in the Cabinet Secretariat, also have positions as advisers (*sanjikan*) in the PMO.

72. Gotōda, *Seiji towa Nanika*, 83–85.

73. Ibid., 84.

74. Ibid., 85.

75. Ibid.

76. Ueda, "Governing in a Crisis, Part 1."

77. Ibid.

78. According to the Cabinet Law, the "cabinet researchers shall, by order, be in charge of the collection, research, and analysis of information relating to important policies of the cabinet" (Article 14–2).

79. Besides the Cabinet Information Research Office, other intelligence-gathering organizations include the Public Security Investigation Agency (under the Justice Ministry), the Ground Self-Defense Force Staff Office Annex (Nibetsu), the Information Analysis, Research, and Planning Bureau (in the Foreign Ministry), and the foreign affairs and security sections in the NPA. The Public Security Investigation Agency collects and analyzes information concerning specific groups—generally left-wing and right-wing. Nibetsu monitors radio transmissions, particularly those of the former Soviet Union, China, and North Korea. The foreign affairs section focuses on anti-Japan operations carried out by these and other communist countries, while the security section follows the movements of political activists and extremists such as the Japan Red Army. See "On the Way to Securing a World Position? Japan's Intelligence Agencies and their Activities," *Japan Quarterly* 29 (April–June 1982): 159–62; Hitomi Nakamura, "Governing in a Crisis, Part 2," *Japan Times Weekly*, May 20–26, 1991.

80. Jin, *Sōridaijin no Isu*, 133. See also Ōkina's view in his "Naikaku Kanbō" (101) about the reorganization of the office, which coincides with Taniguchi's.

81. Information about the origins of the office is based on quotations in Jin, *Sōridaijin no Isu*, 135; and Onda, *Naze Sōridaijin*, 76–77.

82. Mori, *Shushō Kantei*, 137.

83. The office has a total regular staff of eighty-four and a provisional staff from other ministries of seventy. It has five divisions: general affairs, domestic, international, economic, and materials. The functions of the divisions are covered in Kyōikusha, *Naikaku/Sōrifu*, 160–62.

84. Information on this case comes from Jin, *Sōridaijin no Isu*, 135–66; "Securing a World Position," 159–60.

85. Jin writes that information also comes from the major trading companies. *Sōridaijin no Isu*, 137–40.

86. "On the Way to Securing a World Position," 160.

87. Jin, *Sōridaijin no Isu*, 137.

88. Onda, *Naze Sōridaijin*, 78.

89. The Sentaku Islands incident is cited in Jin, *Sōridaijin no Isu*, 138–39; and the cancellation of the Baoshan steel plan project in Onda, *Naze Sōridaijin*, 78.

90. Mori, *Shushō Kantei*, 135.

91. Gotōda, *Seiji towa Nanika*, 85.

92. Tahara, *Nihon no Kanryō*, 14.

93. Ibid., 15.

94. Quoted in Nakamura, "Governing in a Crisis, Part 2."

95. Ibid.

96. Ōkina, "Naikaku Kanbō," 102.

97. The agency was created on the recommendation of the Second Ad Hoc Commission on Administrative Reform in its fifth report released on March 14, 1983. The cabinet approved this recommendation during its meeting on May 24, 1983. And in the fall of 1983, the 100th Extraordinary National Assembly passed two laws related to the establishment of the Management and Coordination Agency.

98. Management and Coordination Agency, *Management and Coordination Agency: Organization and Functions* (Tokyo: Management and Coordination Agency, Prime Minister's Office, 1985), 1.

99. For an account of the deliberations of the Rinchō on setting up a central agency, see Tahara Sōichirō, *Nihon no Daikaizō: Shin Nihon no Kanryō* (Tokyo: Bungei Shunjū, 1986).

100. Ibid., 15–16.

101. The parts of the PMO that are included in the new agency include the personnel and pension bureaus, the Statistical Center, the Youth Affairs Administration, and Northern Territories Affairs Administration.

102. Yamaguchi Asao, "Jōhō Gyōsei o Gyūjiru Gotōda Sōmuchō no Sugomi," *Chūō Kōron*, December 1985, 228–38.

103. Management and Coordination Agency, *Management and Coordination Agency*, 7–9.

104. Technically, appointment to positions at the level of bureau chief and above require cabinet approval. The cabinet, however, usually rubber-stamps the recommendations of the minister, who in turn generally does not intervene very much in the promotion of officials within the ministry. Onda in *Naze Sōridaijin* (68) writes that the Management and Coordination Agency has an impact on the movement and promotion of some agencies that are staffed by officials from more than one ministry, such as the National Land Agency, the Environment Agency, Hokkaidō Development Agency, and the Okinawa Development Agency, but I have not seen anything about this elsewhere.

105. Higuchi Tsuneo, *Tamaki Kazuo no Yuigon* (Tokyo: Asuka Shinsha, 1987), 115.

106. Ibid., 86–87.

107. Higuchi writes that, in October 1986, two Foreign Ministry officials visited Tamaki to discuss the issue of rice imports. During the meeting, Tamaki told them, " If you don't listen to me, I won't go along with your request [for more staff members]." The two officials, who were competing for the administrative vice ministership, simply bowed their heads and said, "Please grant us the favor regarding the staff" (*teiin wa zehi yoroshiku onegaishimasu*). Ibid., 88.

108. Management and Coordination Agency, *Management and Coordination Agency*, 10–16.

109. See Tahara, *Nihon no Daikaizō*; Yamaguchi, "Jōhō Gyōsei," 228–38.

110. Tahara, *Nihon no Daikaizō*, 31–34. The literature put out by the Management and Coordination Agency talks about its "administrative information system" but does not mention anything about a "personnel information system." The agency is now using computers to set up the Decision Support System which "supports planning, drafting, and decision of administrative policies through centralized control of administrative information (using an administrative information database)." Institute of Administrative Management, *The Administrative Management and Reform in Japan* (Tokyo: Gyōsei Kanri Kenkyū Sentā, 1987), 102.

111. Tahara, *Nihon no Daikaizō*, 31–32.

112. Yamaguchi goes so far as to say that the inspection authority will make other ministries act as local agencies of the government: "To oversimplify, administration from now on will be carried out by the Cabinet Secretariat and the Management and Coordination Agency. If the ministries do not follow the instructions of the Cabinet Secretariat, then they will be put under the thumb of the Management and Coordination Agency's strict administrative inspection." Yamaguchi, "Jōhō Gyōsei," 238.

113. Tahara, *Nihon no Daikaizō*, 24.

114. Higuchi, *Tamaki*, 48.

115. Ibid., 108–09.

116. See Yamaguchi, "Jōhō Gyōsei," 228–38. He writes that Gotōda used his personal intelligence network to learn about the activities of Nisugi, then president of the JNR, and other officials who were opposed to privatization. The information played a crucial part in Nakasone's decision to fire Nisugi.

117. Junko Kato argues that the Rinchō was especially important in reforming the pension system. Kato, "Public Pension Reforms in the United States and Japan: A Study of Comparative Public Policy," *Comparative Political Studies* 24 (April 1991): 100–126.

118. The ad hoc cabinet staff office was made up of three seconded officials: Nagatomi Yūichirō from the Finance Ministry, Akiyama Masao from the MITI, and Uchida Katsu from the Foreign Ministry. The office was set up in the Kōtei because there was no room in the Kantei.

119. See Shindō Mineyuki, *Gyōsei Kaikaku to Gendai Seiji* (Tokyo: Iwanami Shoten, 1986), 92–94; Sone Yasunori, "Yarase no Seiji 'Shingikai Hōshiki' o Kenshō," *Chūō Kōron*, 1201 (January 1, 1986): 148–55; Aoki Satoshi, *Nakasone Famirī* (Tokyo: Akebi Shobō, 1986).

120. Muramatsu, "Politics and Policies of the Nakasone Administration," 307–43.

121. According to John Hart, the number in the White House ranges from about three hundred to over six hundred. Hart *The Presidential Branch* (New York: Pergamon Press, 1987), 97–101. For figures on Britain's No. 10 Downing Street, see C. Campbell, *Governments under Stress*, 19.

122. See Kataoka, "Naikaku to Gyōsei," 15.

123. Jin, *Sōridaijin no Isu*, 141.

124. I. M. Destler et al., *Managing on Alliance: The Politics of U.S.-Japanese Relations* (Washington, D.C.: Brookings Institution, 1976), 71.

125. Gotōda, *Seiji towa Nanika*, 76.

Chapter 9
The Prime Minister and Public Policy

1. Karel G. van Wolferen, "The Japan Problem," *Foreign Affairs* 65 (Winter 1987): 288–303; van Wolferen, *The Enigma of Japanese Power: People and Politics in a Stateless Nation* (New York: Alfred A. Knopf, 1989).

2. See John W. Kingdon, *Agendas, Alternatives, and Public Policies* (Boston: Little, Brown, 1984).

3. See Valerie Bunce, *Do New Leaders Make a Difference?* (Princeton, N.J.: Princeton University Press, 1981).

4. See, for example, James L. Sundquist, *Politics and Policy: The Eisenhower, Kennedy and Johnson Years* (Washington, D.C.: Brookings Institution, 1968). Also, Paul C. Light notes that John Kennedy was able to take up a focused set of party proposals that had been refined by the Democratic party during the 1953–60 period when the party was out of power. Light, *The President's Agenda: Domestic Policy Choice from Kennedy to Carter* (Baltimore: Johns Hopkins University Press, 1983).

5. Participants come to associate new leaders with new ideas, so even a change of leadership within a party brings the expectations of a fresh platform. See Bunce, *Do New Leaders Make a Difference?*; Joel D. Aberbach, Robert D. Putnam, and Bert A. Rockman, *Bureaucrats and Politicians in Western Democracies* (Cambridge, Mass.: Harvard University Press, 1981), 248–49.

6. See T. J. Pempel, "The Unbundling of 'Japan, Inc.': The Changing Dynamics of Japanese Policy Formation," *Journal of Japanese Studies* 13 (Summer 1987): 271–306; Michio Muramatsu and Ellis S. Krauss, "The Conservative Policy Line and the Development of Patterned Pluralism," in *The Political Economy of Japan, vol. 1, The Domestic Transformation*, ed. Kozo Yamamura and Yasukichi Yasuba (Stanford, Calif.: Stanford University Press, 1987), 515–54.

7. Gerald L. Curtis, *The Japanese Way of Politics* (New York: Columbia University Press, 1988). Others have described the LDP as a "department store"—a place that has something for everyone.

8. Tanaka Zen'ichirō dates the change in the approach of the LDP from Ikeda Hayato's "low posture" attitude in the early 1960s. Tanaka, *Jimintō Taisei no Seiji Shidōryoku* (Tokyo: Daiichi Hōki, 1981). See also John Creighton Campbell, "Fragmentation and Power: Politicians and Bureaucrats in the Japanese Decision-Making System," paper presented to the Midwest Seminar on Japan, Ann Arbor, Mich. 1988.

9. See J. C. Campbell, "Fragmentation and Power."

10. See Chie Nakane, *Japanese Society* (Berkeley and Los Angeles: University of California Press, 1970); Nobutaka Ike, *Japanese Theory of Democracy* (Boulder, Colo.: Westview Press, 1978).

11. *Business Week*, October 14, 1985, 39.

12. See Colin Campbell, *Governments under Stress: Political Executives and Key Bureaucrats in Washington, London, and Ottawa* (Toronto: University of Toronto Press, 1983).

13. See Sone Yasunori, "Yarase no Seiji 'Shingikai Hōshiki' o Kenshō," *Chūō Kōron* 1201 (January 1, 1986): 148–55.

14. John Creighton Campbell, *How Policies Change: The Japanese Goverenment and the Aging Society* (Princeton, N.J.: Princeton University Press, 1992), chap. 10.

15. Light writes the presidents choose issues according to the benefits they receive in satisfying three goals: (1) reelection, (2) historical achievement, and (3) good policy. Thus, one can analyze prime ministers' choice of issues by looking at their goals and the benefits they receive from promoting certain policies. Light, *President's Agenda*, 62–80.

16. Nakasone was the first—and so far only—prime minister to become a lame duck because he was the first to have been reelected since the LDP limited party presidents to two terms in the mid-1970s.

17. See Imamura Tsunao, "Soshiki no Bunka to Kōsō," in *Gyōseigaku Kōza*, vol. 4, Gyōsei to Soshiki, ed. Tsuji Kiyoaki (Tokyo: Tokyo University Press, 1976), 183–87.

18. See Nakamura Keiichirō, *Miki Seiken: 747 Nichi* (Tokyo: Gyōseimondai Kenkyūjo, 1981).

19. See George R. Packard III, *Protest in Tokyo: The Security Treaty Crisis of 1960* (Princeton, N.J.: Princeton University Press, 1966); Yoshimura Katsuri, *Ikeda Seiken: 1575 Nichi* (Tokyo: Gyōseimondai Kenkyūjo, 1985).

20. Light, *President's Agenda*, 66.

21. See Donald C. Hellmann, *Japanese Foreign Policy and Domestic Politics: The Peace Agreement with the Soviet Union* (Berkeley and Los Angeles: University of California Press, 1969).

22. Light notes that Kennedy worked on education issues as a senator and made aid to education one of his top priorities as president. Light, *President's Agenda*, 22.

23. The analogy came to me after reading reports of the 1989 San Francisco earthquake explaining why some buildings and structures collapsed while others survived with virtually no damage. Some shock waves hit some structures, such as pillars supporting the elevated highways, at a resonant frequency that amplified the shaking and brought about their collapse.

24. Kingdon describes how ideas float around in policy communities and how "policy entrepreneurs"—advocates of policy change—push their ideas in an attempt to educate the public, the decision makers, and other members of the policy community. Kingdon, *Agendas, Alternatives, and Public Policies*, chap. 6.

25. J. C. Campbell, *How Policies Change*, chap. 11; Kent E. Calder, *Crisis and Compensation: Public Policy and Political Stability in Japan, 1949–1986* (Princeton, N.J.: Princeton University Press, 1988), 214–24. See also J. C. Campbell, "Fragmentation and Power"; Campbell, *Contemporary Japanese Budget Politics* (Berkeley and Los Angeles: University of California Press, 1977), 27–28.

26. Light, *President's Agenda*, 86–87. See also Richard Rose, *The Post-modern President: George Bush Meets the World*, 2d ed. (Chatham, N.J.: Chatham House, 1991), 174–78; Patricia Ingraham, "Political Direction and Policy Change in Three Federal Departments," in *The Managerial Presidency*, ed. James P. Pfiffner (Pacific Grove, Calif.:

Brooks/Cole Publishing, 1991), 180–93; Charles O. Jones, "Presidents and Agendas: Who Defines What for Whom?" ibid., 197–213.

27. Kingdon, *Agendas, Alternatives, and Public Policies*, chap. 8.

28. This term is borrowed from Rose's concept of the president as "a policy taster." *Postmodern President*, 174–75.

29. For the "atomistic" view of the U.S. political system, see Anthony King, "The American Policy in the Late 1970s: Building Coalitions in the Sands," in *The New American Political System*, 1st ed., ed. Anthony King (Washington, D.C.: American Enterprise Institute, 1978), 371–95.

30. Daniel I. Okimoto notes the importance of collective norms "to curb selfish, short-term interests" and to "pull together in the face of national adversity." Okimoto, *Between MITI and the Market: Japanese Industrial Policy for High Technology* (Stanford, Calif.: Stanford University Press, 1989), 213–16.

31. Calder, *Crisis and Compensation*.

32. Ibid., 229.

33. Robert J. Spitzer, *The Presidency and Public Policy: The Four Arenas of Presidential Power* (University: University of Alabama Press, 1983). See also Steven A. Shull, *Domestic Policy Formation: Presidential-Congressional Partnership?* (Westport, Conn.: Greenwood Press, 1983).

34. Okimoto divides the LDP's traditional supporters into two groups. Type 1 groups, such as farmers, fishermen, small- and medium-scale businessmen, are those who provide votes to the party in exchange for "favorable legislation, subsidies, generous tax treatment and other promotional policies." Type 2 groups, such as those involved in construction, housing, and real estate, give financial and organizational support in return for LDP assistance in licensing, contracts, and other services. Okimoto, *MITI and the Market*, 194–99.

35. J. C. Campbell, *How Policies Change*, chap. 11.

36. William T. Bianco and Robert H. Bates suggest that a leader can be important in dissuading people from pursuing their short-term, narrow interests and pushing them instead toward their longer-term, broader interests. Bianco and Bates, "Cooperation by Design: Leadership, Structure, and Collective Dilemmas," *American Political Science Review* 84 (March 1990): 133–47.

Chapter 10
Conclusion

1. Harvey C. Mansfield, Jr., *Taming the Prince: The Ambivalence of Modern Executive Power* (New York: Free Press, 1989), 1. See also John W. Gardner, *On Leadership* (New York: Free Press, 1990); James MacGregor Burns, *Leadership* (New York: Harper and Row, 1978).

2. Alexander Hamilton, "No. 70," in *The Federalist Papers*, by Alexander Hamilton, James Madison, and John Jay (New York: Mentor Books, 1963).

3. Thomas E. Cronin commenting on Richard Neustadt's view of the presidency. Cronin, *The State of the Presidency*, 2d ed. (Boston: Little, Brown, 1980), 133.

4. See Richard E. Neustadt, *Presidential Power: The Politics of Leadership from FDR to Carter* (New York: John Wiley and Sons, 1980).

5. See G. W. Jones, "The Prime Minister's Power," in *The British Prime Minister*, 2d ed., ed. Anthony King (Durham, N.C.: Duke University Press, 1985), 195–220, reprinted from *Parliamentary Affairs* 18 (Spring 1965): 167–85. Colin Campbell also notes that "there has been a plethora of literature in Canada maintaining that Pierre Elliott Trudeau has transformed the Prime Ministership into a Presidential institution." C. Campbell, "Political Leadership in Canada: Pierre Elliott Trudeau and the Ottawa Model," in *Presidents and Prime Ministers*, ed. Richard Rose (Washington, D.C.: American Enterprise Institute, 1980), 50.

6. Gotōda Masaharu, *Seiji towa Nanika* (Tokyo: Kōdansha, 1988), 76.

7. Theodore J. Lowi, *The Personal President: Power Invested, Promise Unfulfilled* (Ithaca, N.Y.: Cornell University Press, 1985). See also Hugh Heclo, "The Presidential Illusion," in *The Illusion of Presidential Government*, ed. Hugh Heclo and Lester M. Salamon (Boulder, Colo.: Westview Press, 1981), 1–17.

8. See also James MacGregor Burns, *The Power to Lead: The Crisis of the American Presidency* (New York: Simon and Schuster, 1984); Charles M. Hardin, *Constitutional Reform in America: Essays on the Separation of Powers* (Ames: Iowa State University Press, 1989); Donald L. Robinson, *Government for the Third American Century* (Boulder, Colo.: Westview Press, 1989); James L. Sundquist, *Constitutional Reform and Effective Government* (Washington, D.C.: Brookings Institution, 1986); Bert A. Rockman, *The Leadership Question: The Presidency and the American System* (New York: Praeger, 1984).

9. Paul C. Light, *The President's Agenda: Domestic Policy Choice from Kennedy to Carter* (Baltimore: Johns Hopkins University Press, 1983), 36–37.

10. David A. Stockman, for instance, admitted that neither he nor anyone else really knew what they were doing. Stockman, *Triumph of Politics: Why the Reagan Revolution Failed* (New York: Harper and Row, 1986).

11. Light, *President's Agenda*.

12. Arthur M. Schlesinger, Jr., *The Imperial Presidency* (Boston: Houghton Mifflin, 1973).

13. John D. Steinbruner, *The Cybernetic Theory of Decision: New Dimensions of Political Analysis* (Princeton, N.J.: Princeton University Press, 1974), 123.

14. See Valerie Bunce, *Do New Leaders Make a Difference?* (Princeton, N.J.: Princeton University Press, 1981).

15. Light, *President's Agenda*, 200. See also George Reedy, *The Twilight of the Presidency: From Johnson to Reagan*, rev. ed. (New York: New American Library, 1987).

16. Joel D. Aberbach and Bert A. Rockman, "Mandates or Mandarins? Control and Discretion in the Modern Administrative State," in *The Managerial Presidency*, ed. James P. Pfiffner (Pacific Grove, Calif.: Brooks/Cole Publishing, 1991), 158–65.

17. Rockman, *Leadership Question*, 1.

18. Lowi, *Personal President*, 211. Similarly, James G. March argues that organizations might choose to have ambiguous tastes for a number of reasons. See his "Bounded Rationality, Ambiguity, and the Engineering of Choice," *Bell Economic Journal of Economics* 9:2 (Autumn 1978): 587–608.

19. John Creighton Campbell, "Policy Conflict and Its Resolution within the Governmental System," in *Conflict in Japan*, ed. Ellis S. Krauss, Thomas P. Rohlen, and Patricia G. Steinhoff (Honolulu: University of Hawaii Press, 1984), 325.

20. Kent E. Calder, "Japanese Foreign Economic Policy Formation: Explaining the Reactive State," *World Politics* 40 (July 1988): 518–41.

21. See Walter F. Buckley, "Society as a Complex Adaptive System," in *Modern Systems Research for the Behavioral Scientist*, ed. Walter F. Buckley (Chicago: Aldine, 1968), 490–513; Karl E. Weick, *The Social Psychology of Organizing*, 2d ed. (Reading, Mass.: Addison-Wesley, 1979).

22. Weick, *Social Psychology*, 188.

23. See, in particular, chaps. 6 and 7, above.

24. Daniel I. Okimoto, *Between MITI and the Market: Japanese Industrial Policy for High Technology* (Stanford, Calif.: Stanford University Press, 1989), 210.

25. See Michio Muramatsu and Ellis S. Krauss, "The Conservative Policy Line and the Development of Patterned Pluralism"; and Yutaka Kosai, "The Politics of Economic Management," both in *The Political Economy of Japan*, vol. 1, *The Domestic Transformation*, ed. Kozo Yamamura and Yasukichi Yasuba (Stanford, Calif.: Stanford University Press, 1987), 516–54 and 555–92, respectively.

26. Kent E. Calder, *Crisis and Compensation: Public Policy and Political Stability in Japan, 1949–1986* (Princeton, N.J.: Princeton University Press, 1988), 229.

27. Okimoto, *MITI and the Market*, 206.

28. Ibid., 210.

29. T. J. Pempel, *Policy and Politics in Japan: Creative Conservatism* (Philadelphia: Temple University Press, 1982). See also Gerald L. Curtis, *The Japanese Way of Politics* (New York: Columbia University Press, 1988).

30. Muramatsu and Krauss, "Conservative Policy Line," 533.

31. J. C. Campbell, "Policy Conflict," 300.

32. Chalmers Johnson, *MITI and the Japanese Miracle: The Growth of Industrial Policy, 1925–1975* (Stanford, Calif.: Stanford University Press, 1982), 74.

33. The Foreign Ministry is the most internationalist, the MITI has historically been protectionist, and the Finance Ministry is fairly internationalist but stingy about spending money for defense or foreign aid. Johnson, MITI, 75.

34. John Creighton Campbell, *How Policies Change: The Japanese Government and the Aging Society* (Princeton, N.J.: Princeton University Press, 1992).

35. James G. March, "How We Talk and How We Act: Administrative Theory and Administrative Life," app. G in *Leadership and Ambiguity*, 2d ed., by Michael D. Cohen and James G. March (Boston: Harvard Business School Press, 1986), 282.

36. Okimoto, MITI *and the Market*, 212.

Bibliography

English Language Sources

Aberbach, Joel D., Ellis S. Krauss, Michio Muramatsu, and Bert A. Rockman. "Comparing Japanese and American Administrative Elites." *British Journal of Political Science* 20 (October 1990): 461–88.

Aberbach, Joel D., Robert D. Putnam, and Bert A. Rockman. *Bureaucrats and Politicians in Western Democracies.* Cambridge, Mass.: Harvard University Press, 1981.

Aberbach, Joel D., and Bert A. Rockman. "Clashing Beliefs within the Executive Branch: The Nixon Administration Bureaucracy." *American Political Science Review* 70 (1976): 456–68.

————. "Mandates or Mandarins? Control and Discretion in the Modern Administrative State." In *The Managerial Presidency*, edited by James P. Pfiffner, 158–65. Pacific Grove, Calif.: Brooks/Cole Publishing, 1991.

Alderman, R. K., and Neil Carter. "A Very Tory Coup: The Ousting of Mrs. Thatcher." *Parliamentary Affairs* 44 (April 1991): 125–39.

Alderman, R. K., and Martin J. Smith. "Can British Prime Ministers Be Given the Push by Their Parties?" *Parliamentary Affairs* 43 (July 1990): 260–76.

Allison, Graham T. *Essence of Decision: Explaining the Cuban Missile Crisis.* Boston: Little, Brown, 1971.

Andeweg, Rudy B. "The Dutch Prime Minister: Not Just Chairman, Not Yet Chief?" *West European Politics* 14 (April 1991): 116–32.

Angel, Robert C. "Prime Ministerial Leadership in Japan: Recent Changes in Personal Style and Administrative Organization." *Pacific Affairs* 61 (Winter 1988–89): 583–602.

Anton, Thomas J. *Adminstered Politics: Elite Political Culture in Sweden*. Boston: Martinus Hijhoff, 1980.

Asahi Evening News. (English-language newspaper published in Japan).

Baerwald, Hans H. *Party Politics in Japan*. Boston: Allen and Unwin, 1986.

Barrileaux, Ryan J. "The Presidency: Levels of Analysis." *Presidential Studies Quarterly* 14 (Winter 1984): 73–77.

———. "Toward an Institutionalist Framework for Presidency Studies." *Presidential Studies Quarterly* 12 (Spring 1982): 154–58.

Baumgartner, Frank. *Conflict and Rhetoric in French Policymaking*. Pittsburgh: University of Pittsburgh Press, 1989.

Bell, Gerald D. "Formality versus Flexibility in Complex Organizations." In *Organizations and Human Behavior*, edited by G. D. Bell, 97–106. Englewood Cliffs, N.J.: Prentice-Hall, 1967.

Bianco, William T., and Robert H. Bates. "Cooperation by Design: Leadership, Structure, and Collective Dilemmas." *American Political Science Review* 84 (March 1990): 133–47.

Bond, Jon R., and Richard Fleisher. *The President in the Legislative Arena*. Chicago: University of Chicago Press, 1990.

Buchanan, Bruce. "Constrained Diversity: The Organizational Demands of the Presidency." In *The Managerial Presidency*, edited by James P. Pfiffner, 78–103. Pacific Grove, Calif.: Brooks/Cole Publishing, 1991.

Buckley, Walter F. "Society as a Complex Adaptive System." In *Modern Systems Research for the Behavioral Scientist*, edited by Walter F. Buckley, 490–513. Chicago: Aldine, 1968.

Bunce, Valerie. *Do New Leaders Make a Difference?* Princeton, N.J.: Princeton University Press, 1981.

Burns, James MacGregor. *Leadership*. New York: Harper and Row, 1978.

———. *The Power to Lead: The Crisis of the American Presidency*. New York: Simon and Schuster, 1984.

Calder, Kent E. *Crisis and Compensation: Public Policy and Political Stability in Japan, 1949–1986*. Princeton, N.J.: Princeton University Press, 1988.

———. "Japanese Foreign Economic Policy Formation: Explaining the Reactive State." *World Politics* 40 (July 1988): 518–41.

———. "*Kanryō* vs. *Shomin*: Contrasting Dynamics of Conservative Leadership in Postwar Japan." In *Political Leadership in Contemporary Japan*, edited by Terry Edward MacDougall, 1–28. Michigan Papers in Japanese Studies, No. 1. Ann Arbor: Center for Japanese Studies, University of Michigan, 1982.

Campbell, Colin. *Governments under Stress: Political Executives and Key Bureaucrats in Washington, London, and Ottawa*. Toronto: University of Toronto Press, 1983.

————. *Managing the Presidency: Carter, Reagan, and the Search for Executive Harmony.* Pittsburgh: University of Pittsburgh Press, 1986.

————. "Political Leadership in Canada: Pierre Elliott Trudeau and the Ottawa Model." In *Presidents and Prime Ministers*, edited by Richard Rose and Ezra N. Suleiman, 50–93. Washington, D.C.: American Enterprise Institute, 1980.

Campbell, John Creighton. "Bureaucratic Primacy: Japanese Policy Communities in an American Perspective." *Governance* 2 (January 1989): 2–22.

————. *Contemporary Japanese Budget Politics.* Berkeley and Los Angeles: University of California Press, 1977.

————. "Democracy and Bureaucracy in Japan." In *Democracy in Japan*, edited by Takeshi Ishida and Ellis S. Krauss, 113–38. Pittsburgh: University of Pittsburgh Press, 1989.

————. "Fragmentation and Power: Politicians and Bureaucrats in the Japanese Decision-Making System." Paper presented to the Midwest Seminar on Japan, Ann Arbor, Mich., 1988.

————. *How Policies Change: The Japanese Government and the Aging Society.* Princeton, N.J.: Princeton University Press, 1992.

————. "Policy Conflict and Its Resolution within the Governmental System." In *Conflict in Japan*, edited by Ellis S. Krauss, Thomas P. Rohlen, and Patricia G. Steinhoff, 294–334. Honolulu: University of Hawaii Press, 1984.

Cassese, Sabino. "Is There a Government in Italy? Politics and Administration at the Top." In *Presidents and Prime Ministers*, edited by Richard Rose and Ezra N. Suleiman, 171–202. Washington, D.C.: American Enterprise Institute, 1980.

Cohen, Michael D., and James G. March. *Leadership and Ambiguity: The American College President*, 2d ed. Boston: Harvard Business School Press, 1986.

Cohen, Michael D., James G. March, and Johan P. Olsen, "A Garbage Can Model of Organizational Choice," *Administrative Science Quarterly* 17 (March 1972): 1–25.

————. "People, Problems, Solutions, and the Ambiguity of Relevance." In *Ambiguity and Choice in Organizations*, 2d ed., edited by James G. March and Johan P. Olsen. Bergen: Universitetsforlaget, 1976.

Corwin, Edward S. *The President: Office and Powers 1787–1957*, 4th ed. New York: New York University Press, 1957.

Cronin, Thomas E. *The State of the Presidency.* 2d ed. Boston: Little, Brown, 1980.

Crossman, Richard H. *Inside View: Three Lectures on Prime Ministerial Government.* London: Jonathan Cape, 1972.

————. "Prime Ministerial Government." In *The British Prime Minister*, 2d ed., edited by Anthony King, 175–94. Durham, N.C.: Duke University Press, 1985.

Curtis, Gerald L. "Big Business and Political Influence." In *Modern Japanese Organizations and Decision-Making*, edited by Ezra F. Vogel, 33–70. Berkeley and Los Angeles: University of California Press, 1975.

———. *Election Campaigning Japanese Style*. New York: Columbia University Press, 1971.

———. *The Japanese Way of Politics*. New York: Columbia University Press, 1988.

Cyert, Richard M., and James G. March. *A Behavioral Theory of the Firm*. Englewood Cliffs, N.J.: Prentice-Hall, 1963.

Dahl, Robert A. "Power." In *International Encyclopedia of the Social Sciences*, edited by David L. Sills, 12:405–15. New York: Macmillan and Free Press, 1968.

Daily Yomiuri. (English-language newspaper published in Japan).

Destler, I. M., Hideo Sato, Priscilla Clapp, and Haruhiro Fukui. *Managing an Alliance: The Politics of U.S.-Japanese Relations*. Washington, D.C.: Brookings Institution, 1976.

Destler, I. M., Haruhiro Fukui, and Hideo Sato. *The Textile Wrangle: Conflict in Japanese-American Relations, 1969–1971*. Washington, D.C.: Brookings Institution, 1976.

Dower, John W. *Empire and Aftermath: Yoshida Shigeru and the Japanese Experience, 1878–1954*. Harvard East Asian Monographs, no. 84. Cambridge, Mass.: Council on East Asian Studies, Harvard University, 1988.

Duke, Benjamin. *Japan's Militant Teachers: A History of the Left-Wing Teachers' Movement*. Honolulu: University of Hawaii Press, 1973.

Dunleavy, Patrick, and R. A. W. Rhodes. "Core Executive Studies in Britain." *Public Administration* 68 (Spring 1990): 3–28.

Edinger, Lewis J. *West German Politics*. New York: Columbia University Press, 1986.

Edwards, George C., III. *At the Margins: Presidential Leadership of Congress*. New Haven, Conn.: Yale University Press, 1989.

———. "Director or Facilitator? Presidential Policy Control of Congress." In *The Managerial Presidency*, edited by James P. Pfiffner, 214–23. Pacific Grove, Calif.: Brooks/Cole Publishing, 1991.

Elgie, Robert, and Howard Machin. "France: The Limits to Prime-Ministerial Government in a Semi-Presidential System." *West European Politics* 14 (April 1991): 62–78.

Epstein, Leon D. "Parliamentary Government." In *International Encyclopedia of the Social Sciences*, edited by David L. Stills, 11: 419–26. New York: Macmillan and Free Press, 1968.

———. "What Happened to the British Party Model." *American Political Science Review* 74 (March 1980): 9–22.

Fukui, Haruhiro. "The Liberal Democratic Party Revisited: Continuity and Change in the Party's Structure and Performance." *Journal of Japanese Studies* 10 (Summer 1984): 385–435.

———. *Party in Power: The Japanese Liberal-Democrats and Policymaking*. Berkeley and Los Angeles: University of California Press, 1970.

———. "Studies in Policymaking: A Review of the Literature." In *Policymaking in*

Contemporary Japan, edited by T. J. Pempel, 22–59. Ithaca, N.Y.: Cornell University Press, 1977.

————. "Tanaka Goes to Peking: A Case Study in Foreign Policymaking." In _Policymaking in Contemporary Japan_, edited by T. J. Pempel, 60–102. Ithaca, N.Y.: Cornell University Press, 1977.

Gardner, John W. _On Leadership_. New York: Free Press, 1990.

Halperin, Morton H. _Bureaucratic Politics and Foreign Policy_. Washington, D.C.: Brookings Institution, 1974.

Hamilton, Alexander. "No. 70." In _The Federalist Papers_, by Alexander Hamilton, James Madison, and John Jay. New York: Mentor Books, 1963.

Hardin, Charles M. _Constitutional Reform in America: Essays on the Separation of Power_. Ames: Iowa State University Press, 1989.

Hargrove, Erwin C., and Michael Nelson. _Presidents, Politics, and Policy_. Baltimore: Johns Hopkins University Press, 1984.

Hart, John. "President and Prime Minister: Convergence or Divergence?" _Parliamentary Affairs_ 44 (April 1991): 208–25.

————. _The Presidential Branch_. New York: Pergamon Press, 1987.

Heclo, Hugh. _A Government of Strangers_. Washington, D.C.: Brookings Institution, 1977.

————. "The Presidential Illusion." In _The Illusion of Presidential Government_, edited by Hugh Heclo and Lester M. Salamon, 1–17. Boulder, Colo.: Westview Press, 1981.

————. _Studying the Presidency: A Report to the Ford Foundation_. New York: Ford Foundation, 1977.

Hellmann, Donald C. _Japanese Foreign Policy and Domestic Politics: The Peace Agreement with the Soviet Union_. Berkeley and Los Angeles: University of California Press, 1969.

————. "Japanese Politics and Foreign Policy: Elitist Democracy within an American Greenhouse." In _The Political Economy of Japan_, vol. 2, _The Changing International Context_, edited by Takashi Inoguchi and Daniel I. Okimoto, 345–78. Stanford, Calif.: Stanford University Press, 1988.

Hennessy, Peter. _Whitehall_. New York: Free Press, 1989.

Heywood, Paul. "Governing a New Democracy: The Power of the Prime Minister in Spain." _West European Politics_ 14 (April 1991): 97–115.

Hine, David, and Renato Finocchi. "The Italian Prime Minister." _West European Politics_ 14 (April 1991): 79–96.

Hockin, Thomas A. "The Prime Minister and Political Leadership: An Introduction to Some Restraints and Imperatives." In _Apex of Power: The Prime Minister and Political Leadership in Canada_, 2d ed., edited by Thomas A. Hockin, 2–21. Scarborough, Ont.: Prentice-Hall, 1977.

Hsiao, Gene T. "The Sino-Japanese Rapprochement: A Relationship of Ambivalence." *China Quarterly* (January-March 1974): 103–44.

Ike, Nobutaka. *Japanese Theory of Democracy.* Boulder, Colo.: Westview Press, 1978.

Ingraham, Patricia. "Political Direction and Policy Change in Three Federal Departments." In *The Managerial Presidency,* edited by James P. Pfiffner, 180–93. Pacific Grove, Calif.: Brooks/Cole Publishing, 1991.

Institute of Administrative Management. *Administrative Management and Reform in Japan.* Tokyo: Gyōsei Kanri Kenkyū Sentā, 1987.

Itoh, Hiroshi. *The Japanese Supreme Court: Constitutional Practices.* New York: M. Wiener, 1989.

Japan Economic Institute, *JEI Report.*

Japan Times. (English-language newspaper published in Japan).

Japan Times Weekly. (English-language newspaper published in Japan).

Jenkins, Peter. *Mrs. Thatcher's Revolution: The Ending of the Socialist Era.* Cambridge, Mass.: Harvard University Press, 1988.

Johnson, Chalmers. *MITI and the Japanese Miracle: The Growth of Industrial Policy, 1925–1975.* Stanford, Calif.: Stanford University Press, 1982.

———. "MITI, MPT, and the Telecom Wars: How Japan Makes Policy for High Technology." BRIE Working Paper, no. 21. Berkeley: Berkeley Roundtable on the International Economy, University of California, Berkeley, 1986.

Jones, Charles O. "Presidents and Agendas: Who Defines What for Whom?" In *The Managerial Presidency,* edited by James P. Pfiffner, 197–213. Pacific Grove, Calif.: Brooks/Cole Publishing, 1991.

Jones, George W. "Mrs. Thatcher and the Power of the PM." *Contemporary Record* 3 (April 1990): 2–6.

———. "The Prime Minister's Aides." In *The British Prime Minister,* 2d ed., edited by Anthony King, 72–95. Durham, N.C.: Duke University Press, 1985.

———. "The Prime Minister's Power." In *The British Prime Minister,* 2d ed., edited by Anthony King, 195–220. Durham, N.C.: Duke University Press, 1985. Reprinted from *Parliamentary Affairs* 18 (Spring 1965): 167–85.

———. "The Study of Prime Ministers: A Framework for Analysis." *West European Politics* 14 (April 1991): 1–8.

———. "West European Prime Ministers in Perspective." *West European Politics* 14 (April 1991): 163–78.

———, ed. *West European Prime Ministers.* Special issue of *West European Politics* 14 (April 1991): 1–178.

Kanter, Rosabeth Moss. *Men and Women of the Corporation.* New York: Basic Books, 1979.

Kato, Junko. "Public Pension Reforms in the United States and Japan: A Study of Comparative Public Policy." *Comparative Political Studies* 24 (April 1991): 100–26.

Kellerman, Barbara. *The Political Presidency: Practice of Leadership from Kennedy through Reagan*. New York: Oxford University Press, 1984.

Kernell, Samuel. "The Evolution of the White House Staff." In *The Managerial Presidency*, edited by James P. Pfiffner, 43–59. Pacific Grove, Calif.: Brooks/Cole Publishing, 1991.

————, ed. *Parallel Politics: Economic Policymaking in Japan and the United States*. Washington, D.C.: Brookings Institution, 1991.

Key, Sun Ryang. "Postwar Japanese Political Leadership—A Study of Prime Ministers." *Asian Survey* 13 (November 1973): 1010–20.

Kim, Paul S. *Japan's Civil Service System: Its Structure, Personnel, and Politics*. New York: Greenwood Press, 1988.

King, Anthony. "The American Policy in the Late 1970s: Building Coalitions in the Sand." In *The New American Political System*, 1st ed. edited by Anthony King, 371–95. Washington, D.C.: American Enterprise Institute, 1978.

————. "The British Prime Ministership in the Age of the Career Politician." *West European Politics* 14 (April 1991): 25–47.

————. "Executives." In *Handbook of Political Science*, vol. 5, *Governmental Institutions and Processes*, edited by Fred I. Greenstein and Nelson W. Polsby, 173–265. Reading, Mass.: Addison-Wesley, 1975.

————. "Prime Minister and Cabinet." *Contemporary Record* 4 (September 1990): 22–23.

————, ed. *The British Prime Minister*, 2d ed. Durham, N.C.: Duke University Press, 1985.

Kingdon, John W. *Agendas, Alternatives, and Public Policies*. Boston: Little, Brown, 1984.

Koh, B. C. *Japan's Administrative Elite*. Berkeley and Los Angeles: University of California Press, 1989.

Kosai, Yutaka. "The Politics of Economic Management." In *The Political Economy of Japan*, vol. 1, *The Domestic Transformation*, edited by Kozo Yamamura and Yasukichi Yasuba, 555–92. Stanford, Calif.: Stanford University Press, 1987.

Krauss, Ellis S. "Conflict in the Diet: Toward Conflict Management in Parliamentary Politics." In *Conflict in Japan*, edited by Ellis S. Krauss, Thomas P. Rohlen, and Patricia G. Steinhoff, 243–93. Honolulu: University of Hawaii Press, 1984.

————. "Japanese Parties and Parliament: Changing Leadership Roles and Role Conflict." In *Political Leadership in Japan*, edited by Terry Edward MacDougall, 93–114. Michigan Papers in Japanese Studies, no. 1. Ann Arbor: Center for Japanese Studies, University of Michigan, 1982.

Krauss, Ellis S. and Michio Muramatsu. "The Structure of Interest Group Influence on Policymaking in Japan." Manuscript, [1983].

Kubota, Akira, *Higher Civil Servants in Japan: Their Social Origins, Educational Backgrounds, and Career Patterns*. Princeton, N.J.: Princeton University Press, 1969.

Kyogoku, Jun-ichi. *The Political Dynamics of Japan*. Translated by Nobutaka Ike. Tokyo: University of Tokyo Press, 1987.

Laver, Michael, and Norman Schofield. *Multiparty Government: The Politics of Coalition in Europe*. Oxford: Oxford University Press, 1990.

Leiserson, Michael. "Factions and Coalitions in One-Party Japan: An Interpretation Based on the Theory of Games." *American Political Science Review* 62 (September 1968): 770-87.

Light, Paul C. *The President's Agenda: Domestic Policy Choice from Kennedy to Carter*. Baltimore: Johns Hopkins University Press, 1983.

Lijphart, Arend. *Democracies: Patterns of Majoritarian and Consensus Government in Twenty-One Countries*. New Haven, Conn.: Yale University Press, 1984.

Lincoln, Ed. *Japan: Reaching Economic Maturity*. Washington, D.C.: Brookings Institution, 1985.

Lindblom, Charles E. "The Science of Muddling Through." *Public Administration Review* 14 (Spring 1959): 79–88.

Lowi, Theodore J. *The Personal President: Power Invested, Promise Unfulfilled*. Ithaca, N.Y.: Cornell University Press, 1985.

Lunch, William M. *The Nationalization of American Politics*. Berkeley and Los Angeles: University of California Press, 1987.

MacDougall, Terry Edward. "Asukata Ichio and Some Dilemmas of Socialist Leadership in Japan." In *Political Leadership in Japan*, edited by Terry Edward MacDougall, 51–92. Michigan Papers in Japanese Studies, no. 1. Ann Arbor: Center for Japanese Studies, University of Michigan, 1982.

———. "Democracy and Local Government in Postwar Japan." In *Democracy in Japan*, edited by Takeshi Ishida and Ellis S. Krauss, 139–69. Pittsburgh: University of Pittsburgh Press, 1989.

———, ed. *Political Leadership in Contemporary Japan*. Michigan Papers in Japanese Studies, no. 1. Ann Arbor: Center for Japanese Studies, University of Michigan, 1982.

McKay, David. *Domestic Policy and Ideology: Presidents and the American State, 1964–1987*. Cambridge: Cambridge University Press, 1989.

Mackintosh, John P. *The British Cabinet*, 3d ed. London: Stevens, 1977.

———. *The Government and Politics of Britain*, 3d ed. London: Hutchinson, 1974.

Macridis, Roy C. "Political Executive." In *International Encyclopedia of the Social Sciences*, edited by David L. Sills, 12:228–35. New York: Macmillan and Free Press, 1968.

Madison, James. "No. 51." "No. 62." In *The Federalist Papers*, by Alexander Hamilton, James Madison, and John Jay. New York: Mentor Books, 1963.

Management and Coordination Agency. *Management and Coordination Agency: Organization and Functions*. Tokyo: Management and Coordination Agency, Prime Minister's Office, 1985.

Mansfield, Harvey C., Jr. *Taming the Prince: The Ambivalence of Modern Executive Power*. New York: Free Press, 1989.

March, James G. "Bounded Rationality, Ambiguity, and the Engineering of Choice." *Bell Journal of Economics* 9 (Autumn 1978): 587–608.

———. "How We Talk and How We Act: Administrative Theory and Administrative Life." App. G of Michael D. Cohen and James G. March, *Leadership and Ambiguity*, 2d ed. Boston: Harvard Business School Press, 1986.

———. "The Power of Power." In *Varieties of Political Theory*, edited by David Easton, 39–70. Englewood Cliffs, N.J.: Prentice-Hall, 1966.

March, James G., and Johan P. Olsen, eds. *Ambiguity and Choice in Organizations*, 2d ed. Bergen: Universitetsforlaget, 1979.

March, James G., and Herbert A. Simon. *Organizations*. New York: John Wiley and Sons, 1958.

Massey, Joseph A. *Youth and Politics in Japan*. Lexington, Mass.: Lexington Books, 1976.

Masumi Junnosuke. *Postwar Politics in Japan, 1945–1955*. Translated by Lonny E. Carlile. Berkeley: Institute of East Asian Studies, University of California, 1985.

Mayer, Lawrence C., and John H. Burnett. *Politics in Industrial Societies: A Comparative Perspective*. New York: John Wiley and Sons, 1977.

Mayntz, Renate. "Executive Leadership in Germany: Dispersion of Power or *Kanzlerdemokratie?*" In *Presidents and Prime Ministers*, edited by Richard Rose and Ezra N. Suleiman, 139–70. Washington, D.C.: American Enterprise Institute, 1980.

Mény, Yves. *Government and Politics in Western Europe: Britain, France, Italy, West Germany*. Translated by Janet Lloyd. Oxford: Oxford University, 1990.

Mochizuki, Mike Masato. "Managing and Influencing the Japanese Legislative Process: The Role of Parties and the National Diet." Ph. D. diss., Harvard University, 1982.

Moe, Terry M. "The Politicized Presidency." In *The Managerial Presidency*, edited by James P. Pfiffner, 135–57. Pacific Grove, Calif.: Brooks/Cole Publishing, 1991.

Monbushō. *Outline of Education in Japan 1989*. Tokyo: Asian Cultural Centre for UNESCO, 1989.

Mullins, Kerry, and Aaron Wildavsky. "The Procedural Presidency of George Bush." *Society* 28 (January/February 1991): 49–59.

Murakami, Yasusuke. "The Japanese Model of Political Economy." In *The Political Economy of Japan*, vol. 1, *The Domestic Transformation*, edited by Kozo Yamamura and Yasukichi Yasuba, 33–92. Stanford, Calif.: Stanford University Press, 1987.

Muramatsu, Michio. "In Search of National Identity: The Politics and Policies of the Nakasone Administration." *Journal of Japanese Studies* 13 (Summer 1987): 307–42.

Muramatsu, Michio, and Ellis S. Krauss. "The Conservative Policy Line and the Development of Patterned Pluralism." In *The Political Economy of Japan*, vol. 1, *The Domestic Transformation*, edited by Kozo Yamamura and Yasukichi Yasuba, 516–54. Stanford, Calif.: Stanford University Press, 1987.

―――. "The Dominant Party and Social Coalitions in Japan." In *Uncommon Democracies: The One-Party Dominant Regimes*, edited by T. J. Pempel, 282–305. Ithaca, N.Y.: Cornell University Press, 1990.

Nagai, Michio. "Educational Reform: Developments in the Postwar Years." *Japan Quarterly* 30 (January–March 1985): 14–17.

Nakamura, Hitomi. "Governing in a Crisis, Part 2." *Japan Times Weekly*, May 20–26, 1991.

Nakane, Chie. *Japanese Society*. Berkeley and Los Angeles: University of California Press, 1970.

Nakasone Yasuhiro. "Reflections of a Presidential Prime Minister." *Japan Echo* 15 (Spring 1988): 8–16. Translated from "Sōri kantei o saru ni saishite," *Bungei Shunjū* (December 1987): 94–109.

Nathan, Richard P. *The Administrative Presidency*. New York: John Wiley and Sons, 1983.

―――. "Federalism—The Great 'Composition.'" In *The New American Political System*, 2d ed., edited by Anthony King, 231–61. Washington, D.C.: AEI Press, 1990.

National Police Agency. *Police White Paper 1985*.

Neustadt, Richard E. *Presidential Power: The Politics of Leadership from FDR to Carter*. New York: John Wiley and Sons, 1980.

―――. "White House and Whitehall." In *The British Prime Minister*, 2d ed., edited by Anthony King, 155–74. Durham, N.C.: Duke University Press, 1985.

Norton, Philip. *The British Polity*, 2d ed. New York: Longman, 1991.

―――. "'The Lady's Not for Turning' but What about the Rest? Margaret Thatcher and the Conservative Party 1979–89." *Parliamentary Affairs* 43 (January 1990): 41–76.

Okimoto, Daniel I. *Between MITI and the Market: Japanese Industrial Policy for High Technology*. Stanford, Calif.: Stanford University Press, 1989.

―――. "Political Inclusivity: The Domestic Structure of Trade." In *The Political Economy of Japan*, vol. 2, *The Changing International Context*, edited by Takashi Inoguchi and Daniel I. Okimoto, 305–44. Stanford, Calif.: Stanford University Press, 1988.

O'Leary, Brendan. "An *Taoiseach*: The Irish Prime Minister." *West European Politics* 14 (April 1991): 133–62.

Olsen, Johan P. "Governing Norway: Segmentation, Anticipation, and Consensus Formation." In *Presidents and Prime Ministers*, edited by Richard Rose and Ezra

N. Suleiman, 203–55. Washington, D.C.: American Enterprise Institute, 1980.

"On the Way to Securing a World Position? Japan's Intelligence Agencies and Their Activities." *Japan Quarterly* 29 (April–June 1982): 159–62.

Organization of the Government of Japan. Tokyo: Institute of Administrative Management, 1987.

Packard, George R., III. *Protest in Tokyo: The Security Treaty Crisis of 1960.* Princeton, N.J.: Princeton University Press, 1966.

Park, Yung H. *Bureaucrats and Ministers in Contemporary Japanese Government.* Berkeley: Institute of East Asian Studies, University of California, 1986.

Patterson, Bradley H., Jr. *The Ring of Power: The White House Staff and Its Expanding Role in Government.* New York: Basic Books, 1988.

Pechman, Joseph A., and Keimei Kaizuka. "Taxation." In *Asia's New Giant: How the Japanese Economy Works*, edited by Hugh Patrick and Henry Rosovsky, 317–82. Washington, D.C.: Brookings, 1976.

Pempel, T. J. "The Bureaucratization of Policy Making in Postwar Japan." *American Journal of Political Science* 18 (November 1974): 647–64.

———. *Policy and Politics in Japan: Creative Conservatism.* Philadelphia: Temple University Press, 1982.

———. "Unbundling 'Japan, Inc.': The Changing Dynamics of Japanese Policy Formation." *Journal of Japanese Studies* 13 (Summer 1987): 271–306.

———, ed. *Uncommon Democracies: The One-Party Dominant Regimes.* Ithaca, N.Y.: Cornell University Press, 1990.

Peppers, Donald A. "The Two Presidencies: Eight Years Later." In *Perspectives on the Presidency*, edited by Aaron Wildavsky, 462–71. Boston: Little, Brown, 1975.

Peterson, Mark A. *Legislating Together: The White House and Capitol Hill from Eisenhower to Reagan.* Cambridge, Mass.: Harvard University Press, 1990.

Pfeffer, Jeffrey. *Organizations and Organization Theory.* Boston: Pitman, 1982.

Pfiffner, James P., Introduction. In *The Managerial Presidency*, edited by James P. Pfiffner, xvii–xxii. Pacific Grove, Calif.: Brooks/Cole Publishing, 1991.

———, ed. *The Managerial Presidency.* Pacific Grove, Calif.: Brooks/Cole Publishing, 1991.

Pharr, Susan J. "Liberal Democrats in Disarray: Intergenerational Conflict in the Conservative Camp." In *Political Leadership in Japan*, edited by Terry Edward MacDougall, 29–50. Michigan Papers in Japanese Studies, no. 1. Ann Arbor: Center for Japanese Studies, University of Michigan, 1982.

Prindle, David F. "Toward a Comparative Science of the Presidency: A Pre-Theory." *Presidential Studies Quarterly* 16 (Summer 1986): 467–80.

Pye, Lucian W. *Asian Power and Politics: The Cultural Dimensions of Authority.* Cambridge, Mass.: Belknap Press of Harvard University Press, 1985.

Reed, Steven R. *Japanese Prefectures and Policymaking*. Pittsburgh: University of Pittsburgh Press, 1986.

Reedy, George E. *The Twilight of the Presidency: From Johnson to Reagan*, rev. ed. New York: New American Library, 1987.

Reischauer, Edwin O. *The Japanese Today: Change and Continuity*. Cambridge, Mass.: Belknap Press of Harvard University Press, 1988.

Richardson, Bradley M., and Scott C. Flanagan. *Politics in Japan*. Boston: Little, Brown, 1984.

Ripley, Randall B., and Grace A. Franklin. *Congress, the Bureaucracy, and Public Policy*. 3d ed. Homewood, Ill.: Dorsey Press, 1984.

Robinson, Donald L. *Government for the Third American Century*. Boulder, Colo.: Westview Press, 1989.

Rockman, Bert A. "The American Presidency in Comparative Perspective: Systems, Situations, and Leaders." In *The Presidency and the Political System*, 2d ed., edited by Michael Nelson, 55–79. Washington, D.C.: Congressional Quarterly Press, 1988.

————. *The Leadership Question: The Presidency and the American System*. New York: Praeger, 1984.

Rose, Richard. "British Government: The Job at the Top." In *Presidents and Prime Ministers*, edited by Richard Rose and Ezra N. Suleiman, 1–49. Washington, D.C.: American Enterprise Institute, 1980.

————. *Do Political Parties Matter?* Chatham, N.J.: Chatham House, 1984.

————. "Evaluating the Presidency: A Positive-and-Normative Approach." Studies in Public Policy, no. 184. Glasgow: Centre for the Study of Public Policy, University of Strathclyde, 1990.

————. "Government against Sub-Governments: A European Perspective on Washington." In *Presidents and Prime Ministers*, edited by Richard Rose and Ezra N. Suleiman, 284–347. Washington, D.C.: American Enterprise Institute, 1980.

————. "The Job at the Top: The Presidency in Comparative Perspective." In *The Presidency and Public Policy Making*, edited by George C. Edwards III, Steven A. Shull, and Norman C. Thomas, 3–21. Pittsburgh: University of Pittsburgh Press, 1985.

————. "Organizing Issues In and Organizing Issues Out." In *The Managerial Presidency*, edited by James P. Pfiffner, 105–19. Pacific Grove, Calif.: Brooks/Cole Publishing, 1991.

————. *Politics in England: Persistence and Change*, 5th ed. Glenview, Ill.: Scott, Foresman, 1985.

————. *The Postmodern President: George Bush Meets the World*, 2d ed. Chatham, N.J.: Chatham House, 1991.

———. "Prime Ministers in Parliamentary Democracies." *West European Politics* 14 (April 1991): 9–24.

Rose, Richard, and Ezra N. Suleiman, ed. *Presidents and Prime Ministers.* Washington, D.C.: American Enterprise Institute, 1980.

Rourke, Francis. "Presidentializing the Bureaucracy." In *The Managerial Presidency,* edited by James P. Pfiffner, 123–33. Pacific Grove, Calif.: Brooks/Cole Publishing, 1991.

Salamon, Lester M. "The Presidency and Domestic Policy Formulation." In *The Illusion of Presidential Government,* edited by Hugh Heclo and Lester M. Salamon, 177–201. Boulder, Colo.: Westview Press, 1981.

Samuels, Richard J. *The Business of the Japanese State: Energy Markets in Comparative and Historical Perspective.* Ithaca, N.Y.: Cornell University Press, 1987.

———. "Power Behind the Throne." In *Political Leadership in Contemporary Japan,* edited by Terry Edward MacDougall, 127–44. Michigan Papers in Japanese Studies, no. 1. Ann Arbor: Center for Japanese Studies, University of Michigan, 1982.

Sartori, Giovanni. *Parties and Party Systems: A Framework for Analysis.* Cambridge: Cambridge University Press, 1976.

Satō Seizaburō, Ken'ichi Kōmon, and Shunpei Kumon. *Postwar Politician: The Life of Former Prime Minister Masayoshi Ohira.* Tokyo: Kodansha International, 1990.

Schlesinger, Arthur M., Jr. *The Imperial Presidency.* Boston: Houghton Mifflin, 1973.

Schoppa, Leonard James. *Educational Reform in Japan: A Case of Immobilist Politics.* New York: Routledge, 1991.

Schwarz, John E. "Exploring a New Role in Policy Making: The British House of Commons in the 1970s." *American Political Science Review* 74 (March 1980): 23–27.

Seldon, Anthony. "The Cabinet Office and Coordination 1979–87." *Public Administration* 68 (Spring 1990): 103–21.

Seligman, Lester S. "Leadership: Political Aspects." In *International Encyclopedia of the Social Sciences,* edited by David L. Sills, 9:107–13. New York: Macmillan and Free Press, 1968.

Shull, Steven A. *Domestic Policy Formation: Presidential-Congressional Partnership?* Westport, Conn.: Greenwood Press, 1983.

Simeon, James C. "Prime Minister's Office and White House Office: Political Administration in Canada and the United States." *Presidential Studies Quarterly* 21 (Summer 1991): 559–80.

Simon, Herbert. *The Models of Man.* New York: John Wiley and Sons, 1957.

Smith, Denis. "President and Parliament: The Transformation of Parliamentary Government in Canada." In *Apex of Power: The Prime Minister and Political Leadership in Canada,* 2d ed., edited by Thomas A. Hockin, 308–25. Scarborough, Ont.: Prentice-Hall, 1977.

Smith, Gordon. "The Resources of a German Chancellor." *West European Politics* 14 (April 1991): 48–61.

Smith, Hedrick. *The Power Game: How Washington Works*. New York: Random House, 1988.

Spitzer, Robert J. *The Presidency and Public Policy: The Four Arenas of Presidential Power*. University: University of Alabama Press, 1983.

Steinbruner, John D. *The Cybernetic Theory of Decision: New Dimensions of Political Analysis*. Princeton, N.J.: Princeton University Press, 1974.

Steiner, Jürg. *Amicable Agreement versus Majority Rule: Conflict Resolution in Switzerland*. Chapel Hill: University of North Carolina Press, 1974.

————. *European Democracies*, 2d ed. New York: Longmans, 1991.

Steiner, Jürg, and Robert H. Dorff. "Decision by Interpretation." *British Journal of Politics* 10 (January 1980): 1–13.

Stockman, David A. *The Triumph of Politics: Why the Reagan Revolution Failed*. New York: Harper and Row, 1986.

Stockwin, J. A. A. "Dynamic and Immobilist Aspects of Japanese Politics." In *Dynamic and Immobilist Politics in Japan*, edited by J. A. A. Stockwin, 1–21. London: Macmillan, 1988.

————. *Japan: Divided Politics in a Growth Economy*, 2d ed. New York: W. W. Norton, 1982.

Suleiman, Ezra N. "Presidential Government in France." In *Presidents and Prime Ministers*, edited by Richard Rose and Ezra N. Suleiman, 94–138. Washington, D.C.: American Enterprise Institute, 1980.

Sundquist, James L. *Constitutional Reform and Effective Government*. Washington, D.C.: Brookings Institution, 1986.

————. *Politics and Policy: The Eisenhower, Kennedy, and Johnson Years*. Washington, D.C.: Brookings Institution, 1968.

Thayer, Nathaniel B. *How the Conservatives Rule Japan*. Princeton, N.J.: Princeton University Press, 1969.

Thompson, Brian. "Living with a Supreme Court in Ireland." *Parliamentary Affairs* 44 (January 1991): 33–49.

Thurston, Donald R. *Teachers and Politics in Japan*. Princeton, N.J.: Princeton University Press, 1973.

Tsuji, Kiyoaki. "Decision-Making in the Japanese Government: A Study of Ringisei." In *Political Development in Modern Japan*, edited by Robert E. Ward, 457–75. Princeton, N.J.: Princeton University Press, 1968.

————. "Public Administration in Japan: History and Problems." In *Public Administration in Japan*, edited by Kiyoaki Tsuji, 7–16. Tokyo: Administrative Management Agency, 1982.

Tsurutani, Taketsugu. *Political Change in Japan: Response to Post Industrial Change*. New York: David McKay, 1977.

Tulis, Jeffrey K. *The Rhetorical President*. Princeton, N.J.: Princeton University Press, 1987.

Ueda, Takahiko. "Governing in a Crisis, Part 1." *Japan Times Weekly*, May 13–19, 1991.

Van Wolferen, Karel G. *The Enigma of Japanese Power: People and Politics in a Stateless Nation*. New York: Alfred A. Knopf, 1989.

―――. "The Japan Problem." *Foreign Affairs* 65 (Winter 1987): 288–303.

Walker, Jack L. "Setting the Agenda in the U.S. Senate." *British Journal of Political Science* 7 (October 1977): 423–45.

Ward, Robert E. *Japan's Political System*, 2d ed. Englewood Cliffs, N.J.: Prentice-Hall, 1978.

Watson, Richard A., and Norman C. Thomas. *The Politics of the Presidency*. New York: John Wiley and Sons, 1983.

Wayne, Stephen J. "An Introduction to Research on the Presidency." In *Studying the Presidency*, edited by George C. Edwards III and Stephen J. Wayne. Knoxville: University of Tennessee Press, 1983.

Weick, Karl E. *The Social Psychology of Organizing*, 2d ed. Reading, Mass.: Addison-Wesley, 1979.

Weller, Patrick. *First among Equals: Prime Ministers in Westminster Systems*. Sydney.: George Allen and Unwin, 1985.

Whalley, John. "Foreign Responses to U.S. Tax Reform." In *Do Taxes Matter? The Impact of the Tax Reform Act of 1986*, edited by Joel Slemrod, 286–314. Cambridge, Mass.: MIT Press, 1990.

Wildavsky, Aaron. "The Two Presidencies." In *The Presidency*, edited by Aaron Wildavsky, 230–43. Boston: Little, Brown, 1969. Reprinted from *Trans-Action* 4 (December 1966).

Yomiuri Research Institute. "The Making of an LDP President." *Japan Echo* 14 (1987): 77–84.

Yoshida, Kazuo. "Who'll Pay?" *Look Japan* 33 (May 1987): 5–7.

Japanese Language Sources

Aoki Satoshi. *Nakasone Famirī*. [The Nakasone family]. Tokyo: Akebi Shobō, 1986.

―――. *Rinkyōshin Kaitai*. [An analysis of the National Council on Educational Reform]. Tokyo: Akebi Shobō, 1986.

Arai Shunzō and Morita Hajime. *Ōhira Masayoshi: Bunjin Saisō*. [Ōhira Masayoshi: The cultured prime minister]. Tokyo: Shunjūsha, 1982.

Asahi Nenkan. [Asahi yearbook].

Asahi Shimbun. [Asahi newspaper].

Ebihara Haruyoshi, ed. *Gendai Nihon on Kyōiku Seisaku to Kyōiku Kaikaku*. [Contemporary Japanese education policy and educational reform|. Tokyo: Eideru Kenkyūjo, 1986.

Ebihara Haruyoshi, Nagai Ken'ichi, and Miwa Sadanobu. *Kyōiku Rinchō, Kyōiku Kaikaku*. |The ad hoc council on education and educational reform|. Tokyo: Eideru Kenkyūjo, 1984.

Fujita Sei. *Zeisei Kaikaku, Sono Kiseki to Tenbō*. |Tax reform: Its past and prospects|. Tokyo: Zeimu Keiri Kyōkai, 1987.

Gendai Seiji Jōhō, 1987. |Current political information|. 4th ed. Tokyo: Sekai Nipōsha, 1986.

Gotōda Masaharu. *Seiji towa Nanika*. |What is politics?| Tokyo: Kōdansha, 1988.

Gyōsei, ed. *Rinkyōshin to Kyōiku Kaikaku*. |The National Council on Educational Reform and educational reform|. 5 vols. Tokyo: Gyōsei, 1987.

Gyōsei Kikōzu. |The organization of the Japanese government|. Tokyo: Gyōsei Kanri Sentā, 1988.

Hanta Kensuke. *Kikubari, Mekubari Shusse Jutsu*. |The successful technique of taking care of and watching over others|. Tokyo: Tokyo Shuppan, 1988.

Hara Masahiko and Kawanabe Masahiro. *Kyōiku Rinchō*. |The ad hoc council on education|. Tokyo: Tōken, 1984.

Harada Saburō. "Hyōryū Tsuzukeru Rinkyōshin." |The National Council on Educational Reform continues to drift|. *Ekonomisuto*, 18 March 1986, 52–56.

———. "Rinkyōshin no Nerai to sono Shōrai." |The objectives of the National Council on Educational Reform and its future|. *Jurisuto*, 825 (November 15, 1984): 33–39.

———. *Rinkyōshin to Kyōiku Kaikaku*. |The National Council on Educational Reform and educational reform|. Tokyo: San'ichi Shobō, 1988.

Hatoyama Kunio. "Interview: Hatoyama Kunio." *Gekkan Gendai* 21 (April 1987): 80–83.

Hayashi Shigeru and Tsuji Kiyoaki, eds. *Nihon Naikaku shi–roku*. |A historical chronicle of Japanese Cabinets|. 6 vols. Tokyo: Daiichi Hōki, 1981.

Higuchi Tsuneo. *Tamaki Kazuo no Yuigon*. |Tamaki Kazuo's last will and testament|. Tokyo: Asuka Shinsha, 1987.

Hirahara Haruyoshi. "Kyōiku no Rinen to Rinkyōshin no Yakuwari, Mondaiten." |Ideas for educational reform and the role and issues of the National Council on Educational Reform|. *Jurisuto*, no. 825 (November 15, 1984): 27–32.

Iijima Kiyoshi, Miyazaki Yoshimasa, and Watanabe Tsuneo, eds. *Seiji no Jōshiki Daihyakka*. |The encyclopedia of political common knowledge|. Tokyo: Kōdansha, 1983.

Ikuta Tadahide. "Gotōda Masaharu." *Gekkan Gendai* 21 (April 1987): 66–78.

Imamura Tsunao. "Soshiki no Bunka to Kōsō." |Organizational culture and structure]. In *Gyōseigaku Kōza*, vol. 4, *Gyōsei to Soshiki*, edited by Tsuji Kiyoaki, 183–87. Tokyo: Tokyo Daigaku Shuppankai, 1976.

Inoguchi Takashi. *Gendai Nihon Seiji Keizai no Kōzu: Seifu to Shijo*. [The framework of the contemporary Japanese political economy: Government and the market]. Tokyo: Tōyō Keizai Shimpō sha, 1983.

Inoguchi Takashi and Iwai Tomoaki. "*Zoku-Giin*" *no Kenkyū* [Zoku-giin research]. Tokyo: Nihon Keizai Shimbunsha, 1987.

Ishiyama Morio. *Monbu Kanryō no Gyakushū*. [The counteroffensive of the education ministry bureaucrats]. Tokyo: Kōdansha, 1986.

Itō Daiichi. "Naikaku Seido no Soshikironteki Kentō." [An organizational theory study of the Cabinet system]. In *Naikaku Seido no Kenkyū*, edited by Nihon Gyōsei Gakkai, 33–59. Tokyo: Gyōsei, 1987.

Itō Masaya. *Jimintō Sengokushi: Kenryoku no Kenkyū*. [A history of the LDP's civil war: Research into political power]. Tokyo: Asahi Sonorama, 1982.

———. *Saisō Tori*. [Taking the prime ministership]. Tokyo: PHP Kenkyūjo, 1986.

———. *Shin Jimintō Sengokushi*. [The new history of the LDP's civil war]. Tokyo: Asahi Sonorama, 1983.

Itō Masaya and Fukuoka Masayuki. *Korekara 10-Nen Sengoku Jimintō*. [The LDP: The next decade of civil war]. Tokyo: Daiichi Kikaku Shuppan, 1988.

Iwai Tomoaki. *Rippō Katei*. [The legislative process]. Tokyo: Tokyo Daigaku Shuppankai, 1988.

Iwai Tomoaki and Inoguchi Takashi. "Zeiseizoku no Seiji Rikigaku." [The political dynamics of the tax *zoku*]. *Chūō Kōron*, March 1987, 96–106.

Jin Ikkō. *Sōridaijin no Isu no Nedan*. [The price of the prime minister's chair]. Tokyo: KK Besutoserāzu, 1987.

Kaminishi Akio. *Burēn Seiji*. [Brain trust politics]. Tokyo: Kōdansha, 1985.

Kataoka Hiromitsu. *Naikaku no Kinō to Hosa Kikō*. [The cabinet's function and support structure]. Tokyo: Seibundō, 1982.

———. "Naikaku to Gyōsei." [Cabinet and administration]. In *Naikaku Seido no Kenkyū*, edited by Nihon Gyōsei Gakkai, 1–31. Tokyo: Gyōsei, 1987.

Katō Ichirō, Nagai Michio, Masamura Kimihiro, Mukaibō Takashi. "Kyōiku Kaikaku no Yukue." [The direction of educational reform]. *Jurisuto*, 825 (November 15, 1984): 6–26.

Kawauchi Issei. *Ōhira Seiken: 554 Nichi*. [The Ōhira administration: 554 days]. Tokyo: Gyōseimondai Kenkyūjo, 1982.

Kikuchi Hisashi. *Jimintō Habatsu*. [LDP factions]. Tokyo: Pīpurusha, 1987.

Kishi Nobusuke. "Jikyoku Shokan: Naze Tōkakai o Kaisan shita ka." [A political note: Why I dissolved the Tōkakai]. KSK *Report*, 116 (November 20, 1962).

Kishiro Yasuyuki. *Jimintō Zeseichōsakai*. [The LDP tax research council]. Tokyo: Tōyō Keizai Shimpōsha, 1985.

_____. "Yamanaka Sadanori: Jimintō no Seisaku Keiseiryoku wa Kanryō Soshiki o Koetaka?" |Yamanaka Sadanori: Has the LDP's policy-making power superceded the bureaucracy's?|. *Jimintō toiu Chie: Nihon-teki Seiji Ryoku no Kenkyū*, 116–29. Tokyo: JICC, 1987.

Kiyomiya Ryū. *Fukuda Seiken: 714 Nichi*. |The Fukuda administration: 714 days|. Tokyo: Gyōseimondai Kenkyūjo, 1984.

Kobayashi Yoshiaki. *Tenkanki no Seiji Ishiki*. |Political awareness in transition|. Tokyo: Keiō Tsūshin, 1985.

Kuribayashi Yoshimitsu. *Ōkura Shuzeikyoku*. |The Finance Ministry's tax bureau|. Tokyo: Kōdansha, 1987.

Kuroha Ryōichi. *Rinkyōshin: Dōnaru Kyōiku Kaikaku*. |The National Council on Educational Reform: What will happen with educational reform?|. Tokyo: Nihon Keizai Shimbunsha, 1985.

Kusuda Minoru. *Satō Seiken: 2797 Nichi*. |The Satō administration: 2,797 days|. 2 vols. Tokyo: Gyōseimondai Kenkyūjo, 1983.

Kyōdō Tsūshin sha. *Uriagezei*. |The sales tax|. Tokyo: Kyōdō Tsūshin, 1987.

Kyōikusha, ed. *Binran: Naikaku/Sōrifu*. |The cabinet and the Prime Minister's Office|. Tokyo: Kyōikusha, 1979.

Mainichi Shimbun. |Mainichi newspaper|.

Mainichi Shimbun Seiji-bu, ed. *Shushō Kantei*. |The prime minister's official residence|. Tokyo: Asahi Sonorama, 1988.

Maki Tarō. *Nakasone Seiken: 1806 Nichi*. |The Nakasone administration: 1,806 days|. 2 vols. Tokyo: Gyōseimondai Kenkyūjo, 1988.

Masumi Junnosuke. *Gendai no Seiji*. |Contemporary politics|. 2 vols. Tokyo: Tokyo Daigaku Shuppankai, 1985.

Mori Kishio. *Shushō Kantei no Himitsu*. |The secrets of the prime minister's official residence|. Tokyo: Ushiobunsha, 1981.

Murakami Yasusuke. *Shin Chūma Taishū no Jidai*. |The age of the new middle mass|. Tokyo: Chūō Kōronsha, 1984.

Murakawa Ichirō. *Jimintō no Seisaku Kettei Shisutemu*. |The LDP's policy decision-making system|. Tokyo: Kyōikusha, 1989.

_____. "Jiyūminshutō no Seisaku Kettei Kikō." |The LDP's policy-making structure|. *Jurisuto* 805 (January 1–15, 1984): 216.

_____. "Jiyūminshutō Seimuchōsakai." |The LDP's PARC|. *Jurisuto* 805 (January 1–15, 1984): 46–52.

_____. *Nihon no Seisaku Kettei Katei*. |Japanese policy-making process|. Tokyo: Gyōsei, 1985.

Nagai Ken'ichi and Miwa Sadanobu, eds. *Rinkyōshin, Kyōiku Kaikaku no Dōkō*. |The National Council on Educational Reform and educational reform|. Tokyo: Eideru Kenkyūjo, 1985.

Nakamura Keiichirō. *Miki Seiken: 747 Nichi.* [The Miki administration: 747 days]. Tokyo: Gyōseimondai Kenkyūjo, 1981.

Nakano Shirō. *Tanaka Seiken: 886 Nichi.* [The Tanaka administration: 886 days]. Tokyo: Gyōseimondai Kenkyūjo, 1982.

Nihon Keizai Shimbun. [Japanese economic newspaper].

Nihon Keizai Shimbunsha, ed. *Jimintō Seichōkai.* [The LDP PARC]. Tokyo: Nihon Keizai Shimbunsha, 1983.

Ōkina Hisajirō. "Naikaku Kanbō Sōgo Chōsei Kikan ni Tsuite." [The Cabinet Secretariat's comprehensive coordinative machinery]. In *Naikaku Seido no Kenkyū,* edited by Nihon Gyōsei Gakkai, 89–109. Tokyo: Gyōsei, 1987.

Ōkubo Shōzō. *Hadaka no Sekai.* [The political world laid bare]. Tokyo: Saimaru Shuppankai, 1975.

Ōmori Kazuo. *Rinji Kyōiku Shingikai: Sannenkan no Kiroku.* [The National Council on Educational Reform: Its three-year record]. Tokyo: Hikaru Shobō, 1987.

Ōmori Wataru, Hayashi Shūzō, Kiyomizu Hiroshi, and Yamamoto Sadao. "Konnichi no Naikaku Kinō o Megutte." [The current cabinet's capability]. *Gyōsei Kanri Kenkyū* 35 (September 1986): 3–22.

Onda Mitsugu. *Naze Sōridaijin Nanoka.* [Why the prime minister?]. Tokyo: Pīpurusha, 1988.

Ōtake Hideo. *Gendai Nihon no Seiji Kenryoku Keizai Kenryoku.* [Contemporary Japan's political authority and economic authority]. Tokyo: San'ichi Shobō, 1979.

Sano Kazuyuki. "Kokumin no Teki 'Uriagezei' o Hineridashita Misshitsu no Genkyōtachi." [The behind-the-scenes ringleaders who brought forth the "sales tax," the enemy of the people]. *Gekkan Gendai* 21 (April 1987): 84–90.

Satō Seizaburō and Matsuzaki Tetsuhisa. *Jimintō Seiken.* [The LDP administrations]. Tokyo: Chūō Kōron, 1986.

Seiji Handobukku. [The handbook of politics].

Seikan Yōran. [Handbook of politicians and bureaucrats].

Shindō Mineyuki. *Gyōsei Kaikaku to Gendai Seiji.* [Administrative reform and current politics]. Tokyo: Iwanami Shoten, 1986.

Shiratori Rei, ed. *Nihon no Naikaku.* [Japan's cabinet]. 3 vols. Tokyo: Shinhyōron, 1981.

Sōmuchō, ed. *Sōmuchō Nenji Hōkokusho: Gyōsei Kaikaku no Suishin to 3-nen no Sōmuchō* [Management and Coordination Agency's annual report: The promotion of administrative reform and the third year of the Management and Coordination Agency]. Tokyo: Ōkurashō Insatsu kyoku, 1987.

Sone Yasunori. "Tagen Minshushugi-ron to Gendai Kokka." [Democratic pluralism and the modern state]. *Nenpō Seijigaku* (1982): 117–49.

————. "Yarase no Seiji 'Shingikai Hōshiki' o Kenshō." [Investigating the activist politics of advisory commissions]. *Chūō Kōron* 1201 (January 1, 1986): 148–55.

Sone Yasunori and Iwai Tomoaki. "Seisaku Katei ni Okeru Gikai no Yakuwari." |The legislature's role in the policy process|. *Nenpō Seijigaku* (1987): 149–74.

Tahara Sōichirō. *Abe, Takeshita ni Sun'nari Seiken ga Ikanai Riyū.* |Why Abe and Takeshita won't easily take power|. Tokyo: Kōbunsha, 1986.

————. *Nihon no Daikaizō: Shin Nihon no Kanryō.* |Japan's big reorganization: Japan's new bureaucracy|. Tokyo: Bungei Shunjū, 1986.

————. *Nihon no Kanryō.* |Japan's bureaucracy|. Tokyo: Bungei Shunjū, 1984.

Takanashi Akira. *Gyōsei Kaikaku wa Seikō Suruka.* |Will administrative reform succeed?|. Tokyo: Sōgo Rōdō Kenkyūjo, 1982.

Tanaka Zen'ichirō. *Jimintō no Doramatsurugī.* |The LDP's dramaturgy|. Tokyo: Tokyo Daigaku Shuppankai, 1987.

————. *Jimintō Taisei no Seiji Shidōryoku.* |Political leadership under the LDP system|. Tokyo: Daiichi Hōki, 1981.

Uchida Kanzō. *Habatsu.* |Factions|. Toyko: Kōdansha, 1983.

————. *Rinkyōshin no Kiseki.* |The National Council on Educational Reform|. Tokyo: Daiichi Hōki, 1987.

Uji Toshihiko. *Suzuki Seiken: 863 Nichi.* |The Suzuki administration: 863 days|. Tokyo: Gyōseimondai Kenkyūjo, 1983.

Watanabe Keiichi. "Jimintō Zeisei Chōsakai: Uriagezei e no Michi." |The LDP's tax council: The road to the sales tax|. *Ekonomisuto* 23 February 1987, 125–30.

Watanabe Tsuneo. *Tōshu to Seitō.* |Party leaders and political leaders|. Tokyo: Kōbundō, 1961.

Yagi Atsushi. *Monbu Daijin no Sengoshi.* |The history of postwar education ministers|. Tokyo: Bijinesusha, 1984.

Yamaguchi Asao. "Jōhō Gyōsei o Gyūjiru Gotōda Sōmuchō no Sugomi." |The intimidation of the Gotōda Management and Coordination Agency, which controls the administration of information|. *Chūō Kōron*, December 1985, 228–38.

Yamazumi Masami. "Kyōiku." |Education|. In *imidas* 1989, 795–804. Tokyo: Shūeisha, 1989.

————. "Kyōiku." |Education|. In *imidas* 1990, 1089–98. Tokyo: Shūeisha, 1990.

Yomiuri Shimbun. |Yomiuri newspaper|.

Yoshida Masanobu. *Ōhira Masayoshi no Seijiteki Jinkaku.* |Ōhira Masayoshi's political personality|. Tokyo: Tōkai Daigaku Shuppankai, 1986.

Yoshimura Katsuri. *Ikeda Seiken: 1575 Nichi.* |The Ikeda administration: 1,575 days|. Tokyo: Gyōseimondai Kenkyūjo, 1985.

Index

339

Pitt Series in Policy and Institutional Studies
Bert A. Rockman, Editor